Nissan Sunny
Service and Repair Manual

A K Legg LAE MIMI and Spencer Drayton

Models covered

(3219 - 240 - 6AA2)

Nissan Sunny Saloon, Hatchback and Estate models, including special/limited editions
1.4 litre (1392 cc) and 1.6 litre (1597 cc) petrol engines

Covers major mechanical features of 100 NX Coupe
Does not cover 2.0 GTi, GTi-R, 4x4 or Diesel models

© Haynes Publishing 1997

ABCDE
FGHIJ
KLMN

Printed in the USA

A book in the **Haynes Service and Repair Manual Series**

ISBN 1 85960 219 3

British Library Cataloguing in Publication Data
A catalogue record for this book is available from the British Library.

Haynes Publishing
Sparkford, Yeovil, Somerset BA22 7JJ, England

Haynes North America, Inc
861 Lawrence Drive, Newbury Park, California 91320, USA

Editions Haynes
4, Rue de l'Abreuvoir
92415 COURBEVOIE CEDEX, France

Haynes Publishing Nordiska AB
Box 1504, 751 45 UPPSALA, Sweden

Contents

LIVING WITH YOUR NISSAN SUNNY

Roadside Repairs

Weekly Checks

Lubricants, fluids and tyre pressures

MAINTENANCE

Routine Maintenance and Servicing

Contents

REPAIRS AND OVERHAUL

REFERENCE

The face-lifted Nissan Sunny range was introduced in April 1991 with the 1.4 LS, 1.6 GS and 1.6 GSX carburettor Saloon, Hatchback and Coupe models. 1.4 L, 1.4 LX, 1.6 LX (including the Estate), 1.6 SLX and 1.6 SR models were added to the range in January 1992, and these models and subsequent models are fitted with catalytic converters. The GTi 2.0 litre fuel-injected model (not covered by this manual) was also introduced at this time, being followed in April 1992 by the 2.0 litre GTi-R (also not covered by this manual). The 1.6 L Estate was introduced in February 1993 and at this time all models (1.4 and 1.6 litre) were fitted with multi-point fuel-injected engines. Various limited edition models were introduced from July 1993 on.

All engines are of 16-valve design and are fitted with a range of emissions control systems. The engines are well-proven and, provided regular maintenance is carried out, are unlikely to give trouble.

The Sunny is available in 4-door Saloon, 3- or 5-door Hatchback, 5-door Estate and 3-door Coupe body styles, with a wide range of fittings and interior trim available depending on the model specification.

Fully independent front and rear suspension is fitted, and all models are fitted with a 5-speed manual transmission or 4-speed automatic transmission. A wide range of standard and optional equipment is available within the Sunny range to suit most tastes, including central locking, electric windows, an electric sunroof and an air bag.

For the home mechanic, the Sunny is a straightforward vehicle to maintain, and most of the items requiring attention are easily accessible.

Nissan Sunny 1.4 LX Hatchback

Nissan Sunny 1.6 SLX Hatchback

The Nissan Sunny Team

Haynes manuals are produced by dedicated and enthusiastic people working in close co-operation. The team responsible for the creation of this book included:

Authors	Mark Coombs Spencer Drayton
Sub-editor	Carole Turk
Editor & Page Make-up	Steve Churchill
Workshop manager	Paul Buckland
Photo Scans	John Martin Paul Tanswell
Cover illustration & Line Art	Roger Healing
Wiring diagrams	Matthew Marke

We hope the book will help you to get the maximum enjoyment from your car. By carrying out routine maintenance as described you will ensure your car's reliability and preserve its resale value.

Your Nissan Sunny Manual

The aim of this manual is to help you get the best value from your vehicle. It can do so in several ways. It can help you decide what work must be done (even should you choose to get it done by a garage), provide information on routine maintenance and servicing, and give a logical course of action and diagnosis when random faults occur. However, it is hoped that you will use the manual by tackling the work yourself. On simpler jobs, it may even be quicker than booking the car into a garage and going there twice, to leave and collect it. Perhaps most important, a lot of money can be saved by avoiding the costs a garage must charge to cover its labour and overheads.

The manual has drawings and descriptions to show the function of the various components, so that their layout can be understood. Then the tasks are described and photographed in a clear step-by-step sequence.

Acknowledgements

Thanks are due to the Champion Spark Plug Company, who supplied the illustrations of various spark plug conditions. Thanks are also due to Sykes-Pickavant Limited, who provided some of the workshop tools, and to all those people at Sparkford who helped in the production of this manual.

We take great pride in the accuracy of information given in this manual, but vehicle manufacturers make alterations and design changes during the production run of a particular vehicle of which they do not inform us. No liability can be accepted by the authors or publishers for loss, damage or injury caused by any errors in, or omissions from, the information given.

Working on your car can be dangerous. This page shows just some of the potential risks and hazards, with the aim of creating a safety-conscious attitude.

General hazards

Scalding

• Don't remove the radiator or expansion tank cap while the engine is hot.
• Engine oil, automatic transmission fluid or power steering fluid may also be dangerously hot if the engine has recently been running.

Burning

• Beware of burns from the exhaust system and from any part of the engine. Brake discs and drums can also be extremely hot immediately after use.

Crushing

• When working under or near a raised vehicle, always supplement the jack with axle stands, or use drive-on ramps. *Never venture under a car which is only supported by a jack.*

• Take care if loosening or tightening high-torque nuts when the vehicle is on stands. Initial loosening and final tightening should be done with the wheels on the ground.

Fire

• Fuel is highly flammable; fuel vapour is explosive.
• Don't let fuel spill onto a hot engine.
• Do not smoke or allow naked lights (including pilot lights) anywhere near a vehicle being worked on. Also beware of creating sparks (electrically or by use of tools).
• Fuel vapour is heavier than air, so don't work on the fuel system with the vehicle over an inspection pit.
• Another cause of fire is an electrical overload or short-circuit. Take care when repairing or modifying the vehicle wiring.
• Keep a fire extinguisher handy, of a type suitable for use on fuel and electrical fires.

Electric shock

• Ignition HT voltage can be dangerous, especially to people with heart problems or a pacemaker. Don't work on or near the ignition system with the engine running or the ignition switched on.

• Mains voltage is also dangerous. Make sure that any mains-operated equipment is correctly earthed. Mains power points should be protected by a residual current device (RCD) circuit breaker.

Fume or gas intoxication

• Exhaust fumes are poisonous; they often contain carbon monoxide, which is rapidly fatal if inhaled. Never run the engine in a confined space such as a garage with the doors shut.
• Fuel vapour is also poisonous, as are the vapours from some cleaning solvents and paint thinners.

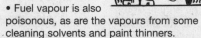

Poisonous or irritant substances

• Avoid skin contact with battery acid and with any fuel, fluid or lubricant, especially antifreeze, brake hydraulic fluid and Diesel fuel. Don't syphon them by mouth. If such a substance is swallowed or gets into the eyes, seek medical advice.
• Prolonged contact with used engine oil can cause skin cancer. Wear gloves or use a barrier cream if necessary. Change out of oil-soaked clothes and do not keep oily rags in your pocket.
• Air conditioning refrigerant forms a poisonous gas if exposed to a naked flame (including a cigarette). It can also cause skin burns on contact.

Asbestos

• Asbestos dust can cause cancer if inhaled or swallowed. Asbestos may be found in gaskets and in brake and clutch linings. When dealing with such components it is safest to assume that they contain asbestos.

Special hazards

Hydrofluoric acid

• This extremely corrosive acid is formed when certain types of synthetic rubber, found in some O-rings, oil seals, fuel hoses etc, are exposed to temperatures above 400°C. The rubber changes into a charred or sticky substance containing the acid. *Once formed, the acid remains dangerous for years. If it gets onto the skin, it may be necessary to amputate the limb concerned.*
• When dealing with a vehicle which has suffered a fire, or with components salvaged from such a vehicle, wear protective gloves and discard them after use.

The battery

• Batteries contain sulphuric acid, which attacks clothing, eyes and skin. Take care when topping-up or carrying the battery.
• The hydrogen gas given off by the battery is highly explosive. Never cause a spark or allow a naked light nearby. Be careful when connecting and disconnecting battery chargers or jump leads.

Air bags

• Air bags can cause injury if they go off accidentally. Take care when removing the steering wheel and/or facia. Special storage instructions may apply.

Diesel injection equipment

• Diesel injection pumps supply fuel at very high pressure. Take care when working on the fuel injectors and fuel pipes.

⚠️ *Warning: Never expose the hands, face or any other part of the body to injector spray; the fuel can penetrate the skin with potentially fatal results.*

Remember...

DO

• Do use eye protection when using power tools, and when working under the vehicle.

• Do wear gloves or use barrier cream to protect your hands when necessary.

• Do get someone to check periodically that all is well when working alone on the vehicle.

• Do keep loose clothing and long hair well out of the way of moving mechanical parts.

• Do remove rings, wristwatch etc, before working on the vehicle – especially the electrical system.

• Do ensure that any lifting or jacking equipment has a safe working load rating adequate for the job.

DON'T

• Don't attempt to lift a heavy component which may be beyond your capability – get assistance.

• Don't rush to finish a job, or take unverified short cuts.

• Don't use ill-fitting tools which may slip and cause injury.

• Don't leave tools or parts lying around where someone can trip over them. Mop up oil and fuel spills at once.

• Don't allow children or pets to play in or near a vehicle being worked on.

The following pages are intended to help in dealing with common roadside emergencies and breakdowns. You will find more detailed fault finding information at the back of the manual, and repair information in the main chapters.

If your car won't start and the starter motor doesn't turn

- [ ] If it's a model with automatic transmission, make sure the selector is in 'P' or 'N'.
- [ ] Open the bonnet and make sure that the battery terminals are clean and tight.
- [ ] Switch on the headlights and try to start the engine. If the headlights go very dim when you're trying to start, the battery is probably flat. Get out of trouble by jump starting (see next page) using a friend's car.

If your car won't start even though the starter motor turns as normal

- [ ] Is there fuel in the tank?
- [ ] Is there moisture on electrical components under the bonnet? Switch off the ignition, then wipe off any obvious dampness with a dry cloth. Spray a water-repellent aerosol product (WD-40 or equivalent) on ignition and fuel system electrical connectors like those shown in the photos. Pay special attention to the ignition coil wiring connector and HT leads. (Note that Diesel engines don't normally suffer from damp.)

A Check that the spark plug HT leads (arrowed) are securely connected by pushing them home.

B Check that the HT leads are securely connected to the distributor cap and the wiring connector is securely connected.

C Check that the HT lead and wiring connector are securely connected to the ignition HT coil.

D Check the security and condition of the battery connections.

Check that electrical connections are secure (with the ignition switched off) and spray them with a water dispersant spray like WD40 if you suspect a problem due to damp

Jump starting

HAYNES HiNT

Jump starting will get you out of trouble, but you must correct whatever made the battery go flat in the first place. There are three possibilities:

1 *The battery has been drained by repeated attempts to start, or by leaving the lights on.*

2 *The charging system is not working properly (alternator drivebelt slack or broken, alternator wiring fault or alternator itself faulty).*

3 *The battery itself is at fault (electrolyte low, or battery worn out).*

When jump-starting a car using a booster battery, observe the following precautions:

✔ Before connecting the booster battery, make sure that the ignition is switched off.

✔ Ensure that all electrical equipment (lights, heater, wipers, etc) is switched off.

✔ Make sure that the booster battery is the same voltage as the discharged one in the vehicle.

✔ If the battery is being jump-started from the battery in another vehicle, the two vehcles MUST NOT TOUCH each other.

✔ Make sure that the transmission is in neutral (or PARK, in the case of automatic transmission).

1 Connect one end of the red jump lead to the positive (+) terminal of the flat battery

2 Connect the other end of the red lead to the positive (+) terminal of the booster battery.

3 Connect one end of the black jump lead to the negative (-) terminal of the booster battery

4 Connect the other end of the black jump lead to a bolt or bracket on the engine block, well away from the battery, on the vehicle to be started.

5 Make sure that the jump leads will not come into contact with the fan, drive-belts or other moving parts of the engine.

6 Start the engine using the booster battery, then with the engine running at idle speed, disconnect the jump leads in the reverse order of connection.

Wheel changing

Some of the details shown here will vary according to model. For instance, the location of the spare wheel and jack is not the same on all cars. However, the basic principles apply to all vehicles.

 Warning: Do not change a wheel in a situation where you risk being hit by other traffic. On busy roads, try to stop in a lay-by or a gateway. Be wary of passing traffic while changing the wheel – it is easy to become distracted by the job in hand.

Preparation

☐ When a puncture occurs, stop as soon as it is safe to do so.
☐ Park on firm level ground, if possible, and well out of the way of other traffic.
☐ Use hazard warning lights if necessary.

☐ If you have one, use a warning triangle to alert other drivers of your presence.
☐ Apply the handbrake and engage first or reverse gear (or Park on models with automatic transmission.

☐ Chock the wheel diagonally opposite the one being removed – a couple of large stones will do for this.
☐ If the ground is soft, use a flat piece of wood to spread the load under the jack.

Changing the wheel

1 The spare wheel and tools are located in the boot, beneath the trim panel and spare tyre cover. The vehicle jack is on the right-hand side of the boot, behind a flap.

2 Unscrew the retainer to remove the spare wheel and prise off the wheel cover.

3 Loosen the wheel nuts slightly.

4 Locate the jack head in the notched jacking point on the sill, then using the wheel brace and trim removal tool as a jack handle, raise the car.

5 Remove the wheel nuts, and the wheel.

6 Fit the spare wheel, fit and hand tighten the wheel nuts, then lower the car and securely tighten the wheel nuts when the wheel is on the ground.

7 Refit the wheel cover, aligning the valve with the wheel cover hole, indicated by the marking (arrowed) on the inside.

Finally...

☐ Remove the wheel chocks.

☐ Stow the jack and tools in the correct locations in the car.

☐ Check the tyre pressure on the wheel just fitted. If it is low, or if you don't have a pressure gauge with you, drive slowly to the nearest garage and inflate the tyre to the right pressure.

☐ Have the damaged tyre or wheel repaired as soon as possible.

Puddles on the garage floor or drive, or obvious wetness under the bonnet or underneath the car, suggest a leak that needs investigating. It can sometimes be difficult to decide where the leak is coming from, especially if the engine bay is very dirty already. Leaking oil or fluid can also be blown rearwards by the passage of air under the car, giving a false impression of where the problem lies.

 Warning: Most automotive oils and fluids are poisonous. Wash them off skin, and change out of contaminated clothing, without delay.

 The smell of a fluid leaking from the car may provide a clue to what's leaking. Some fluids are distinctively coloured. It may help to clean the car and to park it over some clean paper as an aid to locating the source of the leak. Remember that some leaks may only occur while the engine is running.

Sump oil

Engine oil may leak from the drain plug...

Oil from filter

...or from the base of the oil filter.

Gearbox oil

Gearbox oil can leak from the seals at the inboard ends of the driveshafts.

Antifreeze

Leaking antifreeze often leaves a crystalline deposit like this.

Brake fluid

A leak occurring at a wheel is almost certainly brake fluid.

Power steering fluid

Power steering fluid may leak from the pipe connectors on the steering rack.

Towing

When all else fails, you may find yourself having to get a tow home – or of course you may be helping somebody else. Long-distance recovery should only be done by a garage or breakdown service. For shorter distances, DIY towing using another car is easy enough, but observe the following points:

☐ Use a proper tow-rope – they are not expensive. The vehicle being towed must display an 'ON TOW' sign in its rear window.
☐ Always turn the ignition key to the 'on' position when the vehicle is being towed, so that the steering lock is released, and that the direction indicator and brake lights will work.
☐ Only attach the tow-rope to the towing eyes provided.
☐ Before being towed, release the handbrake and select neutral on the transmission.

☐ Note that greater-than-usual pedal pressure will be required to operate the brakes, since the vacuum servo unit is only operational with the engine running.
☐ On models with power steering, greater-than-usual steering effort will also be required.
☐ The driver of the car being towed must keep the tow-rope taut at all times to avoid snatching.
☐ Make sure that both drivers know the route before setting off.
☐ Only drive at moderate speeds and keep the distance towed to a minimum. Drive smoothly and allow plenty of time for slowing down at junctions.
☐ On models with automatic transmission, special precautions apply. If in doubt, do not tow, or transmission damage may result.

Front towing eye on the Sunny 5 door Hatchback

Introduction

There are some very simple checks which need only take a few minutes to carry out, but which could save you a lot of inconvenience and expense.

These "Weekly checks" require no great skill or special tools, and the small amount of time they take to perform could prove to be very well spent, for example;

☐ Keeping an eye on tyre condition and pressures, will not only help to stop them wearing out prematurely, but could also save your life.

☐ Many breakdowns are caused by electrical problems. Battery-related faults are particularly common, and a quick check on a regular basis will often prevent the majority of these.

☐ If your car develops a brake fluid leak, the first time you might know about it is when your brakes don't work properly. Checking the level regularly will give advance warning of this kind of problem.

☐ If the oil or coolant levels run low, the cost of repairing any engine damage will be far greater than fixing the leak, for example.

Underbonnet check points

◀ **1.6 litre petrol**

A *Engine oil level dipstick*
B *Engine oil filler cap*
C *Coolant expansion tank cap and radiator filler cap*
D *Brake fluid reservoir*
E *Screen washer fluid reservoir*
F *Battery*

Engine oil level

Before you start

✔ Make sure that your car is on level ground.
✔ Check the oil level before the car is driven, or at least 5 minutes after the engine has been switched off.

 HAYNES HINT *If the oil is checked immediately after driving the vehicle, some of the oil will remain in the upper engine components, resulting in an inaccurate reading on the dipstick!*

The correct oil

Modern engines place great demands on their oil. It is very important that the correct oil for your car is used (See "Lubricants, fluids and tyre pressures").

Car Care

● If you have to add oil frequently, you should check whether you have any oil leaks. Place some clean paper under the car overnight, and check for stains in the morning. If there are no leaks, the engine may be burning oil *(see "Fault Finding").*

● Always maintain the level between the upper and lower dipstick marks (see photo 3). If the level is too low severe engine damage may occur. Oil seal failure may result if the engine is overfilled by adding too much oil.

1 The engine oil dipstick is located on the front of the engine. Withdraw the dipstick

2 Using a clean rag or paper towel remove all oil from the dipstick. Insert the clean dipstick into the tube as far as it will go, then withdraw it again

3 Note the oil level on the end of the dipstick, which should be between the "H" and "L" marks

4 Oil is added through the filler cap. Unscrew the cap and top-up the level; a funnel may help to reduce spillage. Add the oil slowly, checking the level on the dipstick often. Don't overfill (see "Car Care" *left*)

Coolant level

 Warning: DO NOT attempt to remove the expansion tank pressure cap when the engine is hot, as there is a very great risk of scalding. Do not leave open containers of coolant about, as it is poisonous.

Car Care

● With a sealed-type cooling system, adding coolant should not be necessary on a regular basis. If frequent topping-up is required, it is likely there is a leak. Check the radiator, all hoses and joint faces for signs of staining or wetness, and rectify as necessary.

● It is important that antifreeze is used in the cooling system all year round, not just during the winter months. Don't top-up with water alone, as the antifreeze will become too diluted.

1 The coolant level varies with the temperature of the engine. When the engine is cold, the coolant level should be between the "MIN" and "MAX" marks on the expansion tank. When hot, the level may rise slightly above the "MAX" mark

2 If topping-up is necessary remove the cap from the expansion tank. Although the expansion tank is not pressurised, it is preferable to wait until the engine is cold before topping up the level. Also remove the radiator filler cap.

3 Where necessary, add a mixture of water and antifreeze to the radiator until it is full, then refit and tighten the radiator cap. Add a mixture of water and antifreeze to the expansion tank until the level reaches the "MAX" mark, then refit the tank cap.

Brake fluid level

Note: *Although this procedure is included in "Weekly Checks", the manufacturers only require it to be carried out at 9000 mile/6 month intervals (see Chapter 1).*

Warning:
● *Brake fluid can harm your eyes and damage painted surfaces, so use extreme caution when handling and pouring it.*
● *Do not use fluid that has been standing open for some time, as it absorbs moisture from the air, which can cause a dangerous loss of braking effectiveness.*

HAYNES HiNT • *Make sure that your car is on level ground.*
• *The fluid level in the reservoir will drop slightly as the brake pads wear down, but the fluid level must never be allowed to drop below the "MIN" mark.*

Safety First!

● If the reservoir requires repeated topping-up this is an indication of a fluid leak somewhere in the system, which should be investigated immediately.
● If a leak is suspected, the car should not be driven until the braking system has been checked. Never take any risks where brakes are concerned.

1 The brake fluid reservoir is located at the rear of the engine compartment, on the right-hand side.

2 The "MAX" and "MIN" marks are indicated on the reservoir. The fluid level must be maintained between these marks, and must NEVER fall below the "MIN" mark.

3 If topping-up is necessary, wipe clean the filler cap then unscrew the reservoir cap and carefully lift it out of position, taking care not to damage the level switch float. Inspect the reservoir, if the fluid is dirty the fluid should be renewed (see Chapter 1).

4 Carefully add fluid, taking care not to spill it onto the surrounding components. Use only the specified fluid; mixing different types can cause damage to the system. After topping-up to the correct level, securely refit the cap and wipe off any spilt fluid.

Screen washer fluid level

On models with a headlight washer system, a separate washer reservoir is located behind the screen washer reservoir

Screenwash additives not only keep the winscreen clean during foul weather, they also prevent the washer system freezing in cold weather - which is when you are likely to need it most. Don't top up using plain water as the screenwash will become too diluted, and will freeze during cold weather. *On no account use coolant antifreeze in the washer system - this could discolour or damage paintwork.*

1 The screen washer fluid reservoir is located in the front right-hand corner of the engine compartment, next to the cooling system expansion tank.

2 On some models a level warning light is provided on the instrument panel. On other models press with your finger on the hole in the reservoir cap and withdraw the level tube - the fluid level should be between the upper and lower marks.

3 When topping-up the reservoir, a screenwash additive should be added in the quantities recommended on the bottle. Continue filling until fluid can be seen in the filler neck.

Tyre condition and pressure

It is very important that tyres are in good condition, and at the correct pressure - having a tyre failure at any speed is highly dangerous. Tyre wear is influenced by driving style - harsh braking and acceleration, or fast cornering, will all produce more rapid tyre wear. As a general rule, the front tyres wear out faster than the rears. Interchanging the tyres from front to rear ("rotating" the tyres) may result in more even wear. However, if this is completely effective, you may have the expense of replacing all four tyres at once! Remove any nails or stones embedded in the tread before they penetrate the tyre to cause deflation. If removal of a nail does reveal that the tyre has been punctured, refit the nail so that its point of penetration is marked. Then immediately change the wheel, and have the tyre repaired by a tyre dealer.

Regularly check the tyres for damage in the form of cuts or bulges, especially in the sidewalls. Periodically remove the wheels, and clean any dirt or mud from the inside and outside surfaces. Examine the wheel rims for signs of rusting, corrosion or other damage. Light alloy wheels are easily damaged by "kerbing" whilst parking; steel wheels may also become dented or buckled. A new wheel is very often the only way to overcome severe damage.

New tyres should be balanced when they are fitted, but it may become necessary to re-balance them as they wear, or if the balance weights fitted to the wheel rim should fall off. Unbalanced tyres will wear more quickly, as will the steering and suspension components. Wheel imbalance is normally signified by vibration, particularly at a certain speed (typically around 50 mph). If this vibration is felt only through the steering, then it is likely that just the front wheels need balancing. If, however, the vibration is felt through the whole car, the rear wheels could be out of balance. Wheel balancing should be carried out by a tyre dealer or garage.

1 Tread Depth - visual check
The original tyres have tread wear safety bands (B), which will appear when the tread depth reaches approximately 1.6 mm. The band positions are indicated by a triangular mark on the tyre sidewall (A).

2 Tread Depth - manual check
Alternatively, tread wear can be monitored with a simple, inexpensive device known as a tread depth indicator gauge.

3 Tyre Pressure Check
Check the tyre pressures regularly with the tyres cold. Do not adjust the tyre pressures immediately after the vehicle has been used, or an inaccurate setting will result.

Tyre tread wear patterns

Shoulder Wear

Underinflation (wear on both sides)
Under-inflation will cause overheating of the tyre, because the tyre will flex too much, and the tread will not sit correctly on the road surface. This will cause a loss of grip and excessive wear, not to mention the danger of sudden tyre failure due to heat build-up.
Check and adjust pressures
Incorrect wheel camber (wear on one side)
Repair or renew suspension parts
Hard cornering
Reduce speed!

Centre Wear

Overinflation
Over-inflation will cause rapid wear of the centre part of the tyre tread, coupled with reduced grip, harsher ride, and the danger of shock damage occurring in the tyre casing.
Check and adjust pressures

If you sometimes have to inflate your car's tyres to the higher pressures specified for maximum load or sustained high speed, don't forget to reduce the pressures to normal afterwards.

Uneven Wear

Front tyres may wear unevenly as a result of wheel misalignment. Most tyre dealers and garages can check and adjust the wheel alignment (or "tracking") for a modest charge.
Incorrect camber or castor
Repair or renew suspension parts
Malfunctioning suspension
Repair or renew suspension parts
Unbalanced wheel
Balance tyres
Incorrect toe setting
Adjust front wheel alignment
Note: *The feathered edge of the tread which typifies toe wear is best checked by feel.*

Wiper blades

1 Check the condition of the wiper blades; if they are cracked or show any signs of deterioration, or if the glass swept area is smeared, renew them. Wiper blades should be renewed annually.

2 To remove a windscreen wiper blade, pull the arm fully away from the screen until it locks. Swivel the blade through 90°, press the locking tab with your fingers and slide the blade out of the arm's hooked end.

Battery

Caution: Before carrying out any work on the vehicle battery, read the precautions given in "Safety first" at the start of this manual.

✔ Make sure that the battery tray is in good condition, and that the clamp is tight. Corrosion on the tray, retaining clamp and the battery itself can be removed with a solution of water and baking soda. Thoroughly rinse all cleaned areas with water. Any metal parts damaged by corrosion should be covered with a zinc-based primer, then painted.

✔ Periodically (approximately every three months), check the charge condition of the battery as described in Chapter 5A.

✔ If the battery is flat, and you need to jump start your vehicle, see *Roadside Repairs*.

1 The battery is located on the left-hand side of the engine compartment. The exterior of the battery should be inspected periodically for damage such as a cracked case or cover.

2 Check the tightness of battery clamps (A) to ensure good electrical connections. You should not be able to move them. Also check each cable (B) for cracks and frayed conductors.

HAYNES HINT

Battery corrosion can be kept to a minimum by applying a layer of petroleum jelly to the clamps and terminals after they are reconnected.

3 If corrosion (white, fluffy deposits) is evident, remove the cables from the battery terminals, clean them with a small wire brush, then refit them. Automotive stores sell a tool for cleaning the battery post . . .

4 . . . as well as the battery cable clamps

Bulbs and fuses

✔ Check all external lights and the horn. Refer to the appropriate Sections of Chap-ter 12 for details if any of the circuits are found to be inoperative.

✔ Visually check all accessible wiring connectors, harnesses and retaining clips for security, and for signs of chafing or damage.

 HAYNES HiNT *If you need to check your brake lights and indicators unaided, back up to a wall or garage door and operate the lights. The reflected light should show if they are working properly.*

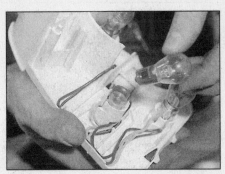

1 If a single indicator light, stoplight or headlight has failed, it is likely that a bulb has blown and will need to be replaced. Refer to Chapter 12 for details. If both stoplights have failed, it is possible that the stop light switch has failed.

2 If more than one indicator light or headlight has failed it is likely that either a fuse has blown or that there is a fault in the circuit (see Chapter 12). The main fuses are located in the fusebox on the driver's side of the facia.

3 Additional fuses and circuit breakers are located in auxiliary fuse boxes in the right-hand and left-hand sides of the engine compartment.

4 To replace a blown fuse, unclip the cover then use the special puller to remove the fuse. Fit a new fuse of the same rating, available from car accessory shops. It is important that you find the reason that the fuse blew - a complete checking procedure is given in Chapter 12.

Lubricants and fluids

Engine . . . . Multigrade engine oil, viscosity SAE10W/40 to 20W/50, to API SG/CD or better

Cooling system . . . . Ethylene glycol-based antifreeze and soft water

Manual gearbox . . . . Hypoid gear oil, viscosity SAE80W to API GL-4

Automatic transmission . . . . Dexron type II automatic transmission fluid (ATF)

Braking system . . . . Hydraulic fluid to SAE J1703F or DOT 4

Power steering . . . . Dexron type II automatic transmission fluid (ATF)

Tyre pressures (cold)

Note: *The correct tyre pressures for your particular car are given on a plate attached to the front door rear pillar on the driver's side, and these should be adhered to where possible. The following pressures are generally applicable, however.*

Tyre size	Front	Rear
Saloon/Hatchback models:		
155SR13	2.2 bar (31 psi)	2.0 bar (28 psi)
175/70 R13 82H	2.2 bar (31 psi)	2.0 bar (28 psi)
Coupe models:		
175/65 R14 82H	2.2 bar (31 psi)	2.0 bar (28 psi)

Chapter 1
Routine maintenance and servicing

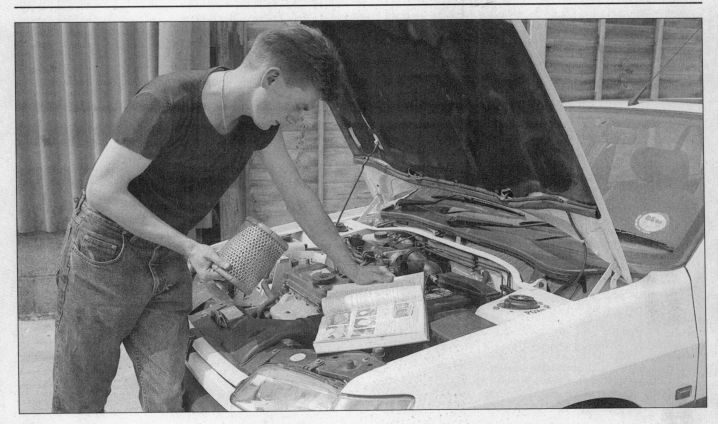

Contents

Degrees of difficulty

Easy, suitable for novice with little experience	Fairly easy, suitable for beginner with some experience	Fairly difficult, suitable for competent DIY mechanic	Difficult, suitable for experienced DIY mechanic	Very difficult, suitable for expert DIY or professional

Lubricants and fluids
Refer to end of "Weekly checks"

Capacities
Engine oil .... 3.2 litres
Cooling system:
    Manual transmission models .... 5.5 litres
    Automatic transmission models .... 5.9 litres
Transmission:
    1.4 litre manual transmission models .... 2.8 litres
    1.6 litre manual transmission models .... 2.9 litres
    All automatic transmission models .... 7.0 litres
Power-assisted steering .... 1.0 litre
Fuel tank .... 50 litres

Engine
Oil filter .... Champion C109

Cooling system
Antifreeze mixture:
    28% antifreeze .... Protection down to -15°C (5°F)
    50% antifreeze .... Protection down to -30°C (-22°F)
Note: *Refer to antifreeze manufacturer for latest recommendations.*

Fuel system
Air filter element:
    Carburettor models .... Champion W247
    Fuel injection models:
        1.4 models .... Champion type not available
        1.6 models .... Champion U548
Fuel filter:
    Carburettor models .... Champion L110
    Fuel injection models .... Champion L215
Idle speed:
    Manual transmission carburettor models .... 750 ± 50 rpm
    Manual transmission fuel injection models .... 700 ± 50 rpm
    Automatic transmission carburettor models .... 850 ± 50 rpm
    Automatic transmission fuel injection models .... 800 ± 50 rpm
Mixture CO%:
    Non-catalytic converter models .... 1.5 ± 0.5
    Catalytic converter models .... 0.5 maximum (not adjustable)

Ignition system
Ignition timing (at idle speed):
    Carburettor models:
        GA14DS (vacuum/EGR boost hose disconnected) .... 0° ± 2° BTDC
        GA14DS (vacuum/EGR boost hose connected) .... 10° ± 5° BTDC
        GA16DS (vacuum/EGR boost hose disconnected) .... 2° ± 2° BTDC
        GA16DS (vacuum/EGR boost hose connected) .... 10° ± 5° BTDC
    Fuel-injected models .... 10° ± 2° BTDC
Spark plugs:
    GA16DS models (1.6 with carburettor) .... Champion RC7YCC4 or RC7YC4
    All other models .... Champion RC9YCC4 or RC9YC4
Spark plug electrode gap .... 1.1 mm (0.043 in)

Brakes
Brake pad friction material minimum thickness .... 2.0 mm
Brake shoe friction material minimum thickness .... 1.5 mm

Auxiliary drivebelt adjustment

	Setting (mm)	Limit (mm)
Alternator:		
With power steering	7 to 9	11
Without power steering	7 to 9	10
Air conditioning compressor	6 to 8	9.5
Power steering pump	4 to 6	7.5

Note: *In all cases, the drivebelt deflection is measured by applying a force of 98 N (10 kg) as described in the text. All figures are quoted for a "used" drivebelt - if a new belt has been fitted, the setting deflection should be decreased by 1 mm.*

Torque wrench settings	Nm	lbf ft
Engine sump drain plug	34	25
Spark plugs	25	18
Air conditioning compressor drivebelt tensioning pulley nut	28	21
Cylinder block coolant drain plug	40	30
Roadwheel nuts	108	80
Seat belt mounting bolts	50	37
Manual transmission:		
Filler/level plug	29	22
Drain plug	29	22
Automatic transmission drain plug	34	25

Maintenance Schedule

The maintenance intervals in this manual are provided with the assumption that you, not the dealer, will be carrying out the work. These are the minimum maintenance intervals recommended by us for vehicles driven daily. If you wish to keep your vehicle in peak condition at all times, you may wish to perform some procedures more often. We encourage frequent maintenance, since it enhances the efficiency, performance and resale value of your car.

When the vehicle is new, it should be serviced by a dealer service department, in order to preserve the factory warranty.

Note: Operations marked with an asterisk should be performed more frequently if the vehicle is used in severe conditions (ie towing a trailer, repeated short distances, dusty conditions etc).

Every 250 miles (400 km) or weekly
- [ ] Refer to "Weekly checks"

Every 9000 miles (15 000 km) or 6 months - whichever comes first
- [ ] Renew the engine oil and filter* (Section 3)
- [ ] Check and adjust the idle speed and mixture settings (Section 4)
- [ ] Renew the spark plugs - models without a catalytic converter (Section 5)
- [ ] Check the brake fluid level (Section 6)
- [ ] Check the power steering fluid level (Section 7)
- [ ] Check the automatic transmission fluid level (Section 8)
- [ ] Check all underbonnet components and hoses for fluid leaks (Section 9)
- [ ] Check manual transmission oil level (Section 10)
- [ ] Check the front and (where fitted) rear brake pads and discs and renew if necessary (Section 11)
- [ ] Check and adjust the handbrake (Section 12)
- [ ] Check and adjust the clutch (Section 13)

Every 18 000 miles (30 000 km) or 12 months - whichever comes first
In addition to the items listed above, carry out the following:
- [ ] Check the condition of the auxiliary drivebelt(s), and renew if necessary (Section 14)
- [ ] Renew the fuel filter (Section 15)
- [ ] Renew the spark plugs - models with a catalytic converter (Section 16)
- [ ] Check the air cleaner automatic temperature control - non-catalyst carburettor models (Section 17)
- [ ] Check the condition of the emissions control system hoses and components (Section 18)

- [ ] Check the operation of the exhaust gas (oxygen) sensor (Section 19)
- [ ] Change the brake fluid (Section 20)
- [ ] Check the steering and suspension components for condition and security (Section 21)
- [ ] Check the condition of the driveshaft rubber gaiters (Section 22)
- [ ] Check the exhaust system (Section 23)
- [ ] Check the wheel alignment and balance (Section 24)
- [ ] Rotate roadwheels (Section 25)
- [ ] Check the rear brake shoes and drums and renew if necessary (Section 26)
- [ ] Check the operation and security of all seat belts (Section 27)
- [ ] Lubricate all hinges and locks (Section 28)
- [ ] Carry out a road test (Section 29)

Every 36 000 miles (60 000 km) or 2 years - whichever comes first
In addition to all the items listed above, carry out the following:
- [ ] Renew the air filter* (Section 30)
- [ ] Check the ignition system components (Section 31)
- [ ] Renew the PCV filter (Section 32)
- [ ] Check the operation of the braking system servo hose and non-return check-valve (Section 33)
- [ ] Renew the coolant (Section 34)

Every 36 000 miles (60 000 km) or 12 months - whichever comes first
Note: *The work given in this Section is only necessary where the vehicle is used in severe conditions (ie towing a trailer, repeated short distances, dusty conditions etc).*
In addition to all the items listed above, carry out the following:
- [ ] Renew the manual transmission oil* (Section 35)
- [ ] Renew the automatic transmission fluid* (Section 36)

1

Underbonnet view of a 1.6 litre fuel-injected model

1 Engine oil filler cap
2 Engine oil dipstick
3 Battery
4 Master cylinder
   brake fluid reservoir
5 Relay box
6 Radiator pressure cap
7 Alternator
8 Braking system
   vacuum servo unit
9 Coolant expansion tank
10 Fuel filter
11 Exhaust gas sensor
12 Air cleaner housing
13 Power steering fluid reservoir
14 Windscreen wiper motor
15 Distributor
16 Windscreen washer reservoir

Front underbody view - 1.6 litre model (1.4 model similar)

1 Centre member
2 Sump drain plug
3 Alternator
4 Radiator cooling fan
5 Brake caliper
6 Lower arm
7 Driveshaft
8 Anti-roll bar
9 Exhaust system front pipe
10 Gearchange linkage
   selector rod
11 Track rod

Rear underbody view - 1.6 litre model (1.4 model similar)

1 Fuel tank
2 Exhaust system intermediate pipe
3 Handbrake cable
4 Exhaust system rear box
5 Anti-roll bar
6 Parallel link
7 Radius rod
8 Fuel tank filler neck

Maintenance procedures

1 Introduction

General information

This Chapter is designed to help the home mechanic maintain his/her vehicle for safety, economy, long life and peak performance.

The Chapter contains a master maintenance schedule, followed by Sections dealing specifically with each task in the schedule. Visual checks, adjustments, component renewal and other helpful items are included. Refer to the accompanying illustrations of the engine compartment and the underside of the vehicle for the locations of the various components.

Servicing your vehicle in accordance with the mileage/time maintenance schedule and the following Sections will provide a planned maintenance programme, which should result in a long and reliable service life. This is a comprehensive plan, so maintaining some items but not others at the specified service intervals, will not produce the same results.

As you service your vehicle, you will discover that many of the procedures can - and should - be grouped together, because of the particular procedure being performed, or because of the close proximity of two otherwise-unrelated components to one

another. For example, if the vehicle is raised for any reason, the exhaust can be inspected at the same time as the suspension and steering components.

The first step in this maintenance programme is to prepare yourself before the actual work begins. Read through all the Sections relevant to the work to be carried out, then make a list and gather together all the parts and tools required. If a problem is encountered, seek advice from a parts specialist, or a dealer service department.

2 Intensive maintenance

If, from the time the vehicle is new, the routine maintenance schedule is followed closely, and frequent checks are made of fluid levels and high-wear items, as suggested throughout this manual, the engine will be kept in relatively good running condition, and the need for additional work will be minimised.

It is possible that there will be times when the engine is running poorly due to the lack of regular maintenance. This is even more likely if a used vehicle, which has not received regular and frequent maintenance checks, is purchased. In such cases, additional work may need to be carried out, outside of the regular maintenance intervals.

If engine wear is suspected, a compression test will provide valuable information regarding the overall performance of the main internal components. Such a test can be used as a basis to decide on the extent of the work to be carried out. If, for example, a compression test indicates serious internal engine wear, conventional maintenance as described in this Chapter will not greatly improve the performance of the engine, and may prove a waste of time and money, unless extensive overhaul work is carried out first.

The following series of operations are those often required to improve the performance of a generally poor-running engine:

Primary operations

a) Clean, inspect and test the battery (see "Weekly checks").
b) Check all the engine-related fluids (see "Weekly checks").
c) Check the condition and tension of the auxiliary drivebelt (Section 14).
d) Renew the spark plugs (Section 5 or 16).
e) Inspect the distributor cap and HT leads - as applicable (Section 31).
f) Check the condition of the air cleaner filter element, and renew if necessary (Section 30).
g) Renew the fuel filter (Section 15).
h) Check the condition of all hoses, and check for fluid leaks (Section 9).
i) Check the idle speed and mixture settings - as applicable (Section 4).

If the primary operations do not prove fully effective, carry out the following secondary operations:

Secondary operations

a) *Check the charging system (Chapter 5A).*
b) *Check the ignition system (Chapter 5B).*
c) *Check the fuel system (Chapter 4).*
d) *Renew the distributor cap and rotor arm - as applicable (Chapter 5B).*
f) *Renew the ignition HT leads - as applicable (Section 31).*

9000 Mile / 6 Month Service

3 Engine oil and filter renewal

1 Frequent oil and filter changes are the most important preventative maintenance procedures which can be undertaken by the DIY owner. As engine oil ages, it becomes diluted and contaminated, which leads to premature engine wear.

2 Before starting this procedure, gather together all the necessary tools and materials. Also make sure that you have plenty of clean rags and newspapers handy, to mop up any spills. Ideally, the engine oil should be warm, as it will drain better, and more built-up sludge will be removed with it. Take care, however, not to touch the exhaust or any other hot parts of the engine when working under the vehicle. To avoid any possibility of scalding, and to protect yourself from possible skin irritants and other harmful contaminants in used engine oils, it is advisable to wear gloves when carrying out this work. Access to the underside of the vehicle will be greatly improved if it can be raised on a lift, driven onto ramps, or jacked up and supported on axle stands (see

"Jacking and Vehicle Support"). Whichever method is chosen, make sure that the vehicle remains level, or if it is at an angle, that the drain plug is at the lowest point.

3 Remove the oil filler cap from the cylinder head cover (twist it anti-clockwise and withdraw it).

4 Using a spanner, or preferably a suitable socket and bar, slacken the drain plug about half a turn. Position the draining container under the drain plug, then remove the plug completely **(see Haynes Hint)**. Recover the sealing ring from the drain plug.

5 Allow some time for the oil to drain, noting that it may be necessary to reposition the container as the oil flow slows to a trickle.

6 After all the oil has drained, wipe the drain plug and the sealing washer with a clean rag. Examine the condition of the sealing washer - renew it if it shows signs of scoring or other damage which may prevent an oil-tight seal. Clean the area around the drain plug opening, and refit the plug complete with the washer. Tighten the plug securely - preferably to the specified torque, using a torque wrench.

7 The oil filter is located at the rear right-hand side of the cylinder block - access is most easily obtained from underneath the vehicle.

8 Move the container into position under the oil filter.

9 Use an oil filter removal tool (if required) to slacken the filter initially, then unscrew it by hand the rest of the way. Empty the oil from the old filter into the container.

10 Use a clean rag to remove all oil, dirt and sludge from the filter sealing area on the engine. Check the old filter to make sure that the rubber sealing ring has not stuck to the engine. If it has, carefully remove it.

11 Apply a light coating of clean engine oil to the sealing ring on the new filter, then screw the filter into position on the engine. Lightly tighten the filter until its sealing ring contacts the block, then tighten it through a further two-thirds of a turn **(see illustration)**.

12 Remove the old oil and all tools from under the vehicle then, if applicable, lower the vehicle to the ground.

13 Fill the engine through the filler hole in the cylinder head cover, using the correct grade and type of oil (refer to *"Weekly Checks"* for details of topping-up). Pour in half the specified quantity of oil first, then wait a few minutes for the oil to drain into the sump. Continue to add oil, a small quantity at a time, until the level is up to the lower mark on the dipstick. Adding a further 1.0 litre will bring the level up to the upper mark on the dipstick.

14 Start the engine and run it for a few minutes, while checking for leaks around the oil filter seal and the sump drain plug. Note that there may be a delay of a few seconds before the low oil pressure warning light goes out when the engine is first started, as the oil circulates through the new oil filter and the engine oil galleries before the pressure builds up. Do not run the engine above idle speed while the warning light is on.

15 Stop the engine, and wait a few minutes for the oil to settle in the sump once more. With the new oil circulated and the filter now completely full, recheck the level on the dipstick, and add more oil as necessary.

HAYNES HiNT

Keep the drain plug pressed into the sump while unscrewing it by hand last couple of turns. As the plug releases, move it away sharply so the stream of oil issuing from the sump runs into the container, not up your sleeve!

3.11 Fitting the oil filter (viewed from below)

OIL CARE FOLLOW THE CODE

OIL BANK LINE
0800 66 33 66

Note: It is antisocial and illegal to dump oil down the drain. To find the location of your local oil recycling bank, call this number free.

4 Idle speed and mixture check and adjustment

1 Before checking the idle speed and mixture setting, always check first the following.

a) *Check that the ignition timing is accurate (Chapter 5).*

b) *Check that the spark plugs are in good condition and correctly gapped (Section 5 or 16).*

c) *Check that the accelerator cable is correctly adjusted (see relevant Part of Chapter 4).*

d) *Check the crankcase breather hoses are secure, with no leaks or kinks (Chapter 4C).*

e) *Check that the air cleaner filter element is clean (Section 30).*

f) *Check that the exhaust system is in good condition (Section 23).*

g) *If the engine is running very roughly, check the compression pressures as described in Chapter 2A.*

h) *On fuel-injected models, check that the fuel injection/ignition system warning light is not illuminated (see relevant Part of Chapter 4).*

2 The idle mixture (exhaust gas CO level) is set at the factory, and should require no further adjustment. If, due to a change in engine characteristics (carbon build-up, bore wear etc) or after a major carburettor overhaul, the mixture becomes incorrect, it can be reset. Note, however, that an exhaust gas analyser (CO meter) will be required to check the mixture and to set it with the necessary standard of accuracy; if this is not available, the car must be taken to a Nissan dealer for the work to be carried out.

3 Take the car on a journey of sufficient length to warm it up to normal operating temperature. **Note:** *Adjustment should be completed within two minutes of return, without stopping the engine. If this cannot be achieved, or if the radiator electric cooling fan operates, wait for the cooling fan to stop. Clear any excess fuel from the inlet manifold by racing the engine two or three times to between 2000 and 3000 rpm, then allow it to idle again.*

4 Ensure that all electrical loads are switched off; if the car does not have a tachometer, connect one following its manufacturer's instructions. Note the idle speed, comparing it with that specified. Proceed as described under the relevant sub-heading.

Carburettor non-catalyst models

5 The idle speed adjusting screw is situated at the rear of the carburettor, and is accessible from behind the air cleaner housing. Screw it in or out as necessary to obtain the specified speed **(see illustration)**.

6 If an exhaust gas analyser is available, follow the manufacturer's instructions to check the exhaust gas CO level. If adjustment

4.5 On carburettor models, the idle speed adjusting screw is situated at the rear of the carburettor (shown with air cleaner removed for clarity)

is required, it is made by altering the mixture adjustment screw which is situated directly below the idle speed adjusting screw.

7 Using a suitable flat-bladed screwdriver, turn the mixture adjustment screw in very small increments until the level is correct; screwing it in (clockwise) weakens the idle mixture and reduces the CO level, screwing it out will richen the mixture and increase the CO level.

8 When adjustments are complete, disconnect any test equipment and recheck the idle speed, adjusting as necessary.

Carburettor catalyst models

9 Adjust the idle speed as described above in paragraph 5.

10 Referring to paragraph 2, check and adjust the idle mixture as follows.

11 Stop the engine and turn off the ignition switch. Disconnect the wiring connector from the exhaust gas sensor (which is screwed into the exhaust manifold) and the air induction solenoid control valve (which is mounted onto the left-hand side of the inlet manifold) (see Chapter 4 for further information).

12 Remove the cap from the top of the exhaust gas take-off pipe which is situated on the left-hand side of the exhaust manifold, and connect the CO meter to the take-off pipe **(see illustration)**.

13 Start the engine, clear excess fuel from the inlet manifold by racing the engine two or three times to between 2000 and 3000 rpm, then allow it to idle again. Check the exhaust gas CO level is within the limits given in the Specifications.

14 If adjustment is required, using a sharp instrument, hook out the tamperproof plug from carburettor to gain access to the mixture adjustment screw, which is situated directly below the idle speed adjusting screw.

15 Using a suitable flat-bladed screwdriver, turn the mixture adjustment screw in very small increments until the level is correct; screwing it in (clockwise) weakens the idle mixture and reduces the CO level, screwing it out will richen the mixture and increase the CO level.

16 When adjustments are complete, disconnect any test equipment and fit a new

4.12 On catalyst carburettor models, the exhaust gas CO level is checked at the take-off pipe (arrowed) on the exhaust manifold

tamperproof plug to the mixture adjustment screw. Refit the cap to the exhaust gas take-off pipe, and reconnect the exhaust gas sensor and solenoid valve wiring connectors.

17 Check the idle speed and, if necessary, readjust.

Fuel-injected models

18 Stop the engine and turn off the ignition switch. Disconnect the wiring connector from the throttle potentiometer, which is mounted onto the side of the throttle housing (see Chapter 4 for further information).

19 Start the engine, clear excess fuel from the inlet manifold by racing the engine two or three times to between 2000 and 3000 rpm, then allow it to idle again. Check that the idle speed is within the limits given in the Specifications. If adjustment is necessary, the idle speed adjusting screw is situated on the right-hand side of the throttle housing **(see illustration)**. Screw it in or out as necessary to obtain the specified speed. When the idle speed is correctly set, switch off the engine and reconnect the throttle potentiometer wiring connector.

20 Experienced home mechanics with a considerable amount of skill and equipment (including a good-quality tachometer and a good-quality, carefully-calibrated exhaust gas analyser) may be able to *check* the exhaust CO level. However, if it is found to be in need of *adjustment*, there must be a fault in the ECCS control system; no adjustment of the mixture is possible.

4.19 On fuel injection models, the idle speed adjusting screw (arrowed) is on the right-hand side of the throttle housing

1

5.2 Disconnecting an HT lead from the spark plug

5.4a Tools required for spark plug removal, gap adjustment and refitting

5.4b Removing a spark plug

21 If the exhaust gas CO content is incorrect, check the operation of the exhaust gas sensor and fuel injection system components using the ECCS control unit self-diagnostic function (see Chapter 4B). If this fails to show the problem, the vehicle must be taken to a Nissan dealer for testing.

5 Spark plug renewal - models without a catalytic converter

1 The correct functioning of the spark plugs is vital for the correct running and efficiency of the engine. It is essential that the plugs fitted are appropriate for the engine (a suitable type is specified at the beginning of this Chapter). If this type is used and the engine is in good condition, the spark plugs should not need attention between scheduled replacement intervals. Spark plug cleaning is rarely necessary, and should not be attempted unless specialised equipment is available, as damage can easily be caused to the firing ends.

2 If the marks on the original-equipment spark plug (HT) leads cannot be seen, mark the leads "1" to "4", to correspond to the cylinder the lead serves (No 1 cylinder is at the transmission end of the engine). Pull the leads from the plugs by gripping the end fitting, not the lead, otherwise the lead connection may be fractured. Note that as the spark plugs are deeply recessed, the HT lead end fittings are extended **(see illustration)**.

3 It is advisable to remove the dirt from the spark plug recesses using a clean brush, vacuum cleaner or compressed air before removing the plugs, to prevent dirt dropping into the cylinders.

4 Unscrew the plugs using a spark plug spanner, suitable box spanner or a deep socket and extension bar **(see illustrations)**. Keep the socket aligned with the spark plug - if it is forcibly moved to one side, the ceramic insulator may be broken off. As each plug is removed, examine it as follows.

5 Examination of the spark plugs will give a good indication of the condition of the engine. If the insulator nose of the spark plug is clean and white, with no deposits, this is indicative of a weak mixture or too hot a plug (a hot plug transfers heat away from the electrode slowly, a cold plug transfers heat away quickly).

6 If the tip and insulator nose are covered with hard black-looking deposits, then this is indicative that the mixture is too rich. Should the plug be black and oily, then it is likely that the engine is fairly worn, as well as the mixture being too rich.

7 If the insulator nose is covered with light tan to greyish-brown deposits, then the mixture is correct and it is likely that the engine is in good condition.

8 The spark plug electrode gap is of considerable importance as, if it is too large or too small, the size of the spark and its efficiency will be seriously impaired. The gap should be set to the value given in the Specifications at the beginning of this Chapter.

9 To set the gap, measure it with a feeler blade, and then bend the outer plug electrode until the correct gap is achieved **(see illustrations)**. The centre electrode should never be bent, as this may crack the insulator and cause plug failure, if nothing worse. If using feeler blades, the gap is correct when the appropriate-size blade is a firm sliding fit.

10 Special spark plug electrode gap adjusting tools are available from most motor accessory shops, or from some spark plug manufacturers.

11 Before fitting the spark plugs, check that the threaded connector sleeves are tight, and that the plug exterior surfaces and threads are clean. See **Haynes Hint** below.

12 Remove the rubber hose (if used), and tighten the plug to the specified torque using the spark plug socket and a torque wrench. Refit the remaining spark plugs in the same manner.

13 Connect the HT leads in their correct order, and refit any components removed for access.

HAYNES HiNT

It is very often difficult to insert spark plugs into their holes without cross-threading them. To avoid this possibility, fit a short length of 5/16 inch internal diameter rubber hose over the end of the spark plug. The flexible hose acts as a universal joint to help align the plug with the plug hole. Should the plug begin to cross-thread, the hose will slip on the spark plug, preventing thread damage to the aluminium cylinder head

5.9a Measuring the spark plug gap with a feeler blade . . .

5.9b . . . and adjusting the gap using a special adjusting tool

6 Brake fluid level check

⚠️ *Warning: Brake hydraulic fluid can harm your eyes and damage painted surfaces, so use extreme caution when handling and pouring it. Do not use fluid that has been standing open for some time, as it absorbs moisture from the air. Excess moisture can cause a dangerous loss of braking effectiveness. Be sure to use only the specified brake hydraulic fluid, since mixing different types of fluid can cause damage to the system.*

1 The brake master cylinder and fluid reservoir is mounted on the front of the vacuum servo unit in the engine compartment. The maximum and minimum marks are indicated on the side of the reservoir, and the fluid level should be maintained between these marks at all times.

2 If topping-up is necessary, first wipe the area around the filler cap with a clean rag before removing the cap. When adding fluid, pour it carefully into the reservoir to avoid spilling it on surrounding painted surfaces. Be sure to use only the specified brake hydraulic fluid, since mixing different types of fluid can cause damage to the system. See *"Lubricants, fluids and tyre pressures"* at the beginning of this Manual.

3 When adding fluid, it is a good idea to inspect the reservoir for contamination. The system should be drained and refilled if deposits, dirt particles or contamination are seen in the fluid.

4 After filling the reservoir to the correct level, make sure that the cap is refitted securely, to avoid leaks and the entry of foreign matter.

5 The fluid level in the master cylinder reservoir will drop slightly as the brake pads and shoes wear down during normal operation. If the reservoir requires repeated replenishing to maintain the proper level, this is an indication of a hydraulic leak somewhere in the system, which should be investigated immediately.

7 Power steering fluid level check

1 The power steering fluid reservoir is on the right-hand side of the engine compartment, in front of the suspension turret.

2 For the check, the car should be parked on level ground, with the front wheels pointing straight-ahead. The engine should be switched off. Note that, for the check to be accurate, the steering **must not** be turned once the engine has stopped.

3 The fluid level should be checked using the dipstick fitted to the underside of the reservoir filler cap. Wipe the area around the filler cap,

7.3 Power steering fluid level dipstick markings
1 "HOT" level range   2 "COLD" level range

then unscrew the cap, and read off the level on the dipstick. If the fluid temperature is between 50 and 80°C (if the vehicle has recently been driven on a reasonable run), the level should be read from the "HOT" range on the dipstick. At fluid temperatures of 0 to 30°C (vehicle has not recently been driven, and engine cold), the level should be read from the "COLD" range on the dipstick **(see illustration)**.

4 If necessary, top-up to the relevant "MAX" mark using the specified type of fluid. Take great care not to allow any dirt or foreign matter to enter the hydraulic system, and do not overfill the reservoir **(see illustration)**. When the level is correct, refit the cap. Note that the need for frequent topping-up of the system indicates a leak, which should be investigated immediately.

8 Automatic transmission fluid level check
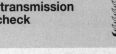

1 Take the vehicle on a short journey to warm the transmission up to normal operating temperature, then park the vehicle on level ground. The fluid level is checked using the dipstick located at the front of the engine compartment, directly below the distributor, which is mounted onto the left-hand end of the cylinder head.

2 With the engine idling and the selector lever in the "P" (Park) position, withdraw the dipstick from the tube, and wipe all the fluid from its end with a clean rag or paper towel. Insert the clean dipstick back into the tube as far as it will go, then withdraw it once more. Note the level on the end of the dipstick, noting that there are two sets of level markings. On one side of the dipstick are the "COLD" upper and lower marks (which are in the form of cut-outs on the edge of the dipstick - for use when the fluid temperature is between 30 and 50°C); on the other side are the "HOT" upper and lower marks (which are in the form of lines marked on the dipstick - for use when the fluid temperature is between 50 and 80°C). If the vehicle is fully warmed-up, the "HOT" marks should be used.

3 If topping-up is necessary, add the required quantity of the specified fluid to the

7.4 Topping-up the power steering fluid level

transmission via the dipstick tube. Use a funnel with a fine mesh gauze, to avoid spillage and to ensure that no foreign matter enters the transmission. Add fluid as necessary until the level is between the relevant set of upper and lower marks on the dipstick. **Note:** *Never overfill the transmission so that the fluid level is above the upper mark.*

4 After topping-up, take the vehicle on a short run to distribute the fresh fluid, then recheck the level again, topping-up if necessary.

5 Always maintain the level between the two dipstick marks. If the level is allowed to fall below the lower mark, various problems, and even severe transmission damage, could result.

9 Hose and fluid leak check

1 Visually inspect the engine joint faces, gaskets and seals for any signs of water or oil leaks. Pay particular attention to the areas around the camshaft cover, cylinder head, oil filter and sump joint faces. Bear in mind that, over a period of time, some very slight seepage from these areas is to be expected - what you are really looking for is any indication of a serious leak. Should a leak be found, renew the offending gasket or oil seal by referring to the appropriate Chapters in this manual.

2 Also check the security and condition of all the engine-related pipes and hoses, and all hydraulic system pipes and hoses. Ensure that all cable-ties or securing clips are in place, and in good condition. Clips which are broken or missing can lead to chafing of the hoses, pipes or wiring, which could cause more serious problems in the future.

3 Carefully check the radiator hoses and heater hoses along their entire length. Renew any hose which is cracked, swollen or deteriorated. Cracks will show up better if the hose is squeezed. Pay close attention to the hose clips that secure the hoses to the cooling system components. Hose clips can pinch and puncture hoses, resulting in cooling system leaks. If the original crimped-type

1

A leak in the cooling system will usually show up as white or rust coloured deposits on the area adjoining the leak

hose clips are used, it may be a good idea to replace them with standard worm-drive clips.

4 Inspect all the cooling system components (hoses, joint faces etc.) for leaks.

5 Where any problems are found on system components, renew the component or gasket with reference to Chapter 3.

6 Where applicable, inspect the automatic transmission fluid cooler hoses for leaks or deterioration.

7 With the vehicle raised, inspect the petrol tank and filler neck for punctures, cracks and other damage. The connection between the filler neck and tank is especially critical. Sometimes a rubber filler neck or connecting hose will leak due to loose retaining clamps or deteriorated rubber.

8 Carefully check all rubber hoses and metal fuel lines leading away from the petrol tank. Check for loose connections, deteriorated hoses, crimped lines, and other damage. Pay particular attention to the vent pipes and hoses, which often loop up around the filler neck and can become blocked or crimped. Follow the lines to the front of the vehicle, carefully inspecting them all the way. Renew damaged sections as necessary. Similarly, whilst the vehicle is raised, take the opportunity to inspect all underbody hydraulic fluid pipes and hoses.

9 From within the engine compartment, check the security of all fuel and hydraulic hose attachments and pipe unions, and inspect the fuel hoses and vacuum hoses for kinks, chafing and deterioration.

10 Manual transmission oil level check

1 Park the car on a level surface. The oil level must be checked before the car is driven, or at least 5 minutes after the engine has been switched off. If the oil is checked immediately after driving the car, some of the oil will remain distributed around the transmission components, resulting in an inaccurate level reading. To improve access, position the car over an inspection pit, or raise the car off the

ground and position it on axle stands (see *"Jacking and Vehicle Support"*), making sure the vehicle remains level to the ground.

2 Wipe clean the area around the filler/level plug, which is on the front face of the transmission. Unscrew the plug and clean it.

3 The oil level should reach the lower edge of the filler/level hole. A certain amount of oil will have gathered behind the filler/level plug and will trickle out when it is removed; this does **not** necessarily indicate that the level is correct. To ensure that a true level is established, wait until the initial trickle has stopped, then add oil as necessary until a trickle of new oil can be seen emerging. The level will be correct when the flow ceases; use only good-quality oil of the specified type **(see illustration)**.

4 Refilling the transmission is an extremely awkward operation; above all, allow plenty of time for the oil level to settle properly before checking it. If a large amount had to be added to the transmission and a large amount flows out on checking the level, refit the filler/level plug, and take the vehicle on a short journey. This will allow the new oil to be distributed fully around the transmission components. On returning, recheck the level when the oil has settled again.

5 If the transmission has been overfilled so that oil flows out as soon as the filler/level plug is removed, check that the car is completely level (front to rear and side to side). If necessary, allow the surplus to drain off into a suitable container.

6 When the level is correct, refit the filler/level plug, tightening it to the specified torque wrench setting. Wash off any spilt oil.

11 Front and (where applicable) rear brake pad check

Front brake pads

1 Firmly apply the handbrake, then jack up the front of the car and support it securely on axle stands (see *"Jacking and Vehicle Support"*). Remove the front roadwheels.

2 For a comprehensive check, the brake pads should be removed and cleaned. The

10.3 Topping-up the manual transmission oil

For a quick check, the thickness of the friction material on each brake pad can be measured through the aperture in the caliper body

operation of the caliper can then also be checked, and the condition of the brake disc itself can be fully examined on both sides. Refer to Chapter 9 for further information **(see Haynes Hint)**.

3 If any pad's friction material is worn to the specified thickness or less, *all four pads must be renewed as a set.*

Rear brake pads

4 Chock the front wheels, then jack up the rear of the vehicle and support it on axle stands (see *"Jacking and Vehicle Support"*). Remove the rear roadwheels.

5 For a quick check, the thickness of friction material remaining on each brake pad can be measured through the top of the caliper body. If any pad's friction material is worn to the specified thickness or less, *all four pads must be renewed as a set.*

6 For a comprehensive check, the brake pads should be removed and cleaned. This will permit the operation of the caliper to be checked, and the condition of the brake disc itself to be fully examined on both sides. Refer to Chapter 9 for further information.

12 Handbrake check and adjustment

Refer to the information in Chapter 9.

13 Clutch check and adjustment

Check that the clutch pedal moves smoothly and easily through its full travel. Check also that the clutch itself functions correctly, with no trace of slip or drag, then adjust the clutch cable as described in Chapter 6. If excessive effort is required to operate the clutch, check first that the cable is correctly routed and undamaged, then remove the pedal to ensure that its pivot is properly greased. Refer to Chapter 6 for further information.

18 000 Mile / 12 Month Service

14 Auxiliary drivebelt check and renewal

1 There are either one, two or three auxiliary drivebelts fitted, depending on specification. The drivebelt arrangements are as follows.

Models without power steering or air conditioning - one drivebelt (drives alternator and coolant pump).

Models with power steering - two drivebelts (one drives the alternator, the other the power steering pump and coolant pump).

Models with power steering and air conditioning - three drivebelts (as for models with power steering, with an additional belt for the air conditioning compressor).

Checking the auxiliary drivebelt

2 Apply the handbrake, then jack up the front of the car and support it on axle stands (see "Jacking and Vehicle Support"). Remove the right-hand front roadwheel.

3 From underneath the front of the car, undo the retaining screws and remove the plastic cover from underneath the wing to gain access to the crankshaft pulley. If necessary, also undo the retaining screws and remove the engine undershield to improve access.

4 Using a socket and extension bar fitted to the crankshaft pulley bolt, rotate the crankshaft so that the entire length of the drivebelt(s) can be examined. Examine the drivebelt(s) for cracks, splitting, fraying or damage. Check also for signs of glazing (shiny patches) and for separation of the belt plies. Renew the belt if worn or damaged.

5 If the condition of the belt is satisfactory, check the drivebelt tension as described below under the relevant sub-heading.

Air conditioning drivebelt

Removal

6 Proceed as described in paragraphs 2 and 3.

7 Disconnect the battery negative lead.

8 Slacken the nut securing the tensioning pulley assembly to the engine.

9 Turn the adjuster bolt to move the tensioner pulley away from the drivebelt until there is sufficient slack for the drivebelt to be removed from the pulleys

Refitting

10 Fit the belt around the pulleys, ensuring that the belt is of the correct type if it is being renewed, and take up the slack in the belt by tightening the adjuster bolt.

11 Tension the drivebelt as described in the following paragraphs.

Tensioning

12 If not already done, proceed as described in paragraphs 2 and 3.

13 Correct tensioning of the drivebelt will ensure that it has a long life. Beware, however, of overtightening, as this can cause wear in the alternator bearings.

14 The belt tension is checked at the mid-point between the pulleys on the top belt run. Referring to the Specifications given at the start of this Chapter, apply the specified force and check that the belt deflection is within the specified range.

15 To adjust the tension, with the tensioner pulley assembly retaining nut slackened, rotate the adjuster bolt until the correct tension is achieved. Once the belt is correctly tensioned, rotate the crankshaft a couple of times and recheck the tension.

16 When the belt is correctly tensioned, tighten the tensioner pulley assembly retaining nut to the specified torque setting, and reconnect the battery negative lead.

17 Refit the cover(s), securely tightening their fasteners, then refit the roadwheel and lower the vehicle to the ground.

Power steering pump drivebelt

Removal

18 Carry out paragraphs 2 and 3.

19 Disconnect the battery negative lead. On models with air conditioning, remove the air conditioning compressor drivebelt.

20 Slacken the power steering pump mounting nuts/bolts (as applicable).

21 Back off the adjuster bolt to relieve the tension in the drivebelt, then slip the drivebelt from the pulleys.

Refitting

22 Fit the belt around the pulleys, ensuring that the belt is of the correct type if it is being renewed, and take up the slack in the belt by tightening the adjuster bolt.

23 Tension the drivebelt as described in the following paragraphs. Where necessary, refit and tension the air conditioning compressor drivebelt as described earlier.

Tensioning

24 If not already done, proceed as described in paragraphs 2 and 3.

25 Correct tensioning of the drivebelt will ensure that it has a long life. Beware, however, of overtightening, as this can cause wear in the alternator bearings.

26 The belt tension is checked at the mid-point between the pulleys on the upper belt run. Referring to the Specifications given at the start of this Chapter, apply the specified force and check that the belt deflection is within the specified range.

27 To adjust, with the upper mounting nut/bolt just holding the power steering pump firm, and the other mounting nut/bolt loosened, turn the adjuster bolt until the correct tension is achieved. Rotate the crankshaft a couple of times, recheck the tension, then securely tighten both the power steering pump mounting nuts/bolts.

28 Refit the cover(s), securely tightening their fasteners, then refit the roadwheel and lower the vehicle to the ground.

Alternator drivebelt

Removal

29 Carry out paragraphs 2 and 3.

30 Disconnect the battery negative lead. On models with air conditioning, remove the air conditioning drivebelt as described earlier. On models with power steering, remove the power steering drivebelt as described earlier.

31 Slacken both the alternator upper and lower mounting nuts/bolts (as applicable) **(see illustration)**.

32 Back off the adjuster bolt to relieve the tension in the drivebelt, then slip the drivebelt from the pulleys **(see illustrations)**.

14.31 Slacken the alternator mounting bolts . . .

14.32a . . . then loosen the adjuster bolt . . .

14.32b . . . and slip the drivebelt off the alternator pulley

Refitting

33 Fit the belt around the pulleys, ensuring that the belt is of the correct type if it is being renewed, and take up the slack in the belt by tightening the adjuster bolt.

34 Tension the drivebelt as described in the following paragraphs. Where necessary, refit the power steering and air conditioning compressor drivebelts as described earlier.

Tensioning

35 If not already done, proceed as described in paragraphs 2 and 3.

36 Correct tensioning of the drivebelt will ensure that it has a long life. Beware, however, of overtightening, as this can cause wear in the alternator bearings.

37 The belt tension is checked at the mid-point between the pulleys on the upper belt run. Referring to the Specifications given at the start of this Chapter, apply the specified force and check that the belt deflection is within the specified range.

38 To adjust, with the upper mounting nut/bolt just holding the alternator firm, and the lower mounting nut/bolt loosened, turn the adjuster bolt until the correct tension is achieved. Rotate the crankshaft a couple of times, recheck the tension, then tighten both the alternator mounting nuts/bolts.

39 Refit the cover(s), securely tightening their fasteners, then refit the roadwheel and lower the vehicle to the ground.

15 Fuel filter renewal

> **Warning: Before carrying out the following operation, refer to the precautions given in "Safety first!" at the beginning of this manual, and follow them implicitly. Petrol is a highly-dangerous and volatile liquid, and the precautions necessary when handling it cannot be overstressed**

1 The fuel filter is situated in the engine compartment, mounted on the left-hand side of the engine compartment bulkhead. Note which way round it is fitted to ensure correct fitting of the new filter.

2 Release the fuel filter from its retaining clips, then release and disconnect the fuel hoses from the filter. On fuel injection models, bear in mind the information given in the relevant Part of Chapter 4 on depressurising the fuel system before the hoses are disconnected **(see illustrations)**.

3 Dispose safely of the old filter; it will be highly inflammable, and may explode if thrown on a fire.

4 Connect the hoses to the new filter and tighten the clips. Where applicable the arrow on the filter must point towards the hose connected to the engine **(see illustration)**.

5 Press the filter into the retaining clips.

15.2a Release the fuel filter from its retaining clips . . .

15.2c . . . and disconnect the hoses

6 Start the engine, and check the filter hoses connections for leaks.

16 Spark plug renewal - models with a catalytic converter

Refer to Section 5.

17 Air cleaner automatic temperature control check

Refer to Chapter 4A, Section 3.

18 Emissions control system check

The emissions control system components and testing are covered in Chapter 4C.

Checking is a simple inspection for obvious signs of damaged or leaking hoses and joints.

19 Exhaust gas sensor check

Carburettor models

On carburettor models, the exhaust gas sensor is tested as described in Section 2 of Chapter 4C.

15.2b . . . then release the hose from the clip . . .

15.4 On refitting, ensure that the filter is fitted so its arrow (arrowed) points in the direction of fuel flow

Fuel-injected models

On fuel-injected models, the exhaust gas sensor can be tested using the ECCS control unit self-diagnosis facility as described in Chapter 4B, Section 11.

20 Brake fluid renewal

> **Warning: Brake hydraulic fluid can harm your eyes and damage painted surfaces, so use extreme caution when handling and pouring it. Do not use fluid that has been standing open for some time, as it absorbs moisture from the air. Excess moisture can cause a dangerous loss of braking effectiveness.**

1 The procedure is similar to that for the bleeding of the hydraulic system as described in Chapter 9, except that the brake fluid reservoir should be emptied by siphoning, using a clean poultry baster or similar before starting, and allowance should be made for the old fluid to be expelled when bleeding a section of the circuit.

2 Working as described in Chapter 9, open the first bleed screw in the sequence, and pump the brake pedal gently until nearly all the old fluid has been emptied from the master cylinder reservoir.

HAYNES HiNT *Old hydraulic fluid is much darker in colour than new fluid, making it easy to distinguish the two.*

3 Top-up to the "MAX" level with new fluid, and continue pumping until only the new fluid remains in the reservoir, and new fluid can be seen emerging from the bleed screw. Tighten the screw, and top the reservoir level up to the "MAX" level line.

4 Work through all the remaining bleed screws in the sequence until new fluid can be seen at all of them. Be careful to keep the master cylinder reservoir topped-up to above the "MIN" level at all times, or air may enter the system and greatly increase the length of the task.

5 When the operation is complete, check that all bleed screws are securely tightened, and that their dust caps are refitted. Wash off all traces of spilt fluid, and recheck the master cylinder reservoir fluid level.

6 Check the operation of the brakes before taking the car on the road.

21 Steering and suspension check

Front suspension and steering check

1 Raise the front of the vehicle, and securely support it on axle stands (see "*Jacking and Vehicle Support*").

2 Visually inspect the balljoint dust covers and the steering rack-and-pinion gaiters for splits, chafing or deterioration **(see illustration)**. Any wear of these components will cause loss of lubricant, together with dirt and water entry, resulting in rapid deterioration of the balljoints or steering gear.

3 On vehicles with power steering, check the fluid hoses for chafing or deterioration, and the pipe and hose unions for fluid leaks. Also check for signs of fluid leakage under pressure from the steering gear rubber gaiters, which would indicate failed fluid seals within the steering gear.

4 Grasp the roadwheel at the 12 o'clock and 6 o'clock positions, and try to rock it **(see illustration)**. Very slight free play may be felt, but if the movement is appreciable, further investigation is necessary to determine the source. Continue rocking the wheel while an assistant depresses the footbrake. If the movement is now eliminated or significantly reduced, it is likely that the hub bearings are at fault. If the free play is still evident with the footbrake depressed, then there is wear in the suspension joints or mountings.

5 Now grasp the wheel at the 9 o'clock and 3 o'clock positions, and try to rock it as before. Any movement felt now may again be caused by wear in the hub bearings or the steering

21.2 Checking a steering gear gaiter

track-rod balljoints. If the inner or outer balljoint is worn, the visual movement will be obvious.

6 Using a large screwdriver or flat bar, check for wear in the suspension mounting bushes by levering between the relevant suspension component and its attachment point **(see illustration)**. Some movement is to be expected as the mountings are made of rubber, but excessive wear should be obvious. Also check the condition of any visible rubber bushes, looking for splits, cracks or contamination of the rubber.

7 With the car standing on its wheels, have an assistant turn the steering wheel back and forth about an eighth of a turn each way. There should be very little, if any, lost movement between the steering wheel and roadwheels. If this is not the case, closely observe the joints and mountings previously described, but in addition, check the steering column universal joints for wear, and the rack-and-pinion steering gear itself.

Suspension strut/ shock absorber check

8 Check for any signs of fluid leakage around the suspension strut/shock absorber body, or from the rubber gaiter around the piston rod. Should any fluid be noticed, the suspension strut/shock absorber is defective internally, and should be renewed. **Note:** *Suspension struts/shock absorbers should always be renewed in pairs on the same axle.*

9 The efficiency of the suspension strut/shock absorber may be checked by bouncing the vehicle at each corner.

21.6 Using a large screwdriver or flat bar, check for wear in the suspension joints

21.4 Grasp the roadwheel at the 12 o'clock and 6 o'clock positions, and try to rock it

Generally speaking, the body will return to its normal position and stop after being depressed. If it rises and returns on a rebound, the suspension strut/shock absorber is probably suspect. Examine also the suspension strut/shock absorber upper and lower mountings for any signs of wear.

22 Driveshaft gaiter check

With the vehicle raised and securely supported on stands, turn the steering onto full lock, then slowly rotate the roadwheel. Inspect the condition of the outer constant velocity (CV) joint rubber gaiters, squeezing the gaiters to open out the folds. Check for signs of cracking, splits or deterioration of the rubber, which may allow the grease to escape, and lead to water and grit entry into the joint. Also check the security and condition of the retaining clips. Repeat these checks on the inner CV joints **(see illustration)**. If any damage or deterioration is found, the gaiters should be renewed (see Chapter 8).

At the same time, check the general condition of the CV joints themselves by first holding the driveshaft and attempting to rotate the wheel. Repeat this check by holding the inner joint and attempting to rotate the driveshaft. Any appreciable movement indicates wear in the joints, wear in the driveshaft splines, or a loose driveshaft retaining nut.

22.1 Checking driveshaft constant velocity joint (CV) joint gaiter

1

23 Exhaust system check

1 With the engine cold (at least an hour after the vehicle has been driven), check the complete exhaust system from the engine to the end of the tailpipe. The exhaust system is most easily checked with the vehicle raised on a hoist, or suitably supported on axle stands (see "*Jacking and Vehicle Support*"), so that the exhaust components are readily visible and accessible.
2 Check the exhaust pipes and connections for evidence of leaks, severe corrosion or damage. Make sure that all brackets and mountings are in good condition, and that all relevant nuts and bolts are tight. Leakage at any of the joints or in other parts of the system will usually show up as a black sooty stain in the vicinity of the leak.
3 Rattles and other noises can often be traced to the exhaust system, especially the brackets and mountings. Try to move the pipes and silencers. If the components are able to contact the body or suspension parts, secure the exhaust system with new mountings. Otherwise separate the joints (if possible) and twist the pipes as necessary to provide additional clearance.

24 Wheel alignment and balance check

Wheel alignment - definitions

1 A vehicle's steering and suspension geometry is defined in four basic settings - all angles are expressed in degrees (toe settings are also expressed as a measurement); the steering axis is defined as an imaginary line drawn through the axis of the suspension strut, extended where necessary to contact the ground.
2 **Camber** is the angle between each roadwheel and a vertical line drawn through its centre and tyre contact patch, when viewed from the front or rear of the car. "Positive" camber is when the roadwheels are tilted outwards from the vertical at the top; "negative" camber is when they are tilted inwards.
3 Camber is not adjustable, and is given for reference only; while it can be checked using a camber checking gauge, if the figure obtained is significantly different from that specified, the vehicle must be taken for careful checking by a professional, as the fault can only be caused by wear or damage to the body or suspension components.
4 **Castor** is the angle between the steering axis and a vertical line drawn through each roadwheel centre and tyre contact patch, when viewed from the side of the car. "Positive" castor is when the steering axis is

tilted so that it contacts the ground ahead of the vertical; "negative" castor is when it contacts the ground behind the vertical.
5 Castor is not adjustable, and is given for reference only; while it can be checked using a castor checking gauge, if the figure obtained is significantly different from that specified, the vehicle must be taken for careful checking by a professional, as the fault can only be caused by wear or damage to the body or suspension components.
6 **Steering axis inclination/SAI** - also known as **kingpin inclination/KPI** - is the angle between the steering axis and a vertical line drawn through each roadwheel centre and tyre contact patch, when viewed from the front or rear of the car. SAI/KPI is not adjustable.
7 **Toe** is the difference, viewed from above, between lines drawn through the roadwheel centres and the car's centre-line. "Toe-in" is when the roadwheels point inwards, towards each other at the front, while "toe-out" is when they splay outwards from each other at the front.
8 The front wheel toe setting is adjusted by screwing the track-rod ends in or out of their track-rods, to alter the effective length of the track-rod assemblies.
9 Rear wheel toe setting is controlled by the position of the eccentrics on the bolts securing the inboard ends of the rear parallel links.

Wheel alignment - checking

10 Due to the special measuring equipment necessary to check the wheel alignment, and the skill required to use it properly, the checking and adjustment of these settings is best left to a Nissan dealer or similar expert. Note that most tyre-fitting shops now possess sophisticated checking equipment.

Wheel balance

11 Accurate wheel balancing requires access to specialised test equipment and as such should be entrusted to a suitably equipped Nissan dealer or a tyre specialist.

25 Rotate wheels

To ensure even tyre wear, the manufacturer recommends that the vehicles tyres are rotated (ie removed and fitted to a different hub) periodically.   The accompanying illustration shows the pattern that should be followed **(see illustration)**. Refer to 'Wheel Changing' in the 'Roadside Repairs' Chapter of this manual which contains an illustrated, step-by step wheel changing procedure. Note that where vehicles are equipped with 'emergency use only' spare tyres, these should be excluded from the rotation pattern.

RADIAL TYRES

4 WHEELS

5 WHEELS

H28749

25.1 Wheel rotation sequence
A Excluding spare   B Including spare

26 Rear brake shoe and drum check - models with rear drum brakes

1 Chock the front wheels, then jack up the rear of the vehicle, and support it securely on axle stands (see "*Jacking and Vehicle Support*").
2 For a quick check, the thickness of friction material remaining on one of the brake shoes can be observed through the hole in the brake backplate which is exposed by prising out the sealing grommet **(see Haynes Hint)**. If a rod of the same diameter as the specified minimum friction material thickness is placed against the shoe friction material, the amount of wear can be assessed. A torch or inspection light will probably be required. If the friction material on any shoe is worn down to the specified minimum thickness or less, all four shoes must be renewed as a set.
3 For a comprehensive check, the brake drum should be removed and cleaned. This will allow the wheel cylinders to be checked, and the condition of the brake drum itself to be fully examined (see Chapter 9).

HAYNES HiNT

For a quick check, the thickness of friction material remaining on one of the brake shoes can be seen through the hole in the brake backplate (arrowed)

27 Seat belt check

1 All vehicles are fitted with three point, inertia reel front and outer rear seat belts, with a two point lap belt for the centre rear seat. Check each seat belt assembly in the following manner:

a) *Inspect the belts webbing for signs of fraying or other damage.*
b) *Check the operation of the buckles and retractor mechanisms.*

 Warning: Do not use any lubricants on the buckle or belt tongue.

c) *Check that all belt anchor points are securely fastened - note that a number of the seat belt mounting bolts are shouldered, to allow the anchor points free rotation.*

2 If there is any evidence of damage, or if the general condition of the belt is poor, then the belt should be renewed as a complete assembly.

 Warning: No attempt should be made to repair the seat belts.

3 If the vehicle has been involved in collision, any seat belts in use at the time should be renewed as a matter of course.
4 Use only warm water and non-detergent soap when cleaning the belt webbing. Never use chemicals that could attack the belt fabric and reduce its effectiveness. Keep the belts fully extended until they have dried - do not apply heat to accelerate drying.

28 Hinge and lock lubrication

Lubricate the hinges of the bonnet, doors and tailgate with a light general-purpose oil. Similarly, lubricate all latches, locks and lock strikers. At the same time, check the security and operation of all the locks, adjusting them if necessary (see Chapter 11).

Lightly lubricate the bonnet release mechanism and cable with a suitable grease.

29 Road test

Instruments and electrical equipment

1 Check the operation of all instruments and electrical equipment.
2 Make sure that all instruments read correctly, and switch on all electrical equipment in turn to check that it functions properly.

Steering and suspension

3 Check for any abnormalities in the steering, suspension, handling or road "feel".
4 Drive the vehicle, and check that there are no unusual vibrations or noises.
5 Check that the steering feels positive, with no excessive "sloppiness", or roughness, and check for any suspension noises when cornering, or when driving over bumps.

Drivetrain

6 Check the performance of the engine, clutch (where applicable), transmission and driveshafts.
7 Listen for any odd noises from the engine, clutch (where applicable) and transmission.
8 Make sure that the engine runs smoothly when idling, and that there is no hesitation when accelerating.

9 Check that, where applicable, the clutch action is smooth and progressive, that the drive is taken up smoothly, and that the pedal travel is not excessive. Also listen for any noises when the clutch pedal is depressed.
10 On manual transmission models, check that all gears can be engaged smoothly, without noise, and that the gear lever action is not abnormally vague or "notchy".
11 On automatic transmission models, make sure that the gearchanges occur smoothly, without snatching, and without an increase in engine speed between changes. Check that all the gear positions can be selected with the vehicle at rest. If any problems are found, they should be referred to a Nissan dealer.
12 Listen for a metallic clicking sound from the front of the vehicle, as the vehicle is driven slowly in a circle with the steering on full lock. Carry out this check in both directions. If a clicking noise is heard, this indicates wear in a driveshaft joint, in which case, renew the joint if necessary.

Braking system

13 Make sure that the vehicle does not pull to one side when braking, and that the wheels do not lock prematurely when braking hard.
14 Check that there is no vibration through the steering when braking.
15 Check that the handbrake operates correctly, without excessive movement of the lever, and that it holds the vehicle stationary on a slope.
16 Test the operation of the brake servo unit as follows. With the engine off, depress the footbrake four or five times to exhaust the vacuum. Hold the brake pedal depressed, then start the engine. As the engine starts, there should be a noticeable "give" in the brake pedal as vacuum builds up. Allow the engine to run for at least two minutes, and then switch it off. If the brake pedal is depressed now, it should be possible to detect a hiss from the servo as the pedal is depressed. After about four or five applications, no further hissing should be heard, and the pedal should feel much harder.

1

36 000 Mile / 2 Year Service

30 Air filter renewal

1 Where necessary, unscrew the air cleaner housing lid retaining nut(s) and screw (as applicable) **(see illustrations)**.
2 Release the lid retaining clips, then lift off the lid and position it clear of the housing **(see illustration)**. If necessary, carefully disconnect the inlet duct from the lid to allow the lid to be removed from the engine compartment.

30.1a On carburettor models, unscrew the retaining nut and bolt (arrowed) . . .

30.1b . . . then release the air cleaner lid retaining clips

30.2 Removing the air cleaner housing lid - fuel injection models

30.3a Removing the air filter element - carburettor models

30.3b Removing the air filter element - fuel injection models

30.6 On refitting, ensure that the lid is securely held in position by all the relevant retaining clips

3 Lift the air cleaner filter element out of the housing, noting which way around it is fitted **(see illustrations)**.

4 Wipe the inside of the air cleaner housing and lid with a clean cloth to remove all traces of dirt and debris.

5 Install the new filter element, ensuring that it is the right way up and is correctly seated in the housing.

6 Refit the air cleaner lid, and secure it in position with its retaining clips **(see illustration)**. Where necessary, refit the lid retaining nut(s) and screw (as applicable), and tighten them securely.

31 Ignition system check

⚠️ *Warning: Voltages produced by an electronic ignition system are considerably higher than those produced by conventional ignition systems. Extreme care must be taken when working on the system with the ignition switched on. Persons with surgically-implanted cardiac pacemaker devices should keep well clear of the ignition circuits, components and test equipment.*

1 The ignition system components should be checked for damage or deterioration as described under the relevant sub-heading.

General component check

2 The spark plug (HT) leads should be checked whenever new spark plugs are installed in the engine. Where necessary, unclip the cover from the distributor.

3 Ensure that the leads are numbered before removing them, to avoid confusion when refitting. Pull the leads from the plugs by gripping the end fitting, not the lead, otherwise the lead connection may be fractured **(see illustration)**.

4 Check inside the end fitting of each lead for signs of corrosion, which will look like a white crusty powder. Push the end fitting back onto the spark plug, ensuring that it is a tight fit on the plug. If not, remove the lead again and use pliers to carefully crimp the metal connector inside the end fitting until it fits securely on the end of the spark plug.

5 Using a clean rag, wipe the entire length of the lead, to remove any built-up dirt and grease. Once the lead is clean, check for burns, cracks and other damage. Do not bend the lead too far, or pull the lead lengthways - the conductor inside might break.

6 Disconnect the other end of the lead from the distributor cap. Again, pull only on the end fitting. Check for corrosion and a tight fit in the same manner as the spark plug end. If an ohmmeter is available, check the resistance of the lead by connecting the meter between the spark plug end of the lead and the segment inside the distributor cap. Refit the lead securely on completion.

7 Check the remaining leads one at a time, in the same way.

8 If new spark plug (HT) leads are required, purchase a set specific to your car and engine.

9 Slacken and remove the distributor cap retaining screws. Remove the cap, and recover the cap seal. Wipe the cap clean, and carefully inspect it inside and out for signs of cracks, carbon tracks (tracking) and worn, burned or loose contacts. Check that the cap's carbon brush is unworn, free to move against spring pressure, and making good contact with the rotor arm. Also inspect the cap seal for signs of wear or damage, and renew if necessary. Slacken the retaining screw, remove the rotor arm from the distributor shaft, and inspect the rotor arm **(see illustrations)**. It is common

31.3 Ensure that the HT leads are clearly numbered before removing them

31.9a The distributor cap is retained by two screws (arrowed)

31.9b Slacken and remove the retaining screw, and pull the rotor arm off the shaft

32.3a On carburettor models, undo the retaining screws . . .

32.3b . . . then remove the PCV filter assembly from the air cleaner lid

32.8 On fuel-injected cars, the PCV filter is fitted to the air cleaner housing base

practice to renew the cap and rotor arm whenever new spark plug (HT) leads are fitted. When fitting a new cap, remove the leads from the old cap one at a time, and fit them to the new cap in the exact same location - do not simultaneously remove all the leads from the old cap, or firing order confusion may occur. On refitting, ensure that the rotor arm is pressed securely onto the distributor shaft, and securely tighten its retaining screw. Ensure that the cap seal is in position, then fit the cap and securely tighten its retaining screws. Where necessary, refit the cover to the distributor.

10 Even with the ignition system in first-class condition, some engines may still occasionally experience poor starting, attributable to damp ignition components. To disperse moisture, an aerosol product 'wet start' can be very effective. Damp start aerosol spray should be used for providing a sealing coat to exclude moisture from the ignition system, and in extreme difficulty, A proprietary cold start aerosol will help to start a car when only a very poor spark occurs.

Ignition timing check and adjustment

11 Check the ignition timing as described in Chapter 5.

32 PCV filter renewal

Carburettor models

1 Undo the air cleaner housing lid retaining nut and screw, and release its retaining clips.
2 Lift the lid, and turn it over to gain access to the PCV filter which is screwed onto the underside of the lid.
3 Undo the two retaining screw and remove. the filter assembly. Remove the filter element from the frame, and discard it **(see illustrations)**.
4 Fit a new PCV filter element and refit the filter assembly to the air cleaner lid, tightening its retaining screws securely.
5 Refit the lid, and secure it in position with its retaining nut, screw and clips.

Fuel-injected models

6 Release the retaining clips, and lift off the air cleaner housing lid.
7 Lift the filter element out from the housing to gain access to the PCV filter.
8 Remove the filter from the air cleaner housing, and wipe clean the area around the filter **(see illustration)**.
9 Fit a new PCV filter to the housing, and refit the air cleaner filter element.
10 Seat the air cleaner lid on the housing, and secure it in position with the retaining clips.

33 Brake servo hose and non-return valve check

Working in the engine bay, examine the brake servo vacuum hose along its whole length, from the inlet manifold to the port on the front of the servo. Look for signs of chaffing, deformation from exposure to heat or kinking; also check the security of all hose connections. If any damage is discovered, the hose assembly should be renewed without delay.

If required, the non-return valve may be disconnected and checked - refer to Chapter 9 for details.

34 Coolant renewal

Cooling system draining, flushing and refilling

⚠️ *Warning: Wait until the engine is cold before starting this procedure. Do not allow antifreeze to come in contact with your skin, or with the painted surfaces of the vehicle. Rinse off spills immediately with plenty of water. Never leave antifreeze lying around in an open container, or in a puddle in the driveway or on the garage floor. Children and pets are attracted by its sweet smell, but antifreeze can be fatal if ingested.*

1 With the engine completely cold, cover the expansion tank cap with a wad of rag, and slowly turn the cap anti-clockwise to relieve the pressure in the cooling system (a hissing sound will normally be heard as the pressure reduces). Wait until any pressure remaining in the system is released, then continue to turn the cap until it can be removed.
2 Move the cabin heater control to the 'HOT' position.
3 Position a suitable container beneath the radiator then gradually slacken the drain plug on the underside of the radiator **(see illustration)**. Allow the coolant to drain into the container. *Caution: Do not allow the coolant to come into contact with the auxiliary drivebelts, or any other unprotected rubber components.*
4 If desired the coolant expansion tank may be unbolted from its mountings, removed from the engine bay and flushed out.
5 Reposition the container, then unscrew and remove the engine block drain plug and air relief plug(s) **(see illustrations)**. Allow the coolant to drain into the container.
6 Once all the coolant has drained, refit the radiator drain plug and tighten it securely. Fill the radiator with clean water until it runs from the engine block drain hole. Refit the engine block drain plug and tighten it securely.
7 Continue pouring water into the radiator until it runs from the air relief hole(s). Refit the air relief plugs and tighten them to the specified torque.
8 Top-up the water level to the 'MAX' level on the expansion tank (see 'Weekly Checks'), then refit and tighten the expansion tank cap.

34.3 Radiator drain plug

34.5a Air relief plug fitted to all engines

34.5b Air relief plug - GA16DE engine only

34.5c Cylinder block drain plug

9 Start the engine and run it until the radiator auxiliary cooling fan cuts in. Raise the engine speed above 3000 rpm two or three times to ensure adequate water circulation, then stop the engine and allow it to cool completely.
10 Repeat the steps given in paragraphs 3 to 9, until the water that drains from the cooling system runs clear.
11 After draining the water from the cooling system as described above, repeat the steps given in paragraphs 6 to 8, this time using water and antifreeze, mixed in the specified ratio. Apply thread locking fluid to the engine block drain plug, then refit and tighten it to the specified torque.
12 Start the engine and run it until it reaches normal operating temperature, then stop the engine and allow it to cool.
13 Check for leaks, particularly around any components that have been disturbed. Check the coolant level in the expansion tank, and top-up if necessary. Note that the system must be cold before an accurate level is indicated in the expansion tank. If the expansion tank cap is removed while the engine is still warm, cover the cap with a thick cloth, and unscrew the cap slowly to gradually relieve the system pressure (a hissing sound will normally be heard). Wait until any pressure remaining in the system is released, then continue to turn the cap until it can be removed.

36 000 Mile / 12 Month Service

Note: *This Service is only necessary where the vehicle is used in severe conditions (ie towing a trailer, repeated short distances, dusty conditions etc).*

35 Manual transmission oil renewal

1 This operation is much quicker and more efficient if the car is first taken on a journey of sufficient length to warm the engine/transmission up to normal operating temperature.
2 Park the car on level ground, switch off the ignition and apply the handbrake firmly. For improved access, jack up the front of the car and support it securely on axle stands (see *"Jacking and Vehicle Support"*). Note that the car must be lowered to the ground and level, to ensure accuracy, when refilling and checking the oil level.
3 Wipe clean the area around the filler/level plug, which is on the front face of the transmission. Unscrew the plug and clean it.
4 Position a suitable container under the drain plug situated on the left-hand side of the transmission differential housing.
5 Allow the oil to drain completely into the container. If the oil is hot, take precautions against scalding. Clean both the filler/level and the drain plugs, being especially careful to wipe any metallic particles off the magnetic inserts.
6 When the oil has finished draining, clean the drain plug threads and those of the transmission casing, then refit the drain plug, tightening it to the specified torque wrench setting. If the car was raised for the draining operation, lower it to the ground.
7 Refilling the transmission is an extremely awkward operation. Above all, allow plenty of time for the oil level to settle properly before checking it. Note that the car must be parked on flat level ground when checking the oil level.
8 Refill the transmission with the exact amount of the specified type of oil, then check the oil level as described in Section 10; if the correct amount was poured into the transmission, and a large amount flows out on checking the level, refit the filler/level plug and take the car on a short journey so that the new oil is distributed fully around the transmission components, then check the level again on your return.
9 When the level is correct, refit the filler/level plug, tightening it to the specified torque wrench setting. Wash off any spilt oil.

36 Automatic transmission fluid renewal

1 Take the vehicle on a short run to warm the transmission up to operating temperature.
2 Park the car on level ground, switch off the ignition and apply the handbrake firmly. For improved access, jack up the front of the car and support it securely on axle stands (see *"Jacking and Vehicle Support"*). Note that the car must be lowered to the ground and level, to ensure accuracy, when refilling and checking the fluid level.
3 Remove the dipstick, then position a suitable container under the transmission.
4 Unscrew the drain plug from the transmission sump, and allow the fluid to drain completely into the container. If the fluid is hot, take precautions against scalding. Clean the drain plug, being especially careful to wipe any metallic particles off the magnetic insert. Discard the original sealing washer; it should be renewed whenever it is disturbed.
5 When the fluid has finished draining, clean the drain plug threads and those of the transmission. Fit a new sealing washer to the drain plug and refit it to the transmission, tightening it to the specified torque setting. If the car was raised for the draining operation, lower it to the ground.
6 Refilling the transmission is an extremely awkward operation, adding the specified type of fluid to the transmission a little at a time via the dipstick tube. Use a funnel with a fine mesh gauze, to avoid spillage and to ensure that no foreign matter enters the transmission. Allow plenty of time for the level to settle properly before checking it as described above. Note that the car must be parked on flat level ground when checking the level.
7 Once the level is up to the MAX mark on the dipstick, refit the dipstick then start the engine and allow it to idle for a few minutes. Switch the engine off and recheck the fluid level, topping-up if necessary. Take the car on a short run to fully distribute the new fluid around the transmission and recheck the fluid level as described in Section 8.

Chapter 2 Part A:
Engine in-car repair procedures

Contents

Degrees of difficulty

Easy, suitable for novice with little experience 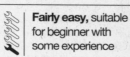	Fairly easy, suitable for beginner with some experience	Fairly difficult, suitable for competent DIY mechanic	Difficult, suitable for experienced DIY mechanic	Very difficult, suitable for expert DIY or professional

Specifications

Engine (general)

Designation	GA
Engine code:	
Carburettor models	GA14DS and GA16DS
Fuel-injected models	GA14DE and GA16DE
Capacity:	
GA14	1392 cc
GA16	1597 cc
Bore:	
GA14	76.0 mm
GA16	73.6 mm
Stroke:	
GA14	88.0 mm
GA16	81.8 mm
Direction of crankshaft rotation	Clockwise (viewed from right-hand side of vehicle)
No 1 cylinder location	At timing chain end of block
Firing order	1-3-4-2
Compression ratio:	
GA14DS	9.5 : 1
GA14DE, GA16DS and GA16DE	9.8 : 1
Cylinder compression pressures	
Standard	13.2 bar
Minimum	11.3 bar
Maximum difference between cylinders	1.0 bar

Camshaft and followers

Drive	Chain
Number of bearings	5

Endfloat:
  Standard:

Carburettor models	0.115 to 0.188 mm
Fuel-injected models	0.070 to 0.143 mm
Service limit (all models)	0.20 mm

Camshaft lobe height:
  Inlet:

Carburettor models	39.880 to 40.070 mm
Fuel-injected models	39.380 to 39.570 mm
Exhaust (all models)	39.880 to 40.070 mm

Bearing journal outer diameter:

No 1 bearing	27.935 to 27.955 mm
Nos 2 to 5 bearings	23.935 to 23.955 mm

Camshaft cylinder head bearing journal internal diameter:

No 1 bearing	28.000 to 28.021 mm
Nos 2 to 5 bearings	24.000 to 24.021 mm

Camshaft journal-to-bearing clearance:

Standard	0.045 to 0.086 mm
Service limit	0.15 mm

Camshaft run-out:

Standard	Less than 0.02 mm
Service limit	0.1 mm
Camshaft follower outer diameter	29.960 to 29.975 mm
Camshaft follower cylinder head bore internal diameter	30.000 to 30.021 mm
Camshaft follower-to-cylinder head bore clearance	0.025 to 0.061 mm

Valve clearances

Cold engine*:

Inlet	0.25 to 0.33 mm
Exhaust	0.32 to 0.40 mm

Hot engine:
  For checking:

Inlet	0.21 to 0.49 mm
Exhaust	0.30 to 0.58 mm

  For adjusting:

Inlet	0.32 to 0.40 mm
Exhaust	0.37 to 0.45 mm

The valve clearances must always be checked with the engine "hot". Although Nissan quote valve clearances for a "hot" and "cold" engine, the valve clearances should only be checked "cold" prior to starting the engine after an overhaul. The valve clearances should then be checked with the engine "hot" once it has been warmed up to normal operating temperature.

Lubrication system

Oil pump type	Gear-type, driven off crankshaft right-hand end

Minimum oil pressure at normal operating temperature:

At idle	0.49 to 1.86 bar
At 3000 rpm	3.43 to 4.41 bar

Oil pump clearances:

Outer gear-to-cover clearance	0.11 to 0.20 mm
Outer gear-to-crescent clearance	0.21 to 0.32 mm
Inner gear-to-crescent clearance	0.217 to 0.327 mm
Outer gear endfloat	0.05 to 0.11 mm
Inner gear endfloat	0.05 to 0.09 mm
Inner gear flange-to-cover bearing surface clearance	0.045 to 0.091 mm

Torque wrench settings

	Nm	lbf ft
Cylinder head cover bolts	4	3
Crankshaft pulley bolt	142	105
Lower timing chain tensioner bolts	9	7
Cylinder head camshaft sprocket access cover nuts/bolts	5	4
Timing chain idler sprocket centre bolt	50	37
Camshaft sprocket retaining bolts	115	84
Lower timing chain front guide bolts	16	12
Lower timing chain rear guide pivot bolt	16	12
Upper timing chain tensioner bolts	8	6
Upper timing chain front guide bolts - early models	8	6

Torque wrench settings (continued)

	Nm	lbf ft
Upper timing chain top guide bolts - early models	11	8
Camshaft bearing cap bolts	11	8
Cylinder head bolts:		
Main bolts:		
Stage 1	29	22
Stage 2	59	43
Fully slacken all the bolts, then tighten through		
Stage 3	29	22
Stage 4 (if an angle tightening gauge is available)	Angle-tighten by 50° to 55°	
Stage 4 (if an angle-tightening gauge is not available)	59 ± 5	43 ± 4
6 mm bolts (to timing chain cover)	8	6
Sump nuts and bolts	8	6
Sump drain plug	35	26
Centre member bolts	88	65
Oil pump:		
Cover retaining screws	5	4
Cover retaining bolt	8	6
Regulator valve bolt	50	37

1 General information

Using this Chapter

Chapter 2 is divided into two Parts; A and B. Repair operations that can be carried out with the engine in the vehicle are described in Part A. Part B covers the removal of the engine/transmission as a unit, and describes the engine dismantling and overhaul procedures.

In Part A the assumption is made that the engine is installed in the vehicle, with all ancillaries connected. If the engine has been removed for overhaul, the preliminary dismantling information which precedes each operation may be ignored.

Engine description

The 1.4 litre (1392 cc) and 1.6 litre (1597 cc) engines are from the GA series of Nissan engines. They are of sixteen-valve, in-line four-cylinder, double overhead camshaft (DOHC) type, mounted transversely at the front of the car with the transmission attached to the left-hand end.

The crankshaft runs in five main bearings. Thrustwashers are fitted to No 3 main bearing (upper half) to control crankshaft endfloat.

The connecting rods rotate on horizontally-split bearing shells at their big-ends. The pistons are attached to the connecting rods by gudgeon pins, which are a sliding fit in the connecting rod small-end eyes being retained by circlips. The aluminium-alloy pistons are fitted with three piston rings - two compression rings and an oil control ring.

The cylinder block is made of cast iron and the cylinder bores are an integral part of the block. On this type of engine the cylinder bores are sometimes referred to as having dry liners.

The inlet and exhaust valves are each closed by coil springs, and operate in guides pressed into the cylinder head; the valve seat inserts are also pressed into the cylinder head, and can be renewed separately if worn.

The camshaft is driven by a timing chain, and operates the sixteen valves via bucket-type followers. The followers are situated directly below the camshafts. Valve clearances are adjusted by shims. The camshafts rotate directly in the cylinder head.

Lubrication is by means of an oil pump, which is driven off the right-hand end of the crankshaft. It draws oil through a strainer located in the sump, and then forces it through an externally-mounted filter into galleries in the cylinder block/crankcase. From there, the oil is distributed to the crankshaft (main bearings) and camshaft. The big-end bearings are supplied with oil via internal drillings in the crankshaft, while the camshaft bearings also receive a pressurised supply. The camshaft lobes and valves are lubricated by splash, as are all other engine components.

Repair operations possible with the engine in the car

The following work can be carried out with the engine in the car:
a) Compression pressure - testing.
b) Cylinder head cover - removal and refitting.
c) Timing chain cover - removal and refitting.
d) Timing chains - removal and refitting.
e) Timing chain tensioners, guides and sprockets - removal and refitting.
f) Camshaft and followers - removal, inspection and refitting.
g) Valve clearances - adjustment.
h) Cylinder head - removal and refitting.
i) Cylinder head and pistons - decarbonising (refer to Part B of this Chapter).
j) Sump - removal and refitting.
k) Oil pump - removal, overhaul and refitting.
l) Crankshaft oil seals - renewal.
m) Engine/transmission mountings - inspection and renewal.
n) Flywheel - removal, inspection and refitting.

Note: *It is possible to remove the pistons and connecting rods (after removing the cylinder head and sump) without removing the engine. However, this is not recommended. Work of this nature is more easily and thoroughly completed with the engine on the bench, as described in Chapter 2B.*

2 Compression test - description and interpretation

1 When engine performance is down, or if misfiring occurs which cannot be attributed to the ignition or fuel systems, a compression test can provide diagnostic clues as to the engine's condition. If the test is performed regularly, it can give warning of trouble before any other symptoms become apparent.

2 The engine must be fully warmed-up to normal operating temperature, the battery must be fully charged, and all the spark plugs must be removed (Chapter 1). The aid of an assistant will also be required.

3 Disable the ignition system by disconnecting the ignition coil HT lead from the distributor cap and earthing it on the cylinder block. Use a jumper lead or similar wire to make a good connection.

4 Fit a compression tester to the No 1 cylinder spark plug hole - the type of tester which screws into the plug thread is to be preferred.

5 Have the assistant hold the throttle wide open, and crank the engine on the starter motor; after one or two revolutions, the compression pressure should build up to a maximum figure, and then stabilise. Record the highest reading obtained.

6 Repeat the test on the remaining cylinders, recording the pressure in each.

7 All cylinders should produce very similar pressures; any difference greater than that specified indicates the existence of a fault. Note that the compression should build up quickly in a healthy engine; low compression

2A

3.3a On some models, remove the rubber plug (arrowed) from the plastic cover . . .

3.3b . . . to gain access to the crankshaft pulley bolt

on the first stroke, followed by gradually increasing pressure on successive strokes, indicates worn piston rings. A low compression reading on the first stroke, which does not build up during successive strokes, indicates leaking valves or a blown head gasket (a cracked head could also be the cause). Deposits on the undersides of the valve heads can also cause low compression.

8 If the pressure in any cylinder is reduced to the specified minimum or less, carry out the following test to isolate the cause. Introduce a teaspoonful of clean oil into that cylinder through its spark plug hole and repeat the test.

9 If the addition of oil temporarily improves the compression pressure, this indicates that bore or piston wear is responsible for the pressure loss. No improvement suggests that leaking or burnt valves, or a blown head gasket, may be to blame.

10 A low reading from two adjacent cylinders is almost certainly due to the head gasket having blown between them; the presence of coolant in the engine oil will confirm this.

11 If one cylinder is about 20 percent lower than the others and the engine has a slightly rough idle, a worn camshaft lobe could be the cause.

12 If the compression reading is unusually high, the combustion chambers are probably coated with carbon deposits. If this is the case, the cylinder head should be removed and decarbonised.

13 On completion of the test, refit the spark plugs and reconnect the ignition HT coil lead.

1 Disconnect the battery negative lead and remove all the spark plugs as described in Chapter 1.

2 Trace No 1 spark plug (HT) lead from the plug back to the distributor cap, and use chalk or similar to mark the distributor body or engine casting nearest to the cap's No 1 terminal. Unclip the distributor cover (where fitted) then undo the cap retaining screws, remove the cap and recover the seal.

3 Apply the handbrake and ensure that the transmission is in neutral, then jack up the front of the vehicle and support it on axle stands (see "*Jacking and Vehicle Support*"). Remove the right-hand roadwheel. Undo the retaining screws and remove the plastic cover from underneath the wing to gain access to the crankshaft pulley bolt **(see illustrations)**.

4 The timing marks are in the form of notches on the crankshaft pulley rim which align with a pointer on the timing chain cover. The notches are spaced at intervals of 5° and go from 20° before top dead centre (BTDC) to 5° after top dead centre (ATDC). The TDC mark is highlighted with yellow paint to aid identification.

5 Using a spanner (or socket and extension bar) applied to the crankshaft pulley bolt, rotate the crankshaft clockwise until the TDC notch on the crankshaft pulley rim is aligned with the pointer on the timing chain cover.

6 With the crankshaft in this position, Nos 1 and 4 cylinders are now at TDC, one of them on the compression stroke. If the distributor rotor arm is pointing at (the previously-marked) No 1 terminal, then No 1 cylinder is correctly positioned; if the rotor arm is pointing at No 4 terminal, rotate the crankshaft one full turn (360°) clockwise until the arm points at the marked terminal. No 1 cylinder will then be at TDC on the compression stroke.

7 Once No 1 cylinder has been positioned at TDC on the compression stroke, TDC for any of the other cylinders can then be located by rotating the crankshaft clockwise 180° at a time and following the firing order (see Specifications).

Removal

1 Disconnect the spark plug (HT) leads from the plugs, and free them from their retaining clips on the top of the cover.

2 Release the retaining clips and disconnect the breather hoses from the rear of the cover **(see illustrations)**.

3 Working in the **reverse** of the sequence shown in illustration 4.11a, slacken and remove the cylinder head cover retaining screws and washers.

4 Lift off the cylinder head cover, and recover the rubber seal from the outer edge of the cover, and the circular seal from each of the cover spark plug holes. On early models, also remove the two semi-circular rubbers from the cut-outs on the right-hand end of the cylinder head; on later models, the rubbers are an integral part of the cover seal.

5 Inspect the cover seals for signs of damage and deterioration, and renew as necessary.

Refitting

6 Carefully clean the cylinder head and cover mating surfaces, and remove all traces of oil.

7 Apply a bead of sealant to the circular cut-outs on the right-hand end of the cylinder head. On early models, fit both the semi-

4.2a Release the clips and disconnect the breather hoses from the right-hand . . .

4.2b . . . and left-hand end (arrowed) of the cylinder head cover

4.7a Apply a bead of sealant to the cylinder head cut-outs

4.7b On early models, install both semi-circular rubbers in the head cut-outs

4.8a Fit the rubber seal to the cover groove . . .

4.8b . . . and fit the spark plug hole seals

4.9 Apply a bead of sealant to the seal as described in the text

4.10 Refit the head cover, ensuring that the seals stay in position

4.11a Cylinder head cover bolt tightening sequence

circular rubbers to the head, ensuring that they are positioned with their flat sides parallel to the head surface (see illustrations).

8 Fit the rubber seal to the cylinder head cover groove, ensuring that it is correctly located along its entire length, and install the four spark plug hole seals, ensuring that they are the correct way around. If necessary, the seals can be held in position using a smear of suitable sealant (see illustrations).

9 Apply a bead of sealant to the cover seal, approximately 1 cm either side of the left-hand exhaust camshaft bearing cap circular cut-out edges (see illustration).

10 Carefully refit the cylinder head cover to the engine, taking great care not to displace any of the rubber seals (see illustration).

11 Make sure the cover is correctly seated, then install the retaining screws and washers.

Working in the sequence shown, tighten the cover screws to the specified torque (see illustrations).

12 Reconnect the breather hoses to the cylinder head cover, and secure them in position with the retaining clips.

13 Connect the HT lead caps to the correct spark plugs, and clip the leads back into the retaining clips. Reconnect the battery negative lead.

5 Crankshaft pulley - removal and refitting

Removal

1 Remove the auxiliary drivebelt(s) as described in Chapter 1.

2 If necessary, position No 1 cylinder at TDC on its compression stroke (Section 3).

3 To prevent crankshaft rotation while the pulley bolt is unscrewed, select top gear and have an assistant apply the brakes firmly. If the engine has been removed from the car, lock the flywheel using a tool similar to the one shown in illustration 15.2 (see Section 15).

4 Unscrew the pulley bolt, along with its washer, and remove the pulley from the crankshaft (see illustration). If the pulley Woodruff key is a loose fit, remove it and store it with the pulley for safe-keeping.

Refitting

5 Refit the Woodruff key (where removed).

6 Align the crankshaft pulley groove with the key, then slide the sprocket onto the crankshaft, and refit the retaining bolt and washer (see illustration).

2A

4.11b Working in sequence, tighten the cover screws to the specified torque

5.4 Unscrew the pulley bolt and washer, and withdraw the crankshaft pulley

5.6 Align the pulley groove (arrowed) with the key, and slide the pulley onto the crankshaft

5.7 Refit the retaining bolt (and washer) and tighten to the specified torque

7 Lock the crankshaft by the method used on removal, and tighten the pulley retaining bolt to the specified torque setting (see illustration).

8 Refit the auxiliary drivebelt(s) and adjust them as described in Chapter 1.

6 Timing chain cover - removal and refitting

Note: If the timing chain cover is to be removed without disturbing the cylinder head, there is a slight risk of oil leakage from chain cover-to-cylinder head joint after refitting. Bearing in mind this information, it is up to the individual owner to decide whether or not it is worth renewing the head gasket when the chain cover is removed.

Removal

1 Remove the coolant pump as described in Chapter 3.

2 Remove the crankshaft pulley as described in Section 5.

3 Remove the sump and oil pump pick-up/strainer as described in Section 12.

4 Undo the two bolts securing the power steering pump mounting bracket to the front of the timing chain cover, then undo the nut/bolt securing the bracket to the pump and remove the bracket (see illustration).

5 Slacken and remove the three retaining bolts, and remove the mounting bracket from the top of the right-hand engine/transmission mounting; where necessary, free the wiring from its retaining clips on the bracket. Unscrew the retaining nuts and bolts, and remove the camshaft sprocket access cover from the right-hand end of the cylinder head. Recover the cover gasket (where fitted) (see illustrations).

6 Unscrew the two retaining bolts, and remove the lower timing chain tensioner from the rear of the chain cover. Recover the tensioner gasket, noting which way up its is fitted (see illustration). Note: Do not rotate the engine whilst the chain tensioner is removed.

7 Slacken and remove the four bolts securing the right-hand end of the cylinder head to the top of the timing chain cover. On early models, it will be necessary to remove the upper timing chain front guide to gain access to one of the bolts.

6.4 Removing the power steering pump mounting bracket

6.5a Undo the retaining bolts (arrowed) and remove the bracket

6.5b Undo the retaining nuts and bolts . . .

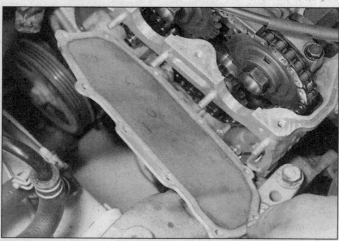

6.5c . . . and remove the sprocket access cover (early model shown, with gasket)

6.6 Timing chains and associated components - early models shown (later models similar)

1 Upper chain top guide bolt*
2 Upper chain top guide*
3 Upper timing chain
4 Exhaust camshaft sprocket
5 Inlet camshaft sprocket
6 Upper chain tensioner
7 Upper chain tensioner bolt
8 Camshaft sprocket bolt
9 Lower chain tensioner bolt
10 Lower chain tensioner
11 Lower chain tensioner gasket
12 Lower chain rear guide
13 Lower chain rear guide pivot bolt
14 Locating dowel and O-ring
15 Upper chain front guide*
16 Upper chain front guide bolt*
17 Idler sprocket shaft
18 Idler sprocket
19 Lower chain front guide
20 Lower chain front guide bolt
21 Lower timing chain
22 Crankshaft sprocket
23 Oil pump drive spacer
24 Timing chain cover
25 Crankshaft pulley
26 Crankshaft pulley bolt
27 Idler sprocket bolt
*Fitted to early models only

6.10 Undo the retaining bolts and remove the mounting bracket from the engine

6.12 Removing the timing chain cover

8 Place a jack with interposed block of wood beneath the engine to take the weight of the engine. Alternatively, attach a hoist or support bar to the engine lifting eyes, and take the weight of the engine.

9 Unscrew the through-bolt from the right-hand engine/transmission mounting, then undo the three retaining bolts and remove the mounting assembly from the engine compartment. Recover the rubbers fitted to the body mounting bracket, if they are loose.

10 Undo the bracket retaining bolts and the bolt securing the alternator adjuster strap to the bracket, and remove the right-hand engine/transmission mounting bracket from the engine (see illustration).

11 Slacken and remove the timing chain cover retaining bolts. Note the correct fitted location of each bolt, as the bolts are of different lengths.

12 Slide the timing chain cover off the end of the crankshaft, and manoeuvre it out of the engine compartment (see illustration). Recover the special sealing collars from the oil galleries and discard them; new ones must

be used on refitting. If the cover locating dowels are a loose fit, remove them and store them with the cover for safe-keeping.

13 Slide the oil pump drive spacer off the end of the crankshaft.

Refitting

14 Prior to refitting the cover, it is recommended that the crankshaft oil seal should be renewed. Carefully lever the old

seal out of the cover using a large flat-bladed screwdriver. Fit the new seal to the cover, making sure its sealing lip is facing inwards. Drive the seal into position until it seats on its locating shoulder, using a suitable tubular drift, such as a socket, which bears only on the hard outer edge of the seal (see illustrations).

15 Ensure that the cover and crankcase mating surfaces are clean and dry.

2A

6.14a Lever out the crankshaft oil seal with a large screwdriver . . .

6.14b . . . and tap the new seal into position with a suitable socket

6.16 Fit the new special sealing collars to the cylinder block oil galleries

6.17 Apply sealant to the timing cover mating surface, and around the coolant pump passage (arrowed)

6.19 Align the oil pump drive spacer with the key, and slide it onto the crankshaft (cover locating dowel locations arrowed)

6.20 Engage the oil pump with the drive spacer, and slide the timing cover into position

6.22a Refit the bolts securing the cylinder head to the top of the timing cover, and tighten them to the specified torque

16 Fit the new special sealing collars to the cylinder block oil galleries (see illustration).
17 Apply a thin coat of suitable sealant to the timing cover crankcase mating surface, not forgetting to apply sealant to the area around the coolant pump passage in the centre of the cover (see illustration). If the cylinder head is in position, also apply sealant to the upper face of the cover.
18 Refit the cover locating dowels to the cylinder block (where removed).
19 Align the oil pump drive spacer groove with the key, then slide the spacer onto the crankshaft (see illustration).
20 Offer up the cover, and position the oil pump inner rotor so that it will engage with the drive spacer as the cover is refitted (see illustration). Slide the cover over the end of

the crankshaft, taking great care not to damage the oil seal lip, and seat it on its locating dowels.
21 Refit the cover retaining bolts in their original locations and tighten them securely, working in several stages.
22 Fit the four 6 mm bolts securing the cylinder head to the chain cover, and tighten them to the specified torque setting. On early models, refit the upper timing chain front guide (see illustrations).
23 Fit a new gasket to the lower chain tensioner, making sure it is fitted the correct way up so its cut-out is aligned with the tensioner oil hole. Install the tensioner and gasket, and tighten its retaining bolts to the specified torque setting (see illustrations).

6.22b On early models, refit the upper timing chain front guide

6.23a Ensure that the gasket cut-out is aligned with the oil hole (arrowed) . . .

6.23b . . . then refit the tensioner to the engine

24 Refit the right-hand engine/transmission mounting bracket to the engine, and securely tighten its retaining bolts. Fit the rubbers to the body mounting bracket (where removed), ensuring that their pins are correctly seated in the bracket holes, and fit the mounting, tightening its retaining bolts to the specified torque setting.

25 Align the right-hand mounting with its body bracket, then insert the through-bolt and tighten its nut to the specified torque setting. Remove the jack from underneath the engine.

26 Ensure that the sprocket access cover and head mating surfaces are clean and dry. Where the cover was originally fitted with a gasket, fit a new gasket to the cylinder head; where the cover was originally fitted using sealant, apply a continuos bead of suitable sealant to the cover mating surface. Install the cover and tighten its retaining nuts and bolts to the specified torque setting.

27 Install the bracket to the top of the right-hand engine/transmission mounting, and tighten its bolts to the specified torque setting.

28 Refit the power steering pump to the engine, and securely tighten its mounting bracket bolts.

29 Install the oil pump pick-up/strainer and sump as described in Section 12.

30 Refit the crankshaft pulley as described in Section 5.

31 Refit the coolant pump as described in Chapter 3.

32 Replenish the engine oil and coolant as described in Chapter 1.

7.4a On early models, remove the top chain upper guide . . .

7.4b . . . then retract the tensioner and remove it from the head

7 Timing chains - removal, inspection and refitting

Note: *The following section refers to "early" and "later" models. The two models can be distinguished from their upper timing chain components; early models have a top and front chain guide for the upper timing chain - these are omitted on later models.*

Removal

1 Position No 1 cylinder at TDC on its compression stroke, as described in Section 3.

2 Remove the cylinder head cover as described in Section 4.

3 Remove the timing chain cover as described in Section 6.

4 On early models, slacken and remove the bolts securing the upper chain top guide in position, and remove it from the head. Retract the upper chain tensioner, and retain it in the retracted position using the hook on the side of the tensioner. Undo the two retaining bolts, and remove the tensioner from the end of the cylinder head **(see illustrations)**.

5 On later models, retract the upper chain tensioner, and hold it in position by inserting a small-diameter rod in front of the tensioner pad. Undo the two retaining bolts, and remove the tensioner from the end of the cylinder head.

6 Slacken the camshaft sprocket retaining bolts, whilst retaining the camshafts with a large open-ended spanner fitted to the flats on the right-hand end of each shaft. Remove each bolt along with its washer **(see illustrations)**.

7 Disengage each sprocket from the end of its respective camshaft, and manoeuvre them out from the cylinder head. If the sprocket locating pins are a loose fit in the camshaft ends, remove them and store them with the sprockets.

8 Disengage the upper timing chain from the idler sprocket, and manoeuvre it out of the cylinder head **(see illustration)**.

9 Unscrew the pivot bolt, and remove the lower chain rear guide from the crankcase **(see illustration)**.

10 Slacken and remove the idler sprocket centre bolt and washer, then lower the sprocket out of position and remove it from the bottom of the cylinder head **(see illustration)**. Recover the idler shaft from the rear of the sprocket.

2A

7.6a Slacken the sprocket retaining bolt whilst holding the camshaft . . .

7.6b . . . then remove the bolt along with its washer

7.8 Manoeuvre the upper timing chain out through the head aperture

7.9 Unscrew the pivot bolt, and remove the lower chain rear guide

7.10 Unscrew the centre bolt and washer, and remove the idler sprocket

7.16 Examine the chain guides for signs of wear such as that shown

7.18 Ensure that the crankshaft is at TDC, then fit the Woodruff key (arrowed) . . .

7.19 . . . and slide on the crankshaft sprocket

11 Disengage the lower timing chain from the crankshaft sprocket, and remove it from the engine.

12 Slide the crankshaft sprocket off the end of the crankshaft. Remove the Woodruff key (if loose) from the crankshaft, and store it with the sprocket for safe-keeping. **Note:** *Do not rotate the crankshaft or camshafts whilst the timing chains are removed.*

Inspection

13 Examine the teeth on the camshaft, idler and crankshaft sprockets for any sign of wear or damage such as chipped, hooked or missing teeth. If there is any sign of wear or damage on either sprocket, *all* sprockets and *both* timing chains should be renewed as a set.

7.20a Fit the shaft to the rear of the idler sprocket . . .

14 Inspect the links of the timing chains for signs of wear or damage on the rollers. The extent of wear can be judged by checking the amount by which the chain can be bent sideways; a new chain will have very little sideways movement. If there is an excessive amount of side play in either timing chain, it must be renewed.

15 Note that it is a sensible precaution to renew the timing chains, regardless of their apparent condition, if the engine has covered a high mileage, or if it has been noted that the chain(s) have sounded noisy when the engine running. Although not strictly necessary, it is always worth renewing the chains and sprockets as a matched set, since it is false economy to run a new chain on worn sprockets and vice-versa. If there is any doubt about the condition of the timing chains and sprockets, seek the advice of a Nissan dealer service department, who will be able to advise you as to the best course of action, based on their previous knowledge of the engine.

16 Examine the chain guides for signs of wear or damage to their chain contact faces, renewing any which are badly marked **(see illustration)**.

17 Check the upper chain tensioner pad for signs of wear, and check that the plunger is free to slide freely in the tensioner body. The condition of the tensioner spring can only be judged in comparison to a new component. Renew the tensioner if its pad is worn or there is any doubt about the condition of its tensioning spring.

Refitting

18 Check the crankshaft is still positioned at TDC (the keyway will be in the 12 o'clock position, seen from the right-hand end of the engine) and refit the Woodruff key to the crankshaft groove **(see illustration)**.

19 Ensure that the crankshaft sprocket is positioned the correct way around, with its timing mark facing away from the crankcase, then align its groove with the key, and slide the sprocket onto the crankshaft **(see illustration)**.

20 Apply a smear of clean engine oil to the idler sprocket shaft, and fit the shaft to the rear of the sprocket so that its flange is positioned between the sprocket and crankcase. Engage the idler sprocket with the lower timing chain, aligning its outer timing mark with one of the chain's coloured (silver) links **(see illustrations)**.

21 Manoeuvre the chain and idler sprocket assembly into position, engaging the chain with the crankshaft sprocket so that its second coloured (silver) link is aligned with the timing mark on the crankshaft sprocket; the timing mark is in the form of a small cut-out on the sprocket hub **(see illustration)**.

22 Check that the idler sprocket and crankshaft sprocket marks are still correctly aligned with the lower chain silver links, then install the idler sprocket centre bolt and washer, and tighten it to the specified torque setting **(see illustration)**.

7.20b . . . then engage the sprocket with the chain, aligning its timing mark with one of the chain's coloured links (arrowed)

7.21 Engage the chain so that its coloured link is correctly aligned with the sprocket timing mark (arrowed)

7.22 Fit the idler sprocket bolt and washer, and tighten to the specified torque

7.23 Timing chain and sprocket coloured links and timing marks
  1 Inlet camshaft sprocket link and mark
  2 Exhaust camshaft sprocket link and mark
  3 Idler sprocket link and mark

7.24 Manoeuvre the upper chain into position, and engage it with the idler sprocket so that the relevant coloured link is correctly aligned with its timing mark (arrowed)

7.25a Engage the inlet camshaft sprocket with the chain, aligning its timing mark (arrowed) with the relevant coloured link . . .

7.25b . . . then install the exhaust camshaft sprocket and align its timing mark (arrowed) with the last coloured link

2A

23 The upper timing chain has three coloured links, one for each of the sprocket timing marks. Note, however, that the links are not spaced at regular intervals. On early models, all three links are silver; the first (inlet camshaft sprocket) link and second (exhaust camshaft sprocket) link are 16 rollers apart, the second and third (idler sprocket) link are also 16 rollers apart, but the gap between the third silver link and the first link is 22 rollers **(see illustration)**. On later models, the gaps between the links are the same, but the idler gear link is easily identified since it is gold in colour (camshaft sprocket links remain silver).
24 Bearing in mind paragraph 23, lower the upper chain into position, making sure its coloured links are facing outwards. Engage the chain with the idler sprocket, aligning its appropriate link with the sprocket inner timing mark **(see illustration)**.

25 Manoeuvre both the inlet and exhaust camshaft sprockets into position, ensuring that their timing marks are facing outwards. **Note:** *Both sprockets are identical.* Engage them with the chain, aligning the inlet sprocket timing mark with the first chain silver link and the exhaust timing mark with the second. Check that all the timing marks are correctly aligned with the upper chain links **(see illustrations)**.
26 Locate the sprockets on the camshafts, aligning their cut-outs with the locating pins. Check that the chain silver links are correctly aligned with each sprocket's timing mark. If not, disengage the sprocket(s) from the chain, and make the necessary adjustments **(see illustration)**.
27 With the timing marks correctly positioned, install the camshaft sprocket

7.26 Locate the sprockets on the camshafts, and check that all the timing marks and coloured links are correctly aligned (arrowed)

7.27 Refit the sprocket retaining bolts and washers, and tighten them to the specified torque setting

7.29a On early models, fit the tensioner with its plunger held in the retracted position, and securely tighten its bolts . . .

7.29b . . . then release the hook (arrowed) and check that the plunger extends from the body

retaining bolts and washers, and tighten them both to the specified torque (see illustration).

28 Fit the lower chain rear guide, and tighten its pivot bolt to the specified torque.

29 On early models, fit the upper chain top guide to the cylinder head, and tighten its retaining bolts to the specified torque setting. Ensure that the upper chain tensioner assembly is held in the retracted position by its hook, and fit the tensioner to the cylinder head. Tighten the tensioner retaining bolts to the specified torque, then release the hook and check that the tensioner pad is forced against the chain (see illustrations).

30 On later models, retract the tensioner pad and hold it in position with a suitable rod. Fit the tensioner to the cylinder head, and tighten its retaining bolts to the specified torque. Withdraw the rod, and check that the tensioner pad is forced against the chain.

31 Refit the cylinder head cover (Section 3).

32 Refit the timing chain cover (Section 6).

---

8 Timing chain tensioners, guides and sprockets - removal, inspection and refitting

Removal

Lower timing chain tensioner

1 Firmly apply the handbrake, then jack up the front of the vehicle and support it on axle stands (see *"Jacking and Vehicle Support"*).

2 From underneath the vehicle, unscrew the two retaining bolts and remove the lower timing chain tensioner from the rear of the chain cover. Recover the tensioner gasket, noting which way up it is fitted. **Note:** *Do not rotate the engine whilst the chain tensioner is removed.*

Upper timing chain tensioner

3 Slacken and remove the three retaining bolts, and remove the mounting bracket from the top of the right-hand engine/transmission mounting.

4 Unscrew the retaining nuts and bolts, and remove the camshaft sprocket access cover from the right-hand end of the cylinder head. Recover the cover gasket (where fitted).

5 On early models, retract the tensioner, and retain it in that position using the hook on the side of the tensioner.

6 On later models, retract the chain tensioner, and hold it in position by inserting a small diameter rod in front of the tensioner pad.

7 Undo the two retaining bolts and remove the tensioner from the end of the cylinder head. **Note:** *Do not rotate the engine whilst the chain tensioner is removed.*

Lower timing chain front guide

8 Remove the timing chains as described in Section 7.

9 Slacken and remove the retaining bolts, and remove the lower chain front guide from the side of the crankcase.

Lower timing chain rear guide

10 Remove the timing chain cover as described in Section 6.

11 Unscrew the pivot bolt, and remove the lower chain rear guide from the crankcase (see illustration).

Upper chain top guide (early models only)

12 Remove the cylinder head cover as described in Section 4.

13 Undo the two retaining bolts, and remove the guide from the top of the camshaft bearing cap.

Upper chain front guide (early models only)

14 Remove the camshaft sprocket access cover from the cylinder head, as described in paragraphs 3 and 4.

15 Undo the two retaining bolts, and remove the guide from the cylinder head (see illustration).

Camshaft sprockets

16 Position No 1 cylinder at TDC on its compression stroke as described in Section 3.

17 Remove the cylinder head cover as described in Section 4.

18 Remove the camshaft sprocket access cover as described in paragraphs 3 and 4 of this Section.

19 Remove both camshaft sprockets and the upper timing chain as described in paragraphs 4 to 7 of Section 7.

Idler sprocket and crankshaft sprocket

20 Remove the timing chains and sprockets as described in Section 7.

Inspection

21 Refer to Section 7.

Refitting

Lower timing chain tensioner

22 Ensure that the tensioner and cover mating surfaces are clean and dry.

23 Fit a new tensioner gasket to the cover, making sure it is fitted the correct way up so its cut-out is aligned with the tensioner oil hole (see illustration 6.23a in Sewction 6).

24 Install the chain tensioner, and tighten its retaining bolts to the specified torque setting.

8.11 Remove the pivot bolt, and withdraw the lower chain rear guide from the cylinder block

8.15 The upper chain front guide is retained by two bolts (arrowed) - early models only

8.25 On early models, prior to refitting retract the plunger and secure it in position with the hook (arrowed)

Upper timing chain tensioner

25 On early models, ensure that the tensioner assembly is held in the retracted position by its hook, and fit it to the cylinder head. Tighten the tensioner retaining bolts to the specified torque, then release the hook and check that the tensioner pad is forced against the chain (see illustration).

26 On later models, retract the tensioner pad, and hold it in position with a suitable rod. Fit the tensioner to the head, and tighten its retaining bolts to the specified torque. Withdraw the rod, and check that the tensioner pad is forced against the chain.

27 Ensure that the sprocket access cover and head mating surfaces are clean and dry. Where the cover was originally fitted with a gasket, fit a new gasket to the cylinder head; where the cover was originally fitted using sealant, apply a continuous bead of suitable sealant to the cover mating surface. Install the cover, and tighten its retaining nuts and bolts to the specified torque setting.

28 Install the bracket to the top of the right-hand engine/transmission mounting, and tighten its bolts to the specified torque setting.

Lower timing chain front guide

29 Fit the guide to the crankcase, and tighten its retaining bolts to the specified torque.

30 Refit the timing chains as described in Section 7.

Lower timing chain rear guide

31 Fit the guide to the crankcase, and tighten its pivot bolt to the specified torque.

32 Refit the timing chain cover as described in Section 6.

Upper chain top guide (early models only)

33 Fit the guide to the top of the camshaft bearing cap, and tighten its retaining bolts to the specified torque.

34 Refit the cylinder head cover as described in Section 4.

Upper chain front guide (early models only)

35 Fit the guide to the cylinder head and tighten its retaining bolts to the specified torque.

36 Refit the sprocket access cover as described in paragraphs 27 and 28.

Camshaft sprockets

37 Refit the camshaft sprockets and upper timing chain as described in paragraphs 23 to 27 of Section 7.

38 On early models, refit the top and front upper chain guides, and tighten the retaining bolts to their specified torque setting.

39 Refit the upper chain tensioner as described in paragraphs 25 to 28.

40 Refit the cylinder head cover as described in Section 4.

Idler sprocket and crankshaft sprocket

41 Refit the timing chains and sprockets as described in Section 7.

9 Valve clearances - checking and adjustment

Note: *The valve clearances must always be checked with the engine "hot". Although Nissan quote valve clearances for a "hot" and "cold" engine, the valve clearances should only be checked "cold", prior to starting the engine after an overhaul. The valve clearances should then be checked again once the engine has been warmed up to normal operating temperature.*

Note: *This is not a routine operation. It should only be necessary at high mileage, after overhaul, or when investigating noise or power loss which may be attributable to the valve gear.*

1 The importance of having the valve clearances correctly adjusted cannot be overstressed, as they vitally affect the performance of the engine. That being said, the check should not be regarded as routine maintenance, and should only be carried out when the valve gear has become noisy, after engine overhaul, or when trying to trace the cause of power loss which may be attributed to the valves. The clearances are checked as follows.

2 Draw the outline of the engine on a piece of paper, numbering the cylinders 1 to 4, with No 1 cylinder at the timing chain end of the engine. Show the position of each valve, together with the specified valve clearance. Above each valve, draw two lines for noting the actual clearance and the amount of adjustment required. **Note:** *Nissan quote two sets of clearance tolerances; one for **checking** the clearance, and a second one to use when **adjusting/setting** the clearance. The checking tolerance is exceptionally large and, although not strictly necessary, it is desirable to have all valve clearances within the adjusting/setting tolerances.*

3 Warm the engine up to normal operating temperature, then switch off. Remove the cylinder head cover as described in Section 4.

9.5 Checking a valve clearance

4 Position No 1 cylinder at TDC on its compression stroke, as described in Section 3.

5 Using feeler blades, measure the clearance between the base of the cam and the follower of the following valves, recording each clearance on the paper (see illustration).

No 1 cylinder inlet and exhaust valves
No 2 cylinder inlet valves
No 3 cylinder exhaust valves

6 Rotate the crankshaft through one complete turn (360°) clockwise until the TDC notch on the crankshaft pulley is realigned with the pointer. No 4 cylinder is now at TDC on its compression stroke.

7 Check the clearances of the following valves, and record them on the paper.

No 2 cylinder exhaust valves
No 3 cylinder inlet valves
No 4 cylinder inlet and exhaust valves

8 Calculate the difference between each measured clearance and the desired value, and record it on the piece of paper. Where a valve clearance differs from the specified value, then the shim for that valve must be replaced with a thinner or thicker shim accordingly.

9 To remove the shim, the follower has to be pressed down against valve spring pressure just far enough to allow the shim to be slid out. To do this, make sure that the cam lobe of the valve on which the shim is to be removed is pointing away from the follower, then rotate the follower so that its notch is at a right-angle to the camshaft centre-line.

10 Using a suitable C-spanner or stout screwdriver, carefully lever down between the camshaft and the edge of the follower, until the follower is depressed sufficiently to allow the shim to be slid out of position. With the shim removed, slowly release the follower. If difficulty is experienced in removing the shims, it will be necessary to remove the camshaft(s) as described in Section 10.

11 The shim size is stamped on the bottom face of the shim (eg. 224 indicates the shim is 2.24 mm thick), but it is advisable to use a micrometer to measure the true thickness of any shim removed, as it may have been reduced by wear. **Note:** *Shims are available in thicknesses between 2.00 mm and 2.98 mm, in steps of 0.02 mm.* The size of shim required is calculated as follows.

2A

12 If the measured clearance is less than specified, subtract the measured clearance from the specified clearance, and subtract the result from the thickness of the existing shim. For example:

Sample calculation - inlet valve clearance too small:

Clearance measured = 0.26 mm
Desired clearance = 0.36 mm (0.32 to 0.40 mm)
Difference = 0.10 mm
Shim thickness fitted = 2.50 mm
Shim thickness required = 2.50 - 0.10 = 2.40 mm

13 If the measured clearance is greater than specified, subtract the specified clearance from the measured clearance, and add the result to the thickness of the existing shim. For example:

Sample calculation - exhaust valve clearance too big:

Clearance measured = 0.51 mm
Desired clearance = 0.41 mm (0.37 to 0.45 mm)
Difference = 0.10 mm
Shim thickness fitted = 2.76 mm
Shim thickness required = 2.76 + 0.10 = 2.86 mm

14 Depress the follower, then slide the required size of shim into position, so that it is fitted with its marked face facing downwards. Ensure that the shim is correctly seated, then repeat the procedure (as required) for the remaining valve(s) which require adjustment.

15 Once all valves have been adjusted, rotate the crankshaft through at least four complete turns in the correct direction of rotation, to settle all disturbed shims in position, then recheck the clearances as described above.

16 With all valve clearances correctly adjusted, refit the cylinder head cover as described in Section 4, and refit all components removed to gain access to the crankshaft pulley.

10 Camshafts and followers - removal, inspection and refitting

Removal

1 Remove the distributor as described in Chapter 5.

2 Remove the camshaft sprockets as described in Section 8.

3 The camshaft right and left-hand end bearing caps are noticeably different to the others, however, the other bearing caps are all similar. On later models, the caps have identification markings cast into the top of each centre bearing cap; the exhaust camshaft caps are marked "E2" to "E5" and the inlet camshaft caps are marked "I2" to "I5"; the No 2 caps being fitted nearest the timing chain end of the engine **(see illustration)**. On early models, the caps may not be marked, and suitable identification marks should be made prior to removal. Using white paint or a suitable marker pen, mark each cap in some way to indicate its correct fitted orientation and position. This will

avoid the possibility of installing the caps in the wrong positions and/or the wrong way around on refitting.

4 Working in the **reverse** of the sequence shown in illustration 10.23, evenly and progressively slacken the camshaft bearing cap retaining bolts by one turn at a time, to relieve the pressure of the valve springs on the bearing caps gradually and evenly. Once the valve spring pressure has been relieved, the bolts can be fully unscrewed and removed. Remove the end bearing caps first, then remove the exhaust camshaft caps followed by the inlet camshaft caps.

5 Lift the camshafts out of the cylinder head.

6 Obtain sixteen small, clean plastic containers, and number them 1 to 16. Alternatively, divide a larger container into sixteen compartments. Using a rubber sucker, withdraw each shim and follower in turn, and place it in its respective container. Do not interchange the cam followers, or the rate of wear will be increased.

Inspection

7 Inspect the cam bearing surfaces of the head and the bearing caps. Look for score marks and deep scratches. Check the camshaft lobes for heat discoloration (blue appearance), score marks, chipped areas or flat spots.

8 Camshaft run-out can be checked by supporting each end of the camshaft on V-blocks, and measuring any run-out at the centre of the shaft using a dial gauge. If the run-out exceeds the specified limit, a new camshaft will be required.

9 Measure the height of each lobe with a micrometer, and compare the results to the figures given in the Specifications at the start of this Chapter. If damage is noted or wear is excessive, new camshaft(s) must be fitted.

10 The camshaft bearing oil clearance should now be checked. There are two possible ways of checking this; the first method is by direct measurement (see paragraphs 11 and 16) and the second by the use of a product called Plastigage (see paragraphs 12 to 16).

11 If the direct measurement method is to be used, fit the bearing caps to the head, using the marks made on removal to ensure that they are correctly positioned. Tighten the

10.3 Inlet and exhaust camshaft bearing cap markings (arrowed)

retaining bolts to the specified torque in the sequence shown in illustration 10.23. Measure the diameter of each bearing cap journal, and compare the measurements obtained with the results given in the Specifications at the start of this Chapter. If any journal is worn beyond the service limit, the cylinder head must be renewed. The camshaft bearing oil clearance can then be calculated by subtracting the camshaft bearing journal diameter from the bearing cap journal diameter.

12 If the Plastigage method is to be used, clean the camshafts, the bearing surfaces in the cylinder head and the bearing caps with a clean, lint-free cloth, then lay the cams in place in the cylinder head.

13 Cut strips of Plastigage, and lay one piece on each bearing journal, parallel with the camshaft centreline. Ensuring that the camshafts are not rotated at all, refit both camshafts as described in paragraphs 19 to 23, ignoring the remark about applying sealant to the bearing cap.

14 Now unscrew the bolts as described in paragraph 4 and carefully lift off the bearing caps, again making sure the camshafts are not rotated.

15 To determine the oil clearance, compare the crushed Plastigage (at its widest point) on each journal to the scale printed on the Plastigage container.

16 Compare the results to this Chapter's Specifications. If the oil clearance is greater than specified, measure the diameter of the cam bearing journal with a micrometer. If the journal diameter is less than the specified limit, renew the camshaft and recheck the clearance. If the clearance is still too great, replace the cylinder head and bearing caps with new parts.

17 Check the cam follower and cylinder head bearing surfaces for signs of wear or damage. If the necessary measuring equipment is available, the amount of wear can be assessed by direct measurement. Compare the measurement of each follower and its cylinder head bore with the measurements given in the Specifications at the start of this Chapter. Renew worn components as necessary.

Refitting

18 Liberally oil the cylinder head cam follower bores and the followers. Carefully refit the followers to the cylinder head, ensuring that each follower is refitted to its original bore. Some care will be required to enter the followers squarely into their bores. Ensure that all the shims are correctly seated in the top of each follower, then liberally oil the camshaft bearing and lobe contact surfaces.

19 Refit the camshafts to their correct locations in the cylinder head. The exhaust camshaft is easily distinguished by the distributor drive slot on its left-hand end. On later models, the shafts also have identification markings - the inlet camshaft is marked "I" and the exhaust camshaft "E".

20 Check that the crankshaft pulley TDC notch is still aligned with the pointer on the timing chain cover. Position each camshaft so that its No 1 cylinder lobes are pointing away from their valves. With the shafts in this position, the sprocket locating pin in the inlet camshaft's right-hand end will be in the 9 o'clock position when viewed from the right-hand end of the engine, while that of the exhaust camshaft will be in the 12 o'clock position.

21 Ensure that the bearing cap and head mating surfaces are completely clean, unmarked and free from oil. Apply a smear of suitable sealant to the exhaust camshaft's left-hand end bearing cap mating surface.

22 Refit the bearing caps, using the identification marks made or noted on removal to ensure that each is installed the correct way round and in its original location.

23 Working in the sequence shown (see illustration), evenly and progressively tighten the camshaft bearing cap bolts by one turn at a time until the caps touch the cylinder head. Then go round again and tighten all the bolts to the specified torque setting. Work only as described, to impose the pressure of the valve springs gradually and evenly on the bearing caps.

24 Refit the camshaft sprockets as described in Section 8. **Note:** *If the cylinder head/camshafts have been overhauled, check the valve clearances "cold" prior to refitting the cylinder head cover (see Section 9).*

25 Refit the distributor as described in Chapter 5.

26 Check the valve clearances as described in Section 9.

11 Cylinder head - removal and refitting

Removal

 HAYNES HINT *To aid refitting, make notes on the locations of all relevant brackets and the routing of hoses and cables before removal.*

1 Disconnect the battery negative lead.
2 Remove the timing chains as described in Section 7.
3 Remove the camshafts as described in Section 10.
4 Note that the following text assumes that the cylinder head will be removed with both inlet and exhaust manifolds attached; this is easier, but makes it a bulky and heavy assembly to handle. If it is wished to remove the manifolds first, proceed as described in the relevant Part of Chapter 4.
5 Working as described in the relevant Part of Chapter 4, disconnect the exhaust system front pipe from the manifold.

10.23 Camshaft bearing cap bolt tightening sequence. Apply sealant to the shaded area of the left-hand exhaust camshaft bearing (inset) cap prior to refitting

6 Remove the air cleaner assembly as described in Chapter 4.
7 On carburettor engines, disconnect the following from the carburettor and inlet manifold, as described in Chapter 4A:
a) *Fuel feed hose and return hose from the fuel pump (plug all openings, to prevent loss of fuel and the entry of dirt into the system).*
b) *Accelerator cable.*
c) *Carburettor wiring connector(s).*
d) *Vacuum servo unit vacuum hose, coolant hose and all other relevant breather/vacuum hoses from the manifold and associated valves.*
e) *Remove the inlet manifold support bracket.*
f) *On models with a catalytic converter, disconnect the exhaust gas sensor wiring connector.*

8 On fuel-injected engines, carry out the following operations as described in the relevant Part of Chapter 4.
a) *Depressurise the fuel system, and disconnect the fuel feed and return hoses from the fuel rail (plug all openings, to prevent loss of fuel and entry of dirt into the fuel system).*
b) *Disconnect the accelerator cable.*
c) *Disconnect the relevant electrical connectors from the throttle housing, inlet manifold and associated components.*
d) *Disconnect the vacuum servo unit hose, coolant hose(s) and all the other relevant/breather hoses from the manifold and associated valves.*
e) *Remove the inlet manifold support brackets.*
f) *On models with a catalytic converter, disconnect the exhaust gas sensor wiring connector.*

9 Slacken the retaining clip(s) and disconnect the coolant hose(s) from the cylinder head.

10 Slacken and remove the 6 mm bolt from the front, left-hand corner of the cylinder head.
11 Working in the **reverse** of the sequence shown in illustration 11.25, progressively slacken the ten main cylinder head bolts by half a turn at a time, until all bolts can be unscrewed by hand.
12 Lift out the cylinder head bolts and recover the washers, noting which way around they are fitted.
13 Lift the cylinder head away; seek assistance if possible, as it is a heavy assembly (especially if complete with manifolds). Remove the gasket from the top of the block, noting the two locating dowels and the oil jet fitted to the top of the cylinder block. If they are a loose fit in the block, remove the locating dowels and oil jet, noting which way round they are fitted, and store them with the head for safe-keeping.
14 If the cylinder head is to be dismantled for overhaul, then refer to Part B of this Chapter.

Preparation for refitting

15 Check the condition of the cylinder head bolts, and particularly their threads, whenever they are removed. Wash the bolts and wipe dry, then check each for any sign of visible wear or damage, renewing any bolt if necessary. Although Nissan do not actually specify that the bolts must be renewed, it is strongly recommended that the bolts should be renewed as a complete set whenever they are disturbed.
16 The mating faces of the cylinder head and cylinder block/crankcase must be perfectly clean before refitting the head. Use a hard plastic or wood scraper to remove all traces of gasket and carbon; also clean the piston crowns. Take particular care, as the surfaces are damaged easily. Also, make sure that the carbon is not allowed to enter the oil and water passages - this is particularly important

2A

for the lubrication system, as carbon could block the oil supply to any of the engine's components. Using adhesive tape and paper, seal the water, oil and bolt holes in the cylinder block/crankcase. To prevent carbon entering the gap between the pistons and bores, smear a little grease in the gap. After cleaning each piston, use a small brush to remove all traces of grease and carbon from the gap, then wipe away the remainder with a clean rag. Clean all the pistons in the same way.

17 Check the mating surfaces of the cylinder block/crankcase and the cylinder head for nicks, deep scratches and other damage. If slight, they may be removed carefully with a file, but if excessive, machining may be the only alternative to renewal.

18 If warpage of the cylinder head gasket surface is suspected, use a straight-edge to check it for distortion. Refer to Part B of this Chapter if necessary.

Refitting

19 Wipe clean the mating surfaces of the cylinder head and cylinder block/crankcase. Check that the two locating dowels are in position at each end of the cylinder block/crankcase surface, and refit the oil jet to the centre of the block.

20 Fit a new gasket to the cylinder block/crankcase surface, aligning it with the oil jet and locating dowels.

21 With the aid of an assistant, carefully refit the cylinder head assembly to the block, aligning it with the locating dowels.

22 Apply a smear of clean oil to the threads, and to the underside of the heads, of the ten main cylinder head bolts.

23 Fit the washer to each head bolt, making sure it is fitted with its tapered edge uppermost.

24 Carefully enter each bolt into its relevant hole (do not drop them in) and screw in, by hand only, until finger-tight.

25 Working progressively and in the sequence shown, tighten the **ten main** cylinder head bolts (Nos 1 to 10 in the accompanying illustration) to their Stage 1 torque setting, using a torque wrench and suitable socket **(see illustration)**. **Note:** Bolts 11 to 15 in the sequence (the 6 mm bolts) should not be tightened now, but only after the ten main bolts have been tightened to Stage 4.

26 Once the ten main bolts have been tightened to their Stage 1 setting, go around again in the specified sequence and tighten them to the specified Stage 2 torque setting.

27 Leave the bolts a minute then, working in the **reverse** of the specified sequence, progressively slacken the head bolts by half a turn at a time, until all bolts can be unscrewed by hand.

28 Tighten the ten main bolts again by hand, then go around again in the specified sequence and tighten these ten bolts to the specified Stage 3 torque setting.

11.25 Cylinder head bolt tightening sequence

29 Finally, go around again in the specified sequence and tighten the ten main head bolts either through the Stage 4 angle setting **or**, if an angle-measuring gauge is not available, to the specified Stage 4 torque setting.

30 With the main cylinder head bolts correctly tightened, fit the five 6 mm bolts (Nos 11 to 15 in the tightening sequence) and tighten them in sequence to their specified torque setting.

31 Reconnect the coolant hose to the cylinder head and securely tightening its retaining clip.

32 Working as described in the relevant Part of Chapter 4, carry out the following tasks:

a) Refit all disturbed wiring, hoses and control cable(s) to the inlet manifold and fuel system components.

b) Reconnect and adjust the accelerator cable.

c) Reconnect the exhaust system front pipe to the manifold. Where applicable, reconnect the exhaust gas sensor wiring connector.

d) Refit the air cleaner assembly and inlet duct.

12.5 Engine/transmission front support bar fixings (arrowed)

33 Refit the camshafts to the head as described in Section 10.

34 Fit the timing chains and sprockets as described in Section 7. **Note:** If the cylinder head has been overhauled, check the valve clearances "cold" prior to refitting the cylinder head cover (see Section 9).

35 Start the engine and warm it up to normal operating temperature, then check the valve clearances as described in Section 9.

12 Sump - removal and refitting

Removal

1 Firmly apply the handbrake, then jack up the front of the vehicle and support it on axle stands (see "Jacking and Vehicle Support"). Disconnect the battery negative lead.

2 To improve access, slacken and remove the retaining screws and remove the plastic undershield(s) from beneath the engine.

3 Drain the engine oil, then clean and refit the engine oil drain plug, tightening it to the specified torque. If the engine is nearing its service interval when the oil and filter are due for renewal, it is recommended that the filter is also removed, and a new one fitted. After reassembly, the engine can then be refilled with fresh oil. Refer to Chapter 1 for further information.

4 Remove the exhaust system front pipe as described in the relevant Part of Chapter 4.

5 Undo the retaining bolts, and remove the small support bars linking the transmission to the cylinder block, from the front and rear of the block **(see illustration)**.

6 Progressively slacken and remove all the sump retaining nuts and bolts.

7 Break the joint by striking the sump with the palm of your hand, then lower the sump and withdraw it from the vehicle **(see illustration)**.
8 While the sump is removed, undo the two retaining bolts and remove the oil pump pick-up/strainer and O-ring from the base of the timing cover **(see illustration)**.
9 Wash the strainer in solvent, and check it for signs of clogging or splitting. Renew it if the pick-up/strainer is damaged in any way.

Refitting

10 Clean all traces of sealant from the mating surfaces of the cylinder block/crankcase and sump, then use a clean rag to wipe out the sump and the engine's interior.

12.7 Removing the sump from the engine

12.8 Remove the oil pump pick-up/strainer from the base of the timing chain cover

12.11 Fit a new O-ring (arrowed) to the oil pump pick-up/strainer recess

12.12 Apply sealant to the groove between the sump mounting bolt holes, and to the inner side of each hole

11 Fit a new O-ring to the recess in the top of the pick-up/strainer, and fit the strainer to the base of the timing cover **(see illustration)**. Securely tighten the strainer bolts.
12 Ensure that the sump and cylinder block/crankcase mating surfaces are clean and dry. Apply a continuous bead of sealant to the mating surface of the sump. Apply the sealant to the groove in the centre of the mating surface between the holes, and around the inner edge of each bolt hole **(see illustration)**.
13 Offer up the sump, locating it on its retaining studs, and refit its retaining nuts and bolts. Tighten the nuts and bolts evenly and progressively to the specified torque.
14 Refit the support bars, tightening their retaining bolts securely.
15 Refit the exhaust front pipe as described in the relevant Part of Chapter 4.
16 Refit the undershields (if removed) and securely tighten their retaining screws.
17 Replenish the engine oil as described in Chapter 1.

13.1 Exploded view of the oil pump components

1 *Timing chain cover*
2 *Outer gear*
3 *Inner gear*
4 *Pump cover screw*
5 *Pump cover bolt*
6 *Oil pressure regulator valve piston*
7 *Spring*
8 *Sealing washer*
9 *Oil pressure regulator valve bolt*

13 Oil pump - removal, inspection and refitting

Removal

1 The oil pump is an integral part of the timing chain cover **(see illustration)**. Remove the cover as described in Section 6.

13.2a Undo the retaining screws and bolts . . .

13.2b . . . and remove the pump cover from the rear of the timing chain cover

13.3a . . . then lift out the pump outer gear . . .

13.3b . . . and inner gear

13.4a Unscrew the pressure regulator valve bolt and sealing washer . . .

13.4b . . . and withdraw the spring and piston from the cover

Inspection

2 Unscrew the retaining screws and bolt, and remove the pump cover from the rear of the timing chain cover **(see illustrations)**.

3 Remove both the oil pump gears from the cover **(see illustrations)**.

4 Unscrew the oil pressure regulator valve bolt from the front edge of the cover, and recover its sealing washer. Withdraw the spring and the valve piston, noting which way the piston is fitted **(see illustrations)**. **Note:** *If necessary, the regulator valve can be dismantled without removing the timing cover from the engine.*

5 Inspect the pump gears, regulator valve piston and the cover for obvious signs of wear or damage.

6 Fit the gears to the cover and, using feeler blades of the appropriate thickness, measure the clearance between the outer gear and cover, and between the tips of inner and outer gear teeth and the crescent which is positioned between them **(see illustrations)**.

7 Using a feeler blade and a straight-edge placed across the top of the cover and the gears, measure the inner and outer gear endfloat **(see illustration)**.

8 If access to the necessary measuring equipment can be gained, measure the diameter of the inner gear and cover bearing surfaces. Subtract the gear outer diameter from the cover inner diameter, and calculate the gear-to-housing clearance.

9 If any measurement is outside the specified limits, or the gears, valve or cover is damaged, the complete timing chain cover assembly should be renewed.

10 If the pump is found to be worn, also check the oil pressure relief valve. To gain access to the relief valve, unscrew the oil filter from the front of the cylinder block. Inspect the valve ball for signs of wear or damage. Depress the valve ball, and check that it moves smoothly and easily, and returns quickly under spring pressure. If not the valve must be renewed. Pull

the valve out from the cylinder block, noting which way round it is fitted. Press the new one into position using a suitable tubular spacer. Fit a new oil filter to the engine (see Chapter 1).

11 Lubricate the gears with clean engine oil, and refit them to the pump body. Ensure that the inner gear is fitted with its flange towards the cover.

12 Ensure that the mating surfaces are clean and dry, and refit the pump cover. Fit the cover retaining bolt and screws, and tighten them to the specified torque settings.

13 Fit the pressure regulator valve ensuring it is the correct way around, and install the spring. Fit a new sealing washer to the valve bolt, and tighten the bolt to the specified torque setting.

Refitting

14 Refit the timing chain cover as described in Section 6.

13.6a Measuring outer gear-to-cover clearance

13.6b Measuring outer gear-to-crescent clearance

13.7 Checking gear endfloat with a straight edge and feeler blade

14 Crankshaft oil seals - renewal

Right-hand (timing chain cover) oil seal

1 Remove the crankshaft pulley as described in Section 5.
2 Carefully lever the oil seal out of position, using a large flat-bladed screwdriver, taking care not to damage the oil pump gears or timing cover.
3 Clean the seal housing, and polish off any burrs or raised edges which may have caused the seal to fail in the first place.
4 Lubricate the lips of the new seal with a smear of grease and offer up the seal, ensuring its sealing lip is facing inwards. Carefully ease the seal into position, taking care not to damage its sealing lip. Drive the seal into position until it seats on its locating shoulder, using a suitable tubular drift, such as a socket, which bears only on the hard outer edge of the seal. Take care not to damage the seal lips during fitting. Note that the seal lips should face inwards.
5 Wash off any traces of oil, then refit the crankshaft pulley as described in Section 5.

Left-hand (flywheel) oil seal

6 Remove the flywheel (Section 15).

15.2 Use the fabricated tool shown to lock the flywheel ring gear and prevent crankshaft rotation

7 Taking care not to mark either the crankshaft or any part of the cylinder block/crankcase, lever the seal evenly out of its housing using a large flat-bladed screwdriver.
8 Clean the seal housing, and polish off any burrs or raised edges which may have caused the seal to fail in the first place.
9 Lubricate with grease the lips of the new seal and the crankshaft shoulder, then offer up the seal to the cylinder block/crankcase.
10 Ease the sealing lip of the seal over the crankshaft shoulder by hand only, and press the seal evenly into its housing until its outer flange seats evenly on the housing lip. If necessary, a soft-faced mallet can be used to tap the seal gently into place.
11 Wash off any traces of oil, then refit the flywheel as described in Section 15.

15 Flywheel - removal, inspection and refitting

Removal

1 Remove the transmission as described in Chapter 7A, then remove the clutch assembly as described in Chapter 6.
2 Prevent the flywheel from turning by locking the ring gear teeth with a similar arrangement to that shown (see illustration). Alternatively, bolt a strap between the flywheel and the cylinder block/crankcase.
3 Slacken and remove the flywheel retaining bolts, and remove the flywheel. Do not drop it, as it is very heavy.
4 If necessary, remove the cover plate from the cylinder block, noting which way round it is fitted. If the cover plate dowels are a loose fit in the block, remove them and store them with the plate for safe-keeping.

Inspection

5 If the flywheel's clutch mating surface is deeply scored, cracked or otherwise damaged, the flywheel must be renewed. However, it may be possible to have it surface-ground; seek the advice of a Nissan dealer or engine reconditioning specialist.
6 If the ring gear is badly worn or has missing teeth, it must be renewed. This job is best left to a Nissan dealer or engine reconditioning specialist. The temperature to which the new ring gear must be heated for installation is critical and, if not done accurately, the hardness of the teeth will be destroyed.

Refitting

7 Install the locating dowels (where removed) and refit the cover plate to the cylinder block.
8 Clean the mating surfaces of the flywheel and crankshaft.
9 Offer up the flywheel, and refit the retaining bolts.
10 Lock the flywheel using the method employed on dismantling, and tighten the retaining bolts to the specified torque.
11 Refit the clutch as described in Chapter 6. Remove the locking tool, and refit the transmission as described in Chapter 7A.

16 Engine/transmission mountings - inspection and renewal

Inspection

1 If improved access is required, raise the front of the car and support it securely on axle stands (see "Jacking and Vehicle Support").
2 Check the mounting rubber to see if it is cracked, hardened or separated from the metal at any point; renew the mounting if any such damage or deterioration is evident (see illustration).

16.2 Engine mounting components

1 Right-hand mounting
2 Right-hand mounting bracket
3 Front mounting
4 Rear mounting
5 Centre member
6 Front mounting (manual transmission)
7 Roll damper (manual transmission)

H28750

2A

16.8 Right-hand engine mounting

16.18 Left-hand engine mounting

16.25 Front engine mounting

3 Check that all the mounting's fasteners are securely tightened; use a torque wrench to check if possible.

4 Using a large screwdriver or a crowbar, check for wear in the mounting by carefully levering against it to check for free play. Where this is not possible, enlist the aid of an assistant to move the engine/transmission back and forth, or from side to side, while you watch the mounting. While some free play is to be expected even from new components, excessive wear should be obvious. If excessive free play is found, check first that the fasteners are correctly secured, then renew any worn components as described below.

Renewal

Right-hand mounting

5 Disconnect the battery negative lead.

6 Place a jack beneath the engine, with a block of wood on the jack head. Raise the jack until it is supporting the weight of the engine.

7 Slacken and remove the retaining bolts, and remove the mounting bracket from the top of the right-hand engine/transmission mounting.

8 Unscrew the nut and through-bolt, then undo the three retaining bolts and remove the right-hand mounting assembly from the engine compartment (see illustration). Recover the rubbers which are fitted to each side of the body mounting bracket.

9 If necessary, undo the retaining bolts and remove the right-hand engine/transmission mounting bracket from the engine.

10 Check carefully for signs of wear or damage on all components, and renew them where necessary.

11 On refitting, fit the mounting bracket (where removed) to the engine, and securely tighten its retaining bolts.

12 Fit the rubbers to the body mounting bracket, ensuring that their pins are correctly seated in the bracket holes. Fit the mounting to the top of the engine bracket, tightening its retaining bolts to the specified torque setting.

13 Align the right-hand mounting with the body bracket, then insert the through-bolt and tighten its nut to the specified torque setting. Remove the jack from underneath the engine.

14 Refit the bracket to the top of the right-hand engine/transmission mounting, and tighten its bolts to the specified torque setting.

15 Reconnect the battery negative lead.

Left-hand mounting

16 Remove the battery as described in Chapter 5.

17 Place a jack and block of wood beneath the transmission, and raise the jack to take the weight of the transmission.

18 Slacken and remove the through-bolt, then undo the three bolts and remove the left-hand mounting from the transmission (see illustration). Recover the rubbers from each side of the mounting bracket and, if necessary, unbolt the mounting bracket from the vehicle body.

19 Check carefully for signs of wear or damage on all components, and renew them where necessary.

20 On refitting, fit the mounting bracket (where removed) and securely tighten its retaining bolts.

21 Refit the rubbers to the mounting bracket, ensuring that their pins are correctly seated in the bracket holes, and manoeuvre the mounting into position. Fit the bolts securing the mounting to the transmission, and tighten them to the specified torque setting.

22 Align the left-hand mounting with its bracket, then insert the through-bolt and tighten to the specified torque setting.

23 Remove the jack from underneath the engine, and reconnect the battery negative lead.

Front mounting

24 Firmly apply the handbrake, jack up the front of the vehicle and support it on axle stands (see "Jacking and Vehicle Support"). Disconnect the battery negative lead.

25 On manual transmission models, using a suitable marker pen mark the outline of the front engine/transmission through-bolt on the mounting bracket to use as a guide on refitting (see illustration).

26 Place a jack beneath the engine, with a block of wood on the jack head. Raise the jack until it is supporting the weight of the engine.

27 Slacken and remove the through-bolt(s) from the mounting.

28 Undo the retaining bolts, and remove the mounting/bracket from the front of the engine.

29 Check carefully for signs of wear or damage on all components, and renew them where necessary. On manual transmission models if renewal of the mounting rubber is

necessary, press the original out from the centre member. Install the new rubber; coating the rubber with soapy water (or washing-up liquid) to ease installation.

30 On refitting, fit the mounting/bracket to the engine, and tighten the retaining bolts to the specified torque.

31 Refit the through-bolt to the mounting, and lightly tighten its nut. Position the engine/transmission so that the front mounting through-bolt is correctly aligned with the mark made prior to removal, then tighten the through-bolt to the specified torque setting. The distance between the centres of the front engine mounting through-bolts must be 55.0 mm ± 1.0 mm.

32 Remove the jack from underneath the transmission, and reconnect the battery negative lead.

33 Lower the vehicle to the ground and reconnect the battery.

Rear mounting

34 If not already done, firmly apply the handbrake, then jack up the front of the vehicle and support it securely on axle stands (see "Jacking and Vehicle Support"). Disconnect the battery negative lead.

35 Slacken and remove the through-bolt from the rear engine/transmission mounting.

36 Undo the bolts securing the mounting bracket in position, and manoeuvre it away from the engine/transmission.

37 Undo the two retaining bolts, and remove the mounting from the centre member. On manual transmission models also remove the roll damper.

38 Check carefully for signs of wear or damage on all components, and renew them where necessary.

39 On reassembly, fit the rear mounting to the centre member, and tighten its retaining bolts to the specified torque.

40 Refit the mounting bracket and tighten its retaining bolts to the specified torque.

41 Align the rear mounting with its bracket, then insert the through-bolt and tighten its nut to the specified torque setting.

42 Remove the jack from underneath the engine, and reconnect the battery negative lead.

43 Lower the vehicle to the ground and reconnect the battery.

Chapter 2 Part B:
Engine removal and general overhaul procedures

Contents

Degrees of difficulty

Easy, suitable for novice with little experience	**Fairly easy,** suitable for beginner with some experience	**Fairly difficult,** suitable for competent DIY mechanic	**Difficult,** suitable for experienced DIY mechanic	**Very difficult,** suitable for expert DIY or professional 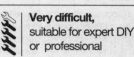

Specifications

Engine codes
See Chapter 2A.

Cylinder head
Maximum gasket face distortion .... 0.1 mm
Cylinder head height .... 117.0 to 118.0 mm

Valves
Valve head diameter:
  Inlet:
    1.4 litre engine .... 28.9 to 29.1 mm
    1.6 litre engine .... 29.9 to 30.1 mm
  Exhaust:
    1.4 litre engine .... 23.9 to 24.1 mm
    1.6 litre engine .... 23.9 to 24.0 mm
Valve stem diameter:
  Inlet .... 5.465 to 5.480 mm
  Exhaust .... 5.445 to 5.460 mm
Overall length:
  Inlet .... 92.00 to 92.50 mm
  Exhaust .... 92.37 to 92.87 mm
Valve guide inner diameter:
  Inlet .... 5.500 to 5.515 mm
  Exhaust .... 5.500 to 5.515 mm
Valve stem-to-guide clearance:
  Inlet .... 0.020 to 0.050 mm
  Exhaust .... 0.040 to 0.070 mm
Valve spring free length .... 41.19 mm
Valve spring out-of-square limit .... 1.80 mm

Cylinder block
Cylinder bore diameter:
  1.4 litre engine:
    Grade 1 .... 73.600 to 73.610 mm
    Grade 2 .... 73.610 to 73.620 mm
    Grade 3 .... 73.620 to 73.630 mm
    Oversizes available .... 0.5 mm and 1.0 mm

Cylinder block (continued)

1.6 litre engine:
Grade 1	76.000 to 76.010 mm
Grade 2	76.010 to 76.020 mm
Grade 3	76.020 to 76.030 mm
Oversizes available	0.5 mm and 1.0 mm

Pistons and connecting rods

Piston diameter:
1.4 litre engine (measured 9.5 mm up from the base of skirt):
Grade 1	73.575 to 73.585 mm
Grade 2	73.585 to 73.595 mm
Grade 3	73.595 to 73.905 mm
0.5 mm oversize piston	74.075 to 74.105 mm
1.0 mm oversize piston	74.575 to 74.605 mm

1.6 litre engine (measured 9.5 mm up from the base of skirt):
Standard piston:
Grade 1	75.975 to 75.985 mm
Grade 2	75.985 to 75.995 mm
Grade 3	75.995 to 76.005 mm
0.5 mm oversize piston	76.475 to 76.505 mm
1.0 mm oversize piston	76.975 to 77.005 mm

Piston-to-bore clearance	0.015 to 0.035 mm
Piston gudgeon pin bore diameter	18.987 to 18.999 mm
Gudgeon pin outer diameter	18.989 to 19.001 mm
Piston-to-gudgeon pin clearance	-0.004 to 0.000 mm (ie. an interference fit)
Connecting rod small-end bush diameter	18.987 to 18.999 mm

Connecting rod small-end bush-to-gudgeon pin clearance:
Standard	0.005 to 0.017 mm
Service limit	0.023 mm
Connecting rod big-end bore diameter	43.000 to 43.013 mm

Connecting rod big-end bearing side clearance:
Standard	0.20 to 0.47 mm
Service limit	0.52 mm

Piston rings

Ring-to-groove clearance:
Standard:
Top compression ring	0.040 to 0.080 mm
Second compression ring	0.030 to 0.070 mm
Service limit	0.2 mm

End gaps:
Standard:
Top compression ring	0.20 to 0.35 mm
Second compression ring	0.37 to 0.52 mm
Oil control ring	0.20 to 0.60 mm
Service limit	1.0 mm

Crankshaft

Endfloat:
Standard	0.06 to 0.18 mm
Service limit	0.3 mm
Run-out	Less than 0.05 mm

Main bearing journal diameter:
Grade 0	49.956 to 49.964 mm
Grade 1	49.948 to 49.956 mm
Grade 2	49.940 to 49.948 mm
Main bearing journal ovality	Less than 0.005 mm
Main bearing journal taper	Less than 0.002 mm

Big-end bearing journal diameter:
Grade 0	39.968 to 39.974 mm
Grade 1	39.962 to 39.968 mm
Grade 2	39.956 to 39.962 mm
Big-end journal ovality	Less than 0.005 mm
Big-end journal taper	Less than 0.002 mm

Main bearing running clearance:
Standard	0.018 to 0.042 mm
Service limit	0.1 mm

Crankshaft (continued)

Big-end bearing running clearance:
Standard	0.010 to 0.035 mm
Service limit	0.1 mm

Main bearing shell thicknesses:

Standard:
Black	1.826 to 1.830 mm
Brown	1.830 to 1.834 mm
Green	1.834 to 1.838 mm
Yellow	1.838 to 1.842 mm
Blue	1.842 to 1.846 mm
0.25 mm undersize	1.957 to 1.965 mm
0.50 mm undersize	2.082 to 2.090 mm

Big-end bearing shell thicknesses:

Standard:
Black	1.505 to 1.508 mm
Brown	1.508 to 1.511 mm
Green	1.511 to 1.514 mm
0.08 mm undersize	1.542 to 1.546 mm
0.12 mm undersize	1.562 to 1.566 mm
0.25 mm undersize	1.627 to 1.631 mm

Torque wrench settings

	Nm	lbf ft
Flywheel bolts	88	65
Rear oil seal housing bolts	8	6
Big-end bearing cap nuts:		
Stage 1	15	11
Stage 2 (if an angle tightening gauge is available)	Angle-tighten by 35° to 40°	
Stage 2 (if an angle-tightening gauge is not available)	25	18
Main bearing cap bolts	50	37
Engine-to-transmission fixing bolts:		
Bolts less than 30 mm long	19	14
Bolts 30 mm long, and longer	35	26
Right-hand engine/transmission mounting:		
Mounting-to-engine mounting bracket bolts	55	41
Through-bolt	49	37
Mounting upper bracket bolts	49	37
Left-hand engine/transmission mounting:		
Through-bolt	49	37
Mounting-to-transmission bolts	49	37
Front engine/transmission mounting bolts:		
Through-bolt	49	37
Mounting-to-engine bolts	49	37
Rear engine/transmission mounting:		
Through-bolt	49	37
Mounting bracket retaining bolts	49	37

1 General information

Included in this Part of Chapter 2 are details of removing the engine from the vehicle, and general overhaul procedures for the cylinder head, cylinder block/crankcase and all other engine internal components.

The information given ranges from advice concerning preparation for an overhaul and the purchase of replacement parts, to detailed step-by-step procedures covering removal, inspection, renovation and refitting of engine internal components.

After Section 6, all instructions are based on the assumption that the engine has been removed from the vehicle. For information concerning in-car engine repair, as well as the removal and refitting of those external components necessary for full overhaul, refer to Part A of this Chapter and to Section 6. Ignore any preliminary dismantling operations described in Part A that are no longer relevant once the engine has been removed from the vehicle.

Apart from torque wrench settings, which are given at the beginning of Part A, all specifications relating to engine overhaul are at the beginning of this Part of Chapter 2.

2 Engine overhaul - general information

It is not always easy to determine when, or if, an engine should be completely overhauled, as a number of factors must be considered.

High mileage is not necessarily an indication that an overhaul is needed, while low mileage does not preclude the need for an overhaul. Frequency of servicing is probably the most important consideration. An engine which has had regular and frequent oil and filter changes, as well as other required maintenance, should give many thousands of miles of reliable service. Conversely, a neglected engine may require an overhaul very early in its life.

Excessive oil consumption is an indication that piston rings, valve seals and/or valve guides are in need of attention. Make sure that oil leaks are not responsible before deciding that the rings and/or guides are worn. Perform a compression test, as described in Part A of this Chapter, to determine the likely cause of the problem.

Check the oil pressure with a gauge fitted in place of the oil pressure switch, and compare it with that specified. If it is extremely low, the main and big-end bearings, and/or the oil pump, are probably worn out.

Loss of power, rough running, knocking or metallic engine noises, excessive valve gear noise, and high fuel consumption may also point to the need for an overhaul, especially if they are all present at the same time. If a complete service does not remedy the situation, major mechanical work is the only solution.

An engine overhaul involves restoring all internal parts to the specification of a new engine. During an overhaul, the pistons and the piston rings are renewed. New main and big-end bearings are generally fitted; if necessary, the crankshaft may be renewed, to restore the journals. The valves are also serviced as well, since they are usually in less-than-perfect condition at this point. While the engine is being overhauled, other components, such as the distributor, starter and alternator, can be overhauled as well. The end result should be an as-new engine that will give many trouble-free miles.

Note: *Critical cooling system components such as the hoses, thermostat and water pump should be renewed when an engine is overhauled. The radiator should be checked carefully, to ensure that it is not clogged or leaking. Also, it is a good idea to renew the oil pump whenever the engine is overhauled.*

Before beginning the engine overhaul, read through the entire procedure, to familiarise yourself with the scope and requirements of the job. Overhauling an engine is not difficult if you follow carefully all of the instructions, have the necessary tools and equipment, and pay close attention to all specifications. It can, however, be time-consuming. Plan on the car being off the road for a minimum of two weeks, especially if parts must be taken to an engineering works for repair or reconditioning. Check on the availability of parts, and make sure that any necessary special tools and equipment are obtained in advance. Most work can be done with typical hand tools, although a number of precision measuring tools are required for inspecting parts to determine if they must be renewed. Often, the engineering works will handle the inspection of parts, and can offer advice concerning reconditioning and renewal.

Note: *Always wait until the engine has been completely dismantled, and until all components (especially the cylinder block/crankcase and the crankshaft) have been inspected, before deciding what service and repair operations must be performed by an engineering works. The condition of these components will be the major factor to consider when determining whether to overhaul the original engine, or to buy a reconditioned unit. Do not, therefore, purchase parts or have overhaul work done on other components until they have been*

thoroughly inspected. As a general rule, time is the primary cost of an overhaul, so it does not pay to fit worn or sub-standard parts.

As a final note, to ensure maximum life and minimum trouble from a reconditioned engine, everything must be assembled with care, in a spotlessly-clean environment.

3 Engine removal - methods and precautions

1 If you have decided that the engine must be removed for overhaul or major repair work, several preliminary steps should be taken.
2 Locating a suitable place to work is extremely important. Adequate work space, along with storage space for the vehicle, will be needed. If a workshop or garage is not available, at the very least, a flat, level, clean work surface is required.
3 Cleaning the engine compartment and engine/transmission before beginning the removal procedure will help keep tools clean and organised.
4 An engine hoist or A-frame will also be necessary. Make sure that the equipment is rated in excess of the combined weight of the engine and transmission. Safety is of primary importance, considering the potential hazards involved in removing the engine/transmission from the vehicle.
5 If this is the first time you have removed an engine, an assistant should ideally be available. Advice and aid from someone more experienced would also be helpful. There are many instances when one person cannot simultaneously perform all of the operations required when lifting the engine out of the vehicle.
6 Plan the operation ahead of time. Before starting work, arrange for the hire of, or obtain, all of the tools and equipment you will need. Some of the equipment necessary to perform engine/transmission removal and installation safely and with relative ease (in addition to an engine hoist) is as follows: a heavy-duty trolley jack, complete sets of spanners and sockets as described in the front of this manual, wooden blocks, and plenty of rags and cleaning solvent for mopping up spilled oil, coolant and fuel. If the hoist must be hired, make sure that you arrange for it in advance, and perform all of the operations possible without it beforehand. This will save you money and time.
7 Plan for the vehicle to be out of use for quite a while. An engineering works will be required to perform some of the work which the do-it-yourselfer cannot accomplish without special equipment. These places often have a busy schedule, so it would be a good idea to consult them before removing the engine, in order to accurately estimate the amount of time required to rebuild or repair components that may need work.

8 Always be extremely careful when removing and refitting the engine/transmission. Serious injury can result from careless actions. Plan ahead and take your time, and a job of this nature, although major, can be accomplished successfully.
9 The engine and transmission is removed from under the vehicle on all models described in this manual.

4 Engine and manual transmission - removal, separation and refitting

Removal

Note: *The engine can be removed from the car only as a complete unit with the transmission; the two are then separated for overhaul. The engine/transmission is lowered out of position, and withdrawn from under the vehicle. To allow adequate clearance underneath the vehicle, there should be at least 75 cm between the front bumper and the ground when the vehicle is raised and supported.*
1 Park the vehicle on firm, level ground. Chock the rear wheels, then firmly apply the handbrake. Apply the handbrake, then jack up the front of the vehicle. Securely support it on axle stands (see *"Jacking and Vehicle Support"*), bearing in mind the note at the start of this Section.
2 Remove both front roadwheels.
3 Undo all the retaining screws, and remove the undershields from underneath and around the engine.
4 Remove the bonnet as described in Chapter 11.
5 Drain the cooling system (see Chapter 1), saving the coolant if it is fit for re-use.
6 Drain the transmission oil as described in Chapter 1. Refit the drain and filler plugs, and tighten them to their specified torque settings.
7 If the engine is to be dismantled, working as described in Chapter 1, drain the oil and if required remove the oil filter. Clean and refit the drain plug, tightening it to the specified torque.
8 Remove the battery as described in Chapter 12.
9 Where necessary remove the coolant expansion tank and bracket with reference to Chapter 3.
10 Remove the auxiliary drivebelt(s) as described in Chapter 1.
11 Working as described in Chapter 5, remove the alternator.
12 On models with air conditioning, unbolt the compressor and position it clear of the engine. Support the weight of the compressor by tying it to the vehicle body, to prevent any excess strain being placed on the compressor lines whilst the engine is removed. **Do not** disconnect the refrigerant lines from the compressor (see the warnings given in Chapter 3, Section 10).

4.17 Disconnect the gearchange linkage support rod (1) and selector rod (2) from the transmission

4.18a Undo the four bolts and washers . . .

4.18b . . . and remove the centre member from underneath the engine/transmission

13 Remove the power steering pump as described in Chapter 10, however it is not necessary to disconnect the hydraulic fluid lines from it.

14 Working on each side in turn unbolt the front brake calipers from the steering knuckles and tie them to one side. **Do not** disconnect the hydraulic hoses.

15 Refer to Chapter 10 and disconnect the front suspension lower balljoints on both sides.

16 Refer to Chapter 8 and disconnect the driveshafts from each side of the transmission. There is no need to remove the driveshafts completely.

17 Detach the gearchange rod and support rod from the transmission (refer to Chapter 7A if necessary) **(see illustration)**. Also disconnect the clutch cable as described in Chapter 6.

18 Slacken and remove the four bolts and washers securing the centre member to the vehicle body, and lower the assembly away from the engine **(see illustrations)**.

19 Refer to Chapter 4A or 4B (as applicable) and remove the exhaust front downpipe from the vehicle.

20 Remove the radiator, complete with hoses and cooling fans, as described in Chapter 3.

21 Where necessary remove the front anti-roll bar with reference to Chapter 10.

22 On carburettor engines, disconnect the following from the carburettor and inlet manifold, as described in Chapter 4A:

 a) Air cleaner housing.

 b) Fuel feed hose and return hose from the fuel pump (plug all openings, to prevent loss of fuel and the entry of dirt into the system).

 c) Accelerator cable.

 d) Carburettor wiring connector(s).

 e) Vacuum servo unit vacuum hose, coolant hose, and all other relevant breather/vacuum hoses from the manifold and associated valves.

 f) Where applicable, remove the inlet manifold support bracket.

 g) On models with a catalytic converter, disconnect the exhaust gas sensor wiring connector.

23 On fuel injection engines, carry out the following operations as described in Chapter 4B.

 a) Remove the air cleaner inlet duct.

 b) Depressurise the fuel system, and disconnect the fuel feed and return hoses from the fuel rail (plug all openings, to prevent loss of fuel and entry of dirt into the fuel system).

 c) Disconnect the accelerator cable.

 d) Disconnect the relevant electrical connectors from the throttle housing, inlet manifold and associated components. Free the wiring from the manifold, and position it clear of the cylinder head so that it does not hinder removal.

 e) Disconnect the vacuum servo unit hose, coolant hose(s), and all the other relevant/breather hoses from the manifold and associated valves.

 f) Where applicable, remove the inlet manifold support bracket(s).

24 Slacken the retaining clips, and disconnect the heater hoses and all other relevant cooling system hoses from the engine, noting each hose's correct fitted location.

25 Referring to Chapter 5, disconnect the wiring connectors from the distributor, ignition HT coil and the power transistor unit. Free the wiring loom from any relevant retaining clips, so that it is free from the cylinder head and will not hinder the removal procedure. Also undo the retaining bolts, and disconnect all the relevant earth leads from the head and inlet manifold **(see illustration)**.

26 Disconnect the speedometer cable and any remaining wiring connectors from the transmission.

27 Manoeuvre the engine hoist into position, and attach it to the cylinder head using suitable lifting brackets. Raise the hoist until it is supporting the weight of the engine.

28 Using a suitable marker pen, mark the outline of the front engine/transmission through-bolt on the mounting bracket to use as a guide on refitting. Slacken and remove the nut and withdraw the through-bolt from the mounting. Slacken and remove the nut and through-bolt from the rear engine/transmission mounting **(see illustrations)**. Unbolt and remove the engine front mounting and bracket with reference to Part A.

2B

4.25 Unscrew the bolt(s) and free all earth lead(s) from the cylinder head

4.28a Prior to removal, mark the position of the front engine/transmission mounting through-bolt (arrowed) on its bracket

4.28b Slacken and remove the rear engine/transmission mounting through-bolt (arrowed)

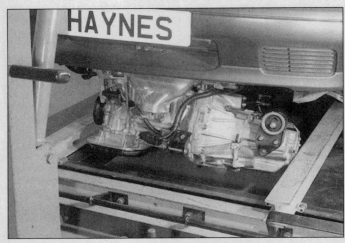

4.32 Carefully lower the engine/ transmission downwards and out of position

4.50 Tighten the centre member mounting bolts to the specified torque

29 Unscrew the nut and through-bolt from the right-hand engine/transmission mounting, then undo the retaining bolts and remove the mounting assembly from the engine compartment. Recover the rubbers which are fitted to each side of the body mounting bracket, if they are loose.

30 Slacken and remove the through-bolt from the left-hand engine/transmission mounting. Undo the three bolts securing the mounting to the transmission, and manoeuvre the mounting out of position. Recover the rubbers from each side of the mounting bracket, if they are loose.

31 Make a final check that any components which would prevent the removal of the engine/transmission from the car have been removed or disconnected. Ensure that components such as the gearchange link rods are secured so that they cannot be damaged on removal.

32 If available, a low trolley should be placed under the engine/transmission assembly, to facilitate its easy removal from under the vehicle. Lower the engine/transmission assembly, making sure that nothing is trapped or damaged. Enlist the help of an assistant during this procedure, as it may be necessary to tilt the assembly slightly to clear the body panels (see illustration). Great care must be taken to ensure that no components are trapped and damaged during the removal procedure.

33 Withdraw the assembly from under the vehicle.

Separation

34 With the engine/transmission assembly removed, support the assembly on suitable blocks of wood, on a workbench (or failing that, on a clean area of the workshop floor).

35 Unscrew the retaining bolts, and remove the starter motor from the transmission.

36 Ensure that both engine and transmission are adequately supported, then slacken and remove the bolts securing the transmission

housing to the engine. Note the correct fitted positions of each bolt (and, where fitted, the relevant brackets) as they are removed, to use as a reference on refitting.

37 Carefully withdraw the transmission from the engine, ensuring that the weight of the transmission is not allowed to hang on the input shaft while it is engaged with the clutch friction disc.

38 If they are loose, remove the locating dowels from the engine or transmission, and keep them in a safe place.

Refitting

39 If the engine and transmission have been separated, perform the operations described below in paragraphs 41 to 45. If not, proceed as described from paragraph 46 onwards.

40 Apply a smear of high-melting-point grease to the splines of the transmission input shaft. Do not apply too much, otherwise there is a possibility of the grease contaminating the clutch friction plate.

41 Ensure that the locating dowels are correctly positioned in the engine or transmission, and that the release bearing is correctly engaged with the fork.

42 Carefully offer the transmission to the engine, until the locating dowels are engaged. Ensure that the weight of the transmission is not allowed to hang on the input shaft as it is engaged with the clutch friction plate.

43 Refit the transmission housing-to-engine bolts, ensuring that all the necessary brackets are correctly positioned, and tighten them to the specified torque setting.

44 Refit the starter motor and tighten the retaining bolts.

45 Position the engine/transmission assembly under the vehicle, then reconnect the hoist and lifting tackle to the engine lifting brackets.

46 With the aid of an assistant, lift the assembly up into the engine compartment, making sure that it clears the surrounding components.

47 Refit the rubbers to the left-hand engine/transmission mounting bracket, ensuring that their pins are correctly seated in the bracket holes. Manoeuvre the mounting into position, then fit the bolts securing it to the transmission and tighten them to the specified torque setting. Insert the through-bolt and nut, tightening it by hand only at this stage.

48 Fit the rubbers to the right-hand body mounting bracket, ensuring that their pins are correctly seated in the bracket holes. Refit the mounting to the top of its bracket, and tighten its retaining bolts to the specified torque setting. Insert the through-bolt and nut, tightening it by hand only at this stage.

49 Refit the through-bolt and nut to the rear engine/transmission mounting, tightening it by hand only.

50 Refit the centre member beneath the engine compartment and tighten the bolts (see illustration).

51 Refit the front engine mounting bracket and tighten the bolts, then insert the through-bolt and nut. Position the engine/transmission so that the front mounting through-bolt is correctly aligned with the mark made prior to removal, then tighten to the specified torque setting. The distance between the centres of the front engine mounting through-bolts must be 55.0 mm ± 1.0 mm.

52 Rock the engine/transmission to settle it in position, then tighten the remaining engine mounting through-bolts to their specified torque settings.

53 The remainder of the refitting procedure is a direct reversal of the removal sequence, noting the following points:

a) Ensure that the wiring harness is correctly routed and retained by all the relevant retaining clips, and all connectors are correctly and securely reconnected.

b) Prior to refitting the driveshafts to the transmission, renew the driveshaft oil seals as described in Chapter 7A.

c) *Ensure that all coolant hoses are correctly reconnected and securely retained by their retaining clips.*

d) *Adjust the accelerator cable as described in the relevant Part of Chapter 4.*

e) *Connect and adjust the clutch cable as described in Chapter 6.*

f) *Refit and adjust the auxiliary drivebelt(s) as described in Chapter 1.*

g) *Refill the engine and transmission with correct quantity and type of lubricant, as described in the relevant Sections of Chapter 1.*

h) *Refill the cooling system as described in Chapter 1.*

i) *On completion, start the engine and check for leaks.*

5 Engine and automatic transmission - removal, separation and refitting

Removal

Note: *The engine can be removed from the car only as a complete unit with the transmission; the two are then separated for overhaul. The engine/transmission is lowered out of position, and withdrawn from under the front of the vehicle. To allow adequate clearance underneath the vehicle, there should be at least 75 cm between the front bumper and the ground when the vehicle is raised and supported.*

1 Carry out the operations described in paragraphs 1 to 33 of Section 4 with the following changes. When draining the automatic transmission fluid refer to Chapter 1, and instead of the procedure given in paragraph 17 disconnect the selector cable from the transmission as described in Chapter 7B.

Separation

2 With the engine/transmission assembly removed, support the assembly on suitable blocks of wood, on a workbench (or failing that, on a clean area of the workshop floor).

3 Unscrew the retaining bolts, and remove the starter motor from the transmission.

4 Undo the retaining bolts, and remove the cover plate from the sump flange to gain access to the torque converter retaining bolts. Slacken and remove the visible bolt then, using a socket and extension bar to rotate the crankshaft pulley, undo the remaining bolts securing the torque converter to the driveplate as they become accessible. There are four bolts in total.

5 To ensure that the torque converter does not fall out as the transmission is removed, secure it in position using a length of metal strip bolted to one of the starter motor bolt holes.

6 Ensure that both engine and transmission are adequately supported, then slacken and remove the bolts securing the transmission housing to the engine. Note the correct fitted positions of each bolt (and, where fitted, the relevant brackets) as they are removed, to use as a reference on refitting.

7 Carefully withdraw the transmission from the engine. If they are loose, remove the locating dowels from the engine or transmission, and keep them in a safe place.

Refitting

8 If the engine and transmission have been separated, perform the operations described below in paragraphs 8 to 13. If not, proceed as described from paragraph 14 onwards.

9 Prior to joining, ensure that the torque converter is correctly engaged with the transmission. This can be checked by measuring the distance from the converter mounting bolt holes to the transmission mating surface; if the converter is correctly seated, this distance will be at least 21.1 mm.

10 Ensure that the locating dowels are correctly positioned in the engine or transmission.

11 Carefully offer the transmission to the engine, and engage it on the locating dowels. Refit the transmission housing-to-engine bolts, ensuring that all the necessary brackets are correctly positioned, and tighten them to the specified torque settings.

12 Remove the torque converter retaining strap (if fitted on removal). Align the torque converter holes with the those in the driveplate, and insert the retaining bolts.

13 Tighten the torque converter retaining bolts to the specified torque setting, then refit the cover plate to the sump and securely tighten its retaining bolts.

14 Refit the starter motor and tighten the retaining bolts.

15 Position the engine/transmission assembly under the vehicle, then reconnect the hoist and lifting tackle to the engine lifting brackets.

16 With the aid of an assistant, lift the assembly up into the engine compartment, making sure that it clears the surrounding components.

17 Refit the rubbers to the left-hand engine/transmission mounting bracket, ensuring that their pins are correctly seated in the bracket holes. Manoeuvre the mounting into position, then fit the bolts securing it to the transmission and tighten them to the specified torque setting. Insert the through-bolt and nut, tightening it by hand only at this stage.

18 Fit the rubbers to the right-hand body mounting bracket, ensuring that their pins are correctly seated in the bracket holes. Refit the mounting to the top of its bracket, and tighten its retaining bolts to the specified torque setting. Insert the through-bolt and nut, tightening it by hand only at this stage.

19 Refit the through-bolt and nut to the rear engine/transmission mounting, tightening it by hand only.

20 Refit the crossmember beneath the engine compartment and tighten the bolts.

21 Refit the front engine mounting bracket and tighten the bolts, then insert the through-bolt and nut. Position the engine/transmission so that the front mounting through-bolt is correctly aligned with the mark made prior to removal, then tighten to the specified torque setting.

22 Rock the engine/transmission to settle it in position, then tighten the remaining engine mounting through-bolts to their specified torque settings.

23 The remainder of the refitting procedure is a direct reversal of the removal sequence, noting the following points:

a) *Ensure that the wiring harness is correctly routed and retained by all the relevant retaining clips, and all connectors are correctly and securely reconnected.*

b) *Prior to refitting the driveshafts to the transmission, renew the driveshaft oil seals as described in Chapter 7B.*

c) *Ensure that all coolant hoses are correctly reconnected and securely retained by their retaining clips.*

d) *Adjust the accelerator cable as described in the relevant Part of Chapter 4.*

e) *Connect and adjust the selector and kickdown cables as described in Chapter 7B.*

f) *Refit and adjust the auxiliary drivebelt(s) as described in Chapter 1.*

g) *Refill the engine and transmission with correct quantity and type of lubricant, as described in the relevant Sections of Chapter 1.*

h) *Refill the cooling system as described in Chapter 1.*

i) *On completion, start the engine and check for leaks.*

6 Engine overhaul - dismantling sequence

1 It is much easier to dismantle and work on the engine if it is mounted on a portable engine stand. These stands can often be hired from a tool hire shop. Before the engine is mounted on a stand, the flywheel should be removed, so that the stand bolts can be tightened into the end of the cylinder block/crankcase.

2 If a stand is not available, it is possible to dismantle the engine with it blocked up on a sturdy workbench, or on the floor. Be extra-careful not to tip or drop the engine when working without a stand.

3 If you are going to obtain a reconditioned engine, all the external components must be removed first, to be transferred to the replacement engine (just as they will if you are doing a complete engine overhaul yourself). These components include the following (**see illustration**):

a) *Alternator, power steering pump and/or air conditioning compressor mounting brackets (as applicable).*

b) *Distributor, HT leads and spark plugs (Chapters 1 and 5).*
c) *Coolant pump and thermostat/coolant outlet housing(s) (Chapter 3).*
d) *The carburettor/fuel injection system components (see relevant Part of Chapter 4).*
e) *All electrical switches and sensors, and the engine wiring harness.*
f) *Inlet and exhaust manifolds (see relevant Part of Chapter 4).*
g) *Fuel pump - carburettor models (Chapter 4A).*
h) *Engine mountings (Part A of this Chapter).*
i) *Flywheel/driveplate (Part A of this Chapter).*

Note: *When removing the external components from the engine, pay close attention to details that may be helpful or important during refitting. Note the fitted position of gaskets, seals, spacers, pins, washers, bolts, and other small items.*

4 If you are obtaining a "short" engine (which consists of the engine cylinder block/crankcase, crankshaft, pistons and connecting rods all assembled), then the cylinder head, sump, oil pump, and timing chains will have to be removed also.

5 If you are planning a complete overhaul, the engine can be dismantled, and the internal components removed, in the order given below, referring to Part A of this Chapter unless otherwise stated.

a) *Inlet and exhaust manifolds (Chapter 4A or 4B).*
b) *Sump.*
c) *Timing chain(s) and sprockets.*
d) *Cylinder head.*
e) *Flywheel.*
f) *Piston/connecting rod assemblies.*
g) *Crankshaft.*

6 Before beginning the dismantling and overhaul procedures, make sure that you have all of the correct tools necessary. Refer to *"Tools and working facilities"* in the *Reference* Section of this manual for further information.

7 Cylinder head - dismantling

Note: *New and reconditioned cylinder heads are available from the manufacturer, and from engine overhaul specialists. Be aware that some specialist tools are required for the dismantling and inspection procedures, and new components may not be readily available. It may therefore be more practical and economical for the home mechanic to purchase a reconditioned head, rather than dismantle, inspect and recondition the original head.*

1 Remove the cylinder head as described in Part A of this Chapter (as applicable).
2 If not already done, remove the inlet and exhaust manifolds with reference to the relevant Part of Chapter 4.

6.3 Exploded view of the cylinder block and associated components

1 Flywheel retaining bolt
2 Flywheel
3 Cover plate
4 Oil seal
5 Oil seal housing
6 Cylinder block
7 Locating dowels and O-rings
8 Piston rings
9 Circlips
10 Gudgeon pin
11 Piston
12 Connecting rod
13 Main bearing inserts and thrustwashers
14 Crankshaft
15 Connecting rod big-end cap
16 Main bearing caps
17 Sump
18 Drain plug
19 Sealing washer
20 Big-end bearing inserts

3 If not already done, remove the camshaft followers and shims as described in Part A.
4 Using a valve spring compressor, compress each valve spring in turn until the split collets can be removed. Release the compressor, and lift off the spring retainer, spring and spring seat. Using a pair of pliers, carefully extract the valve stem seal from the top of the guide **(see illustration)**.
5 If, when the valve spring compressor is screwed down, the spring retainer refuses to free and expose the split collets, gently tap the top of the tool, directly over the retainer, with a light hammer. This will free the retainer.

7.4 Pull the valve stem oil seal off the guide using a pair of pliers

6 Withdraw the valve through the combustion chamber.

7 It is essential that each valve is stored together with its collets, retainer, spring, and spring seat. The valves should also be kept in their correct sequence, unless they are so badly worn that they are to be renewed. If they are going to be kept and used again, place each valve assembly in a labelled polythene bag or similar small container **(see illustration)**. Note that No 1 valve is nearest to the timing chain end of the engine.

8 Cylinder head and valves - cleaning and inspection

1 Thorough cleaning of the cylinder head and valve components, followed by a detailed inspection, will enable you to decide how much valve service work must be carried out during the engine overhaul. **Note:** *If the engine has been severely overheated, it is best to assume that the cylinder head is warped - check carefully for signs of this.*

Cleaning

2 Scrape away all traces of old gasket material from the cylinder head.

3 Scrape away the carbon from the combustion chambers and ports, then wash the cylinder head thoroughly with paraffin or a suitable solvent.

4 Scrape off any heavy carbon deposits that may have formed on the valves, then use a power-operated wire brush to remove deposits from the valve heads and stems.

Inspection

Note: *Be sure to perform all the following inspection procedures before concluding that the services of a machine shop or engine overhaul specialist are required. Make a list of all items that require attention.*

Cylinder head

5 Inspect the head very carefully for cracks, evidence of coolant leakage, and other damage. If cracks are found, a new cylinder head should be obtained.

6 Use a straight-edge and feeler blade to check that the cylinder head surface is not distorted **(see illustration)**. If it is, it may be possible to have it machined, provided that the cylinder head is not reduced to less than the specified height.

7 Examine the valve seats in each of the combustion chambers. If they are severely pitted, cracked, or burned, they will need to be renewed or re-cut by an engine overhaul specialist. If they are only slightly pitted, this can be removed by grinding-in the valve heads and seats with fine valve-grinding compound, as described below.

8 Check the valve guides for wear by inserting the relevant valve, and checking for side-to-side motion of the valve. A very small

7.7 Place each valve and its associated components in a labelled polythene bag

amount of movement is acceptable. If the movement seems excessive, remove the valve. Measure the valve stem diameter (see below), and renew the valve if it is worn. If the valve stem is not worn, the wear must be in the valve guide, and the guide must be renewed. The renewal of valve guides is best carried out by a Nissan dealer or engine overhaul specialist, who will have the necessary tools available.

9 If renewing the valve guides, the valve seats are to be re-cut or re-ground only *after* the guides have been fitted.

Valves

10 Examine the head of each valve for pitting, burning, cracks, and general wear. Check the valve stem for scoring and wear ridges. Rotate the valve, and check for any obvious indication that it is bent. Look for pits and excessive wear on the tip of each valve stem. Renew any valve that shows any such signs of wear or damage.

11 If the valve appears satisfactory at this stage, measure the valve stem diameter at several points using a micrometer **(see illustration)**. Any significant difference in the readings obtained indicates wear of the valve stem. Should any of these conditions be apparent, the valve(s) must be renewed.

12 If the valves are in satisfactory condition, they should be ground (lapped) into their respective seats, to ensure a smooth, gas-tight seal. If the seat is only lightly pitted, or if it has been re-cut, fine grinding compound

8.6 Using a straight edge and feeler blade to measure cylinder head gasket face distortion

only should be used to produce the required finish. Coarse valve-grinding compound should *not* be used, unless a seat is badly burned or deeply pitted. If this is the case, the cylinder head and valves should be inspected by an expert, to decide whether seat re-cutting, or even the renewal of the valve or seat insert (where possible) is required.

13 Valve grinding is carried out as follows. Place the cylinder head upside-down on a bench.

14 Smear a trace of (the appropriate grade of) valve-grinding compound on the seat face, and press a suction grinding tool onto the valve head. With a semi-rotary action, grind the valve head to its seat, lifting the valve occasionally to redistribute the grinding compound **(see illustration)**. A light spring placed under the valve head will greatly ease this operation.

15 If coarse grinding compound is being used, work only until a dull, matt even surface is produced on both the valve seat and the valve, then wipe off the used compound, and repeat the process with fine compound. When a smooth unbroken ring of light grey matt finish is produced on both the valve and seat, the grinding operation is complete. *Do not grind-in the valves any further than absolutely necessary, or the seat will be prematurely sunk into the cylinder head.*

16 When all the valves have been ground-in, carefully wash off *all* traces of grinding compound using paraffin or a suitable solvent, before reassembling the cylinder head.

2B

8.11 Measuring a valve stem diameter

8.14 Grinding-in a valve

9.1a Fit the spring seat . . .

9.1b . . . and press a new oil seal onto the valve guide using a socket

9.2 Lubricate the valve stem, and slide the valve into its respective guide

Valve components

17 Examine the valve springs for signs of damage and discoloration. The specified Nissan procedure for checking the condition of valve springs involves measuring the force necessary to compress each spring to a specified height. This is not possible without the use of the Nissan special test equipment, and therefore spring checking must be entrusted to a Nissan dealer. A rough idea of the condition of the spring can be gained by measuring the spring free length, and comparing it to the length given in this Chapter's Specifications.

18 Stand each spring on a flat surface, and position a square alongside the edge of the spring. Measure the gap between the upper edge of the spring and the square, and compare it to the out-of-square limit given in the Specifications.

19 If any of the springs are damaged, distorted or have lost their tension, obtain a complete new set of springs. It is normal to renew the valve springs as a matter of course if a major overhaul is being carried out.

20 Renew the valve stem oil seals regardless of their apparent condition.

9 Cylinder head - reassembly

1 Refit the spring seat then, working on the first valve, dip the new valve stem seal in fresh engine oil. Carefully locate it over the valve and onto the guide. Take care not to damage the seal as it is passed over the valve stem. Use a suitable socket or metal tube to press the seal firmly onto the guide **(see illustrations)**.

2 Lubricate the stems of the valves, and insert the valves into their original locations **(see illustration)**. If new valves are being fitted, insert them into the locations to which they have been ground.

3 Locate the valve spring on top of its seat, ensuring that the spring is fitted with its closer-pitched coils at the bottom, then refit the spring retainer **(see illustrations)**.

4 Compress the valve spring, and locate the split collets in the recess in the valve stem **(see illustration)**. Release the compressor, then repeat the procedure on the remaining valves.

HAYNES HiNT *Use a little dab of grease to hold the collets in position on the valve stem while the spring compressor is released.*

5 With all the valves installed, place the cylinder head on the bench and, using a hammer and interposed block of wood, tap the end of each valve stem to settle the components.

6 The cylinder head and associated components may now be refitted as described in Part A of this Chapter.

10 Piston/connecting rod assembly - removal

1 Remove the sump, timing chain(s) and cylinder head as described in Part A of this Chapter (as applicable).

2 If there is a pronounced wear ridge at the top of any bore, it may be necessary to remove it with a scraper or ridge reamer, to avoid piston damage during removal. Such a ridge indicates excessive wear of the cylinder bore.

3 Each connecting rod and bearing cap should be stamped with its respective cylinder number, No 1 cylinder being at the timing chain end of the engine **(see illustration)**. If no markings are visible, using a hammer and centre-punch, paint or similar, mark each connecting rod and big-end bearing cap with its respective cylinder number on the flat machined surface provided.

9.3a Fit the spring with its closer-pitched coils at the bottom . . .

9.3b . . . and fit the spring retainer

9.4 Install the collets, noting the use of grease to help keep the collets in position

10.3 Connecting rods are stamped with their relevant cylinder number (arrowed)

11.5 Main bearing cap identification numbers (arrowed)

4 Turn the crankshaft to bring pistons 1 and 4 to BDC (bottom dead centre).

5 Unscrew the nuts from No 1 piston big-end bearing cap. Take off the cap, and recover the bottom half bearing shell. If the bearing shells are to be re-used, tape the cap and the shell together.

6 To prevent the possibility of damage to the crankshaft bearing journals, tape over the connecting rod bolt threads.

7 Using a hammer handle, push the piston up through the bore, and remove it from the top of the cylinder block. Recover the bearing shell, and tape it to the connecting rod for safe-keeping.

8 Loosely refit the big-end cap to the connecting rod, and secure with the nuts - this will help to keep the components in their correct order.

9 Remove No 4 piston assembly in the same way.

10 Turn the crankshaft through 180° to bring pistons 2 and 3 to BDC (bottom dead centre), and remove them in the same way.

11 Crankshaft - removal

1 Remove the sump, timing chain(s) and flywheel as described in Part A of this Chapter (as applicable).

2 Remove the pistons and connecting rods, as described in Section 10. **Note:** *If no work is to be done on the pistons and connecting rods, there is no need to remove the cylinder head, or to push the pistons out of the cylinder bores. The pistons should just be pushed far enough up the bores that they are positioned clear of the crankshaft journals.*

3 Check the crankshaft endfloat as described in Section 14, then proceed as follows.

4 Undo the retaining bolts, and remove the rear oil seal housing from the left-hand (flywheel) end of the cylinder block. If the locating dowels are a loose fit, remove them and store them with the housing for safe-keeping.

5 The main bearing caps should be numbered 1 to 5 from the timing chain end of the engine **(see illustration)**. If not, using white paint or a suitable marker pen, mark each cap in some way as to indicate its

correct fitted orientation and position. This will avoid the possibility of installing the caps in the wrong positions and/or the wrong way around on refitting.

6 Working in the **reverse** of the sequence shown in illustration 18.26 (see Section 18), slacken the main bearing cap retaining bolts by a turn at a time. Once all bolts are loose, unscrew and remove them from the cylinder block.

7 Withdraw the bearing caps, and recover the lower main bearing shells. Tape each shell to its respective cap for safe-keeping.

8 Carefully lift out the crankshaft, taking care not to displace the upper main bearing shells.

9 Recover the upper bearing shells from the cylinder block, and tape them to their respective caps for safe-keeping. Remove the thrustwasher halves from the side of No 3 main bearing, and store them with the bearing cap.

12 Cylinder block/crankcase - cleaning and inspection

Cleaning

1 Remove all external components and electrical switches/sensors from the block. For complete cleaning, the core plugs should ideally be removed. Drill a small hole in the plugs, then insert a self-tapping screw into the hole. Pull out the plugs by pulling on the screw with a pair of grips, or by using a slide hammer.

2 Scrape all traces of sealant from the cylinder block/crankcase, taking care not to damage the gasket/sealing surfaces.

3 Remove all oil gallery plugs (where fitted). The plugs are usually very tight - they may have to be drilled out, and the holes re-tapped. Use new plugs when the engine is reassembled.

4 If any of the castings are extremely dirty, all should be steam-cleaned.

5 After the castings are returned, clean all oil holes and oil galleries one more time. Flush all internal passages with warm water until the water runs clear. Dry thoroughly, and apply a light film of oil to all mating surfaces and cylinder bores, to prevent rusting. If you have access to compressed air, use it to speed up the drying process, and to blow out all the oil holes and galleries.

 Warning: Wear eye protection when using compressed air!

6 If the castings are not very dirty, you can do an adequate cleaning job with hot (as hot as you can stand!), soapy water and a stiff brush. Take plenty of time, and do a thorough job. Regardless of the cleaning method used, be sure to clean all oil holes and galleries very thoroughly, and to dry all components well. Protect the cylinder bores as described above, to prevent rusting.

12.7 Cleaning a cylinder block threaded hole using a suitable tap

7 All threaded holes must be clean, to ensure accurate torque readings during reassembly. To clean the threads, run the correct-size tap into each of the holes to remove rust, corrosion, thread sealant or sludge, and to restore damaged threads **(see illustration)**. If possible, use compressed air to clear the holes of debris produced by this operation.

 A good alternative is to inject an aerosol water-dispersant lubricant into each hole, using the long tube usually supplied, but make sure that you wear eye protection when cleaning out these holes in this way!

8 Apply suitable sealant to the new oil gallery plugs, and insert them into the holes in the block. Tighten them securely.

9 If the engine is not going to be reassembled right away, cover it with a large plastic bag to keep it clean; protect all mating surfaces and the cylinder bores as described above, to prevent rusting.

Inspection

10 Visually check the casting for cracks and corrosion. Look for stripped threads in the threaded holes. If there has been any history of internal water leakage, it may be worthwhile having an engine overhaul specialist check the cylinder block/crankcase with special equipment. If defects are found, have them repaired if possible, or obtain a new block.

11 Check each cylinder bore for scuffing and scoring. Check for signs of a wear ridge at the top of the cylinder, indicating that the bore is excessively worn.

12 Check the bore of each cylinder for scuffing and scoring.

13 Measure the diameter of each cylinder bore 10 mm from the top of the bore, both parallel to the crankshaft axis and at right-angles to it. Repeat the procedure measuring the bore diameter 60 mm from the top, and then 100 mm from the top, so that a total of six measurements are taken. Using the measurements obtained, calculate the cylinder taper and cylinder out-of-round dimensions. **Note:** *The cylinder bore grades are stamped on the cylinder block, on the*

2B

12.13 The cylinder bore grades can be determined from the four-digit code (A) stamped on the base of the block. The five-digit code (B) is for the main bearing bores

flywheel end of the cylinder block base; there are two sets of codes - the four-digit code is for the cylinder bores, the first number in the sequence is for No 1 cylinder and the last for No 4 (the five-digit code is for the cylinder block main bearing bores - see Section 18) **(see illustration).**

14 Check the pistons and rings as described in Section 13. The piston-to-bore clearance can be calculated by subtracting the piston diameter from the cylinder bore diameter measurement.

15 Compare all results with the Specifications at the beginning of this Chapter. If any measurement exceeds the service limit specified, the cylinder must be rebored, where possible, to the next oversize and new pistons fitted, or the cylinder block must be renewed. Seek the advice of an engine overhaul specialist as to the best course of action. Pistons are available in two oversizes - 0.5 mm and 1.0 mm.

16 If the cylinder bores and pistons are in reasonably good condition, and not worn to the limits, and if the piston-to-bore clearances can be maintained properly, then it may only be necessary to renew the piston rings.

17 If this is the case, the bores should be honed, to allow the new rings to bed in correctly and provide the best possible seal. The conventional type of hone has spring-loaded stones, and is used with a power drill. You will also need some paraffin or honing oil and rags. The hone should be moved up and down the bore to produce a cross-hatch pattern, and plenty of honing oil should be used. Ideally the cross-hatch lines should intersect at approximately a 60° angle. Do not take off more material than is necessary to produce the required finish. If new pistons are being fitted, the piston manufacturers may specify a finish with a different angle, so their instructions should be followed. Do not withdraw the hone from the bore while it is still being turned - stop it first. After honing a bore, wipe out all traces of the honing oil. If equipment of this type is not available, or if you are not sure whether you are competent to undertake the task yourself, an engine overhaul specialist will carry out the work at moderate cost.

13 Piston/connecting rod assembly - inspection

1 Before the inspection process can begin, the piston/connecting rod assemblies must be cleaned, and the original piston rings removed from the pistons.

2 Carefully expand the old rings over the top of the pistons. The use of two or three old feeler blades will be helpful in preventing the rings dropping into empty grooves **(see illustration)**. Be careful not to scratch the piston with the ends of the ring. The rings are brittle, and will snap if they are spread too far. They're also very sharp - protect your hands and fingers. Always remove the rings from the top of the piston. Keep each set of rings with its piston if the old rings are to be re-used.

3 Scrape away all traces of carbon from the top of the piston. A hand-held wire brush (or a piece of fine emery cloth) can be used, once the majority of the deposits have been scraped away.

4 Remove the carbon from the ring grooves in the piston, using an old ring. Break the ring in half to do this (be careful not to cut your fingers - piston rings are sharp). Be careful to remove only the carbon deposits - do not remove any metal, and do not nick or scratch the sides of the ring grooves.

5 Once the deposits have been removed, clean the piston/connecting rod assembly with paraffin or a suitable solvent, and dry thoroughly. Make sure that the oil return holes in the ring grooves are clear.

6 Using a micrometer, measure the piston diameter at right-angles to the gudgeon pin axis (at the specified distance up from the bottom of the skirt), and compare the results with the Specifications at the beginning of this Chapter. The piston size grade is stamped onto the piston crown. Renew any piston which has worn beyond its specified limits.

7 Check the ring-to-groove clearance by inserting each ring from the outside, together with a feeler blade between the ring's top surface and the piston land. If the ring-to-groove clearance is excessive, renew the rings and recheck the clearance. If the clearance is still excessive, even with new piston rings, then the piston must be renewed.

8 Check the ring end gaps by inserting each ring into the cylinder bore and pushing it in with the piston crown to ensure that it is square in the bore. Push the ring down into the bore until the piston skirt is level with the block mating surface, then withdraw the piston. Using feeler blades, measure the piston ring end gap. If the ring end gap is excessive, renew the rings and repeat the checking procedure. If the clearance is still excessive, even with new piston rings, then the cylinder bores must be rebored/renewed (see Section 12).

13.2 Using a feeler blade to ease piston ring removal

9 Carefully inspect each piston for cracks around the skirt, around the gudgeon pin holes, and at the piston ring "lands" (between the ring grooves).

10 Look for scoring and scuffing on the piston skirt, holes in the piston crown, or burned areas at the edge of the crown. If the skirt is scored or scuffed, the engine may have been suffering from overheating, and/or abnormal combustion which caused excessively-high operating temperatures. The cooling and lubrication systems should be checked thoroughly. Scorch marks on the sides of the pistons show that blow-by has occurred. A hole in the piston crown, or burned areas at the edge of the piston crown, indicates that abnormal combustion (pre-ignition, knocking, or detonation) has been occurring. If any of the above problems exist, the causes must be investigated and corrected, or the damage will occur again. The causes may include incorrect ignition timing, inlet air leaks, or a faulty injector (as applicable).

11 Corrosion of the piston, in the form of pitting, indicates that coolant has been leaking into the combustion chamber and/or the crankcase. Again, the cause must be corrected, or the problem may persist in the rebuilt engine.

12 Examine each connecting rod carefully for signs of damage, such as cracks around the big-end and small-end bearings. Check that the rod is not bent or distorted. Damage is highly unlikely, unless the engine has been seized or badly overheated. Detailed checking of the connecting rod assembly can only be carried out by a Nissan dealer or engine repair specialist with the necessary equipment.

13 If necessary, the piston and connecting rods can be separated and reassembled as follows.

14 Using a small flat-bladed screwdriver, prise out the circlips, and push out the gudgeon pin **(see illustration)**. If necessary, support the piston, and tap the pin out using a suitable hammer and punch, taking great care not to mark the piston/connecting rod bores.

 Gudgeon pin removal will be considerably eased if the piston is warmed (to approximately 60 to 70°C)

13.14a Prise out the circlips, then press the gudgeon pin out of the piston

13.14b To ease gudgeon pin removal, gently heat the piston by submerging it in hot water

13.20 Correct connecting rod/piston fitting orientation

1 Piston grade number
2 Front marking (arrowed)
3 Connecting rod oil hole
4 Connecting rod cylinder number marking (maybe on opposite side of rod)

first. Warm the piston by submerging it in a pan of hot water, then remove the assembly and press the gudgeon pin out, taking great care not to burn your hands (see illustration). Identify the piston, gudgeon pin and rod to ensure correct reassembly. Discard the circlips - new ones must be used on refitting.

15 Examine the gudgeon pin, piston bore and connecting rod small-end bearing for signs of wear or damage. If the necessary measuring equipment is available, the amount of wear can be assessed by direct measurement, and the piston-to-gudgeon pin, and gudgeon pin-to-small-end clearances can be calculated.

16 If the gudgeon pin and connecting rod small-end bush are worn or the specified clearance is exceeded, this can be cured by renewing both the pin and bush. Bush renewal, however, is a specialist job - press facilities are required, and the new bush must be reamed accurately.

17 If the gudgeon pin-to-piston clearance is greatly exceeded, both the piston and pin should be renewed as a matched pair. Note that this clearance is not as critical as the gudgeon pin-to-small-end clearance, since the pin is retained by circlips.

18 The connecting rods themselves should not need renewal, unless seizure or some other major mechanical failure has occurred. Check the alignment of the connecting rods visually, and if the rods are not straight, take them to an engine overhaul specialist for a more detailed check.

19 Examine all components, and obtain any new parts from your Nissan dealer.

20 Position the piston so that the front marking on the piston crown (either in the form of an arrow or a dot) is positioned correctly in relation to the oil hole in the connecting rod shaft **(see illustration)**. With the piston and rod correctly mated, the piston front marking will face towards the timing chain end of the engine, and the connecting rod oil hole will face the rear of the cylinder block.

21 Apply a smear of clean engine oil to the gudgeon pin. Slide it into the piston and through the connecting rod small-end **(see illustration)**. **Note:** *Gudgeon pin installation will be greatly eased if the piston is first warmed (see paragraph 14).* If necessary, tap the pin into position using a hammer and suitable punch, whilst ensuring that the piston is securely supported.

22 Check that the piston pivots freely on the rod, then secure the gudgeon pin in position with two new circlips **(see illustration)**. Ensure that each circlip is correctly located in its groove in the piston.

14 Crankshaft - inspection

Checking crankshaft endfloat

1 If the crankshaft endfloat is to be checked, this must be done when the crankshaft is still installed in the cylinder block/crankcase, but is free to move (see Section 11).

2 Check the endfloat using a dial gauge in contact with the end of the crankshaft. Push the crankshaft fully one way, and then zero the gauge. Push the crankshaft fully the other way, and check the endfloat **(see illustration)**. The result can be compared with the specified amount, and will give an indication as to whether new thrustwashers are required.

3 If a dial gauge is not available, feeler blades can be used. First push the crankshaft fully towards the flywheel end of the engine, then use feeler blades to measure the gap between the No 4 crankpin web and No 3 main bearing thrustwasher.

13.21 Press the gudgeon pin into position . . .

13.22 . . . and secure it in position with two new circlips

14.2 Using a dial gauge to measure crankshaft endfloat

2B

14.11a Using a micrometer to measure a crankshaft main bearing journal diameter

14.11b Using a micrometer to measure a big-end bearing journal diameter

Inspection

4 Clean the crankshaft using paraffin or a suitable solvent, and dry it, preferably with compressed air if available.

 Warning: Wear eye protection when using compressed air! Be sure to clean the oil holes with a pipe cleaner or similar probe, to ensure that they are not obstructed.

5 Check the main and big-end bearing journals for uneven wear, scoring, pitting and cracking.

6 Big-end bearing wear is accompanied by distinct metallic knocking when the engine is running (particularly noticeable when the engine is pulling from low speed) and some loss of oil pressure.

7 Main bearing wear is accompanied by severe engine vibration and rumble - getting progressively worse as engine speed increases - and again by loss of oil pressure.

8 Check the bearing journal for roughness by running a finger lightly over the bearing surface. Any roughness (which will be accompanied by obvious bearing wear) indicates that the crankshaft requires regrinding (where possible) or renewal.

9 Crankshaft run-out can be checked by supporting each end of the crankshaft on V-blocks, and measuring any run-out at the centre of the shaft using a dial gauge. If the run-out exceeds the specified limit, a new crankshaft will be required.

10 If the crankshaft has been reground, check for burrs around the crankshaft oil holes (the holes are usually chamfered, so burrs should not be a problem unless regrinding has been carried out carelessly). Remove any burrs with a fine file or scraper, and thoroughly clean the oil holes as described previously.

11 Using a micrometer, measure the diameter of the main and big-end bearing journals, and compare the results with the Specifications **(see illustrations)**. By measuring the diameter at a number of points around each journal's circumference, you will be able to determine whether or not the journal is out-of-round. Take the measurement at each end of the journal, near the webs, to determine if the journal is tapered. Compare the results obtained with those given in the Specifications.

12 Check the oil seal contact surfaces at each end of the crankshaft for wear and damage. If the seal has worn a deep groove in the surface of the crankshaft, consult an engine overhaul specialist. Repair may be possible, but otherwise a new crankshaft will be required.

13 Nissan produce undersize bearing shells for both the main bearings and big-end bearings. There are two undersizes of main bearing shells (0.25 and 0.50 mm) and three undersizes of big-end bearing shells (0.08, 0.12 and 0.25 mm). Refer to your Nissan dealer for further information on parts availability. If undersize bearing shells are available, and the crankshaft has worn beyond the specified limits, providing that the crankshaft journals have not already been reground, it may be possible to have the crankshaft reconditioned, and to fit the undersize shells. Seek the advice of your Nissan dealer or engine specialist on the best course of action.

15 Main and big-end bearings - inspection

1 Even though the main and big-end bearings should be renewed during the engine overhaul, the old bearings should be retained for close examination, as they may reveal valuable information about the condition of the engine. The bearing shells are graded by thickness, the grade of each shell being indicated by the colour code marked on it.

2 Bearing failure can occur due to lack of lubrication, the presence of dirt or other foreign particles, overloading the engine, or corrosion. Regardless of the cause of bearing failure, the cause must be corrected (where applicable) before the engine is reassembled, to prevent it from happening again **(see illustration)**.

3 When examining the bearing shells, remove them from the cylinder block/crankcase, the main bearing caps, the connecting rods and the connecting rod big-end bearing caps. Lay them out on a clean surface in the same general position as their location in the engine. This will enable you to match any bearing problems with the corresponding crankshaft journal. *Do not* touch any shell's bearing surface with your fingers while checking it, or the delicate surface may be scratched.

4 Dirt and other foreign matter gets into the engine in a variety of ways. It may be left in the engine during assembly, or it may pass through filters or the crankcase ventilation system. It may get into the oil, and from there into the bearings. Metal chips from machining operations and normal engine wear are often present. Abrasives are sometimes left in engine components after reconditioning, especially when parts are not thoroughly cleaned using the proper cleaning methods. Whatever the source, these foreign objects often end up embedded in the soft bearing material, and are easily recognised. Large particles will not embed in the bearing, and will score or gouge the bearing and journal. The best prevention for this cause of bearing failure is to clean all parts thoroughly, and

15.2 Typical bearing failures

A Scratched by dirt; dirt embedded in bearing material
B Lack of oil; overlay wiped out
C Improper seating; bright (polished) sections
D Tapered journal; overlay gone from entire surface
E Radius ride
F Fatigue failure; craters or pockets

keep everything spotlessly-clean during engine assembly. Frequent and regular engine oil and filter changes are also recommended.

5 Lack of lubrication (or lubrication breakdown) has a number of interrelated causes. Excessive heat (which thins the oil), overloading (which squeezes the oil from the bearing face) and oil leakage (from excessive bearing clearances, worn oil pump or high engine speeds) all contribute to lubrication breakdown. Blocked oil passages, which usually are the result of misaligned oil holes in a bearing shell, will also oil-starve a bearing, and destroy it. When lack of lubrication is the cause of bearing failure, the bearing material is wiped or extruded from the steel backing of the bearing. Temperatures may increase to the point where the steel backing turns blue from overheating.

6 Driving habits can have a definite effect on bearing life. Full-throttle, low-speed operation (labouring the engine) puts very high loads on bearings, tending to squeeze out the oil film. These loads cause the bearings to flex, which produces fine cracks in the bearing face (fatigue failure). Eventually, the bearing material will loosen in pieces, and tear away from the steel backing.

7 Short-distance driving leads to corrosion of bearings, because insufficient engine heat is produced to drive off the condensed water and corrosive gases. These products collect in the engine oil, forming acid and sludge. As the oil is carried to the engine bearings, the acid attacks and corrodes the bearing material.

8 Incorrect bearing installation during engine assembly will lead to bearing failure as well. Tight-fitting bearings leave insufficient bearing running clearance, and will result in oil starvation. Dirt or foreign particles trapped behind a bearing shell result in high spots on the bearing, which lead to failure.

9 *Do not* touch any shell's bearing surface with your fingers during reassembly; there is a risk of scratching the delicate surface, or of depositing particles of dirt on it.

10 As mentioned at the beginning of this Section, the bearing shells should be renewed as a matter of course during engine overhaul; to do otherwise is false economy. Refer to Section 18 for details of bearing shell selection.

16 Engine overhaul - reassembly sequence

1 Before reassembly begins, ensure that all new parts have been obtained, and that all necessary tools are available. Read through the entire procedure, to familiarise yourself with the work involved, and to ensure that all items necessary for reassembly of the engine are at hand. In addition to all normal tools and materials, thread-locking compound will be needed. A suitable tube of liquid sealant will also be required for the joint faces that are fitted without gaskets; it is recommended that Nissan's Genuine Liquid Gasket (available from your Nissan dealer) is used.

2 In order to save time and avoid problems, engine reassembly can be carried out in the following order:
a) *Crankshaft (Section 18).*
b) *Piston/connecting rod assemblies (Section 19).*
c) *Cylinder head (See Part A).*
d) *Timing chain(s) and cover (See Part A).*
e) *Sump (See Part A).*
f) *Flywheel (See Part A).*
g) *Engine external components.*

3 At this stage, all engine components should be absolutely clean and dry, with all faults repaired. The components should be laid out (or in individual containers) on a completely clean work surface.

17 Piston rings - refitting

1 Before fitting new piston rings, the ring end gaps must be checked as follows.

2 Lay out the piston/connecting rod assemblies and the new piston ring sets, so that the ring sets will be matched with the same piston and cylinder during the end gap measurement and subsequent engine reassembly.

3 Insert the top ring into the first cylinder, and push it down the bore using the top of the piston. This will ensure that the ring remains square with the cylinder walls. Push the ring

down into the bore until the piston skirt is level with the block mating surface, then withdraw the piston.

4 Measure the end gap using feeler blades, and compare the measurements with the figures given in the Specifications **(see illustration)**.

5 If the gap is too small (unlikely if genuine Nissan parts are used), it must be enlarged, or the ring ends may contact each other during engine operation, causing serious damage. Ideally, new piston rings providing the correct end gap should be fitted. As a last resort, the end gap can be increased by filing the ring ends very carefully with a fine file. Mount the file in a vice with soft jaws, slip the ring over the file with the ends contacting the file face, and slowly move the ring to remove material from the ends. Take care, as piston rings are sharp, and are easily broken.

6 With new piston rings, it is unlikely that the end gap will be too large. If the gaps are too large, check that you have the correct rings for your engine and for the particular cylinder bore size.

7 Repeat the checking procedure for each ring in the first cylinder, and then for the rings in the remaining cylinders. Remember to keep rings, pistons and cylinders matched up.

8 Once the ring end gaps have been checked and if necessary corrected, the rings can be fitted to the pistons. **Note:** *Always follow any instructions supplied with the new piston ring sets - different manufacturers may specify different procedures. Do not mix up the top and second compression rings, as they have different cross-sections.*

9 The oil control ring (lowest on the piston) is installed first. It is composed of three separate components. Slip the expander into the groove, then install the upper side rail into the groove between the expander and the ring land, then install the lower side rail in the same manner **(see illustrations)**.

10 Install the second ring next. **Note:** *The second ring and top ring are different, and can be identified by their cross-sections.* Making sure the ring is the correct way up, fit the ring into the middle groove on the piston, taking care not to expand the ring any more than is necessary **(see illustrations)**.

17.4 Measuring a piston ring end gap

17.9a Fit the oil control ring expander . . .

17.9b . . . then install the side rails as described in text

2B

11 Install the top ring in the same way, making sure the ring is the correct way up. Where the ring is symmetrical, fit it with its identification marking facing upwards.

12 With all the rings in position on the piston, space the ring end gaps as shown **(see illustration)**.

13 Repeat the above procedure for the remaining pistons and rings.

18 Crankshaft - refitting and main bearing running clearance check

Selection of new bearing shells

Note: *This information applies only to standard size bearing shells. Undersize shells are not graded.*

1 New bearing shells are selected using the identification marks on the crankshaft and cylinder block.

2 The crankshaft markings are stamped on the side of No 1 cylinder crankweb (at the timing chain end of the crankshaft). The five-digit code refers to the main bearing journal diameters - the first number in the sequence is for No 1 bearing journal, and the last for No 5 journal **(see illustration)**. **Note:** *On some models, there is also a four-digit code stamped on the web; these numbers are for the big-end bearing (crankpin) journals (see Section 19).*

3 The cylinder block markings are stamped on the flywheel end of the cylinder block base. The

18.2 Crankshaft main bearing journal codes (1) and big-end bearing journal codes (2)

18.3 The five-digit code (A) denotes main bearing bore grades, while the four-digit code (B) is for the cylinder bore grades

17.10a Piston ring fitting diagram

five-digit code is for the main bearing bores - the first number in the sequence is for No 1 main bearing journal, and the last for No 5 journal (the four-digit code is for the cylinder bore size grades) **(see illustration)**.

4 Obtain the identification number of both the relevant crankshaft journal and the cylinder block bearing bore, and select the correct grade of main bearing shell required for each journal, using the relevant following table. The grade of each shell is indicated by a dab of paint on the side of the shell.

Crankshaft code	Bearing shell grade	Block code
0	0	Black
0	1	Brown
0	2	Green
1	0	Brown
1	1	Green
1	2	Yellow
2	0	Green
2	1	Yellow
2	2	Blue

Main bearing running clearance check

5 Clean the backs of the bearing shells, and the bearing locations in both the cylinder block and the main bearing caps.

6 Press the bearing shells into their locations, ensuring that the tab on each shell engages in the notch in the cylinder block/crankcase or main bearing ladder location. Take care not to touch any shell's bearing surface with your fingers. Note that all the upper bearing shells are grooved, and have oil holes in them; the lower shells are plain **(see illustrations)**. If the

17.10b Install the rings with their identification marking (arrowed) uppermost

17.12 Position the piston ring end gaps as shown

original bearing shells are being used for the check, ensure that they are refitted in their original locations. The clearance can be checked in either of two ways.

7 One method (which will be difficult to achieve without a range of internal micrometers or internal/external expanding calipers) is to refit the main bearing caps/ladder (as applicable) to the cylinder block, with the bearing shells in place. With the casting retaining bolts correctly tightened, measure the internal diameter of each assembled pair of bearing shells. If the diameter of each corresponding crankshaft journal is measured and then subtracted from the bearing internal diameter, the result will be the main bearing running clearance.

8 The second (and more accurate) method is to use a product called Plastigauge. This consists of a fine thread of perfectly-round plastic, which is compressed between the

18.6a Align the tabs in the upper grooved shells with the crankcase cut-outs (arrowed)

18.6b Align the tabs in the lower plain shells with the cap cut-outs (arrowed)

18.10 Plastigauge in place on a crankshaft journal main bearing

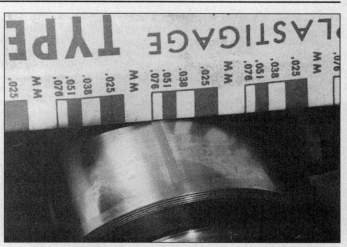

18.14 Measure the width of the Plastigage using the scale on the card provided

bearing shell and the journal. When the shell is removed, the plastic is deformed, and can be measured with a special card gauge supplied with the kit. The running clearance is determined from this gauge. Plastigauge should be available from a motor factor or car accessory shop. The procedure for using Plastigauge is as follows.

9 With the main bearing upper shells in place, carefully lay the crankshaft in position. Do not use any lubricant; the crankshaft journals and bearing shells must be perfectly clean and dry.

10 Cut several lengths of the appropriate-size Plastigauge (they should be slightly shorter than the width of the main bearings), and place one length on each crankshaft journal axis **(see illustration)**.

11 With the main bearing lower shells in position, refit the main bearing caps using the identification markings to ensure each cap is fitted correctly. Refit the main bearing cap bolts and, working in the sequence shown in illustration 18.26, tighten them evenly and progressively to the specified torque setting. Take care not to disturb the Plastigauge, and *do not* rotate the crankshaft at any time during this operation.

12 Working in **reverse** to the sequence shown in illustration 18.26, progressively slacken the bearing cap retaining bolts by one turn at a time. Once all bolts are loose, unscrew them and remove them from the cylinder block.

13 Remove the main bearing caps, again taking great care not to disturb the Plastigauge, nor to rotate the crankshaft.

14 Compare the width of the crushed Plastigauge on each journal to the scale printed on the Plastigauge envelope, to obtain the main bearing running clearance. Compare the clearance measured with that given in the Specifications at the start of this Chapter **(see illustration)**.

15 If the clearance is not as specified, the bearing shells may be the wrong size (or excessively worn, if the original shells are being re-used). Before deciding that different-size shells are required, make sure that no dirt or oil was trapped between the bearing shells and the main bearing ladder or block when the clearance was measured. If the Plastigauge was wider at one end than at the other, the crankshaft journal may be tapered.

16 If the clearance is not as specified with the original bearing shells, repeat the checking procedure using new bearing shells. If the clearance is not as specified even with new bearing shells, then seek the advice of a Nissan dealer or suitable engine overhaul specialist. They will be able to advise you on the best course of action, and whether or not it will be necessary to have the crankshaft journals reground and fit undersize shells.

17 Where necessary, obtain the required grades of bearing shell, and repeat the running clearance checking procedure as described above.

18 On completion, carefully scrape away all traces of the Plastigauge material from the crankshaft and bearing shells. Use your fingernail, or a wooden or plastic scraper which is unlikely to score the bearing surfaces.

Final crankshaft refitting

19 Carefully lift the crankshaft out of the cylinder block once more.

20 Place the bearing shells in their locations as described in paragraph 5 and 6. If new shells are being fitted, ensure that all traces of protective grease are cleaned off using paraffin. Wipe dry the shells and connecting rods with a lint-free cloth. Liberally lubricate each bearing shell in the cylinder block/crankcase with clean engine oil **(see illustration)**.

21 Using a little grease, stick the upper thrustwashers to each side of the No 3 main bearing upper location; ensure that the oilway grooves on each thrustwasher face outwards (away from the cylinder block) **(see illustration)**.

22 Lower the crankshaft into position, and check the crankshaft endfloat as described in Section 14.

23 Thoroughly degrease the mating surfaces of the cylinder block and the main bearing caps.

24 Lubricate the lower bearing shells in the main bearing caps with clean engine oil. Make sure that the locating lugs on the shells engage with the corresponding recesses in the caps.

25 Fit the main bearing caps, using the identification marks to ensure that they are installed in the correct locations and are fitted the correct way round. Insert the retaining bolts, tightening them by hand only.

2B

18.20 Lubricate the main bearing shells with clean engine oil . . .

18.21 . . . then fit the thrustwasher halves, making sure that their grooved faces are facing away from the crankcase

26 Working in the sequence shown, tighten the bearing cap retaining bolts to approximately half the specified torque setting (see illustration). Then go around in the same sequence and tighten the bolts to the full specified torque setting. Check that the crankshaft rotates freely before proceeding any further.

27 Fit the piston/connecting rod assemblies as described in Section 19.

28 Ensure that the mating surfaces of the rear oil seal housing and cylinder block are clean and dry. Note the correct fitted depth of the oil seal then, using a large flat-bladed screwdriver, lever the seal out of the housing.

29 Fit the new crankshaft seal to the housing, making sure that its sealing lip is facing inwards. Tap the seal squarely into the housing until it is positioned at the same depth as the original was noted prior to removal.

30 Apply a bead of suitable sealant to the oil seal housing mating surface, and make sure that the locating dowels are in position. Slide the housing over the end of the crankshaft, and into position on the cylinder block. Tighten the housing retaining bolts to the specified torque setting.

31 Refit the flywheel, timing chains and sump as described in Part A of this Chapter.

19 Piston/connecting rod assembly - refitting and big-end bearing running clearance check

Selection of new bearing shells

Note: *This information applies only to standard size bearing shells. Undersize shells are not graded.*

1 New bearing shells are selected using the identification marks on the crankshaft.

2 The crankshaft markings are stamped either on the side of No 1 cylinder crankweb (at the timing chain end of the crankshaft) or on the side of No 4 cylinder crankweb (at the flywheel/driveplate end of the crankshaft). The four-digit code refers to the big-end (crankpin) journal diameters - the first number in the sequence is for No 1 crankpin, and the last for No 4 crankpin. The five-digit code stamped on No 1 cylinder crankweb refers to main bearing journal sizes (see Section 18).

3 Obtain the identification number of both the relevant crankshaft journal and the cylinder block bearing bore, and select the correct grade of main bearing shell required for each journal using the relevant following table. The grade of each shell is indicated by a dab of paint on the side of the shell.

Crankshaft code	Bearing shell grade
0	White (or no colour)
1	Brown
2	Green

Big-end bearing running clearance check

4 Clean the backs of the bearing shells, and the bearing locations in both the connecting rod and bearing cap.

5 Press the bearing shells into their locations, ensuring that the tab on each shell engages in the recess in the connecting rod and cap (see illustration). Take care not to touch any shell's bearing surface with your fingers, and ensure that the shells are correctly installed so that the upper shell oil hole is correctly aligned with connecting rod oil hole. If the original bearing shells are being used for the check, ensure that they are refitted in their original locations. The clearance can be checked in either of two ways.

6 One method is to refit the big-end bearing cap to the connecting rod, ensuring that they are fitted the correct way round, with the bearing shells in place. With the cap retaining nuts correctly tightened, use an internal micrometer or vernier caliper to measure the internal diameter of each assembled pair of bearing shells. If the diameter of each corresponding crankshaft journal is measured and then subtracted from the bearing internal diameter, the result will be the big-end bearing running clearance.

7 The second, and more accurate, method is to use Plastigauge (see Section 18).

8 Ensure that the bearing shells are correctly fitted. Place a strand of Plastigauge on each (cleaned) crankpin journal.

9 Refit the (clean) piston/connecting rod assemblies to the crankshaft, and refit the big-end bearing caps, using the marks made or noted on removal to ensure that they are fitted the correct way round.

10 Tighten the bearing cap nuts as described below in paragraph 22. Take care not to disturb the Plastigauge, nor to rotate the connecting rod during the tightening sequence.

11 Dismantle the assemblies without rotating the connecting rods. Use the scale printed on the Plastigauge envelope to obtain the big-end bearing running clearance.

12 If the clearance is not as specified, the bearing shells may be the wrong size (or excessively worn, if the original shells are being re-used). Make sure that no dirt or oil was trapped between the bearing shells and the caps or connecting rods when the clearance was measured. If the Plastigauge was wider at one end than at the other, the crankpins may be tapered.

13 If the clearance is not as specified with the original bearing shells, repeat the checking procedure using new bearing shells. If the clearance is not as specified even with new bearing shells, then seek the advice of a Nissan dealer or suitable engine overhaul specialist. They will be able to advise you on the best course of action, and whether or not it will be necessary to have the crankpin journals reground and fit undersize shells.

14 Where necessary, obtain the required grades of bearing shell, and repeat the running clearance checking procedure as described above.

8 4 2 6 10

ENGINE FRONT

3 1 5 9

7

H27231

18.26 Main bearing cap bolt tightening sequence

19.5 Fit each bearing shell to its connecting rod, aligning its tab with the rod cut-out (arrowed)

19.19 Ensure that the piston rings end gaps are correctly spaced, then clamp them in position with piston ring compressor

19.20 Insert the piston/connecting rod assembly into its respective cylinder, and gently tap it into position

15 On completion, carefully scrape away all traces of the Plastigauge material from the crankshaft and bearing shells. Use your fingernail, or a wooden or plastic scraper which is unlikely to score the bearing surfaces.

Final piston/connecting rod refitting

16 Note that the following procedure assumes that the crankshaft and main bearing ladder/caps are in place (see Section 18).

17 Ensure that the bearing shells are correctly fitted as described in paragraphs 4 and 5. If new shells are being fitted, ensure that all traces of the protective grease are cleaned off using paraffin. Wipe dry the shells and connecting rods with a lint-free cloth.

18 Lubricate the cylinder bores, the pistons, and piston rings, then lay out each piston/connecting rod assembly in its respective position.

19 Start with assembly No 1. Make sure that the piston rings are still spaced as described in Section 17, then clamp them in position with a piston ring compressor **(see illustration)**.

20 Insert the piston/connecting rod assembly into the top of cylinder No 1. Ensure that the piston front marking (in the form of either an arrow or a dot) on the piston crown is on the timing chain side of the bore. Using a block of wood or hammer handle against the piston crown, tap the assembly into the cylinder until the piston crown is flush with the top of the cylinder **(see illustration)**.

21 Ensure that the bearing shell is still correctly installed. Liberally lubricate the crankpin and both bearing shells. Taking care not to mark the cylinder bores, tap the

piston/connecting rod assembly down the bore and onto the crankpin. Refit the big-end bearing cap, tightening its retaining nuts finger-tight at first. Note that the faces with the identification marks must match (which means that the bearing shell locating tabs abut each other).

22 Tighten the bearing cap retaining nuts to their Stage 1 torque setting, using a torque wrench and suitable socket. Then tighten them either through the specified Stage 2 angle setting or, if an angle-measuring gauge is not available, to the specified Stage 2 torque setting.

23 Rotate the crankshaft. Check that it turns freely; some stiffness is to be expected if new components have been fitted, but there should be no signs of binding or tight spots.

24 Refit the remaining three piston/connecting rod assemblies in the same way.

25 Refit the cylinder head, timing chain(s) and sump as described in Part A of this Chapter.

20 Engine - initial start-up after overhaul

1 With the engine refitted in the vehicle, double-check the engine oil and coolant levels. Make a final check that everything has been reconnected, and that there are no tools or rags left in the engine compartment.

2 Remove the spark plugs, and disable the ignition system by disconnecting the ignition HT coil lead from the distributor cap, and earthing it on the cylinder block. Use a jumper lead or similar wire to make a good connection.

3 Turn the engine on the starter until the oil pressure warning light goes out. Refit the spark plugs, and reconnect the spark plug (HT) leads, referring to Chapter 1 for further information. Reconnect the HT leads to the distributor.

4 Start the engine, noting that this may take a little longer than usual, due to the fuel system components having been disturbed.

5 While the engine is idling, check for fuel, water and oil leaks. Don't be alarmed if there are some odd smells and smoke from parts getting hot and burning off oil deposits.

6 Assuming all is well, keep the engine idling until hot water is felt circulating through the top hose, then switch off the engine.

7 Check the ignition timing and the idle speed settings (as appropriate), then switch the engine off.

8 After a few minutes, recheck the oil and coolant levels as described in Chapter 1, and top-up as necessary.

9 If they were tightened as described, there is no need to re-tighten the cylinder head bolts once the engine has first run after reassembly.

10 If new pistons, rings or crankshaft bearings have been fitted, the engine must be treated as new, and run-in for the first 500 miles (800 km). *Do not* operate the engine at full-throttle, or allow it to labour at low engine speeds in any gear. It is recommended that the oil and filter be changed at the end of this period.

2B

Chapter 3
Cooling, heating and ventilation systems

Contents

Degrees of difficulty

Easy, suitable for novice with little experience	Fairly easy, suitable for beginner with some experience	Fairly difficult, suitable for competent DIY mechanic 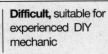	Difficult, suitable for experienced DIY mechanic	Very difficult, suitable for expert DIY or professional

Specifications

General
Radiator cap opening pressure . . . . 0.78 to 0.98 bars (11.0 to 14.0 psi)

Thermostat
Opening temperature:
Starts to open . . . . 76.5°C
Fully closed . . . . 5°C below opening temperature
Maximum valve lift (approximate) . . . . 8 mm at 90°C

Electric cooling fan
Cut-in temperature:
Models with single fan . . . . 82 to 88°C
Models with twin fans:
Primary fan . . . . 82 to 88°C
Secondary fan . . . . 102 to 108°C

Torque wrench settings

	Nm	lbf ft
Coolant pump pulley securing bolts	7	5
Coolant pump securing bolts	7	5
Thermostat cover securing bolts	7	5
Thermostat housing securing bolts	7	5

1 General information and precautions

General information

The engine cooling/cabin heating system is of pressurised type, comprising a coolant pump driven by a V-belt from the crankshaft pulley, a crossflow radiator, a coolant expansion tank, an electric cooling fan, a thermostat, heater matrix, and all associated hoses and switches.

The system functions as follows. The coolant pump pumps cold water around the cylinder block and head passages, and through the inlet manifold, heater matrix and carburettor/throttle body to the thermostat housing.

When the engine is cold, the coolant is returned from the thermostat housing to the coolant pump. When the coolant reaches a predetermined temperature, the thermostat opens, and the coolant passes through the top hose to the radiator. As the coolant circulates through the radiator, it is cooled by the inrush of air when the car is in forward motion. The airflow is supplemented by the action of the electric cooling fan when necessary. Upon reaching the bottom of the radiator, the coolant has now cooled, and the cycle is repeated.

When the engine is at normal operating temperature, the coolant expands, and some of it is released through the valve in the radiator pressure cap, and displaced into the expansion tank. Coolant collects in the tank, and is returned to the radiator when the system cools.

On some models, the coolant is also passed through the engine oil cooler.

The electric cooling fan(s) mounted in front of the radiator are controlled by a thermostatic switch. At a predetermined coolant temperature, the switch/sensor actuates the fan.

Precautions

 Warning: Do not attempt to remove the radiator pressure cap, or to disturb any part of the cooling system, while the engine is hot, as there is a high risk of scalding. If the radiator pressure cap must be removed before the engine and radiator have fully cooled (even though this is not recommended), the pressure in the cooling system must first be relieved. Cover the cap with a thick layer of cloth, to avoid scalding, and slowly unscrew the pressure cap until a hissing sound is heard. When the hissing has stopped, indicating that the pressure has reduced, slowly unscrew the pressure cap until it can be removed; if more hissing sounds are heard, wait until they have stopped before unscrewing the cap completely. At all times, keep your face well away from the pressure cap opening, and protect your hands.

Warning: Do not allow antifreeze to come into contact with your skin, or with the painted surfaces of the vehicle. Rinse off spills immediately, with plenty of water. Never leave antifreeze lying around in an open container, or in a puddle in the driveway or on the garage floor. Children and pets are attracted by its sweet smell, but antifreeze can be fatal if ingested.

Warning: If the engine is hot, the electric cooling fan may start rotating even if the engine is not running. Be careful to keep your hands, hair, and any loose clothing well clear when working in the engine compartment.

2 Cooling system hoses - disconnection and renewal

1 The number, routing and pattern of hoses will vary according to model, but the same basic procedure applies. Before commencing work, make sure that the new hoses are to hand, along with new hose clips if needed. It is good practice to renew the hose clips at the same time as the hoses.

2 Drain the cooling system, as described in Chapter 1, saving the coolant if it is fit for re-use. Squirt a little penetrating oil onto the hose clips if they are corroded.

3 Release the hose clips from the hose concerned. Three types of clip are used; worm-drive, spring and "sardine-can". The worm-drive clip is released by turning its screw anti-clockwise. The spring clip is released by squeezing its tags together with pliers, at the same time working the clip away

from the hose stub. The "sardine-can" clips are not re-usable, and are best cut off with snips or side cutters.

4 Unclip any wires, cables or other hoses which may be attached to the hose being removed. Make notes for reference when reassembling if necessary.

5 Release the hose from its stubs with a twisting motion. Be careful not to damage the stubs on delicate components such as the radiator. If the hose is stuck fast, the best course is often to cut it off using a sharp knife, but again be careful not to damage the stubs.

6 Before fitting the new hose, smear the stubs with washing-up liquid or a suitable rubber lubricant to aid fitting. Do not use oil or grease, which may attack the rubber.

7 Fit the hose clips over the ends of the hose, then fit the hose over its stubs. Work the hose into position. When satisfied, locate and tighten the hose clips.

8 Refill the cooling system as described in Chapter 1. Run the engine, and check that there are no leaks.

9 Recheck the tightness of the hose clips on any new hoses after a few hundred miles.

10 Top-up the coolant level if necessary.

3 Radiator - removal, inspection and refitting

Removal

Note: If leakage is the reason for removing the radiator, bear in mind that minor leaks can often be cured using proprietary radiator sealing compound, with the radiator in situ.

1 Disconnect the battery negative lead.

2 Drain the cooling system as described in Chapter 1.

3 Disconnect the top, bottom and expansion tank coolant hoses from the radiator (on models with automatic transmission, the fluid cooler hoses are connected to the bottom of the radiator) **(see illustration)**.

4 To improve the clearance available, remove the cooling fan(s) and shroud assembly, as described in Section 5.

5 Working at the top of the radiator, unscrew the bolts securing the radiator mounting

3.3 On models with automatic transmission, disconnect the fluid cooler hoses from the radiator

brackets to the upper body panel **(see illustration)**.

6 Withdraw the mounting brackets, and recover the upper mounting rubbers if they are loose.

7 Carefully tilt the radiator back towards the engine, then lift the radiator from the engine compartment **(see illustration)**. Recover the lower mounting rubbers if they are loose.

Inspection

8 If the radiator has been removed due to suspected blockage, it may be flushed out as described in Chapter 1. Clean dirt and debris from the radiator fins, using an air line (in which case, wear eye protection) or a soft brush. Be careful, as the fins are sharp, and easily damaged.

9 If necessary, a radiator specialist can perform a "flow test" on the radiator, to establish whether an internal blockage exists.

10 A leaking radiator must be referred to a specialist for permanent repair. Do not attempt to weld or solder a leaking radiator, as damage to the plastic components may result. In an emergency, minor leaks from the radiator can be cured by using a suitable radiator sealing compound, in accordance with its manufacturer's instructions, with the radiator in situ. If the radiator is to be sent for repair, or is to be renewed, remove all hoses, and the cooling fan switch.

11 Inspect the condition of the radiator mounting rubbers, and renew them if necessary.

3.5 Removing a radiator upper mounting bolt

3.7 Carefully lift the radiator from the engine bay - arrows indicate lower mountings

Refitting

12 Refitting is a reversal of removal, bearing in mind the following points:
  a) *Ensure that the radiator lower lugs engage correctly with the lower mounting rubbers.*
  b) *On completion, refill the cooling system as described in Chapter 1.*

4 Thermostat - removal, testing and refitting

Removal

Note: *Suitable sealant (liquid gasket) will be required when refitting the thermostat housing.*

1 The thermostat is located in a housing bolted to the side of the coolant pump, at the timing chain end of the engine.
2 Disconnect the battery negative lead.
3 Drain the cooling system as described in Chapter 1.
4 Detach the coolant hose from the thermostat cover **(see illustration)**.
5 Where applicable, disconnect the wiring plug from the cooling fan switch located in the thermostat cover.
6 Where applicable, release the wiring harness from the clip on the thermostat cover, and move it to one side.

4.7 Unscrew the securing bolts, and remove the thermostat cover from the housing

4.13 Refit the thermostat to the housing - ensure that the air bleed valve (arrowed) is correctly aligned with the casting

4.4 Slacken the clip and detach the coolant hose from the thermostat cover

7 Unscrew the securing bolts, and remove the thermostat cover from the housing **(see illustration)**. If the cover is stuck to the housing, tap it gently, or rock it back and forth to free it - **do not** lever between the mating faces.
8 Lift the thermostat from the housing, noting that the bleed valve is located at the top.

Testing

9 A rough test of the thermostat may be made by suspending it with a piece of string in a container full of water. Heat the water to bring it to the boil - the thermostat must open by the time the water boils. If not, renew it.
10 If a thermometer is available, the precise opening temperature of the thermostat may be determined; compare with the figures given in the Specifications. The opening temperature is also marked on the thermostat.
11 A thermostat which fails to close as the water cools must also be renewed.

Refitting

12 Commence refitting by thoroughly cleaning the mating faces of the cover and the housing.
13 Refit the thermostat to the housing, noting that the spring loaded side faces into the housing. Check that the air bleed valve is correctly aligned with the housing casting **(see illustration)**.
14 Apply a continuous bead of sealant (liquid gasket) to the housing mating face of the thermostat cover, taking care not to apply excess sealant, which may enter the cooling system.
15 Fit the cover to the thermostat housing, then refit the securing bolts, and tighten to the specified torque.
16 Where applicable, fit the wiring harness to the clip on the thermostat cover and reconnect the wiring plug to the cooling fan switch.
17 Reconnect the coolant hose to the thermostat cover.
18 Refill the cooling system as described in Chapter 1.
19 Reconnect the battery negative lead.

5 Electric cooling fan(s) - testing, removal and refitting

Testing

1 Current is supplied to the cooling fan(s) is via a fuse and the ignition switch. On all except carburettor models, the circuit is completed by the engine temperature sensor, via the engine management electronic control unit. The sensor is located in the inlet manifold, at the rear (timing chain end) of the cylinder head. On carburettor models, the circuit is completed by the cooling fan switch, which is located in the thermostat cover, bolted to the coolant pump at the timing chain end of the engine. On models with air conditioning and/or automatic transmission, two cooling fans are fitted.
2 Detailed fault diagnosis can be carried out by a Nissan dealer using suitable test equipment, but basic diagnosis can be carried out as follows.
3 If the fan does not appear to work, run the engine until normal operating temperature is reached, then allow it to idle. The fan should cut in within a few minutes (before the temperature gauge needle enters the red section). If not, switch off the ignition and disconnect the cooling fan motor wiring connector.
4 The motor can be tested by disconnecting it from the wiring loom, and connecting a 12-volt supply directly to it. The motor should operate - if not, the motor, or the motor wiring, is faulty.
5 If the motor operates when tested as described, the fault must lie in the engine wiring harness, the engine management electronic control unit, or the temperature sensor. The temperature sensor/switch can be tested as described in Section 6. Any further fault diagnosis should be referred to a suitably-equipped Nissan dealer - **do not** attempt to test the electronic control unit.

Removal

6 Disconnect the battery negative lead.
7 Disconnect the motor wiring connector(s) **(see illustration)**.

5.7 Disconnect the motor wiring from the cooling fan(s)

3

8 Unscrew the shroud securing screws from, then lift out the cooling fan assembly **(see illustration).**

Refitting

9 Refitting is a reversal of removal.

---

6 Cooling system electrical switches - testing, removal and refitting

---

Cooling fan switch - carburettor models

Testing

1 The switch is located in the end of the thermostat cover, on the end of the coolant pump, at the timing chain end of the engine.

2 The switch can be tested by removing it, and checking that the switching action occurs at the correct temperature (heat the sensor in a container of water, and monitor the temperature with a thermometer).

3 There should be no continuity between the switch terminals, until the specified cooling fan cut-in temperature is reached, when continuity (and zero resistance) should exist between the terminals.

Removal

4 Disconnect the battery negative lead.

5 Allow the engine to cool completely, then depressurise and partially drain the cooling system to just below the level of the sensor (as described in Chapter 1). Alternatively, have ready a suitable bung to plug the aperture in the housing when the sensor is removed.

6 Disconnect the wiring plug from the sensor.

7 Carefully unscrew the sensor and, where applicable, recover the sealing ring. If the system has not been drained, plug the sensor aperture to prevent further coolant loss.

Refitting

8 If the sensor was originally fitted using sealing compound, clean the sensor threads thoroughly, and coat them with fresh sealing compound.

9 If the sensor was originally fitted using a sealing ring, use a new sealing ring on refitting.

10 Refitting is a reversal of removal, but refill (or top-up) the cooling system as described in Chapter 1.

11 On completion, start the engine and run it until it reaches normal operating temperature. Continue to run the engine until the cooling fan cuts in and out correctly.

Engine temperature sensor

General

12 The engine temperature sensor (where fitted) provides information to the engine management electronic control unit to control the fuel and ignition systems, and the radiator cooling fan (fuel-injected engines only).

5.8 Unscrew the shroud securing screws from, then lift out the cooling fan assembly

Testing

13 On all models, the sensor is located in the inlet manifold, at the rear (timing chain end) of the cylinder head.

14 The sensor contains a thermistor - an electronic component whose electrical resistance decreases at a predetermined rate as its temperature rises.

15 The fuel injection/engine management ECU supplies the sensor with a set voltage and then, by measuring the current flowing in the sensor circuit, it determines the engine temperature. This information is then used, in conjunction with other inputs, to control the fuel injection/engine management system, and the engine cooling fan.

16 If the sensor circuit should fail to provide adequate information, the ECU back-up facility will override the sensor signal. In this event, the ECU assumes a predetermined setting which will allow the fuel injection/engine management system to run, albeit at reduced efficiency. When this occurs, the engine warning light on the instrument panel will come on, and the advice of a Nissan dealer should be sought. The sensor itself can be tested by removing it, and checking the resistances at various temperatures using an ohmmeter (heat the sensor in a container of water, and monitor the temperature with a thermometer). The resistance values are given in the Specifications. *Do not* attempt to test the circuit with the sensor fitted to the engine, and the wiring connector fitted, as there is a high risk of damaging the ECU.

17 Refer to the relevant Part of Chapter 4 for further details of the fuel injection/engine management system.

Removal and refitting

18 Proceed as described previously for the cooling fan switch on carburettor models.

Coolant temperature gauge sender

Testing

19 The sender is located in the rear of the cylinder head, at the flywheel end of the engine.

20 The temperature gauge is fed with a stabilised voltage from the instrument panel feed (via the ignition switch and a fuse). The

gauge earth is controlled by the sender. The sender contains a thermistor - an electronic component whose electrical resistance decreases at a predetermined rate as its temperature rises. When the coolant is cold, the sender resistance is high, current flow through the gauge is reduced, and the gauge needle points towards the blue (cold) end of the scale. As the coolant temperature rises and the sender resistance falls, current flow increases, and the gauge needle moves towards the upper end of the scale. If the sender is faulty, it must be renewed.

21 If the gauge develops a fault, first check the other instruments; if they do not work at all, check the instrument panel electrical feed. If the readings are erratic, there may be a fault in the voltage stabiliser, which will necessitate renewal of the stabiliser (the stabiliser is integral with the instrument panel printed circuit board - see Chapter 12). If the fault lies in the temperature gauge alone, check it as follows:

22 If the gauge needle remains at the "cold" end of the scale when the engine is hot, disconnect the sender wiring plug, and earth the relevant wire to the cylinder head. If the needle then deflects when the ignition is switched on, the sender unit is proved faulty, and should be renewed. If the needle still does not move, remove the instrument panel (Chapter 12) and check the continuity of the wire between the sender unit and the gauge, and the feed to the gauge unit. If continuity is shown, and the fault still exists, then the gauge is faulty, and the gauge should be renewed.

23 If the gauge needle remains at the "hot" end of the scale when the engine is cold, disconnect the sender wire. If the needle then returns to the "cold" end of the scale when the ignition is switched on, the sender unit is proved faulty, and should be renewed. If the needle still does not move, check the remainder of the circuit as described previously.

Removal and refitting

24 The procedure is similar to that described previously in this Section for the engine temperature sensor. On some models, access to the switch is poor, and other components may need to be removed (or hoses, wiring, etc moved to one side) before the sender unit can be reached.

Air conditioning system temperature sensor

Testing

25 The sensor is integral with the air conditioning temperature control unit, located on the side of the heater/air conditioning unit behind the facia. Testing should be entrusted to a Nissan dealer.

Removal and refitting

26 Removal and refitting should be entrusted to a Nissan dealer suitably equipped to test the unit.

7.4 Unscrew the securing bolts, and remove the coolant pump pulley

7.6 Unscrew the coolant pump securing bolts9

7 Coolant pump - removal, inspection and refitting

Removal

1 Disconnect the battery negative lead.
2 Drain the cooling system (Chapter 1).
3 Remove the auxiliary drivebelt(s) (Chapter 1).
4 Unscrew the securing bolts, and remove the coolant pump pulley **(see illustration)**. It will be necessary to counterhold the pulley in order to unscrew the bolts, and this is most easily achieved by wrapping an old drivebelt tightly around the pulley to act in a similar manner to a strap wrench.
5 Unbolt the thermostat housing from the stub on the coolant pump, and move the housing to one side, taking care not to strain the sensor/switch wiring (refer to Section 4). If the housing is stuck, tap it gently with a soft-faced mallet - **do not** lever between the mating faces. If necessary to improve access, disconnect the wiring and the coolant hose, and remove the housing.
6 Unscrew the securing bolts, and withdraw the coolant pump **(see illustration)**. If the pump is stuck, tap it gently using a soft-faced mallet - **do not** lever between the pump and cylinder block mating faces.

Inspection

7 Check the pump body and impeller for signs of excessive corrosion. Turn the impeller, and check for stiffness due to corrosion, or roughness due to excessive end play.

8 No spare parts are available for the pump, and if faulty, worn or corroded, a new pump should be fitted.

Refitting

9 Commence refitting by thoroughly cleaning all traces of sealant from the mating faces of the pump and cylinder block, and from the thermostat housing.
10 Apply a continuous bead of sealant (liquid gasket) to the cylinder block mating face of the pump, taking care not to apply excessive sealant, which may enter the pump itself. Similarly, apply a bead of sealant to the thermostat housing mating face of the pump **(see illustrations)**.
11 Place the pump in position in the cylinder block, then refit and tighten the bolts. Note that the threads of the two lower bolts should be coated with thread-locking compound **(see illustration)**.
12 Refit the pump pulley, then refit the securing bolts and tighten to the specified torque. Counterhold the pulley using an old drivebelt as during removal.
13 Apply a continuous bead of sealant (liquid gasket) to the coolant pump mating face of the thermostat housing, again taking care not to apply excessive sealant.
14 Place the thermostat housing in position on the pump stub, then refit the securing bolts, and tighten to the specified torque.
15 Refit and tension the auxiliary drivebelt(s) as described in Chapter 1.
16 Refill the cooling system (Chapter 1).
17 Reconnect the battery negative lead.

8 Heater/ventilation system - general information

1 The heater/ventilation system consists of a four-speed blower motor (housed behind the facia), face level vents in the centre and at each end of the facia, and air ducts to the front footwells.
2 The control unit is located in the facia, and the controls operate flap valves to deflect and mix the air flowing through the various parts of the heating/ventilation system. The flap valves are contained in the air distribution housing, which acts as a central distribution unit, passing air to the various ducts and vents.
3 Cold air enters the system through the grille at the rear of the engine compartment. If required, the airflow is boosted by the blower fan, and then flows through the various ducts, according to the settings of the controls. Stale air is expelled through ducts at the rear of the vehicle. If warm air is required, the cold air is passed over the heater matrix, which is heated by the engine coolant.
4 On models fitted with air conditioning, a recirculation switch enables the outside air supply to be closed off, while the air inside the vehicle is recirculated. This can be used to prevent unpleasant odours entering from outside the vehicle, but should only be used briefly, as the recirculated air inside the vehicle will soon become stale.

9 Heater/ventilation components - removal and refitting

Heater/ventilation control unit

Removal

1 Disconnect the battery negative lead.
2 Remove the trim panel from the centre instrument cluster, as described in Chapter 11.
3 Withdraw the control unit forwards from the facia, and disconnect the wiring plugs from the rear of the unit.

3

7.10a Apply sealant to the cylinder block mating face . . .

7.10b . . . and thermostat housing mating face of the coolant pump

7.11 The threads of the two lower bolts (arrowed) should be coated with thread-locking compound

9.9 Detach the heater unit coolant hoses from the ports at the bulkhead (arrowed)

9.16 Removing the complete heater unit

4 Pull out the securing clip, and disconnect the temperature control cable from the lever on the rear of the unit, then withdraw the unit.

Refitting

5 Refitting is a reversal of removal, but reconnect the temperature control cable as follows:
a) Move the temperature control lever on the control unit to the fully hot position.
b) Move the air mix door lever on the heater unit to the fully hot position.
c) Reconnect the end of the cable to the lever on the heater unit, then push the securing clip over the cable.

Temperature control cable

6 Removal of the control cable is described previously in this Section as part of the heater/ventilation control unit removal and refitting procedure.

Complete heater assembly

 Warning: On models fitted with air conditioning, do not attempt to remove the cooling unit, which is located between the heater blower motor casing and the main heater assembly. Removal of the cooling unit entails disconnection of refrigerant lines - refer to Section 10 for precautions to be observed. If in any doubt as to the procedure to follow on models with air conditioning, consult a Nissan dealer for advice.

Note: *This is an involved procedure, and it is recommended that the following Section is read thoroughly before commencing work. Plenty of time should be allowed to complete the operation. During dismantling, make notes on the routing of all wiring and cables, and the locations of all fixings, to aid reassembly.*

Removal

7 Disconnect the battery negative lead.
8 Set the heater control to 'HOT', then drain the cooling system as described in Chapter 1.

9 Working in the engine bay, slacken the clips and detach the heater unit coolant hoses from the ports at the bulkhead (see illustration). Recover the rubber grommets.
10 Working inside the vehicle, under the glovebox, remove the two securing screws (one on each side of the glovebox), then lower the glovebox from the facia.
11 With reference to Chapter 11, carry out the following:
a) Remove the securing screws and withdraw the lower panels from the driver and passenger side of the facia.
b) Remove the centre facia panel and surround.
12 Extract the fixings and withdraw the metal reinforcing bracket which fits across the glovebox aperture.
13 Refer to information given earlier in this Section and remove the heater control unit.
14 Detach the ducting from the right hand side of the heater unit, then unhook the control cables from the actuator levers on the left hand side of the unit.
15 Detach the heater register centre duct from the heater unit.
16 Remove the securing screws/nuts and withdraw the heater unit from the bulkhead, carefully manoeuvring it away from the upper ducting (see illustration).

9.22 Removing the heater matrix from the heater unit

Refitting

17 To refit the assembly, reverse the steps described for removal, bearing in mind the following points:
a) Make sure that all wiring and cables are routed as noted during dismantling.
b) Make sure that all air ducts are securely reconnected.
c) Refit the facia components with reference to Chapter 11.
d) On completion, refill and bleed the cooling system as described in Chapter 1.

Heater matrix

Removal

18 Remove the complete heater assembly as described previously in this Section.
19 Remove the plastic heater matrix retaining clip from the end of the heater assembly.
20 Release the securing clip, and disconnect the actuating rod from the lever on the heater assembly air flap.
21 Unhook the actuating rod spring from the water valve lever on the heater matrix, and withdraw the actuating rod.
22 Withdraw the heater matrix from the heater assembly casing (see illustration).

Refitting

23 Refitting is a reversal of removal, but refit the heater assembly as described previously in this Section.

Heater blower motor

Removal

24 Disconnect the battery negative lead.
25 Working under the glovebox, remove the two securing screws (one on each side of the glovebox), then lower the glovebox from the facia.
26 Remove the three securing screws, and withdraw the passenger's side lower facia panel from the facia.
27 Remove the securing screws, and withdraw the metal reinforcing bracket which fits across the glovebox aperture.

28 Disconnect the cooling air hose from the bottom of the motor casing.

29 Remove the two securing screws, noting the locations of any brackets secured by the screws, then withdraw the motor assembly from the heater casing.

Refitting

30 Refitting is a reversal of removal, but ensure that any brackets are positioned as noted before removal, and make sure that the cooling air hose is reconnected.

Heater blower motor resistor

Removal

31 The resistor is located at the bottom of the heater casing, behind the blower motor.

32 Disconnect the battery negative lead.

33 Working under the glovebox, remove the two securing screws (one on each side of the glovebox), then lower the glovebox from the facia.

34 For improved access, remove the blower motor as described in the previous sub-Section.

35 Disconnect the wiring plug from the resistor.

36 Remove the two securing screws, and withdraw the resistor from the blower unit case.

Refitting

37 Refitting is a reversal of removal.

Heater air flap motors

Removal

38 Two air flap motors are fitted, one in the air inlet ducting next to the blower motor, and one on the right-hand side of the main heater casing.

39 For access to the motor in the air inlet ducting, proceed as described in paragraphs 41 to 43 inclusive.

40 For access to the motor on the main heater casing, remove the driver's side lower facia panel, as described in Chapter 11.

41 Disconnect the battery negative lead.

42 To remove a motor, disconnect the wiring plug and the actuator rod from the motor assembly, then unscrew the two securing nuts, and withdraw the motor complete with its mounting bracket.

Refitting

43 Refitting is a reversal of removal, but make sure that the actuating rod is correctly reconnected to the motor.

10 Air conditioning system - general information and precautions

General information

1 An air conditioning system is available on certain models. It enables the temperature of incoming air to be lowered, and also dehumidifies the air, which makes for rapid demisting and increased comfort.

2 The cooling side of the system works in the same way as a domestic refrigerator. Refrigerant gas is drawn into a belt-driven compressor, and passes into a condenser mounted on the front of the radiator, where it loses heat and becomes liquid. The liquid passes through an expansion valve to an evaporator, where it changes from liquid under high pressure to gas under low pressure. This change is accompanied by a drop in temperature, which cools the evaporator. The refrigerant returns to the compressor, and the cycle begins again.

3 Air blown through the evaporator passes to the air distribution unit, where it is mixed with hot air blown through the heater matrix to achieve the desired temperature in the passenger compartment.

4 The heating side of the system works in the same way as on models without air conditioning (see Section 8).

5 The system is electronically-controlled. Any problems with the system should be referred to a Nissan dealer.

Precautions

6 With an air conditioning system, it is necessary to observe special precautions whenever dealing with any part of the system, or its associated components. If for any reason the system must be disconnected, entrust this task to your Nissan dealer or a refrigeration engineer.

 Warning: The refrigeration circuit contains a liquid refrigerant (Freon). The refrigerant is potentially dangerous, and should only be handled by qualified persons. If it is splashed onto the skin, it can cause frostbite. It is not itself poisonous, but in the presence of a naked flame (including a cigarette), it forms a poisonous gas. Uncontrolled discharging of the refrigerant is dangerous, and potentially damaging to the environment. For all these reasons, it is dangerous to disconnect any part of the system without specialised knowledge and equipment.

7 Do not operate the air conditioning system if it is known to be short of refrigerant, as this may damage the compressor.

11 Air conditioning components - removal and refitting

 Warning: Do not attempt to open the refrigerant circuit. Refer to the precautions given in Section 10.

The only operation which can be carried out easily without discharging the refrigerant is renewal of the compressor drivebelt - this procedure is described in Chapter 1. All other operations must be referred to a Nissan dealer or an air conditioning specialist.

If necessary for access to other components, the compressor can be unbolted and moved aside, *without disconnecting its flexible hoses*, after removing the drivebelt.

3

Chapter 4 Part A:
Fuel/exhaust systems - carburettor models

Contents

Degrees of difficulty

Easy, suitable for novice with little experience	Fairly easy, suitable for beginner with some experience	Fairly difficult, suitable for competent DIY mechanic	Difficult, suitable for experienced DIY mechanic	Very difficult, suitable for expert DIY or professional

Specifications

Fuel pump

Type	Mechanical, driven by eccentric on inlet camshaft

Carburettor

Type	Nikki 21L
Choke type	Automatic

Carburettor data

For idle speed and mixture settings, refer to Chapter 1 Specifications.

1.4 litre models without a catalytic converter:

	Primary	Secondary
Throttle chamber bore	28 mm	32 mm
Venturi diameter	22 mm	30 mm
Main jet	96	135
Main air bleed	70	60
Slow jet	40	80
Slow air bleed	80	80
Power jet	55	
Float height setting:		
Float upper edge to carburettor body (carburettor inverted)	10 ± 0.5 mm	
Float lower edge to carburettor body (carburettor upright)	43.5 ± 0.5 mm	
Throttle valve fast idle setting:		
Manual transmission	0.62 ± 0.07 mm	
Automatic transmission	0.79 ± 0.07 mm	
Choke pull-down setting:		
Stage 1	1.22 ± 0.14 mm	
Stage 2	2.15 ± 0.32 mm	

4A

Carburettor data (continued)

	Primary	Secondary

1.4 litre models with a catalytic converter:

	Primary	Secondary
Throttle chamber bore	30 mm	34 mm
Venturi diameter	22 mm	30 mm
Main jet	88	135
Main air bleed	70	60
Slow jet	50	80
Slow air bleed	80	80
Float height setting:		
Float upper edge to carburettor body (carburettor inverted)	10 ± 0.5 mm	
Float lower edge to carburettor body (carburettor upright)	43.5 ± 0.5 mm	
Throttle valve fast idle setting:		
Manual transmission	0.59 ± 0.07 mm	
Automatic transmission	0.75 ± 0.07 mm	
Choke pull-down setting:		
Stage 1	1.44 ± 0.13 mm	
Stage 2	2.42 ± 0.32 mm	

1.6 litre models without a catalytic converter:

	Primary	Secondary
Throttle chamber bore	30 mm	34 mm
Venturi diameter	22 mm	30 mm
Main jet	100	135
Main air bleed	80	60
Slow jet	40	80
Slow air bleed	80	80
Power jet	55	
Float height setting:		
Float upper edge to carburettor body (carburettor inverted)	10 ± 0.5 mm	
Float lower edge to carburettor body (carburettor upright)	43.5 ± 0.5 mm	
Throttle valve fast idle setting:		
Manual transmission	0.59 ± 0.07 mm	
Automatic transmission	0.75 ± 0.07 mm	
Choke pull-down setting:		
Stage 1	1.22 ± 0.14 mm	
Stage 2	2.15 ± 0.32 mm	

1.6 litre models with a catalytic converter:

	Primary	Secondary
Throttle chamber bore	30 mm	34 mm
Venturi diameter	22 mm	30 mm
Main jet	92	135
Main air bleed	70	60
Slow jet	50	80
Slow air bleed	80	80
Float height setting:		
Float upper edge to carburettor body (carburettor inverted)	10 ± 0.5 mm	
Float lower edge to carburettor body (carburettor upright)	43.5 ± 0.5 mm	
Throttle valve fast idle setting	0.63 ± 0.07 mm	
Choke pull-down setting:		
Stage 1	1.44 ± 0.13 mm	
Stage 2	2.42 ± 0.32 mm	

Recommended fuel

Minimum octane rating:

Models without a catalytic converter ("non-catalyst" models):

GA14DS engine	95 RON unleaded or 91 RON leaded (eg UK "4-star")
GA16DS engine	95 RON unleaded or 97 RON leaded (eg UK "4-star")
Models with a catalytic converter ("catalyst" models)	95 RON unleaded. Leaded fuel (eg UK "4-star") must **not** be used

Torque wrench settings

	Nm	lbf ft
Fuel pump retaining bolts	19	14
Fuel tank retaining bolts	34	24
Inlet manifold retaining nuts and bolts	19	14
Exhaust manifold retaining nuts and bolts	19	14
Exhaust system fasteners:		
Front pipe-to-manifold nut	31	23
Front pipe mounting bolt	23	17
Front pipe-to-intermediate pipe/catalytic converter nuts	49	36
Catalytic converter-to-tailpipe bolts	49	36
Intermediate pipe-to-tailpipe bolts	49	36

2.1a Release the air cleaner housing lid from the inlet duct . . .

2.1b . . . then disconnect the hot-air inlet hose

2.2 Remove the filter element and lift off the mounting frame

1 General information and precautions

The fuel system consists of a fuel tank mounted under the rear of the car, a mechanical fuel pump, and a carburettor. The fuel pump is operated by an eccentric on the inlet camshaft, and is mounted on the rear of the cylinder head. The air cleaner contains a disposable paper filter element, and incorporates a flap valve air temperature control system which allows cold air from the outside of the car and warm air from the exhaust manifold to enter the air cleaner in the correct proportions.

The fuel pump lifts fuel from the fuel tank via a filter, which is mounted onto the engine compartment bulkhead, and supplies it to the carburettor. Excess fuel is returned from the pump to the fuel tank. Further details on the carburettor and exhaust system can be found in Sections 10 and 16.

 Warning: Many of the procedures in this Chapter require the removal of fuel lines and connections, which may result in some fuel spillage. Before carrying out any operation on the fuel system, refer to the precautions given in "Safety first!" at the beginning of this manual, and follow them implicitly. Petrol is a highly-dangerous and volatile liquid, and the precautions necessary when handling it cannot be overstressed.

2 Air cleaner assembly - removal and refitting

Removal

1 Release the retaining clips, then slacken and remove the air cleaner housing lid retaining nut and screw. Free the lid from the inlet duct, then slacken the retaining clip and disconnect the hot air inlet hose from the base of the lid. Position the lid clear of the base (see illustrations).
2 Lift out the filter element and remove the mounting frame (see illustration).
3 Undo the retaining bolt, and disconnect the breather hose from the front of the air cleaner housing base. Lift up the base, then disconnect the necessary vacuum hose(s) (noting their correct fitted locations) from the hot idle compensator and air temperature control valve switch, as they become accessible. On models with a catalytic converter, also disconnect the air induction valve (AIV) hose (see illustrations).
4 Remove the housing lid and base as an assembly, and recover the housing seal from the top of the carburettor.
5 To remove the inlet duct, undo the two retaining bolts and free it from the resonator. If necessary, the resonator box can then be unbolted and removed from the vehicle.

Refitting

6 Refitting is a reverse of the removal procedure, ensuring that all ducts and hoses are securely reconnected to their original locations, and do not become trapped as the housing is refitted.

3 Air cleaner air temperature control system - information and component renewal

Information

1 The system, fitted to non-catalyst models, is controlled by a heat-sensitive vacuum switch mounted in the base of the air cleaner housing. When the engine is started from cold, the switch is open, and allows inlet manifold depression to act on the air temperature control valve diaphragm in the air inlet nozzle. This vacuum causes the diaphragm to rise, drawing a flap valve across the cold air inlet, thus allowing only (warmed) air from around the exhaust manifold to enter the air cleaner.
2 As the temperature of the exhaust-warmed air in the air cleaner rises, the bi-metallic strip in the vacuum switch deforms, closing the switch to shut off vacuum supply to the air temperature control valve assembly. As the vacuum supply is cut, the flap is gradually lowered across the hot-air inlet until, when the engine is fully warmed up to normal operating temperature, only cold air from the front of the car is entering the air cleaner.
3 To check the system, allow the engine to cool down completely, then disconnect the inlet duct from the front of the air cleaner inlet nozzle; the flap valve in the nozzle should be

4A

2.3a Disconnect the breather hose (arrowed), and undo the mounting bolt . . .

2.3b . . . then lift up the housing base and disconnect the various vacuum hoses . . .

2.3c . . . and on catalyst models, the air induction valve (AIV) hose (arrowed)

securely seated across the hot-air inlet. Start the engine; the flap should immediately rise to close off the cold air inlet, and should then lower steadily as the engine warms up until it is eventually seated across the hot-air inlet again.

4 To check the vacuum switch, disconnect the vacuum pipe from the control valve when the engine is running, and place a finger over the pipe end. When the engine is cold, full inlet manifold vacuum should be present in the pipe; when the engine is at normal operating temperature, there should be no vacuum in the pipe.

5 To check the air temperature control valve assembly, remove the valve assembly from the air cleaner lid (see below). Disconnect the vacuum pipe, and suck hard at the control valve stub; the flap should rise to shut off the cold air inlet.

6 If either component is faulty, it must be renewed.

Vacuum switch - renewal

7 Remove the air cleaner housing as described in Section 2.

8 Bend up the tangs on the switch retaining clip, and remove the clip (see illustration). Withdraw the switch and seal from the housing. Examine the seal for signs of damage or deterioration, and renew if necessary.

9 Fit the seal to the switch, and install the assembly in the housing. Ensure that the switch is pressed firmly against the housing, and refit the retaining clip, securing it in position by bending down the clip tangs.

10 Refit the air cleaner housing (Section 2).

Air temperature control valve - renewal

11 Remove the air cleaner housing and lid as described in Section 2.

12 Undo the three screws, and remove the air temperature control valve from the housing lid (see illustration). Disconnect the vacuum hose and remove the valve assembly.

13 Undo the retaining screw, then free the vacuum diaphragm unit from the flap valve and remove it from the duct.

14 Fit the new diaphragm unit, attach it to the flap valve, and tighten its retaining screw.

15 Connect the vacuum hose and refit the valve assembly to the housing lid, tightening its retaining screws securely.

3.12 Removing the air temperature control valve assembly from the air cleaner lid

3.8 Air temperature control valve vacuum switch (arrowed). Hot idle compensator valve is also shown

16 Refit the air cleaner (Section 2).

4 Fuel pump - testing, removal and refitting

Note: Refer to the warning note in Section 1 before proceeding.

Testing

1 To test the fuel pump without removing it from the engine (see illustration), disconnect the outlet pipe which leads to the carburettor, and hold a wad of rag over the pump outlet while an assistant spins the engine on the starter. Keep the hands away from the electric cooling fan. Regular spurts of fuel should be ejected as the engine turns.

2 The pump can also be tested after it has been removed. With the pump outlet pipe disconnected but the inlet pipe still connected, hold a wad of rag by the outlet. Operate the pump lever by hand, moving it in and out; if the pump is in a satisfactory condition, the lever should move and return smoothly, and a strong jet of fuel should be ejected.

Removal

3 Identify the pump inlet, outlet and return hoses, and slacken the retaining clips. Place wads of rag beneath the hose unions to catch any spilled fuel, then disconnect both hoses from the pump. Plug the hose ends to minimise fuel loss. If necessary, remove the air cleaner housing to improve access to the pump.

4.1 The fuel pump is mounted on the left-hand end of the cylinder head

4 Slacken and remove the bolts securing the pump to the rear of the cylinder head. Remove the pump along with its insulating spacer; discard the spacer, a new one must be used on refitting.

Refitting

5 Ensure that the pump and cylinder head mating surfaces are clean and dry, then offer up the new insulating spacer. Refit the pump to the cylinder head, and tighten the pump retaining bolts to the specified torque setting.

6 Reconnect the inlet, outlet and return hoses to their relevant pump unions, and securely tighten their retaining clips.

5 Fuel gauge sender unit - removal and refitting

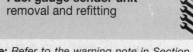

Note: Refer to the warning note in Section 1 before proceeding.

Removal

1 Disconnect the battery negative lead.

2 To gain access to the sender unit, remove the rear seat back as described in Chapter 11.

3 Undo the retaining screws, and lift up the access cover to expose the sender unit.

4 Disconnect the wiring connector from the sender unit, and tape the connector to the vehicle body to prevent it disappearing behind the tank.

5 Mark the hoses for identification purposes, then slacken the feed and return hose retaining clips. Disconnect both hoses from the top of the sender unit, and plug the hose ends. Tape the hoses to the vehicle body to prevent them disappearing behind the tank.

6 Note the alignment marks on the sender unit and tank - if no marks exist, make some.

7 The sender unit is retained by a large ring - unscrew the locking ring and remove the unit from the tank. This is best accomplished by using a screwdriver on the raised ribs of the locking ring. Carefully tap the screwdriver to turn the ring anti-clockwise until it can be unscrewed by hand.

8 Carefully lift the sender unit from the top of the fuel tank, taking great care not to bend the sender unit float arm, or to spill fuel onto the interior of the vehicle. As the sender unit is being removed, unclip the fuel filter from the base of the tank, and remove the sender unit and filter as an assembly.

9 Recover the rubber sealing ring and discard it; a new one must be used on refitting.

10 Wash the filter assembly in fuel. Examine the filter for signs of clogging or splitting, and renew if necessary.

Refitting

11 Refitting is a reversal of the removal procedure, noting the following points:

a) Fit a new rubber sealing ring to the fuel tank.

b) Ensure that the filter is clipped securely in

position before seating the sender unit in the tank.
c) *Align the sender unit arrow with the mark on the tank, and securely tighten the locking ring.*
d) *Ensure that the feed and return hoses are correctly reconnected, and are securely retained by their clips.*

6 Fuel tank - removal and refitting

Note: *Refer to the warning note in Section 1 before proceeding.*

Removal

1 Before removing the fuel tank, all fuel must be drained from the tank. Since a fuel tank drain plug is not provided, it is therefore preferable to carry out the removal operation when the tank is nearly empty. Before proceeding, disconnect the battery negative lead, and syphon or hand-pump the remaining fuel from the tank.
2 Jack up the rear of the car and support on axle stands (see *"Jacking and Vehicle Support"*). Chock the front roadwheels.
3 Disconnect the fuel filler tube from the body of the vehicle.
4 Disconnect the fuel lines and the return line. The feed and return lines are of different diameters so they do not need to be identified.
5 Support the fuel tank with a trolley jack and piece of wood.
6 If equipped, remove the bolts from the heat shield located on the front side of the fuel tank.
7 Disconnect the electrical connectors from the level sender.
8 Unscrew and remove the mounting bolts attaching the fuel tank to the underbody.
9 Slowly lower the fuel tank out of position, disconnecting any other relevant vent pipes as they become accessible (where necessary). Remove the tank from underneath the vehicle, and recover the tank mounting rubbers, noting their correct fitted positions.
10 If the tank is contaminated with sediment or water, remove the sender unit (Section 5) and swill the tank out with clean fuel. The tank is injection-moulded from a synthetic material, and if damaged, it should be renewed. However, in certain cases, it may be possible to have small leaks or minor damage repaired. Seek the advice of a suitable specialist before attempting to repair the fuel tank.

Refitting

11 Refitting is the reverse of the removal procedure, noting the following points:
a) *When lifting the tank back into position, reconnect all the relevant breather hoses, and take great care to ensure that none of the hoses become trapped between the tank and vehicle body. Tighten the fuel tank mounting bolts to the specified torque setting.*

b) *Ensure that all pipes and hoses are correctly routed,. and securely held in position with their retaining clips.*
c) *On completion, refill the tank with fuel, and check for signs of leakage prior to taking the vehicle out on the road.*

7 Accelerator cable - removal, refitting and adjustment

Removal

1 Unhook and release the accelerator inner cable from the carburettor throttle cam.
2 Slacken the outer cable locknut and adjuster nut, then free the outer cable from its mounting bracket **(see illustration)**.
3 Working back along the length of the cable, free it from any relevant retaining clips or ties, whilst noting its correct routing.
4 Working inside the vehicle, remove the lower facia panel from the driver's side of the facia, as described in Chapter 11.
5 Reach up behind the facia, and detach the inner cable end fitting from the top of the accelerator pedal.
6 Undo the bolts securing the outer cable end fitting to the bulkhead, then withdraw the cable through the bulkhead and into the passenger compartment.

Refitting

7 From inside the vehicle, feed the cable through the hole in the bulkhead.
8 When the end of the cable appears in the engine compartment, pull the cable through the bulkhead, and route it correctly around the engine compartment.
9 Return to the inside of the vehicle, and secure the outer cable end fitting to the bulkhead by securely tightening its retaining bolts. Clip the inner cable into position on the top of the accelerator pedal.
10 Make sure that the cable is securely retained, then refit the lower panel to the facia (see Chapter 11).
11 From within the engine compartment, work along the cable, and ensure that it is secured in position with all the relevant retaining clips and ties, and correctly routed.
12 Locate the outer cable in its mounting bracket, and reconnect the inner cable to the throttle cam. Adjust the cable as described below.

Adjustment

13 Loosen the adjustment nuts and make sure that the throttle cam is resting against its stop.
14 Tighten the nut furthest from the cam until the cam just starts to move. Now loosen the nut 1.5 to 2 turns and tighten the locknut.
15 Have an assistant depress the accelerator pedal, and check that the throttle cam opens fully and returns smoothly to its stop. If necessary, readjust the cable as described

7.2 Slacken the locknut (arrowed) and free the accelerator cable from its mounting bracket

8 Accelerator pedal - removal and refitting

Removal

1 Remove the lower facia panel from the driver's side of the facia, as described in Chapter 11.
2 Reach up behind the facia, and detach the inner cable from the top of the accelerator pedal.
3 Undo the two mounting bolts securing the pedal mounting bracket to the bulkhead, and remove the pedal assembly from underneath the facia.
4 If necessary, remove the retaining clip from the end of the accelerator pedal pivot shaft, then slide the pedal out of position and recover the return spring from the mounting bracket.
5 Examine the mounting bracket and pedal pivot points for signs of wear, and renew as necessary.

Refitting

6 Refitting is a reversal of the removal procedure, applying a little multi-purpose grease to the pedal pivot shaft. On completion, adjust the accelerator cable as described in Section 7.

9 Unleaded petrol - general information and usage

Note: *The information given in this Chapter is correct at the time of writing, and applies only to petrols currently available in the UK. If updated information is thought to be required, check with a Nissan dealer. If travelling abroad, consult one of the motoring organisations (or a similar authority) for advice on the petrols available, and their suitability for your vehicle.*

1 The fuel recommended by Nissan is given in the Specifications Section of this Chapter.
2 RON and MON are different testing standards; RON stands for Research Octane Number (also written as RM), while MON

4A

stands for Motor Octane Number (also written as MM).

3 All Nissan Sunny carburettor models are designed to run on fuel with a minimum octane rating of 95 (RON). All models with a catalytic converter must be run on unleaded fuel **only**. Under no circumstances should leaded fuel be used, as this may damage the catalyst. On models without a catalytic converter, either unleaded or leaded fuel can be used without modification.

10 Carburettor - general information

Models without a catalytic converter

1 The Nikki 21 L series carburettor is a downdraught progressive twin venturi instrument, with a vacuum-controlled secondary throttle **(see illustration)**. The choke control is semi-automatic in operation.

2 The carburettor is constructed in three main bodies; these are the upper body, the main body, and the throttle body (which contains the throttle assembly). An insulating block, placed between the main carburettor body and the throttle body, prevents excess heat transference to the main body.

3 During slow running and at idle, fuel sourced from the float chamber passes into the idle channel through a metered idle jet. Here it is mixed with a small amount of air from a calibrated air bleed. The resulting mixture is drawn through a channel, to be discharged from the idle orifice under the throttle valve. A tapered mixture screw is used to vary the outlet, and this ensures fine control of the idle mixture. An idle cut-off valve is used to prevent run-on when the engine is shut down. It utilises a 12-volt solenoid plunger to block the idle channel when the ignition is switched off.

4 A progression slot provides extra enrichment as it is uncovered by the opening of the throttle valve during initial acceleration.

5 Under normal operating conditions, fuel is drawn through a calibrated main jet, into the base of the auxiliary venturi. An emulsion tube is placed in the auxiliary venturi, capped with a main air bleed. The fuel is mixed with air, drawn in through the holes in the emulsion tube. The resulting mixture is discharged into the main airstream via the main nozzle.

6 The carburettor is also equipped with an accelerator pump, to provide an initial spurt of extra fuel during sudden acceleration. The accelerator pump is mechanically operated by a lever which is connected to the throttle linkage. A solenoid valve, controlled by a thermostatic switch, is fitted to the accelerator pump circuit to vary the pump output. With the engine cold, the solenoid valve is opened, and the pump gives maximum output. Once the engine reaches

10.1 Exploded view of the carburettor - non-catalyst model (catalyst model similar)

1 Secondary emulsion tube	16 Main body	29 Accelerator pump control
2 Idle-up control solenoid	17 Float level inspection	solenoid
3 Choke bi-metallic coil cover	window	30 Gasket
4 Upper body	18 Secondary main jet	31 Adjustment screw
5 Float chamber gasket	19 Primary idle jet	32 Throttle damper
6 Accelerator pump lever	20 Needle valve	33 Throttle body
7 Bracket	21 Float	34 Idle speed adjusting
8 Bracket	22 Float pivot pin	screw
9 Secondary venturi	23 Accelerator pump piston	35 Choke link rod
10 Secondary progression jet	24 Primary idle fuel jet	36 Throttle lever
11 Idle-up jet	25 Accelerator pump weight	37 Accelerator pump link rod
12 Primary main air bleed	26 Accelerator pump ball	38 Idle mixture (exhaust gas
13 Primary auxiliary venturi	valve	CO) adjustment screw
14 Part-load enrichment	27 Idle cut-off valve solenoid	39 Tamperproof cap
valve	28 Secondary throttle valve	
15 Primary main jet	diaphragm	

operating temperature, the solenoid valve closes, and the pump output is reduced.

7 The idle speed is set by an adjustable screw. The adjustable mixture screw is sealed during production with a tamperproof plug to prevent unnecessary adjustment.

8 When an electrical load is placed on the alternator (or the power steering is in operation), the idle speed will tend to drop, since both the alternator and the power steering pump are engine-driven. To counteract this stalling tendency, an idle-up solenoid is fitted to the carburettor. The solenoid opens a bypass fuel-and-air channel to increase the idle speed.

9 The choke is controlled by an electrically-heated bi-metallic coil spring which is linked to the choke valve. The choke is operated by slowly depressing the accelerator pedal. Once the engine is running, an electrical supply is applied to the bi-metallic coil. This heats the bi-metallic coil, causing it to unwind and open up the choke valve.

Models with a catalytic converter

10 The Nikki carburettor fitted to models with a catalytic converter is basically the same as that fitted to non-catalytic converter models described above. The only major difference is that the carburettor is electronically controlled by the ECC (electronically controlled carburettor) control unit (which also controls the ignition system - see Chapter 5). This is made possible by the fitting of an air/fuel ratio solenoid valve to the carburettor, this is opened and closed rapidly under the control of the ECC control unit, to richen or weaken the air/fuel mixture ratio by opening or closing the compensating air bleed and main jet.

11 The electrical side of the system consists of the ECC control unit, and all the sensors that provide it with information.

12 The principal information required by the control unit is provided by the boost pressure sensor and the crank angle sensor (which is housed in the distributor). The boost pressure sensor informs the ECC unit of the load on the engine, and the crank angle sensor informs the unit of the engine speed and crankshaft position (see Chapter 5 for further information).

13 Additional information to refine air/fuel mixture control comes from the following sensors:

a) **Coolant temperature sensor** - informs control unit of the engine temperature.
b) **Throttle valve switch** - informs control unit whether the throttle is closed or open.
c) **Ignition switch** - informs the control unit when the engine is being started.
d) **Neutral switch** - informs the control unit when the transmission is in neutral.
e) **Clutch switch** - informs the control unit when the clutch is engaged/disengaged.
f) **Vehicle speed sensor** (mounted in the speedometer) - informs the control unit of the vehicle speed.

g) **The exhaust gas sensor** - sends the control unit information on the amount of oxygen in the exhaust gases (see Part C of this Chapter).

14 All the signals received by the control unit are compared with set values pre-programmed (mapped) into its memory; based on this information, the control unit selects the response appropriate to those values, and accordingly controls the ignition coil (via the power transistor, varying the ignition timing as required), the air/fuel ratio solenoid valve, the accelerator pump, idle-up and idle cut-off solenoid valves, and the exhaust gas sensor. The mixture, idle speed and ignition timing are constantly varied by the control unit, to provide the best settings for starting (with either a hot or cold engine), engine warm-up, idle, cruising and acceleration.

15 To reduce emissions and improve driveability when the engine is cold, an electrical heating element (controlled by the ECC unit) is fitted between the carburettor and inlet manifold to quickly warm-up the carburettor on cold starts. When the engine is up to normal operating temperature, the ECC unit closes the idle cut-off valve when the engine is on the overrun (effectively cutting off the fuel supply to the engine) to improve fuel economy and reduce exhaust emissions.

16 In order to further reduce exhaust emissions, an exhaust gas recirculation (EGR) system and air induction system is fitted to some models. Refer to Part C of this Chapter for further information on these systems.

11 Carburettor - removal and refitting

Note: *Refer to the warning note in Section 1 before proceeding.*

Removal

1 Disconnect the battery negative terminal. Partially drain the cooling system as described in Chapter 1.

2 Remove the air cleaner housing as described in Section 2.

3 Free the accelerator inner cable from the carburettor throttle cam, then slacken the

outer cable locknut and adjuster nut, and free the outer cable from its mounting bracket.

4 Trace the wiring back from the carburettor electrical components to its wiring connector(s), and disconnect them from the main wiring harness **(see illustration)**. On models with a catalytic converter, also disconnect the mixture heater connector situated at the front of the manifold.

5 Slacken the retaining clip, and disconnect the fuel feed hose from the carburettor **(see illustration)**. Place wads of rag around the union to catch any spilled fuel. Plug the hose as soon as it is disconnected, to minimise fuel loss and prevent dirt entry into the system.

6 Make a note of the correct fitted positions of all the relevant vacuum pipes and breather hoses, to ensure that they are correctly positioned on refitting, then release the retaining clips (where fitted) and disconnect them from the carburettor.

7 Slacken and remove the four retaining bolts securing the carburettor to the manifold, and remove the carburettor assembly from the car. Remove the insulating spacer (non-catalyst models) or heating element (catalyst models), and plug the inlet manifold port with a wad of clean cloth to prevent the possible entry of foreign matter.

Refitting

8 Refitting is the reverse of the removal procedure, noting the following points:

a) *Prior to refitting, ensure that the carburettor, inlet manifold and insulating spacer/heating element sealing faces are clean and flat. Refit them to the manifold, and securely tighten the carburettor retaining bolts.*
b) *Use the notes made on dismantling to ensure that all hoses are refitted to their original positions and, where necessary, are securely held by their retaining clips.*
c) *Ensure that all wiring is correctly routed and securely reconnected.*
d) *Reconnect and adjust the accelerator cable as described in Section 7.*
e) *Refit the air cleaner housing as described in Section 2.*
f) *On completion, top-up the cooling system then check and, if necessary, adjust the idle speed and mixture settings as described in Chapter 1.*

4A

11.4 Carburettor wiring connectors

11.5 Slacken the retaining clip (arrowed) and disconnect the fuel hose from the carburettor

12 Carburettor - fault diagnosis, overhaul and adjustments

Diagnosis

1 If a carburettor fault is suspected, always check first that the ignition timing is accurate, that the spark plugs are in good condition and correctly gapped, that the accelerator and choke cables are correctly adjusted, and that the air cleaner filter element is clean; see the relevant Sections of Chapter 1 or of this Chapter. If the engine is running very roughly, first check the valve clearances and the compression pressures as described in Chapter 2A.

2 If careful checking of all of the above produces no improvement, the carburettor must be removed for cleaning and overhaul.

3 Note that in the rare event of a complete carburettor overhaul being necessary, it may prove more economical to renew the carburettor as a complete unit. Check the price and availability of a replacement carburettor and of its component parts before starting work; note that most sealing washers, screws and gaskets are available in kits, as are some of the major sub-assemblies. In most cases, it will be sufficient to dismantle the carburettor and to clean the jets and passages.

Overhaul

Note: *Refer to the warning note in Section 1 before proceeding.*

4 Disconnect the throttle return spring, and inspect the accelerator pump operating lever for wear. Remove the accelerator pump lever retaining spring, circlip and clip, and disconnect the pump lever and spring assembly.

5 Remove the clip, and disconnect the choke connecting rod.

6 Remove the retaining screws, and detach the carburettor upper body. If the top is tight, a gentle tap with a plastic hammer is usually sufficient to free it. Do not lever the assemblies apart, as there is a risk of damaging the mating surfaces.

7 Inspect the float chamber for corrosion and calcium build-up.

8 Remove the accelerator pump inlet spring, retaining clip, strainer and ball; invert the carburettor over a cupped hand to catch these parts.

9 Unscrew the brass plug, and remove the accelerator pump outlet spring, weight and ball; invert the carburettor over a cupped hand to catch these parts.

10 Remove the accelerator pump bellows and piston assembly from the upper body, and check the assembly for fatigue and damage.

11 Tap out the float pin, and remove the float, needle valve and float chamber gasket. **Note:** *In some instances, the needle valve seat is not removable.*

12.22 Release the wires from the wiring connector by depressing the lock tongue with a small, flat-bladed screwdriver as shown

12 Note the correct location of all the jets and air bleeds prior to removal; these notes can then be used to ensure that the jets are correctly positioned on refitting.

13 Where necessary, remove all primary and secondary jets and air bleeds, using a close-fitting screwdriver. **Note:** *Do not attempt to remove the secondary slow air bleeds from the carburettor.*

14 Remove each plug, and unscrew the primary idle-up and secondary slow jets from the main body. Unscrew the primary idle air bleed.

15 Remove the two screws, and detach the auxiliary venturis. Unscrew the primary and secondary combined air corrector and emulsion tubes from the auxiliary venturis.

16 Remove the float chamber plug, and unscrew the primary main jet from its place in the side of the float chamber. Unscrew the secondary main jet, and remove it from the bottom of the float chamber.

17 Remove the idle mixture adjustment screw tamperproof cap. Turn the screw in until it seats lightly, counting the **exact** number of turns required to do this, then unscrew it. On refitting, turn the screw in until it seats lightly, then back the screw off by the number of turns noted on removal, to return the screw to its original location. **Note:** *A special tool is required to remove the mixture screw.*

18 If necessary, the various solenoids can be unscrewed and removed from the carburettor body, noting their correct fitted positions. As each solenoid is removed, recover its spring and plunger and, where fitted, the solenoid sealing washer. Each solenoid can be tested by applying 12 volts across its terminals - as the voltage is applied, the solenoid plunger should be drawn into the solenoid body.

19 On models with a catalytic converter, if the fuel/air ratio solenoid is to be removed, free its wiring from the connector as

described in paragraph 22. Remove the two retaining screws, and withdraw the solenoid valve. Recover the sealing rings from the solenoid and discard them; new ones must be used on refitting.

20 Clean the jets, carburettor body assemblies, float chamber and internal drillings. An air line may be used to clear the internal passages once the carburettor is fully dismantled.

Caution: If high-pressure air is directed into drillings and passages where a diaphragm is fitted, the diaphragm is likely to be damaged. Aerosol cans of carburettor cleaner are widely available, and can prove very useful in helping to clear internal passages of stubborn obstructions.

21 Use a straight edge to check all carburettor body assembly mating surfaces for distortion.

22 Although all electrical components are connected to the same wiring connectors, each one can be renewed individually once its wiring has been released from the relevant connector. To free the wiring, lift the tangs on the side of the wiring connector, and free the retaining clip from the rear of the connector. Using a small, flat-bladed screwdriver, free the relevant wires of the component to be removed, and push them out of the connector **(see illustration)**. Note the correct fitted location of each wire, and take great care not to damage the wiring terminals as they are removed. Slide the wires of the new component into position in the connector, check they are securely retained, then clip the retaining clip into position on the rear of the connector. **Note:** *Ensure that the wires are correctly seated in the connector. If they are not, a poor electrical connection will be made when the two halves of the connector are joined, which could result in the carburettor electrical components not functioning correctly.*

12.26 Float height setting can be checked as described in text using the inspection window (arrowed)

23 On reassembly, renew any worn components, and fit a complete set of new gaskets and seals. A gasket and seal kit is available from your Nissan dealer.

24 Reassembly is a reversal of the dismantling procedure. Ensure that all jets are securely locked in position, but do not overtighten them. Ensure that all mating surfaces are clean and dry, and that all body sections are correctly assembled with their fuel and air passages correctly aligned. Check the float height when reassembling the carburettor. Prior to refitting the carburettor, set the throttle valve fast idle and choke pull-down settings as described below.

Adjustments

Idle speed and mixture settings

25 Refer to Chapter 1.

Float height (fuel level) setting

26 **Note:** *The float height setting can be checked without removing the carburettor, by checking the fuel level in the inspection window on the carburettor body. With the car parked on level ground, and the engine idling at the specified speed, the fuel level should be between the marks on each side of the inspection window* **(see illustration)**. *If not, the float height must be adjusted as follows.* First invert the carburettor body so that the float is at the top.

27 Raise the float fully, then lower it slowly until it contacts the needle valve tip. Hold the float in this position, and measure the distance between the upper edge of the float and the sealing face of the upper body. This should be as given in the Specifications at the start of this Chapter. To adjust the setting, **carefully** bend the pivot arm.

28 Turn the carburettor body the correct way up, then measure the distance between the lower edge of the float and the sealing face of the upper body. This should be as given in the Specifications at the start of this Chapter. To adjust the setting, **carefully** bend the float stopper arm.

Throttle valve fast idle setting

29 Remove the three screws, and detach the bi-metallic cover assembly and fixing ring.

30 Invert the carburettor, then open the throttle slightly and place the fast idle arm

12.31a Position the fast idle arm on the second step of the cam as shown . . .

12.31b . . . then measure the clearance (A) between the primary throttle valve and bore

against the second step of the fast idle cam. The adjustment screw will force open the throttle plate, to leave a small clearance.

31 Ensure that the choke flap is fully closed, then use the shank of a twist drill to measure the clearance "A" between the wall of the throttle bore and the throttle valve **(see illustrations)**. Refer to the Specifications at the start of this Chapter for the required drill size.

32 Adjust as necessary by turning the fast idle adjustment screw as required.

33 Refit the fixing ring and bi-metallic coil housing, ensuring that the spring locates in

the slot of the choke lever. Secure loosely with the three screws.

34 Align the cut mark on the bi-metallic cover with the correct mark on the choke assembly housing, and tighten the three screws.

Choke pull-down setting

35 Operate the carburettor choke linkage to fully close the choke valve, and hold the linkage in this position.

36 Attach a hand-held vacuum pump to the choke pull-down diaphragm, and apply a vacuum to the diaphragm so that the

4A

diaphragm rod is pulled fully into the diaphragm body. In the absence of a vacuum pump, the rod can be pushed into the diaphragm using a small screwdriver.

37 With the rod fully retracted, use the shank of a suitable twist drill to measure the clearance between the edge of the choke valve and bore, and compare this to the clearance given in the Specifications. **Note:** *If the carburettor temperature is below 5°C (41°F), use the stage 1 clearance; above 16.5°C (62°F), refer to the stage 2 clearance.*

38 If necessary, adjust the clearance by **carefully** bending the pull-down tongue in the appropriate direction **(see illustration)**.

13 Electronically-controlled carburettor components - removal and refitting

Note: *The following procedures are only applicable to those models fitted with a catalytic converter.*

Boost pressure sensor

1 The boost pressure sensor is mounted onto the left-hand front suspension mounting turret, where it is located next to the power transistor.

2 To remove the sensor, first disconnect the battery negative terminal.

3 Undo the two retaining screws and remove the boost pressure sensor, disconnecting its wiring connector and vacuum hose as they become accessible **(see illustration)**.

4 Refitting is the reverse of removal.

Power transistor

5 See Chapter 5.

Fuel/air ratio solenoid valve

6 Refer to Section 12.

Carburettor solenoid valves

7 Refer to Section 12, paragraphs 18 and 22.

12.38 Choke pull-down setting

1 *Pull-down adjustment tongue*	4 *Diaphragm*
2 *Vacuum pump*	5 *Choke valve-to-bore clearance*
3 *Pull-down vacuum unit*	

It is not necessary to remove the carburettor from the vehicle, but access can be considerably improved by removing the air cleaner housing as described in Section 2.

Throttle valve switch

8 Undo the two screws, and free the switch from the right-hand side of the carburettor **(see illustration)**. If necessary, remove the air cleaner housing to improve access to the switch.

9 Free the switch wiring from the connector as described in paragraph 22 of Section 12, and remove the switch.

10 Refitting is the reverse of removal. On completion, adjust the switch as follows.

11 Warm the engine up to normal operating temperature, then stop it and disconnect the carburettor wiring connector containing the throttle switch wiring connectors. Referring to the accompanying illustration, use two pieces of wire to connect the terminals of the idle

13.3 Boost pressure sensor wiring connector (1) and vacuum hose (2)

13.8 Throttle valve switch (arrowed) is mounted on the right-hand side of the carburettor

13.11 Adjusting the throttle valve switch. Disconnect the wiring connector, and bridge the idle cut-off solenoid wiring connectors with two pieces of wire. Connect the multimeter to the arrowed terminals of the carburettor side of the connector, and adjust the switch as described in text

cut-off valve solenoid; this is necessary to allow the engine to start. Connect a multimeter set to its resistance across the switch terminals **(see illustration)**.

12 Start the engine, and allow it to idle. Slowly increase the engine speed to approximately 2000 rpm; continuity should exist between the switch terminals. Slowly decrease the engine speed whilst observing the meter; at 1200 rpm the switch should operate, and an open-circuit will be present between the switch terminals. If adjustment is necessary, carefully bend the tang until the switch operates as described.

13 Once the switch is correctly adjusted, stop the engine and reconnect the wiring connector.

Coolant temperature sensor

14 Refer to Chapter 3.

ECC control unit

15 The ECC control unit is situated either under one of the front seats or under the facia in front of the centre console. Prior to removal, disconnect the battery negative terminal.

16 To gain access to the control unit, remove the seat or centre console as applicable (see Chapter 11).

17 Undo the retaining screws, and release the control unit from its mounting bracket. Disconnect the wiring connector(s) and remove the unit from the vehicle.

18 Refitting is the reverse of removal, ensuring that the wiring connector is securely reconnected.

Crank angle sensor

19 The crank angle sensor is an integral part of the distributor, and cannot be renewed separately. If the sensor is faulty, the complete distributor body assembly must be renewed. Refer to Chapter 5 for further information.

Clutch switch

20 The clutch switch is located on the pedal bracket behind the facia. To remove the switch, first disconnect the battery negative lead. If necessary, to improve access, remove the driver's side lower facia panel as described in Chapter 11.

21 Disconnect the wiring plug from the switch, then slacken the locknut and unscrew the switch from its mounting bracket.

22 Refitting is a reversal of removal. Ensure that the clutch is correctly adjusted (see Chapter 6) then adjust the switch as follows.

23 Connect a multi-meter, set to its resistance function, across the switch terminals. Position the switch so there is continuity between the terminals when the pedal is in the at-rest position, and an open-circuit when the pedal is lightly depressed. Once the switch is correctly adjusted, securely tighten the locknut and reconnect the wiring.

Neutral switch

24 Refer to Chapter 7A.

Power steering idle-up switch

25 The power steering idle-up switch is screwed into the power steering feed pipe, in the right-hand rear corner of the engine compartment. Prior to removal, position the front wheels in the straight-ahead position, then disconnect the battery negative terminal.

26 Locate the switch and disconnect its wiring connector.

27 Unscrew the switch and plug its opening in the pipe, working quickly to minimise fluid loss and prevent dirt entering into the hydraulic system. Recover the switch sealing washer.

28 Refitting is the reverse of removal, using a new sealing washer.

Vehicle speed sensor

29 The vehicle speed sensor is an integral part of the speedometer. Refer to Chapter 12 for removal and refitting details.

14 Inlet manifold - removal and refitting

Note: *Refer to the warning note in Section 1 before proceeding.*

Removal

1 Remove the carburettor as described in Section 11.

2 Drain the cooling system as described in Chapter 1.

3 Make a note of the correct fitted locations of all the relevant inlet manifold vacuum and coolant hose connections. Disconnect them from the manifold and, where necessary, from the associated vacuum valves. To avoid confusion on refitting, it may be wise to label each hose as it is disconnected.

4 On models with a catalytic converter, unscrew the union nut and free the EGR pipe, linking the inlet and exhaust manifolds, from the control valve on the left-hand end of the inlet manifold.

5 Disconnect the wiring connector from the coolant temperature sensor on the right-hand end of the manifold. Where necessary, undo the retaining bolt and free the earth lead from the manifold.

6 Undo the retaining bolts and remove the support bracket from the underside of the manifold.

7 Make a final check that all the relevant vacuum/breather hoses have been disconnected from the manifold.

8 Unscrew the retaining nuts and bolts, then manoeuvre the manifold away from the head and out of the engine compartment.

9 Remove the manifold gasket and discard it.

Refitting

10 Refitting is the reverse of the removal procedure, noting the following points:

a) *Ensure that the manifold and cylinder head mating surfaces are clean and dry, and fit the new gasket to the head studs. Install the manifold, and tighten its retaining nuts and bolts to the specified torque setting.*

b) *Ensure that all relevant hoses are reconnected to their original positions, and are securely held (where necessary) by their retaining clips.*

c) *Refit the carburettor as described in Section 11.*

d) *On completion, refill the cooling system as described in Chapter 1.*

4A

15.1 Exhaust manifold and associated components - models with a catalytic converter

1 Hot-air inlet hose
2 EGR pipe
3 Exhaust sensor wiring connector
4 Exhaust gas sampling pipe

16.6a Undo the three nuts securing the front pipe to the manifold . . .

15 Exhaust manifold - removal and refitting

Removal

1 Disconnect the hot-air inlet hose from the manifold shroud, and remove it from the vehicle (see illustration).
2 On models with a catalytic converter, trace the wiring back from the exhaust gas sensor to its wiring connector, and disconnect it from the main wiring harness. Also unscrew the union nuts and free the EGR pipe, air induction pipe and the exhaust gas sampling pipe from the side of the manifold.
3 On all models, slacken and remove the retaining screws, and remove the shroud from the top of the exhaust manifold.
4 Firmly apply the handbrake, then jack up the front of the vehicle and support it on axle stands (see "Jacking and Vehicle Support").
5 Undo the nuts securing the exhaust front pipe to the manifold, and the bolt securing the front pipe to its mounting bracket. Free the front pipe from the manifold, and recover the gasket.
6 Undo the retaining nuts and bolts securing the manifold to the head. Manoeuvre the manifold out of the engine compartment, and discard the manifold gaskets.

Refitting

7 Refitting is the reverse of the removal procedure, noting the following points:
a) Examine all the exhaust manifold studs for signs of damage and corrosion; remove all traces of corrosion, and repair or renew any damaged studs.

b) Ensure that the manifold and cylinder head sealing faces are clean and flat, and fit the new manifold gaskets. Tighten the manifold retaining nuts and bolts to the specified torque.
c) Reconnect the front pipe to the manifold using the information given in Section 16.

16 Exhaust system - general information and component removal

General information

1 On models without a catalytic converter, the exhaust system consists of three sections; the front pipe, the intermediate pipe and silencer box, and the tailpipe and main silencer box.
2 On models with a catalytic converter, the exhaust system consists of four sections, the front pipe, the catalytic converter, the intermediate pipe and silencer box, and the tailpipe and main silencer box.
3 The system is suspended throughout its entire length by rubber mountings, and all exhaust sections are joined by flanged joints which are secured together by nuts and/or bolts.

Removal

4 Each exhaust section can be removed individually, or the complete system can be removed as a unit.
5 To remove the system or part of the system, first jack up the front or rear of the car, and support it on axle stands (see "Jacking and Vehicle Support"). Alternatively, position the car over an inspection pit or on car ramps.

Front pipe

6 Undo the nuts securing the front pipe to the manifold, and the bolt securing the front pipe to its mounting bracket (see illustrations). Separate the front pipe from the manifold and collect the gasket.
7 Slacken and remove the two nuts/bolts and springs securing the front pipe flange joint to the intermediate pipe/catalytic converter (as applicable). Withdraw the front pipe from underneath the vehicle, and recover the gasket from the joint.

Catalytic converter (where fitted)

8 Slacken and remove the two nuts/bolts and springs (as applicable) securing the front pipe flange joint to the catalytic converter.
9 Unscrew the two bolts securing the intermediate pipe to the catalytic converter, and recover the gasket from between the two.
10 Free the catalytic converter from the front pipe, and recover the gasket.

Intermediate pipe

11 On models with a catalytic converter, unscrew the two bolts securing the

16.6b . . . and the bolt securing the front pipe to its mounting bracket

intermediate pipe to the catalytic converter, and recover the gasket from between the two.

12 On models without a catalytic converter, undo the two nuts/bolts and springs (as applicable) securing the front pipe flange joint to the intermediate pipe, then separate the joint and recover the gasket.

13 On all models, slacken and remove the bolt securing the mounting rubber to the rear of the intermediate pipe.

14 Undo the two bolts securing the tailpipe to the intermediate pipe, then manoeuvre the intermediate pipe out from underneath the vehicle. Recover the gasket from the tailpipe joint.

Tailpipe

15 Slacken and remove the two bolts securing the tailpipe to the intermediate pipe.

16 Unhook the tailpipe from its mounting rubbers, then remove it from the vehicle and recover the gasket.

Complete system

17 Undo the nuts securing the front pipe to the manifold, and the bolt securing the front pipe to its mounting bracket. Separate the front pipe from the manifold, and collect the gasket.

18 With the aid of an assistant, free the system from all its mounting rubbers, and manoeuvre it out from underneath the vehicle.

Heat shield(s)

19 The heat shields (where fitted) are secured in position by a mixture of nuts, bolts and clamps. When an exhaust section is renewed, transfer any relevant heat shields from the original over to the new section before installing the exhaust section on the vehicle.

Refitting

20 Each section is refitted by a reverse of the removal sequence, noting the following points:
  a) *Ensure that all traces of corrosion have been removed from the flanges, and renew all necessary gaskets (see illustration).*
  b) *Inspect the rubber mountings for signs of damage or deterioration, and renew as necessary.*
  c) *Prior to tightening the exhaust system fasteners to the specified torque, ensure that all rubber mountings are correctly located, and that there is adequate clearance between the exhaust system and vehicle underbody.*

16.20 Renew all gaskets (front pipe shown)

4A

Chapter 4 Part B:
Fuel/exhaust systems - fuel injection models

Contents

Degrees of difficulty

Easy, suitable for novice with little experience	Fairly easy, suitable for beginner with some experience	Fairly difficult, suitable for competent DIY mechanic	Difficult, suitable for experienced DIY mechanic	Very difficult, suitable for expert DIY or professional

Specifications

General

System type .... Nissan Electronic Concentrated Control System (ECCS) multi-point injection

Application:
  1.4 litre models .... Engine code GA14DE
  1.6 litre models .... Engine code GA16DE

Throttle potentiometer wiring connector - manual transmission models

Fuel system data

For idle speed and mixture settings, refer to Chapter 1 Specifications.
Fuel pump type .... Electric, immersed in tank
Fuel pump regulated constant pressure (approximate) .... 3.0 bars

Fuel system component test data

Fuel pump resistance (at fuel gauge sender unit connection) .... 0.7 ohms
Throttle potentiometer resistances **(see illustrations to right):**
  Meter connected between terminals "A" and "B" or "1" and "2":
    Throttle valve closed .... 0.5 kilohm
    Throttle valve partially open .... 0.5 to 4 kilohms
    Throttle valve fully open .... approx. 4 kilohm
Fuel injector resistance .... 10 ohms
Auxiliary air control (AAC) valve resistance .... 10 ohms
Fast idle control device (FICD) solenoid valve:
  Apply 12 volts across solenoid terminals .... Solenoid should click, indicating correct operation

Power steering pressure switch:
  Steering wheel being turned .... Continuity between switch terminals
  Steering wheel stationary .... Open-circuit between switch terminals

Coolant temperature sensor resistances:
  At 20°C (68°F) .... 2.1 to 2.9 kilohms
  At 90°C (194°F) .... 0.24 to 0.26 kilohms
  At 110°C (230°F) .... 0.14 to 0.15 kilohms

Throttle potentiometer wiring connector - automatic transmission models

Knock sensor wiring connector

Note: *All resistance readings given are approximate values, and should be used as a guide only. Before condemning a component as faulty, have your findings confirmed by a Nissan dealer.*

Recommended fuel

Models with a catalytic converter .... 95 RON unleaded. Leaded fuel (eg UK "4-star") must **not** be used

4B

Torque wrench settings

	Nm	lbf ft
Throttle housing retaining bolts:		
Stage 1	10	7
Stage 2	20	15
Fuel rail retaining bolts:		
Stage 1	10	7
Stage 2	24	18
Inlet manifold nuts and bolts	20	15
Exhaust manifold nuts and bolts	21	16
Exhaust system fasteners:		
Front pipe-to-manifold nuts	32	24
Front pipe mounting bolt	23	18
Front pipe-to-intermediate pipe/catalytic converter nuts	49	36
Catalytic converter-to-tailpipe bolts	49	36
Intermediate pipe-to-tailpipe bolts	49	36

1 General information and precautions

The fuel system consists of a fuel tank mounted under the rear of the car with an electric fuel pump immersed in it, a fuel filter, fuel feed and return lines. The fuel pump supplies fuel to the fuel rail which acts as a reservoir for the four fuel injectors which inject fuel into the inlet tracts. A fuel filter is incorporated in the feed line from the pump to the fuel rail to ensure that the fuel supplied to the injectors is clean.

Refer to Section 6 for further information on the operation of the fuel injection system, and Section 16 for information on the exhaust system.

All fuel injection models are fitted with a catalytic converter.

Warning: Many of the procedures in this Chapter require the removal of fuel lines and connections, which may result in some fuel spillage. *Before carrying out any operation on the fuel system, refer to the precautions given in "Safety first!" at the beginning of this manual, and follow them implicitly. Petrol is a highly-dangerous and volatile liquid, and the precautions necessary when handling it cannot be overstressed. Residual pressure will remain in the fuel lines long after the vehicle was last used. Before disconnecting any fuel line, depressurise the fuel system as described in Section 7.*

2 Air cleaner assembly - removal and refitting

Removal

1 Release the retaining clips, then lift off the air cleaner housing lid along with its seal.
2 Lift out the filter element, noting which way around it is fitted.
3 Unscrew the mounting bolts, release the hoses and disconnect the inlet duct from the left-hand end of the air cleaner housing. Note the two location holes and rubbers **(see illustrations)**.
4 Release the clip and disconnect the crankcase ventilation hose from the base of the air cleaner housing **(see illustrations)**.

2.3a Unscrew the bolt by the battery . . .

2.3b . . . and the bolt on the inner wing . . .

2.3c . . . then disconnect the hoses . . .

2.3d . . . and lift the inlet duct from the location holes

2.4a Release the clip . . .

2.4b . . . and disconnect the crankcase ventilation hose

2.5a Remove the bolt . . .

2.5b . . . loosen the retaining clip . . .

2.5c . . . remove the housing from the top of the throttle housing . . .

5 Slacken and remove the housing retaining bolt and retaining clip, then free the housing from the top of the throttle housing. As the housing is being removed disconnect the small vacuum hose. If necessary, remove the sealing ring from the top of the throttle housing (see illustrations).

Refitting

6 Refitting is a reversal of the relevant removal procedure, ensuring that all hoses are properly reconnected, and that all ducts are correctly seated and securely held by their retaining clips.

3 Accelerator cable - removal, refitting and adjustment

Refer to Chapter 4A, Section 7, substituting "throttle body" for all references to the carburettor. If necessary, remove the air cleaner housing (see Section 2) to improve access to the throttle body end of the cable (see illustration).

4 Accelerator pedal - removal and refitting

Refer to Chapter 4A, Section 8, substituting "throttle body" for all references to the carburettor.

3.1 Accelerator cable connection to the throttle body on the fuel injection engine

5 Unleaded petrol - general information and usage

Note: *The information given in this Chapter is correct at the time of writing, and applies only to petrols currently available in the UK. If updated information is thought to be required, check with a Nissan dealer. If travelling abroad, consult one of the motoring organisations (or a similar authority) for advice on the petrols available, and their suitability for your vehicle.*

1 The fuel recommended by Nissan is given in the Specifications Section of this Chapter.
2 RON and MON are different testing standards; RON stands for Research Octane Number (also written as RM), while MON stands for Motor Octane Number (also written as MM).
3 All Nissan Sunny models are designed to run on fuel with a minimum octane rating of 95 (RON). All models with a catalytic converter must be run on unleaded fuel **only**. Under no circumstances should leaded fuel be used, as this may damage the catalyst. On models without a catalytic converter, either unleaded or leaded fuel can be used without modification.

6 Fuel injection system - general information

1 All multi-point injection models are fitted with a combined fuel injection/ignition (engine management) system, otherwise known as the Electronic Concentrated Control System (ECCS). Refer to Chapter 5 for information on the ignition side of the system, the fuel injection side of the system operates as follows.
2 The fuel pump, immersed in the fuel tank, supplies fuel from the fuel tank to the fuel rail, via a filter mounted on the engine compartment bulkhead. Fuel supply pressure is controlled by the pressure regulator, on the end of the fuel rail, which lifts to allow excess fuel to return to the tank when the optimum operating pressure of the fuel system is exceeded.

2.5d . . . and disconnect the vacuum hose

3 The electrical control system consists of the ECCS control unit, along with the following sensors:
a) **Throttle potentiometer** - informs the ECCS control unit of the throttle valve position, and the rate of throttle opening/closing.
b) **Coolant temperature sensor** - informs the ECCS control unit of engine temperature.
c) **Airflow meter** - informs the ECCS control unit of the mass and temperature of the air passing through the inlet duct.
d) **Crank angle sensor** (housed in the distributor) - informs the ECCS control unit of the engine speed and crankshaft position (see Chapter 5 for further information).
e) **Vehicle speed sensor** (built into the speedometer) - informs the ECCS control unit of the vehicle speed.
f) **Power steering and air conditioning system switches** (where fitted) - informs the ECCS control unit if the system(s) are in operation, to allow it to adjust the idle speed to compensate for the extra load on the engine.
g) **Exhaust gas sensor** (catalyst models only) - informs the ECCS control unit of the oxygen content of the exhaust gases (see Part C of this Chapter for further information).
4 All the above signals are analysed by the ECCS control unit. Based on this information, the ECCS control unit selects the response appropriate to those values, and controls the fuel injectors (varying their pulse width - the

4B

length of time each injector is held open - to provide a richer or weaker mixture, as appropriate). The mixture and idle speed are constantly varied by the ECCS control unit to provide the best settings for cranking, starting (with either a hot or cold engine) and engine warm-up, idle, cruising, and acceleration.

5 The ECCS control unit also has full control over the engine idle speed via the auxiliary air control (AAC) valve. The valve, which is fitted to the throttle housing, controls the opening of an air passage which bypasses the throttle valve. When the throttle valve is closed, the ECCS control unit controls the opening of the valve, which regulates the amount of air which flows through the valve, and so controls the idle speed.

6 The throttle housing has a built-in fast idle facility, which is controlled by a thermostatic valve. When the engine is cold, the wax capsule in the valve (which is fitted to the throttle housing), is at its smallest, and the fast idle cam holds the throttle valve slightly open. As the engine warms up, the wax capsule expands, forcing the valve plunger upwards, which in turn rotates the fast idle cam to the required position.

7 There is also a fast idle control (FICD) solenoid valve which is controlled by the ECCS control unit. The solenoid valve controls the opening of an air passage which bypasses the throttle valve, and this is used to raise the idle speed when either the power steering and/or air conditioning systems are in operation. **Note:** *On some models, the valve may be fitted but will not be operational.*

8 On models with a catalytic converter, the ECCS control unit also controls the exhaust and evaporative emission control systems, which are described in detail in Chapter 4C.

9 If there is an abnormality in any of the readings obtained from sensors, the ECCS control unit switches to its back-up mode. If this happens, it ignores the abnormal sensor signal, and assumes a pre-programmed value which will allow the engine to continue running, albeit at reduced efficiency. If the ECCS control unit enters its back-up mode, the warning light on the instrument panel will come on, and the relevant fault code will be stored in the ECCS control unit memory.

10 If the warning light comes on, the vehicle should be taken to a Nissan dealer at the earliest opportunity. Once there, a complete test of the engine management system can be carried out, using a special electronic diagnostic test unit which is simply plugged into the system's diagnostic connector. **Note:** *The ECCS control unit also has a self-diagnostic mode which can be accessed by the DIY mechanic. See Section 11 for further information.*

7 Fuel system - depressurisation

Note: *Refer to the warning note in Section 1 before proceeding.*

 Warning: The following procedure will merely relieve the pressure in the fuel system - remember that fuel will still be present in the system components, and take precautions accordingly before disconnecting any of them. Use clean rags wrapped around the connections to catch escaping fuel, and dispose of any fuel-soaked rags with care. Plug or tape over any open fuel lines, to prevent further loss of fuel or ingress of dirt.

1 The fuel system referred to in this Section is defined as the tank-mounted fuel pump, the fuel filter, the fuel rail and injectors, the pressure regulator, and the metal pipes and flexible hoses of the fuel lines between these components. All these contain fuel which will be under pressure while the engine is running and/or while the ignition is switched on. The pressure will remain for some time after the ignition has been switched off, and must be relieved before any of these components are disturbed for servicing work.

2 Identify and remove the fuel pump fuse from the vehicle fusebox - the fuses are not numbered as such, but can be identified from the label inside the fusebox cover, or from the wiring diagrams at the end of this manual.

3 Start the engine, and allow it to run until it stalls.

4 Try to start the engine at least twice more, to ensure that all residual pressure has been relieved.

5 Disconnect the battery negative terminal.

6 For safety, the fuel pump fuse should not be refitted until all work on the fuel system has been completed. If you refit the fuse now, **do not** switch on the ignition until work is completed.

8 Fuel pump - removal and refitting

Note: *Refer to the warning note in Section 1 before proceeding.*

Removal

1 The pump is removed as an assembly along with the fuel gauge sender unit. Remove the sender unit, and separate it from the fuel pump as described in Section 9.

2 If necessary, unclip the filter element from the base of the fuel pump, then release the retaining clips, and separate the fuel pump from its plastic covers.

3 Wash the pump filter in a high flash-point solvent. Examine the filter for signs of clogging or splitting, and renew if necessary.

Refitting

4 Where necessary, reassemble the pump and covers, and refit the filter.

5 Ensure that the covers are clipped securely onto the pump, then join the pump to the sender unit and install the assembly as described in Section 9.

9 Fuel gauge sender unit - removal and refitting

Note: *Refer to the warning note in Section 1 before proceeding.*

Removal

1 Disconnect the battery negative lead.

2 To gain access to the sender unit, remove the rear seat cushion as described in Chapter 11.

3 Undo the retaining screws, and lift up the access cover to expose the sender unit.

4 Disconnect the wiring connector(s) from the fuel gauge sender unit, and tape the connector to the vehicle body to prevent it disappearing behind the tank.

5 Depressurise the fuel system as described in Section 7. Mark the hoses for identification purposes, then slacken the feed and return hose retaining clips. Disconnect both hoses from the top of the sender unit, and plug the hose ends.

6 Note the correct fitted position of the alignment mark on the sender unit (the arrow should be pointing towards the front of the vehicle). If no alignment mark exists, make one.

7 On models where the sender unit is retained by a large ring, unscrew the locking ring and remove it from the tank. This is best accomplished by using a screwdriver on the raised ribs of the locking ring. Carefully tap the screwdriver to turn the ring anti-clockwise until it can be unscrewed by hand.

8 On models where the sender unit is bolted to the tank, slacken and remove all the retaining bolts and washers.

9 On all models, carefully lift the sender unit from the top of the fuel tank, taking great care not to bend the sender unit float arm, or to spill fuel onto the interior of the vehicle. As the sender unit is being removed, disconnect the pump wiring connector from its base; reach into the tank, and depress the retaining clip to release the fuel pump from the base of the tank. The fuel pump and sender unit can then be removed as an assembly.

10 Recover the rubber sealing ring and discard it; a new one must be used on refitting.

11 Slacken the retaining clip, then disconnect the fuel pump hose from the underside of the sender unit, and separate the pump and sender unit.

12 Wash the pump filter in a high flash-point solvent. Examine the filter for signs of clogging or splitting, and renew if necessary.

Refitting

13 Refitting is a reversal of the removal procedure, noting the following points:

a) *Reassemble the fuel pump and sender unit, ensuring that the hoses are correctly reconnected to their original locations, and are securely held by their retaining clips.*

b) *Fit a new rubber sealing ring to the fuel tank.*

c) *Ensure that the fuel pump is clipped securely into position before seating the sender unit in the tank.*

d) *Where the unit is retained by a locking ring, align the sender unit arrow with the mark on the tank, and securely tighten the locking ring.*

e) *Where the unit is retained by bolts, align the marks made on removal, and securely tighten all the bolts.*

f) *Ensure that the fuel pump is clipped securely in position before seating the sender unit in the tank.*

g) *Ensure that the feed and return hoses are correctly reconnected, and are securely retained by their clips.*

h) *Prior to refitting the access cover, reconnect the battery, then start the engine and check the fuel hoses for signs of leaks.*

10 Fuel tank - removal and refitting

Refer to Chapter 4A, Section 6, noting that it will be necessary to depressurise the fuel system before the feed and return hoses are disconnected from the fuel sender unit (see Section 7).

11 Fuel injection system - diagnosis and adjustment

Diagnosis

General information

1 If a fault appears in the fuel injection/ignition system, first ensure that all the system wiring connectors are securely connected and free of corrosion. Then ensure that the fault is not due to poor maintenance - ie, check that the air cleaner filter element is clean, that the spark plugs are in good condition and correctly gapped, that the valve clearances are correctly adjusted, the cylinder compression pressures are correct, the ignition timing is correct, and that the emission control systems are operating correctly, referring to Chapters 1, 2, and 4 for further information.

2 If these checks fail to reveal the cause of the problem, a quick check of the fuel injection/ignition circuits can be performed by setting the ECCS control unit to its self-diagnostic mode "2". In mode "2", the ECCS control unit will reveal any fault codes stored in its memory, using the engine check light in the instrument panel and the red LED on the right-hand side of the control unit.

3 Faults detected by ECCS control unit are stored in its memory, until the starter motor has been operated 50 times. If the fault is not detected again within this period, it will automatically be erased from the memory. Fault codes can also be erased from the memory by setting the control unit to self-diagnostic mode "2" and then switching it back to mode "1", as described below, or by leaving the battery disconnected for more than 24 hours.

Setting the self-diagnostic modes

4 Remove the fusebox cover inside the car, to gain access to the diagnostic connector which is clipped to the base of the fusebox.

5 Turn the ignition switch to the "ON" position, but do not start the engine. The ECCS control unit is now in self-diagnostic mode "1".

6 Using a spare piece of wire, connect the "IGN" terminal of the diagnostic connector to the "CHK" terminal **(see illustration)**. Keep the terminals connected for at least 2 seconds, then disconnect the wire. The ECCS control unit is now in self-diagnostic mode "2".

7 In mode "2", the control unit will reveal any fault codes stored in its memory.

8 The code is revealed using a series of long (0.6 second) and short (0.3 second) flashes of the instrument panel engine check light and the red LED on the right-hand side of the control unit. The long flashes, which indicate the first digit of the fault code, will be given out first, then after a gap of approximately 0.9 seconds, the short flashes, which indicate the second digit of the fault code, will follow. There will be a gap of 2.1 seconds before any other codes are revealed. Once all codes have been revealed, the ECU will continuously run through the code(s) stored in its memory, revealing each one in turn with a gap of 2.1 seconds between each code. The fault codes are as follows:

Code number	Faulty circuit
11	Crank angle sensor circuit
12	Airflow meter circuit
13	Coolant temp. sensor circuit
21	Ignition signal circuit
34	Knock sensor circuit
43	Throttle potentiometer circuit
55	All circuits operating correctly

Note: *If both codes 11 and 21 are displayed, check the crank angle sensor circuit before checking the rest of the ignition circuit.*

9 On models with a catalytic converter, with the control unit in mode "2", if the engine is started it will automatically enter its exhaust gas sensor check mode. In this mode, the light and LED indicate the condition of the exhaust gases. When the light and LED are illuminated, the exhaust gas mixture is lean, and when they are off, the mixture is rich. To

11.6 Connect the IGN and CHK terminals using a jumper wire

check the sensor, with the control unit in self-diagnostic mode "2", start the engine and warm it up to normal operating temperature. Once it is warm, raise the engine speed to approximately 2000 rpm, and hold it there for approximately 2 minutes whilst observing the instrument panel light or control unit LED. If the exhaust gas sensor is functioning correctly, the light/LED should flash on and off at least 5 times every 10 seconds.

10 When all the checks are complete, exit the self-diagnostic mode "2". If the engine has not been started, this can be achieved by reconnecting the "IGN" and "CHK" terminals of the diagnostic connector again for at least two seconds. If the engine is running, exit mode "2" by switching the ignition switch to the "OFF" position and disconnecting the battery negative terminal.

11 If a more detailed check of the fuel injection/ignition system is required, take the vehicle to a Nissan dealer. They will have access to the special electronic diagnostic test unit which is plugged into the system's diagnostic connector, and can carry out a full check of the system components.

Adjustment

12 All fuel injection models covered by this manual are fitted with a catalytic converter, and only the base idle speed is adjustable. Refer to Chapter 1 for the adjustment procedures.

12 Throttle housing - removal and refitting

Note: *Refer to the warning note in Section 1 before proceeding.*

1 Disconnect the battery negative terminal.

2 Remove the air cleaner housing as described in Section 2.

3 Depress the retaining clips and disconnect the wiring connectors from the throttle potentiometer, the auxiliary air control valve, the airflow meter and the fast idle control device (FICD) solenoid valve.

4 Free the accelerator inner cable from the throttle cam. Slacken the outer cable locknut and adjuster nut, then free the outer cable from its mounting bracket.

4B

12.7 Throttle housing retaining bolts (arrowed)

13.3 Fuel rail feed and return hoses (arrowed)

13.4 Disconnecting the injector wiring

5 Make a note of the correct fitted positions of all the relevant vacuum pipes and breather hoses, to ensure that they are correctly positioned on refitting, then release the retaining clips (where fitted) and disconnect them from the throttle housing.

6 Release the retaining clips, disconnect the coolant hoses from each side of the throttle housing, and plug the hose ends. Work quickly, to minimise coolant loss.

7 Slacken and remove the bolts securing the throttle housing assembly to the inlet manifold, and remove it from the engine compartment **(see illustration)**. Remove the gasket and discard it; a new one must be used on refitting. Plug the inlet manifold port with a wad of clean cloth, to prevent the possible entry of foreign matter.

Refitting

8 Refitting is a reverse of the removal procedure, bearing in mind the following points:

a) Ensure that the mating surfaces of the manifold and throttle housing are clean and dry, and fit a new gasket to the manifold. Fit the throttle body then, working in a diagonal sequence, tighten the retaining bolts to the specified Stage 1 torque setting. Go around again in sequence, and tighten them to the specified Stage 2 torque setting.

b) Ensure that all hoses are correctly reconnected and, where necessary, that their retaining clips are securely tightened.

c) On completion, adjust the accelerator

cable using the information given in Section 3. On automatic transmission models, also check the kickdown cable adjustment as described in Chapter 7B.

13 Fuel injection system components - removal and refitting

Fuel rail and injectors

Note: *Refer to the warning note in Section 1 before proceeding.*

Note: *If a faulty injector is suspected, before condemning the injector, it is worth trying the effect of one of the proprietary injector-cleaning treatments.*

1 Disconnect the battery negative terminal. To improve access to the fuel rail, remove the air cleaner housing as described in Section 2.

2 Disconnect the vacuum pipe from the fuel pressure regulator.

3 Depressurise the fuel system as described in Section 7, then slacken the retaining clips and disconnect the fuel feed and return hoses from the left-hand end of the fuel rail **(see illustration)**. Label the hoses if wished, to avoid confusion on refitting.

4 Depress the retaining tangs, and disconnect the wiring connectors from the four injectors **(see illustration)**.

5 Slacken and remove the fuel rail retaining bolts, then carefully ease the fuel rail and injector assembly out from the inlet manifold, and remove it from the vehicle. Recover the spacers fitted between the rail and manifold,

and remove each injector seal from the manifold.

6 To remove the injectors, undo the two retaining bolts and remove the retaining plate from the relevant injector. Push the injector out of position, and recover the sealing rings **(see illustrations)**. Repeat the procedure as required to remove any other injectors.

7 Discard the seals and sealing rings; new ones must be used on refitting.

8 Refitting is a reversal of the removal procedure, noting the following points:

a) Fit new O-rings to all disturbed injectors, and fit new injector seals to the manifold.

b) Apply a smear of engine oil to the O-rings to aid installation, then ease the injectors into the fuel rail.

c) Fit a new seal to each injector, and ease the fuel rail assembly into position in the manifold. Fit the spacers between the rail and manifold then, working in a diagonal sequence from the centre outwards, tighten the bolts to their specified Stage 1 torque setting. Go around again in sequence, and tighten them to the specified Stage 2 torque.

d) On completion, start the engine and check for fuel leaks.

Fuel pressure regulator

Note: *Refer to the warning note in Section 1 before proceeding.*

9 Disconnect the battery negative terminal.

10 Disconnect the vacuum hose from the fuel pressure regulator, which is mounted on the left-hand end of the fuel rail **(see illustration)**.

13.6a Unscrew the retaining bolts . . .

13 6b . . . and remove the injector from the fuel rail

13.10 Fuel pressure regulator (arrowed) is mounted on the left-hand end of the rail

11 Depressurise the fuel system as described in Section 7, then slacken the retaining clips and disconnect the fuel hose from base of the regulator.

12 Undo the two retaining bolts, and remove the regulator from the end of the fuel rail. Recover the sealing ring fitted to the regulator and discard it; a new one must be used on refitting.

13 Refitting is the reverse of removal, using a new sealing ring. On completion, start the engine and check for fuel leaks.

Throttle potentiometer

14 The throttle potentiometer is mounted onto the right-hand side of the throttle housing **(see illustration)**. Prior to removal, disconnect the battery negative terminal.

15 Disconnect the wiring connector from the throttle potentiometer.

16 Using a dab of white paint or a suitable marker pen, make alignment marks between the potentiometer and the throttle housing.

17 Undo the two retaining screws, and remove the potentiometer.

18 On refitting, offer up the potentiometer, making sure its lever is correctly engaged with the throttle valve spindle lever.

19 Align the marks made prior to removal, and lightly tighten the retaining screws. Adjust the potentiometer as follows:

20 Using a multi-meter set to the resistance scale, check that the potentiometer resistance readings are as given in the Specifications at the start of this Chapter. If necessary, slacken the retaining screws and reposition the potentiometer until its resistances are as shown.

21 When the potentiometer is correctly positioned, securely tighten its retaining screws and reconnect the wiring connector.

22 Reconnect the battery negative terminal.

Auxiliary air control (AAC) valve

23 The auxiliary air control (AAC) valve is mounted onto the front of the throttle body. Prior to removal, disconnect the battery negative terminal.

24 Disconnect the wiring connector from the control valve **(see illustration)**.

25 Undo the retaining screws, then remove the valve from the throttle body and recover the gasket.

13.14 Throttle potentiometer (arrowed) is mounted on the right-hand side of the throttle housing

26 If necessary, with the valve removed, separate the two halves of the valve by removing the retaining screws, then recover the sealing ring. Check that the valve plunger is free to move easily, and returns quickly under spring pressure. If not, the valve assembly must be renewed.

27 Refitting is the reverse of removal, using a new gasket.

Airflow meter

28 The airflow meter is mounted onto the right-hand side of the throttle body. Prior to removal, disconnect the battery negative terminal.

29 Disconnect the wiring connector from the airflow meter **(see illustration)**.

30 Undo the retaining screws, then remove the meter from the throttle body **(see illustration)**. Recover its sealing ring (where fitted).

31 Refitting is the reverse of removal, using a new sealing ring (where applicable) and tightening its retaining screws securely.

Fast idle control device (FICD) solenoid valve

32 The fast idle control device (FICD) solenoid valve is screwed into the front of the throttle body **(see illustration)**. Prior to removal, disconnect the battery negative terminal. If necessary, remove the air cleaner housing as described in Section 2 to improve access to the valve.

33 Disconnect the wiring connector from the solenoid.

13.24 Auxiliary air control (AAC) valve wiring connector (1) and retaining screws (2)

34 Unscrew the solenoid valve from the body, and recover the plunger, spring and sealing washer.

35 Refitting is the reverse of removal, using a new sealing washer. Ensure that the solenoid plunger and spring are fitted in the correct order, and the correct way around.

Fast idle thermostatic valve (fast idle cam)

36 The fast idle thermostatic valve is fitted to the left-hand side of the throttle body. Prior to removal, disconnect the battery negative terminal.

37 Remove the air cleaner housing as described in Section 2.

38 Unscrew the nut and washer, then withdraw the fast idle cam retaining plate, spring, spacer and lever, noting each component's correct fitted position.

39 Undo the retaining screw, and remove the fast idle valve retaining plate. Lift the valve out of position, and recover its sealing ring.

40 Refitting is the reverse of removal. Use a new sealing ring, and ensure that all the fast idle cam components are refitted in their original positions.

Crank angle sensor and power transistor

41 The crank angle sensor and power transistor are integral parts of the distributor, and cannot be renewed separately. If either is faulty, the complete distributor body assembly must be renewed. Refer to Chapter 5 for further information.

4B

13.29 Disconnect the wiring connector . . .

13.30 . . . then undo the retaining screws (arrowed) and remove the airflow meter

13.32 The fast idle control device (FICD) (arrowed) is screwed into the front of the throttle housing

Coolant temperature sensor

42 Refer to Chapter 3.

ECCS control unit

43 The ECCS control unit is situated just in front of the centre console, mounted onto the transmission tunnel floor. Prior to removal, disconnect the battery negative terminal.
44 To gain access to the control unit, undo the retaining screws and release the retaining clips, then remove the small trim panel from each side of the front of the centre console.
45 Undo the retaining screws, and release the control unit from its mounting bracket. Disconnect the wiring connector(s), and remove the unit from the vehicle.
46 Refitting is the reverse of removal, ensuring that the wiring connector is securely reconnected.

Neutral switch - manual transmission models

47 Refer to Chapter 7A.

Starter inhibitor/reversing light switch - automatic transmission models

48 Refer to Chapter 7B.

ECCS control unit and fuel pump relays

49 Refer to Chapter 12.

Power steering idle-up switch

50 The power steering idle-up switch is screwed into the power steering feed pipe, in the right-hand rear corner of the engine compartment. Prior to removal, set the front wheels in the straight-ahead position, then disconnect the battery negative terminal.
51 Locate the switch and disconnect its wiring connector.
52 Unscrew the switch, recover its sealing washer, and plug the opening in the pipe. Work quickly, to minimise fluid loss and to prevent dirt entering the hydraulic system.

53 Refitting is the reverse of removal, using a new sealing washer.

Air conditioning system idle-up switch

54 The air conditioning switch is screwed into the air conditioning pipe, in the left-hand front corner of the engine compartment. Removal and refitting of the switch requires the air conditioning system to be discharged and recharged (Chapter 3, Section 10); this should not be attempted by the home mechanic.

Vehicle speed sensor

55 The vehicle speed sensor is an integral part of the speedometer. Refer to Chapter 12 for removal and refitting details.

14 Inlet manifold - removal and refitting

Removal

1 Drain the cooling system (Chapter 1).
2 Carry out the operations described in paragraphs 1 to 6 of Section 12, and disconnect all components from the throttle housing.
3 Make a note of the correct fitted locations of all the relevant inlet manifold vacuum hose connections, and disconnect them from the manifold and (where necessary) from the associated vacuum valves. To avoid confusion on refitting, it may be wise to label each hose as it is disconnected.
4 Unscrew the union nut and free the EGR pipe linking the inlet and exhaust manifolds, from the control valve on the left-hand end of the inlet manifold (see illustration).
5 Disconnect the wiring connectors from the injectors and the engine coolant temperature sensor. Free the wiring from any relevant retaining clips, and position it clear of the manifold. Where necessary, also undo the retaining bolt(s) and free the earth lead(s) from the manifold (see illustration).

14.4 Unscrew the union nut (arrowed) and disconnect the EGR pipe from the valve

6 Undo the retaining bolts and remove the support bracket from the underside of the manifold.
7 Depressurise the fuel system as described in Section 7, then slacken the retaining clips and disconnect the fuel feed and return hoses from the left-hand end of the fuel rail. Plug the hose and rail unions, to minimise fuel loss and to prevent dirt entering the system.
8 Make a final check that all the necessary vacuum/breather hoses have been disconnected from the manifold then, working in the **reverse** of the sequence shown in illustration 14.10, slacken and remove the manifold retaining nuts and bolts.
9 Manoeuvre the manifold away from the head, and out of the engine compartment. Remove the manifold gasket and discard it.

Refitting

10 Refitting is the reverse of the removal procedure, noting the following points:
  a) Ensure that the manifold and cylinder head mating surfaces are clean and dry, and fit the new gasket to the head studs. Install the manifold, and tighten its retaining nuts and bolts to the specified torque setting in the order shown (see illustration).

14.5 Undo the bolts, and free the earth leads (arrowed) from the right-hand end of the manifold

H27255

14.10 Inlet manifold nut and bolt tightening sequence

15.2 Removing the exhaust manifold shroud

15.3 Unscrew the union nut, and free the EGR pipe from the side of the manifold

b) Ensure that all relevant hoses are reconnected to their original positions, and are securely held (where necessary) by their retaining clips.

c) Adjust the accelerator cable as described in Section 3.

d) On completion, refill the cooling system as described in Chapter 1.

15 Exhaust manifold - removal and refitting

Removal

1 Trace the wiring back from the exhaust gas sensor to its wiring connector, and disconnect it from the main wiring harness.

2 Slacken and remove the retaining screws, and remove the shroud from the top of the exhaust manifold (see illustration).

3 Where necessary, unscrew the union nut, and free the EGR pipe from the side of the manifold (see illustration). Note that it may be necessary to slacken the inlet manifold end of the pipe, and the pipe mounting bolts (where fitted), in order to free the pipe from the manifold.

4 Firmly apply the handbrake, then jack up the front of the vehicle and support it on axle stands (see "Jacking and Vehicle Support").

5 Undo the nuts securing the exhaust front pipe to the manifold, and the bolt securing the front pipe to its mounting bracket. Free the front pipe from the manifold, and recover the gasket(s).

6 Working in the reverse of the sequence shown in illustration 15.8, slacken and remove the manifold retaining nuts and bolts.

7 Manoeuvre the manifold out of the engine compartment, and discard the manifold gasket(s).

Refitting

8 Refitting is the reverse of the removal procedure, noting the following points:

a) Examine all the exhaust manifold studs for signs of damage and corrosion; remove all traces of corrosion, and repair or renew any damaged studs.

b) Ensure that the manifold and cylinder head sealing faces are clean and flat, and fit the new manifold gasket(s). Tighten the manifold retaining nuts and bolts to the specified torque in the order shown (see illustration).

c) Reconnect the front pipe to the manifold, using the information given in Section 16.

16 Exhaust system - general information and component removal

General information

1 On models without a catalytic converter, the exhaust system consists of three sections; the front pipe, the intermediate pipe and silencer box, and the tailpipe and main silencer box.

2 On models with a catalytic converter, the exhaust system consists of four sections, the front pipe, the catalytic converter, the intermediate pipe and silencer box, and the tailpipe and main silencer box. Some models may be fitted with two catalytic converters, one located next to the exhaust manifold.

3 The system is suspended throughout its entire length by rubber mountings, and all exhaust sections are joined by flanged joints which are secured together by nuts and/or bolts.

4B

15.8 Exhaust manifold nut and bolt tightening sequence

Removal

4 Each exhaust section can be removed individually or, alternatively, the complete system can be removed as a unit.

5 To remove the system or part of the system, first jack up the front or rear of the car, and support it on axle stands (see *"Jacking and Vehicle Support"*). Alternatively, position the car over an inspection pit, or on car ramps.

Front pipe

6 On models with a catalytic converter, trace the wiring back from the exhaust gas sensor to its wiring connector. Disconnect the connector, and free the wiring from any relevant retaining clips so that it is free to be removed with the front pipe.

7 On all models, undo the nuts securing the front pipe to the manifold, and the bolt securing the front pipe to its mounting bracket. Separate the front pipe from the manifold, and collect the gaskets.

8 Slacken and remove the two nuts/bolts and springs (as applicable) securing the front pipe flange joint to the intermediate pipe/catalytic converter (as applicable). Withdraw the front pipe from underneath the vehicle, and recover the gasket from the joint. Note that it may be necessary to undo the bolts and release the mounting bracket from the vehicle body to allow the front pipe to be withdrawn.

Catalytic converter (where fitted)

9 Slacken and remove the two nuts/bolts and springs (as applicable) securing the front pipe flange joint to the catalytic converter.

10 Unscrew the two nuts/bolts securing the intermediate pipe to the catalytic converter, and recover the gasket from between the two.

11 Free the catalytic converter from the front pipe, and recover the gasket.

Intermediate pipe

12 On models with a catalytic converter, unscrew the two bolts securing the intermediate pipe to the catalytic converter, and recover the gasket from between the two.

13 On models without a catalytic converter, undo the two nuts securing the front pipe flange joint to the intermediate pipe, then separate the joint and recover the gasket.

14 On all models, slacken and remove the bolt securing the mounting rubber to the rear of the intermediate pipe.

15 Undo the two bolts securing the tailpipe to the intermediate pipe, then manoeuvre the intermediate pipe out from underneath the vehicle. Recover the gasket from the tailpipe joint.

Tailpipe

16 Slacken and remove the two bolts securing the tailpipe to the intermediate pipe.

17 Unhook the tailpipe from its mounting rubbers, then remove it from the vehicle and recover the gasket.

Complete system

18 On models with a catalytic converter, trace the wiring back from the exhaust gas sensor to its wiring connector. Disconnect the connector, and free the wiring from any relevant retaining clips so that it is free to be removed with the exhaust system.

19 Undo the nuts securing the front pipe to the manifold, and the bolt securing the front pipe to its mounting bracket. Separate the front pipe from the manifold, and collect the gaskets.

20 With the aid of an assistant, free the system from all its mounting rubbers, and manoeuvre it out from underneath the vehicle.

Heat shield(s)

21 The heat shields (where fitted) are secured in position by a mixture of nuts, bolts and clamps. When an exhaust section is renewed, transfer any relevant heat shields from the original over to the new section before installing the exhaust section on the vehicle.

Refitting

22 Each section is refitted by a reverse of the removal sequence, noting the following points:

a) *Ensure that all traces of corrosion have been removed from the flanges, and renew all necessary gaskets.*

b) *Inspect the rubber mountings for signs of damage or deterioration, and renew as necessary.*

c) *Prior to tightening the exhaust system fasteners to the specified torque, ensure that all rubber mountings are correctly located, and that there is adequate clearance between the exhaust system and vehicle underbody/suspension components, etc.*

Chapter 4 Part C:
Emission control systems

Contents

Degrees of difficulty

Easy, suitable for novice with little experience	**Fairly easy,** suitable for beginner with some experience	**Fairly difficult,** suitable for competent DIY mechanic	**Difficult,** suitable for experienced DIY mechanic	**Very difficult,** suitable for expert DIY or professional

1 General information

1 All Nissan Sunny models covered in this manual are capable of using unleaded petrol, and also have various other features built into the fuel system to help minimise harmful emissions. Non-catalyst carburettor models can also use leaded petrol (see Chapter 4A Specifications).

2 All models are fitted with a crankcase emissions control system, along with the following systems, according to model:

Non-catalyst carburettor models
- *idle compensator system and a dashpot.*

Catalyst carburettor models without EGR
- *catalytic converter, idle compensator system, and a dashpot.*

Catalyst carburettor models with EGR
- *catalytic converter, exhaust gas recirculation (EGR) system, evaporative emissions control system, air induction system, idle compensator system, and a dashpot.*

Multi-point injection models
- *catalytic converter, exhaust gas recirculation (EGR) system, idle compensator system, and evaporative emissions control system.*

3 The various emissions control systems operate as follows.

Crankcase emissions control

4 To reduce the emission of unburned hydrocarbons from the crankcase into the atmosphere, the engine is sealed, and the blow-by gases and oil vapour are drawn from inside the crankcase, through the PCV valve, into the inlet tract, to be burned by the engine during normal combustion.

5 Under conditions of high manifold vacuum, the gases will be sucked positively out of the crankcase. Under conditions of low manifold vacuum, the gases are forced out of the crankcase by the (relatively) higher crankcase pressure; if the engine is worn, the raised crankcase pressure (due to increased blow-by) will cause some of the flow to return under all manifold conditions.

Catalytic converter

6 To minimise the amount of pollutants which escape into the atmosphere, some models are fitted with a catalytic converter in the exhaust system. On all models where a catalytic converter is fitted, the system is of the "closed-loop" type, in which an exhaust gas sensor provides the fuel system control unit constant feedback, enabling the unit to adjust the mixture to provide the best possible conditions for the converter to operate.

7 The sensor's tip is sensitive to oxygen, and sends the control unit a varying voltage depending on the amount of oxygen in the exhaust gases; if the inlet air/fuel mixture is too rich, the sensor sends a high-voltage signal. The voltage falls as the mixture weakens. Peak conversion efficiency of all major pollutants occurs if the inlet air/fuel mixture is maintained at the chemically-correct ratio for the complete combustion of petrol - 14.7 parts (by weight) of air to 1 part of fuel (the "stoichiometric" ratio). The sensor output voltage alters in a large step at this point, the control unit using the signal change as a reference point, and correcting the inlet air/fuel mixture accordingly by altering the fuel injector pulse width (injector opening time). On later models, the sensor has a built-in heating element (controlled by the control unit), to quickly bring the sensor's tip to an efficient operating temperature.

Evaporative emissions control system

8 To minimise the escape of unburned hydrocarbons into the atmosphere, an evaporative emissions control system is fitted to models with a catalytic converter. The fuel tank filler cap is sealed, and a carbon canister collects the petrol vapours generated in the tank (fuel-injected models) or tank and carburettor float chamber (carburettor models) when the car is parked. It stores them until the vapours can be cleared into the inlet tract when the engine is running.

9 The system is controlled by vacuum in the inlet manifold sensed near the throttle valve, and a control solenoid valve on models fitted with EGR. A constant purge line with a calibrated orifice allows a small proportion of vapour to be drawn into the inlet manifold at all times the engine is running.

10 To ensure that the engine runs correctly when it is cold and/or idling, and to protect the catalytic converter from the effects of an over-rich mixture, the solenoid valve is not opened by the control unit until the engine has warmed up and is under load. Once these conditions are met, the valve solenoid is modulated on and off to allow the stored vapour to pass into the inlet manifold.

Exhaust gas recirculation (EGR) system

11 This system reduces the emission of certain pollutants produced in high temperature areas of the combustion chambers. This is achieved by taking some of the (inert) exhaust gases from the exhaust manifold and recirculating them back into the inlet manifold, via a pipe linking the two. The exhaust gas recirculation (EGR) valve is fitted to the inlet manifold end of the pipe.

12 On carburettor models, the system is controlled by the thermal vacuum valve (TVV) and the back-pressure transducer (BPT) valve. When the engine is cold, the vacuum supply to the EGR valve is cut, and the valve remains closed. When the engine reaches operating temperature, the valve opens, allowing the vacuum supply to act on the EGR valve, via the BPT valve. The BPT valve is sensitive to the exhaust gas back pressure, and regulates the EGR valve on and off accordingly. When the back pressure is high, the BPT valve closes, allowing the vacuum supply to act on the EGR valve, opening the valve. When the back pressure drops, the BPT valve opens, cutting off the vacuum supply to the EGR valve, and so closing the valve.

13 On fuel-injected models, the system is controlled by the ECCS control unit, via a solenoid valve and the back-pressure transducer (BPT) valve; the solenoid valve also operates the evaporative emissions control system. When the engine is cold, the ECCS control unit keeps the solenoid valve closed, cutting off the vacuum supply to the EGR valve. When the engine reaches operating temperature, the ECCS control unit opens the solenoid valve, allowing the vacuum supply to act on the EGR valve, via the BPT valve **(see illustration)**. The BPT valve is sensitive to the exhaust gas back pressure, and regulates the EGR valve on and off accordingly. When the back pressure is high, the BPT valve closes, allowing the vacuum supply to act on the EGR valve, opening the valve. When the back pressure drops, the BPT valve opens, cutting off the vacuum supply to the EGR valve, and so closing the valve.

Air induction system

14 The air induction system reduces emissions of unburned hydrocarbon particles (HC) and carbon monoxide (CO) by passing filtered air directly into the exhaust manifold, so that a considerable proportion of these substances remaining in the exhaust gases after combustion are burned up in the manifold before reaching the catalytic converter. The system consists of the air induction valve (AIV) and a solenoid valve, and is controlled by the ECCS control unit.

15 To ensure that the engine runs correctly when it is cold and/or idling, the solenoid valve is not opened by the control unit until the engine has warmed up and is under load. When both these conditions are met, the valve solenoid is then modulated on and off to allow the fresh, filtered air to enter the exhaust manifold. The system functions by using the pressure variations in the exhaust gases to draw air through from the filter housing, so that there is no need for a separate air pump. The AIV only allows gases to flow only one way, so that there is no risk of hot exhaust gases flowing back into the filter.

1.13 EGR system back-pressure transducer (BPT)

Idle compensator system

16 The idle compensator system prevents the idle mixture becoming excessively rich at high engine temperatures. This is achieved by supplying additional air into the inlet manifold when the engine temperature is high. The system consists solely of the idle compensator valve which is fitted to the air cleaner housing.

17 The compensator valve has a bi-metallic strip which is sensitive to temperature. At low temperatures, the valve is closed. As the temperature in the air cleaner housing increases, the bi-metallic strip in the valve deforms, and the valve gradually opens. This allows a charge of fresh, filtered air from the air cleaner housing to enter the manifold, and so weakens the idle mixture. Some models are fitted with two compensator valves.

Dashpot

18 The dashpot is fitted to reduce the amount of unburnt hydrocarbons in the exhaust gases on the overrun. It does this by preventing the throttle valve from being snapped shut, such as when the driver lifts off suddenly at high engine speeds. The dashpot acts as a damper, and slowly closes throttle valve during its final stages. This reduces the amount of unburnt hydrocarbons in the exhaust gases by preventing the excessively-high inlet manifold vacuum which would otherwise draw unburnt fuel into the exhaust.

2.4 Carbon canister hose union identification - carburettor models
For A, B and C, refer to text

2 Emission control systems - testing and component renewal

Note: *Refer to Section 1 for information on which systems are fitted to each relevant model.*

Crankcase emissions control

1 This system requires no attention, other than to check that the hose(s) are clear and undamaged, and to renew the PCV filter (where fitted) at the intervals given in Chapter 1.

Evaporative emissions control system

Testing - carburettor models

2 If the system is thought to be faulty, disconnect the hoses from the carbon canister and thermal vacuum valve (TVV), and check that they are clear by blowing through them.

3 To check the TVV, which is screwed into the right-hand end of the inlet manifold, with the engine cold, disconnect both hoses from the valve. Connect a length of hose to one of the valve ports, and blow down it; the valve should be closed to the passage of air. Start the engine and warm it up to normal operating temperature. With the engine warm, again blow down the valve ports; the valve should now be open, and allow air to pass freely. If the valve does not perform as expected, it is faulty and must be renewed.

4 The carbon canister and associated valves can be tested as follows **(see illustration)**. The canister is located in the left-hand rear corner of the engine compartment.

5 Trace hose "A" back from the canister, and disconnect it from the T-piece connector. Start the engine and suck on the hose; there should be no sign of leakage, and the engine speed should increase slightly. Reconnect the hose to the T-piece.

6 Trace hose "C" back from the canister, and disconnect it from the carburettor float chamber. Start the engine and blow down the hose; there should be no sign of leakage. Reconnect the hose to the carburettor.

7 Trace hose "B" back from the canister, and disconnect it from the inlet manifold. With the engine stopped, blow and suck on the hose; there should be no sign of leakage. Reconnect the hose to the manifold.

8 If any trace of leakage is found whilst performing the checks described in paragraphs 5 to 7, the canister and valve assembly is faulty, and must be renewed.

Testing - fuel-injected models

9 If the system is thought to be faulty, disconnect the hoses from the carbon canister and solenoid control valve, and check that they are clear by blowing through them. The canister is located in the left-hand rear corner of the engine compartment, and the solenoid valve is mounted onto the rear of the inlet manifold.

2.10 Carbon canister hose union identification - fuel injected models
For A and B, refer to text

2.13 Evaporative emission control system solenoid valve test details - fuel-injected models
For A, B and C, refer to text

10 To check the canister, disconnect the hoses from the canister (see illustration), and blow down port "A" of the canister; there should be no sign of leakage. Blow down each of the ports "B" in turn. Both ports should be clear, and should freely pass air. If the checks do not give the expected results, the canister and valve assembly is faulty and must be renewed.

11 The solenoid valve can be checked as follows, referring to illustration 2.13. If necessary, remove the valve as described later to improve access.

12 Blow down port "A", and check that no air flows out of port "B", but that air flows out of port "C".

13 Connect a fused 12-volt supply to the solenoid valve as shown (see illustration). With the voltage applied, blow down port "A", and check that air passes through the valve and flows out of port "B" but not out of port "C".

14 If the solenoid valve does not perform as expected, it is faulty and must be renewed.

Carbon canister - renewal

15 The carbon canister is located on the left-hand rear of the engine compartment (see illustration).

2.15 Carbon canister assembly - fuel-injected models

16 Make a note of the correct fitted location of each hose on the canister. To avoid the possibility of connecting the hoses incorrectly on refitting, make identification marks between each hose and its canister union.

17 Release the retaining clips (where fitted) and disconnect the hoses from the top of the canister.

18 Free the canister from its mounting bracket, and remove it from the engine compartment.

19 Refitting is a reverse of the removal procedure, ensuring that the hoses are correctly reconnected.

Thermal vacuum valve (TVV) renewal - carburettor models

20 The thermal vacuum valve (TVV) is screwed into the right-hand end of the inlet manifold (see illustration). The engine and manifold should be cold before removing the valve.

21 Either partially drain the cooling system (as described in Chapter 1) to just below the level of the valve, or have ready a suitable plug which can be used to plug the valve aperture in the manifold whilst it is removed. If a plug is used, take great care not to damage the manifold, and do not use anything which will allow foreign matter to enter the cooling system.

22 Disconnect both hoses from the valve.

23 Carefully unscrew the valve from the manifold, and recover the sealing ring (where applicable).

24 Refitting is the reverse of removal, using a new sealing ring (where fitted). If a sealing ring was not fitted to the valve, apply a smear of sealing compound to its threads prior to refitting.

Solenoid control valve renewal

25 The solenoid control valve is mounted onto the rear of the inlet manifold. To improve access, remove the air cleaner housing (see Section 2).

26 To renew the solenoid valve, disconnect the battery negative terminal, then depress the retaining clip and disconnect the wiring connector from the valve.

27 Make a note of the correct fitted location of each hose on the valve. To avoid the possibility of connecting the hoses incorrectly on refitting, make identification marks between each hose and its valve union.

28 Release the retaining clips (where fitted) then disconnect the hoses from the valve, and free the valve from its mounting bracket.

29 Refitting is a reverse of the removal procedure, ensuring that the hoses are correctly reconnected.

Exhaust gas recirculation (EGR) system

Testing - carburettor models

30 If the system is thought to be faulty, disconnect the hoses from the exhaust gas recirculation (EGR) valve, the back-pressure transducer (BPT) valve and thermal vacuum valve (TVV), and check that they are clear by blowing through them. If all is well, reconnect all hoses.

31 The thermal vacuum valve can be checked as described in paragraph 3.

2.20 On carburettor models, the TVV valve (arrowed) is screwed into the right-hand end of the inlet manifold

4C

2.35 EGR valve - fuel injection model (other models similar)

2.39 BPT valve details - carburettor model (other models similar)
1 Retaining screws   2 Vacuum pipes

32 To check the operation of the EGR valve, disconnect the vacuum hose from the top of the valve, and fit a length of hose to the valve union. Suck on the hose end; check that the valve diaphragm is pulled up, and returns quickly when the vacuum is released. This can be checked by placing a finger lightly against the underside of the valve where the movement of the diaphragm can be felt. If the valve operation is sticky or the diaphragm does not move at all, the EGR valve must be renewed.

33 If the TVV is known to be operating correctly, the BPT valve can be checked as follows. Warm the engine up to normal operating temperature, and disconnect the vacuum hose from the EGR valve. Place a finger over the end of the disconnected hose, and rev the engine in short bursts. As the engine speed (and exhaust gas pressure) increases, a vacuum should be felt in the pipe. As the engine speed falls, the vacuum should be switched off by the BPT valve. If this is not the case, the BPT valve is faulty and should be renewed.

Testing - fuel-injected models

34 The system can be tested as described in the previous sub-section, ignoring the information about the TVV. Instead of the TVV, a solenoid control valve is fitted. The solenoid valve is the same valve as controls the evaporative emissions control system, and can be tested as described earlier in this Section.

Exhaust gas recirculation (EGR) valve - renewal

35 Disconnect the vacuum hose from the EGR valve, which is mounted on the left-hand end of the inlet manifold **(see illustration)**. Where necessary, remove the air cleaner housing to improve access to the valve. On some models, access can be further improved by first removing the BPT valve (see below).

36 Slacken the union nuts, and disconnect the EGR pipe and BPT valve pipe from the EGR valve.

37 Unscrew the two retaining nuts/bolts and washers, and remove the valve from the manifold. Remove the gasket and discard it.

38 Refitting is the reverse of removal, using a new gasket.

Back-pressure transducer (BPT) valve - renewal

39 The BPT valve is mounted on the left-hand side of the inlet manifold **(see illustration)**. Where necessary, remove the air cleaner housing to improve access to the valve.

40 Disconnect both vacuum hoses from the top of the valve.

41 Undo the two retaining bolts and remove the valve from the manifold, disconnecting it from the exhaust gas pipe.

42 Refitting is the reverse of removal

Thermal vacuum valve renewal - carburettor models

43 The procedure is described earlier in this Section.

Solenoid control valve renewal - fuel-injected models

44 The procedure is described earlier in this Section.

Exhaust emissions control system

Testing - carburettor models

45 Adjust the idle mixture (exhaust gas CO content) as described in Chapter 1.

46 Remove the fusebox cover, to gain access to the diagnostic connector which is clipped to the base of the fusebox.

47 Using multi-meter set to its voltage function, connect the probes of the meter to the check connector as shown **(see illustration)**

48 Start the engine, raise the engine speed to approximately 2000 rpm, and hold it there for approximately 2 minutes whilst observing the meter. If the exhaust gas sensor is functioning correctly, the meter reading should switch from 0 volts to approximately 12 volts at least 5 times every 10 seconds. If not, the sensor is probably faulty. A more detailed check of the sensor and catalytic converter can be carried out by a Nissan dealer.

2.47 On carburettor models with a catalyst, connect the multi-meter to the fusebox check connector as shown, and test the exhaust gas sensor as described in text

2.51a Disconnect the exhaust gas sensor wiring . . .

2.51b . . . and release it from the clip

2.52 The exhaust gas sensor is screwed into the manifold

Testing - fuel-injected models

49 If the CO level at the tailpipe is too high, the operation of the exhaust gas sensor should be tested using the ECCS control unit self-diagnosis facility as described in Chapter 4B. Detailed testing of the sensor and catalytic converter must be left to a Nissan dealer.

Catalytic converter - renewal

50 Refer to Part A or B of this Chapter (as applicable).

Exhaust gas sensor - renewal

Note: *The exhaust gas sensor is delicate, and it will not work if it is dropped or knocked, if its power supply is disrupted, or if any cleaning materials are used on it.*

51 Trace the wiring back from the exhaust gas sensor, which is screwed into the exhaust manifold. Disconnect the wiring connector, and free the wiring from any relevant retaining clips or ties (see illustrations).

52 Unscrew the sensor, and remove it along with its sealing washer (see illustration).

53 Refitting is a reverse of the removal procedure, using a new sealing washer. Prior to installing the sensor, apply a smear of high-temperature grease to the sensor threads.

Ensure that the sensor is securely tightened. Check that the wiring is correctly routed, and in no danger of contacting either the exhaust system or the engine.

Air induction system

Testing

54 If the system is thought to be faulty, disconnect the hoses from the air induction solenoid control valve and the air induction valve (AIV), and check that they are clear by blowing through them. The solenoid valve is located on the left-hand end of the inlet manifold, and the air induction valve (AIV) is mounted on the left-hand suspension mounting turret.

55 The solenoid valve can be checked as follows. If preferred, remove the valve as described in paragraphs 69 to 73 to improve access.

56 Connect a 12-volt supply to the solenoid valve as shown (see illustration). Blow down port "A" - air should pass through the valve, and flow out of port "B". Blow down port "C", and check that no air flows through the valve.

57 If the solenoid valve does not perform as expected, it is faulty and must be renewed.

58 To check the AIV, first remove it as described in paragraphs 68 and 69 then check it as follows.

59 Blow down port "B" (see illustration), and check that no air passes through the valve. Apply a vacuum to port "A" of the valve, then blow down port "B" - air should pass through the valve, and flow out of port "C". Blow down port "C", and check that no air passes through the valve, both with and without a vacuum applied to port "A".

60 If the AIV does not perform as expected, it is faulty and must be renewed.

Air induction solenoid control valve - renewal

61 The solenoid control valve is mounted on the left-hand end of the inlet manifold.

62 To renew the solenoid valve, disconnect the battery negative terminal. then depress the retaining clip and disconnect the wiring connector from the valve.

63 Make a note of the correct fitted location of each hose on the valve. To avoid the possibility of connecting the hoses incorrectly on refitting, make identification marks between each hose and its valve union.

4C

2.56 Air induction solenoid valve test details - carburettor models with a catalyst

2.59 Air induction valve port details - carburettor catalyst models

A *Vacuum pipe from solenoid valve*

B *From air cleaner housing*
C *To exhaust manifold*

64 Release the retaining clips (where fitted), and disconnect the hoses from the valve.
65 Free the valve from its mounting bracket, and remove it from the engine compartment.
66 Refitting is a reverse of the removal procedure, ensuring that the hoses are correctly reconnected.

Air induction valve (AIV) - renewal

67 The AIV is mounted on the left-hand suspension turret.
68 To renew the valve, slacken the retaining clips (where fitted), and disconnect the hoses from the valve **(see illustration)**.
69 Undo the mounting bolts and remove the valve from the engine compartment.
70 Refitting is the reverse of removal, ensuring that the hoses are correctly reconnected and securely retained by their clips.

Idle compensator system

Testing

71 Remove the air cleaner housing lid and filter as described in Chapter 1 for access to the valve **(see illustration)**.
72 The operation of the valve(s) can be checked using a thermometer and a hairdryer. Position the thermometer as close as possible to the valve, then gently heat the valve using the hairdryer. Where one valve is fitted, the valve should remain closed below 55°C (131°F), start to open between 55° and 65°C (131° and 149°F), and be fully open at 65°C (149°F). Where two valves are fitted, the first one should operate as already described and the second one should remain closed below 65°C (149°F), start to open between 65° and 75°C (149° and 167°F), and be fully open at 75°C (167°F). Allow the valve to cool, and check that it closes fully.
73 If the valve does not open and close as specified; it is faulty and must be renewed.

Idle compensator valve - renewal

74 Remove the air cleaner filter element as described in Chapter 1.

75 Disconnect the hose from the base of the valve, then undo the retaining screws and remove it from the air cleaner housing.
76 Refitting is the reverse of removal.

Dashpot

Testing

77 Push the dashpot rod into the dashpot, making sure that the rod enters the dashpot slowly, then release the rod and check that it returns quickly. If not, the dashpot must be renewed.

Dashpot - renewal

78 On carburettor models, undo the two retaining screws, and remove the dashpot assembly from the side of the carburettor.
79 On fuel-injected models, unscrew the retaining nut, and lift the dashpot out of its throttle body mounting bracket.
80 Refitting is the reverse of removal. On completion, start the engine and warm it up to normal operating temperature. With the engine idling, have an assistant slowly depress the accelerator pedal, while you observe the engine speed. Note the engine speed at which the adjustment screw comes into contact with the end of the dashpot rod. This should happen at 1900 ± 200 rpm. If adjustment is necessary, slacken the locknut and rotate the screw as required. Recheck the dashpot contact speed, tightening the locknut securely when the screw is correctly adjusted.

3 Catalytic converter - general information and precautions

The catalytic converter is a reliable and simple device which needs no maintenance in itself, but there are some facts of which an owner should be aware if the converter is to function properly for its full service life.
a) DO NOT use leaded petrol in a car with a catalytic converter - the lead will coat the

precious metals, reducing their converting efficiency, and will eventually destroy the converter.
b) Always keep the ignition and fuel systems well-maintained in accordance with the manufacturer's schedule (see Chapter 1).
c) If the engine develops a misfire, do not drive the car at all (or at least as little as possible) until the fault is cured.
d) DO NOT push- or tow-start the car - this will soak the catalytic converter in unburned fuel, causing it to overheat when the engine does start.
e) DO NOT switch off the ignition at high engine speeds - ie do not "blip" the throttle immediately before switching off.
f) DO NOT use fuel or engine oil additives - these may contain substances harmful to the catalytic converter.
g) DO NOT continue to use the car if the engine burns oil to the extent of leaving a visible trail of blue smoke.
h) Remember that the catalytic converter operates at very high temperatures. DO NOT, therefore, park the car in dry undergrowth, over long grass, or over piles of dead leaves, after a long run.
i) Remember that the catalytic converter is FRAGILE - do not strike it with tools during servicing work.
j) In some cases, a sulphurous smell (like that of rotten eggs) may be noticed from the exhaust. This is common to many catalytic converter-equipped cars when new - once the car has covered a few thousand miles, the problem should disappear.
k) The catalytic converter, used on a well-maintained and well-driven car, should last for between 50 000 and 100 000 miles, but if the converter is no longer effective, it must be renewed.

2.68 Air induction valve (AIV) is secured to the body by two bolts (arrowed)

2.71 Idle compensator valve (arrowed) is mounted onto the base of the air cleaner housing

Chapter 5 Part A:
Starting and charging systems

Contents

Degrees of difficulty

Easy, suitable for novice with little experience		Fairly easy, suitable for beginner with some experience		Fairly difficult, suitable for competent DIY mechanic		Difficult, suitable for experienced DIY mechanic		Very difficult, suitable for expert DIY or professional	
									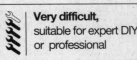

Specifications

General

System type	12 volt, negative earth

Battery

Capacity	60 or 65 amp/hour

Alternator

Type	Hitachi or Mitsubishi
Rating:	
Carburettor models	65 amp
Fuel injection models	70 amp
Minimum brush length:	
Hitachi	6.0 mm
Mitsubishi	8.0 mm

Starter motor

Type	Hitachi or Mitsubishi - pre-engaged

Torque wrench setting	Nm	lbf ft
Alternator lower mounting bolt	44	33
Alternator mounting bracket to block	44	33
Alternator upper adjustment link:		
To engine	19	14
To alternator	19	14
Starter motor mounting bolts	36	27
Inlet manifold support bracket	26	19

5A

---

1 General information and precautions

General information

The engine electrical system consists mainly of the charging and starting systems. Because of their engine-related functions, these components are covered separately from the body electrical devices such as the lights, instruments, etc (which are covered in Chapter 12). The ignition system is described in Part B of this Chapter.

The electrical system is of 12-volt negative earth type.

The battery may be of low-maintenance or "maintenance-free" (sealed for life) type, and is charged by the alternator, which is belt-driven from the crankshaft pulley. The starter motor is of the pre-engaged type, incorporating an integral solenoid. On starting, the solenoid moves the drive pinion into engagement with the flywheel ring gear before the starter motor is energised. Once the engine has started, a one-way clutch prevents the motor armature being driven by the engine until the pinion disengages from the flywheel. On some models the starter motor has reduction gears.

Precautions

Further details of the various systems are given in the relevant Sections of this Chapter. While some repair procedures are given, the usual course of action is to renew the component concerned. The owner whose interest extends beyond mere component renewal should obtain a copy of the "*Automobile Electrical & Electronic Systems Manual*", available from the publishers of this manual.

It is necessary to take extra care when working on the electrical system, to avoid damage to semi-conductor devices (diodes and transistors), and to avoid the risk of personal injury. In addition to the precautions given in "*Safety first!*", observe the following when working on the system:

Always remove rings, watches, etc before working on the electrical system. Even with the battery disconnected, capacitive discharge could occur if a component's live terminal is earthed through a metal object. This could cause a shock or nasty burn.

Do not reverse the battery connections. Components such as the alternator, ECCS control unit (where applicable), or any other components having semi-conductor circuitry, could be irreparably damaged.

If the engine is being started using jump leads and a slave battery, connect the batteries *positive-to-positive* and *negative-to-negative* (see "*Jump starting*"). This also applies when connecting a battery charger.

Never disconnect the battery terminals, the alternator, any electrical wiring, or any test instruments, when the engine is running.

Do not allow the engine to turn the alternator when the alternator is not connected.

Never "test" for alternator output by "flashing" the output lead to earth.

Never use an ohmmeter of the type incorporating a hand-cranked generator for circuit or continuity testing.

Always ensure that the battery negative lead is disconnected when working on the electrical system.

Before using electric-arc welding equipment on the car, disconnect the battery, alternator and components such as electronic control units, to protect them from the risk of damage.

Certain radio/cassette units fitted as standard equipment by Nissan have a built-in security code, to deter thieves. If the power source to the unit is cut, the anti-theft system will activate. Even if the power source is immediately reconnected, the radio/cassette unit will not function until the correct security code has been entered. Therefore, if you do not know the correct security code for the radio/cassette unit, **do not** disconnect the battery negative terminal, or remove the radio/cassette unit from the vehicle. Refer to your Nissan dealer for further information on whether the unit fitted to your car has a security code.

2 Battery - testing and charging

Standard and low-maintenance battery - testing

1 If the vehicle covers a small annual mileage, it is worthwhile checking the specific gravity of the electrolyte every three months, to determine the state of charge of the battery. Use a hydrometer to make the check, and compare the results with the following table:

	Above 25°C	Below 25°C
Fully-charged	1.21 to 1.23	1.27 to 1.29
70% charged	1.17 to 1.19	1.23 to 1.25
Fully-discharged	1.05 to 1.07	1.11 to 1.13

Note that the specific gravity readings assume an electrolyte temperature of 15°C (60°F); for every 10°C (48°F) below 15°C (60°F), subtract 0.007. For every 10°C (48°F) above 15°C (60°F), add 0.007.

2 If the battery condition is suspect, first check the specific gravity of electrolyte in each cell. A variation of 0.040 or more between any cells indicates loss of electrolyte, or deterioration of the internal plates.

3 If the specific gravity variation is 0.040 or more, the battery should be renewed. If the cell variation is satisfactory but the battery is discharged, it should be charged as described later in this Section.

Maintenance-free battery - testing

4 In cases where a "sealed for life" maintenance-free battery is fitted, topping-up and testing of the electrolyte in each cell is not possible. The condition of the battery can therefore only be tested using a battery condition indicator or a voltmeter.

5 Certain models may be fitted with a maintenance-free battery, with a built-in charge condition indicator. The indicator is located in the top of the battery casing, and indicates the condition of the battery from its colour. If the indicator shows green, then the battery is in a good state of charge. If the indicator turns darker, eventually to black, then the battery requires charging, as described later in this Section. If the indicator shows clear/yellow, then the electrolyte level in the battery is too low to allow further use, and the battery should be renewed. **Do not** attempt to charge, load or jump start a battery when the indicator shows clear/yellow.

6 If testing the battery using a voltmeter, connect the voltmeter across the battery, and compare the result with those given in the Specifications under "charge condition". The test is only accurate if the battery has not been subjected to any kind of charge for the previous six hours. If this is not the case, switch on the headlights for 30 seconds, then wait four to five minutes before testing the battery after switching off the headlights. All other electrical circuits must be switched off,

so check that the doors and tailgate are fully shut when making the test.

7 If the voltage reading is less than 12.2 volts, then the battery is discharged, whilst a reading of 12.2 to 12.4 volts indicates a partially-discharged condition.

8 If the battery is to be charged, remove it from the vehicle and charge it as described later in this Section.

Standard and low-maintenance battery - charging

Note: *The following is intended as a guide only. Always refer to the manufacturer's recommendations (often printed on a label attached to the battery) before charging a battery.*

9 Charge the battery at a rate equivalent to 10% of the battery capacity (eg for a 45 Ah battery charge at 4.5 A) and continue to charge the battery at this rate until no further rise in specific gravity is noted over a four-hour period.

10 Alternatively, a trickle charger charging at the rate of 1.5 amps can safely be used overnight.

11 Specially rapid "boost" charges which are claimed to restore the power of the battery in 1 to 2 hours are not recommended, as they can cause serious damage to the battery plates through overheating.

12 While charging the battery, note that the temperature of the electrolyte should never exceed 37.8°C (100°F).

Maintenance-free battery - charging

Note: *The following is intended as a guide only. Always refer to the manufacturer's recommendations (often printed on a label attached to the battery) before charging a battery.*

13 This battery type takes considerably longer to fully recharge than the standard type, the time taken being dependent on the extent of discharge, but it can take anything up to three days.

14 A constant-voltage type charger is required, to be set, when connected, to 13.9 to 14.9 volts, with a charger current below 25 amps. Using this method, the battery should be usable within three hours, giving a voltage reading of 12.5 volts, but this is for a partially-discharged battery and, as mentioned, full charging can take far longer.

15 If the battery is to be charged from a fully-discharged state (condition reading less than 12.2 volts), have it recharged by your Nissan dealer or local automotive electrician, as the charge rate is higher, and constant supervision during charging is necessary.

3.2 Loosen the nuts (arrowed) to disconnect the battery terminals

3 Battery - removal and refitting

Removal

Note: *If the vehicle has a security coded radio, check that you have a copy of the code number before disconnecting the battery cable; refer to Chapter 12 for details.*

1 The battery is located on the left-hand side of the engine compartment.

2 Loosen the nuts and disconnect both cables from the battery terminals **(see illustration)**. Always disconnect the negative cable first and connect it up last.

3 Unscrew the nuts and remove the hold-down clamp from the top of the battery. Unhook the clamp rods from the lower bracket.

4 Lift the battery out of the engine compartment and, if necessary, remove the plastic battery tray. If required, the battery mounting bracket can also be unbolted and removed from the engine compartment.

Refitting

5 Refitting is a reversal of removal, but smear petroleum jelly on the terminals when reconnecting the leads, and always reconnect the positive lead first, and the negative lead last.

4 Alternator/charging system - testing in vehicle

Note: *Refer to the warnings given in "Safety first!" and in Section 1 of this Chapter before starting work.*

1 If the ignition warning light fails to illuminate when the ignition is switched on, first check the alternator wiring connections for security. If satisfactory, check that the warning light bulb has not blown, and that the bulbholder is secure in its location in the instrument panel. If the light still fails to come on, check the continuity of the warning light feed wire from

the alternator to the bulbholder. If all is satisfactory, the alternator is at fault, and should be taken to an auto-electrician for testing and repair.

2 If the ignition warning light illuminates when the engine is running, stop the engine and check that the drivebelt is correctly tensioned (see Chapter 2A), and that the alternator connections are secure. If all is so far satisfactory the alternator should be renewed, or taken to an auto-electrician for testing and repair.

3 If the alternator output is suspect, even though the warning light functions correctly, the regulated voltage may be checked as follows.

4 Connect a voltmeter across the battery terminals, and start the engine.

5 Increase the engine speed until the voltmeter reading remains steady; the reading should be approximately 12 to 13 volts, and no more than 14 volts.

6 Switch on as many electrical accessories (eg, the headlights, heated rear window and heater blower) as possible, and check that the alternator maintains the regulated voltage at around 13 to 14 volts.

7 If the regulated voltage is not as stated, this may be due to worn brushes, weak brush springs, a faulty voltage regulator, a faulty diode, a severed phase winding, or worn or damaged slip-rings. The alternator should taken to an auto-electrician for testing and repair.

5 Alternator - removal and refitting

Removal

1 Disconnect the battery negative lead.

2 Slacken the auxiliary drivebelt as described in Chapter 1, and disengage it from the alternator pulley.

3 Remove the rubber covers (where fitted) from the alternator terminals, then unscrew the retaining nut(s) and disconnect the wiring from the rear of the alternator. Where necessary, also undo the retaining screw and disconnect the earth lead.

4 Unscrew the alternator upper and lower mounting bolts and washers, then manoeuvre the alternator away from its mounting brackets and out of position. Recover the spacer (where fitted) from between the alternator and the adjuster strap.

Refitting

5 Refitting is a reversal of removal, tensioning the auxiliary drivebelt as described in Chapter 1, and ensuring that the alternator mountings are securely tightened.

6 Alternator brushes and regulator - inspection and renewal

A number of different types of alternator have been fitted to Sunny models, and the availability of spares is limited. If it is suspected that the brushes require renewal, consult a Nissan dealer or an automotive electrical specialist for advice. Most specialists will be able to supply and fit new brushes at reasonable cost.

7 Starting system - testing

Note: *Refer to the precautions given in "Safety first!" and in Section 1 of this Chapter before starting work.*

1 If the starter motor fails to operate when the ignition key is turned to the appropriate position, the following possible causes may be to blame:

a) The battery is faulty.

b) The electrical connections between the switch, solenoid, battery and starter motor are somewhere failing to pass the necessary current from the battery through the starter to earth.

c) The solenoid is faulty.

d) The starter motor is mechanically or electrically defective.

2 To check the battery, switch on the headlights. If they dim after a few seconds, this indicates that the battery is discharged - recharge (see Section 3) or renew the battery. If the headlights glow brightly, operate the ignition switch and observe the lights. If they dim, then this indicates that current is reaching the starter motor, therefore the fault must lie in the starter motor. If the lights continue to glow brightly (and no clicking sound can be heard from the starter motor solenoid), this indicates that there is a fault in the circuit or solenoid - see following paragraphs. If the starter motor turns slowly when operated, but the battery is in good condition, then this indicates that either the starter motor is faulty, or there is considerable resistance somewhere in the circuit.

3 If a fault in the circuit is suspected, disconnect the battery leads (including the earth connection to the body), the starter/solenoid wiring and the engine/transmission earth strap. Thoroughly clean the connections, reconnect the leads and wiring, then use a voltmeter or test light to check that full battery voltage is available at the battery positive lead connection to the solenoid, and that the earth is sound. Smear petroleum jelly around the battery terminals to prevent corrosion - corroded connections are amongst the most frequent causes of electrical system faults.

5A

4 If the battery and all connections are in good condition, check the circuit by disconnecting the wire from the solenoid blade terminal. Connect a voltmeter or test light between the wire end and a good earth (such as the battery negative terminal), and check that the wire is live when the ignition switch is turned to the "start" position. If it is, then the circuit is sound - if not, the circuit wiring can be checked as described in Chapter 12.

5 The solenoid contacts can be checked by connecting a voltmeter or test light between the battery positive feed connection on the starter side of the solenoid, and earth. When the ignition switch is turned to the "start" position, there should be a reading or lighted bulb, as applicable. If there is no reading or lighted bulb, the solenoid is faulty and should be renewed.

6 If the circuit and solenoid are proved sound, the fault must lie in the starter motor. Remove it and have it tested by an automotive electrician. It may be possible to have the starter motor overhauled by a specialist, but check on the availability and cost of spares before proceeding, as it may prove more economical to obtain a new or exchange motor.

8 Starter motor - removal and refitting

Removal

1 Disconnect the battery negative lead.
2 So that access to the motor can be gained both from above and below, firmly apply the handbrake, then jack up the front of the vehicle and support it on axle stands (see "*Jacking and Vehicle Support*").
3 To improve access to the starter motor, undo the bolts securing the inlet manifold support bracket(s), and move the bracket(s) clear of the starter motor. Note that it is not necessary to remove the brackets completely.
4 Slacken and remove the retaining nut, and disconnect the main battery cable from the starter motor solenoid. Also disconnect the wiring connector from the solenoid **(see illustration)**.
5 Unscrew the starter motor mounting bolts, supporting the motor as the bolts are withdrawn, and manoeuvre the starter motor out from underneath the engine. To provide additional working room, turn the wheels on full lock.

Refitting

6 Refitting is a reversal of removal.

9 Oil pressure warning light switch - removal and refitting

Removal

1 The switch is located at the rear of the cylinder block, towards its right-hand end. Access to the switch is improved if the vehicle is jacked up and supported on axle stands (see "*Jacking and Vehicle Support*"), so that the switch can be reached from underneath.
2 Disconnect the battery negative lead.
3 Remove the protective sleeve from the wiring plug (where applicable), then disconnect the wiring from the switch.
4 Unscrew the switch and recover the sealing washer (where fitted). Be prepared for oil spillage. If the switch is to be left removed from the engine for any length of time, plug the hole to prevent excessive oil loss.

Refitting

5 Where the switch was fitted with a sealing washer, examine the sealing washer for signs of damage or deterioration, and if necessary renew it. Where no sealing washer was fitted, clean the switch and apply a smear of sealant to its threads.
6 Refit the switch, tightening it securely, and reconnect the wiring connector.
7 Lower the vehicle to the ground, then check and if necessary, top-up the engine oil as described in Chapter 1.

8.4 Disconnecting the wiring (arrowed) from the starter motor

Chapter 5 Part B:
Ignition system

Contents

Degrees of difficulty

Easy, suitable for novice with little experience		Fairly easy, suitable for beginner with some experience		Fairly difficult, suitable for competent DIY mechanic		Difficult, suitable for experienced DIY mechanic		Very difficult, suitable for expert DIY or professional	

Specifications

General

System type:
Carburettor non-catalyst models	Breakerless electronic ignition
Carburettor catalyst models	Breakerless electronic ignition controlled by ECC control unit
Fuel-injection models	Breakerless electronic ignition controlled by ECCS control unit
Firing order	1-3-4-2 (No 1 at timing chain end)

Ignition timing:
Carburettor models:	
GA14DS (vacuum/EGR boost hose disconnected)	0° ± 2° BTDC
GA14DS (vacuum/EGR boost hose connected)	10° ± 5° BTDC
GA16DS (vacuum/EGR boost hose disconnected)	2° ± 2° BTDC
GA16DS (vacuum/EGR boost hose connected)	10° ± 5° BTDC
Fuel-injected models	10° ± 2° BTDC

Ignition HT coil resistances (approximate):
Carburettor models:	
Primary windings	1.0 ohm
Secondary windings	10 000 ohms
Fuel-injected models (where applicable):	
Primary windings	2.0 ohm
Secondary windings	12 000 ohms

Torque wrench settings	Nm	lbf ft
Distributor mounting bolts	10	7

1 General information

Carburettor models without a catalytic converter

On these models, a breakerless electronic ignition system is used. The system comprises solely of the HT ignition coil and the distributor, both of which are mounted on the left-hand end of the cylinder head, the distributor being driven off the end of the exhaust camshaft.

The distributor contains a toothed reluctor mounted onto its shaft, and the IC ignition unit which is fixed to its body. The system operates as follows.

When the ignition is switched on but the engine is stationary, the IC ignition unit prevents current flowing through the ignition system primary (LT) circuit.

As the crankshaft rotates, the reluctor moves through the magnetic field created by the IC ignition unit. When the reluctor teeth are correctly positioned, a small AC voltage is created. The IC ignition unit uses this voltage to switch and complete the ignition system primary (LT) circuit.

As the reluctor teeth move out of alignment, the AC voltage changes, and the IC ignition unit switches again to interrupt the primary (LT) circuit. This causes a high voltage to be induced in the coil secondary (HT) windings, which then travels down the HT lead to the distributor and onto the relevant spark plug.

In addition to system components described above, the system has an ignition timing vacuum control. The system is controlled by one or two thermal vacuum valves (TVV) screwed into the right-hand end of the inlet manifold - non-catalyst models have one TVV and catalyst models have two TVV's. Each valve is fitted in the vacuum line to the distributor vacuum diaphragm and their purpose is to retard ignition timing during the engine warm-up period.

Carburettor models with a catalytic converter, and all fuel-injected models

On these models, the ignition system is integrated with the fuel system, to form a combined fuel/ignition system which is controlled by the ECC control unit (carburettor models) or ECCS control unit (fuel-injected models) (see the relevant Part of Chapter 4 for further information on the fuelling side of the system).

The distributor contains a crank angle sensor which informs the control unit of engine speed and crankshaft position. Based on this information, and the information received from its other sensors, the control unit then calculates the correct ignition timing setting, and switches the power transistor unit on and off accordingly. This causes a high voltage to be induced in the coil secondary (HT) windings (located inside the distributor), which then travels via the distributor rotor arm and HT leads to the relevant spark plug.

2 Ignition system - testing

Warning: Voltages produced by an electronic ignition system are considerably higher than those produced by conventional ignition systems. Extreme care must be taken when working on the system with the ignition switched on. Persons with surgically-implanted cardiac pacemaker devices should keep well clear of the ignition circuits, components and test equipment.

Carburettor models without a catalytic converter

Note: *Refer to the warning given in Section 1 before starting work. Always switch off the ignition before disconnecting or connecting any component, and when using a multi-meter to check resistances.*

General

1 The components of electronic ignition systems are normally very reliable; most faults are far more likely to be due to loose or dirty connections, or to "tracking" of HT voltage due to dirt, dampness or damaged insulation, than to the failure of any of the system's components. **Always** check all wiring thoroughly before condemning an electrical component, and work methodically to eliminate all other possibilities before deciding that a particular component is faulty.

2 The practice of checking for a spark by holding the live end of an HT lead a short distance away from the engine is **not** recommended; not only is there a high risk of a powerful electric shock, but the HT coil or power transistor unit will very likely be damaged. Similarly, **never** try to "diagnose" misfires by pulling off one HT lead at a time.

Engine will not start

3 If the engine either will not turn over at all, or only turns very slowly, check the battery and starter motor. Connect a voltmeter across the battery terminals (meter positive probe to battery positive terminal), then disconnect the ignition coil HT lead from the distributor cap and earth it. Note the voltage reading obtained while turning over the engine on the starter for (no more than) ten seconds. If the reading obtained is less than approximately 9.5 volts, first check the battery, starter motor and charging system as described in the relevant Sections of this Chapter.

4 If the engine turns over at normal speed but will not start, check the HT circuit by connecting a timing light (following the equipment manufacturer's instructions) and turning the engine over on the starter motor; if the light flashes, voltage is reaching the spark plugs, so these should be checked first. If the light does not flash, check the HT leads themselves, followed by the distributor cap, carbon brush and rotor arm using the information given in Chapter 1.

5 If there is a spark, check the carburettor, referring to Chapter 4A for further information.

6 If there is still no spark, check the voltage at the ignition HT coil "+" terminal; it should be the same as the battery voltage (ie, at least 11.7 volts). If the voltage at the coil is more than 1 volt less than that at the battery, check the feed back through the fusebox and ignition switch to the battery and its earth until the fault is found.

7 If the feed to the HT coil is sound, check the coil's primary and secondary winding resistance as described later in this Section; renew the coil if faulty, but be careful to check carefully the condition of the LT connections themselves before doing so, to ensure that the fault is not due to dirty or poorly-fastened connectors.

8 If the HT coil is in good condition, the fault is probably within the IC ignition unit. Testing of the unit should be entrusted to a Nissan dealer.

9 The ignition timing retard system thermal vacuum valve (TVV) can be checked as described for similar components in Part C of Chapter 4. Check the vacuum delay valve (VDV) by blowing through it from both sides of the valve. The valve should pass air freely when blown through from the distributor side of the valve, but resistance should be felt when air is blown through from the carburettor side of the valve; if not, renew the VDV. On refitting, ensure that the valve is installed the correct way round, with its brown side facing the carburettor.

Engine misfires

10 An irregular misfire suggests either a loose connection or intermittent fault on the primary circuit, or an HT fault on the coil side of the rotor arm.

11 With the ignition switched off, check carefully through the system, ensuring that all connections are clean and securely fastened. If the equipment is available, check the LT circuit as described above.

12 Check that the HT coil, the distributor cap and the HT leads are clean and dry. Check the leads themselves and the spark plugs (by substitution, if necessary), then check the distributor cap, carbon brush and rotor arm as described in Chapter 1.

13 Regular misfiring is almost certainly due to a fault in the distributor cap, HT leads or spark plugs. Use a timing light (paragraph 4 above) to check whether HT voltage is present at all leads.

14 If HT voltage is not present on any particular lead, the fault will be in that lead, or in the distributor cap. If HT is present on all leads, the fault will be in the spark plugs; check and renew them if there is any doubt about their condition.

15 If no HT is present, check the HT coil; its secondary windings may be breaking down under load.

Carburettor models with a catalytic converter, and all fuel-injected models

16 If a fault appears in the ignition system, first ensure that the fault is not due to a poor electrical connection or poor maintenance; ie, check that the air cleaner filter element is clean, that the spark plugs are in good condition and correctly gapped, and that the engine breather hoses are clear and undamaged, referring to Chapter 1 for further information. Also check that the accelerator cable is correctly adjusted, as described in the relevant Part of Chapter 4. If the engine is running very roughly, check the compression pressures and, where possible, the valve clearances, as described in the relevant Part of Chapter 2.

17 The only ignition system checks which can be carried out by the home mechanic are those described in Chapter 1. If necessary, the system wiring and wiring connectors can be checked as described in Chapter 12, ensuring that the control unit wiring connector(s) have first been disconnected.

18 On fuel-injected models, a quick check of the system can be carried out using the control unit self-diagnosis mode (see Chapter 4B, Section 11).

19 If the above checks fail to reveal the cause of the problem, the vehicle should be taken to a suitably-equipped Nissan dealer for testing.

3.2a Disconnect the HT lead . . .

3.2b . . . and wiring connector from the ignition coil . . .

3.3 . . . then undo the two bolts (arrowed) and remove the coil from its bracket

3 Ignition coil (non-catalyst carburettor models) - removal, testing and refitting

Note: *This Section applies to non-catalyst carburettor models only.*

Removal

1 The ignition coil is mounted on the left-hand end of the cylinder head. Prior to removal, disconnect the battery negative terminal.
2 Disconnect the HT lead from the coil, then depress the retaining clip and disconnect the coil wiring connector **(see illustrations)**.
3 Slacken and remove the retaining nut and bolt, and remove the coil from its mounting bracket on the cylinder head **(see illustration)**.

4.2a Remove the screws . . .

Testing

4 Testing of the coil consists of using a multimeter set to its resistance function, to check the primary (LT "+" to "-" terminals) and secondary (LT "+" to HT lead terminal) windings. Compare the results obtained to those given in the Specifications at the start of this Chapter. Note that the resistance of the coil windings will vary slightly according to the coil temperature - the results in the Specifications are approximate values for when the coil is at 20°C.
5 Check that there is no continuity between the HT lead terminal and the coil body.
6 If the coil is faulty, renew it.

Refitting

7 Refitting is a reversal of the relevant removal procedure, ensuring that the wiring connector and HT lead are securely reconnected.

4 Distributor - removal and refitting

Removal

1 Disconnect the battery negative terminal.
2 Unclip the cover (where fitted), then slacken and remove the distributor cap retaining screws. Remove the cap, position it clear of the distributor body, and recover the cap seal **(see illustrations)**.

3 Depress the retaining clip, and disconnect the wiring connector(s) from the distributor **(see illustration)**.
4 On non-catalyst carburettor models, disconnect the hose(s) from the vacuum diaphragm unit.
5 Check the cylinder head and distributor flange for alignment marks. If no marks are visible, using a scriber or suitable marker pen, mark the relationship of the distributor body to the cylinder head.
6 Unscrew and remove the two mounting bolts, and withdraw the distributor from the cylinder head **(see illustration)**. Remove the O-ring from the end of the distributor body and discard it; a new one must be used on refitting.

Refitting

7 Lubricate the new O-ring with a smear of engine oil, and fit it to the groove in the distributor body. Examine the distributor cap seal for wear or damage, and renew if necessary.
8 Align the distributor rotor shaft drive coupling key with the slots in the camshaft end, noting that the slots are offset to ensure that the distributor can only be fitted in one position. Carefully insert the distributor into the cylinder head, whilst rotating the rotor arm slightly to ensure that the coupling is correctly engaged **(see illustration)**.
9 Align the marks noted or made on removal, and install the distributor retaining bolts, tightening them lightly only **(see illustration)**.

5B

4.2b . . . and lift off the distributor cap

4.3 Disconnect the wiring from the distributor

4.6 Unscrewing the distributor mounting bolts

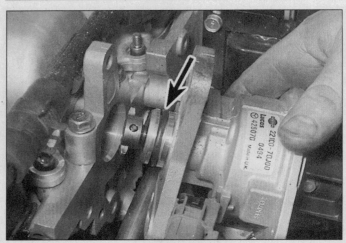

4.8 Fit a new O-ring (arrowed) and refit the distributor, aligning its drive coupling with the camshaft slot

4.9 Align the marks made prior to removal (arrowed), and refit the distributor mounting bolts

10 Ensure that the seal is correctly located in its groove, then refit the cap assembly to the distributor and tighten its retaining screws securely **(see illustrations)**. Fold the waterproof cover back over the distributor cap, ensuring that it is correctly located.
11 Reconnect the distributor wiring connector and where applicable the vacuum hose(s) to the diaphragm unit.
12 Check and, if necessary, adjust the ignition timing as described in Section 7, then tighten the distributor mounting bolts to the specified torque.

5 IC ignition unit (non-catalyst carburettor models) - removal and refitting

Removal

1 Remove the distributor as described in Section 4.

2 Remove the rotor arm.

Hitachi distributor

3 Using a dab of paint or suitable marker pen, make an identification mark on the top of the distributor toothed reluctor. The mark can then be used to ensure that the reluctor is installed the right way up.
4 Slide the reluctor off the distributor shaft, and recover the roll pin. If necessary, the rotor can be drawn off using a suitable legged puller.
5 Carefully disconnect the wiring connectors from the ignition unit, noting each wire's correct fitted position.
6 Undo the retaining screws, and remove the IC ignition unit from the distributor.

Mitsubishi distributor

7 Remove the cover from the distributor.
8 Disconnect the wiring then unscrew the screw and remove the adapter post.
9 Undo the retaining screws, and remove the IC ignition unit from the distributor.

Refitting

10 Refitting is a reversal of removal, but on the Hitachi distributor use a feeler blade to check that the air gap between the reluctor and stator is between 0.3 and 0.5 mm. If necessary loosen the screws and adjust the position of the stator as required.
Refit the distributor as described in Section 4.

6 Ignition power transistor unit - removal and refitting

Carburettor models with a catalytic converter

1 The power transistor unit is situated in the engine compartment, mounted onto the left-hand suspension mounting turret.
2 Disconnect the battery negative terminal, then disconnect the wiring connector from the power transistor.

4.10a Fit the seal to the distributor body . . .

4.10b . . . then refit the cap and securely tighten its retaining screws

3 Undo the retaining bolts, and remove the power transistor from the vehicle.

4 Refitting is the reverse of removal.

All fuel-injected models

5 On fuel-injected models, the power transistor is an integral part of the distributor, and cannot be renewed separately. If the unit is faulty, the complete distributor body assembly must be renewed.

7 Ignition timing - checking and adjustment

1 To check the ignition timing, a stroboscopic timing light will be required.

2 The timing marks are in the form of notches on the crankshaft pulley rim, which align with a pointer on the timing chain cover. The notches are spaced at intervals of 5°, and go from 20° before top dead centre (BTDC) to 5° after top dead centre (ATDC). The TDC mark is highlighted with paint to aid identification **(see illustration)**.

3 Start the engine, warm it up to normal operating temperature, and then switch off. Check the ignition timing as described under the relevant sub-heading.

Carburettor models

4 Disconnect the vacuum hose from the distributor vacuum diaphragm unit (non-catalyst models) or the boost pressure sensor (catalyst models), which is mounted on the left-hand suspension mounting turret. Plug the hose end.

5 Connect the timing light to No 1 cylinder (nearest the timing chain) plug lead as described in the timing light manufacturer's instructions.

6 Start the engine, allowing it to idle at the specified speed, and point the timing light at the crankshaft pulley. The relevant timing mark should be aligned with the pointer on the timing chain cover (see Specifications for the correct timing setting).

7 If adjustment is necessary, slacken the two distributor mounting bolts, then slowly rotate the distributor body as required until the crankshaft pulley marks are correctly positioned. Once the marks are correctly aligned, hold the distributor stationary, and tighten its mounting bolts to the specified torque. Recheck that the timing marks are still correctly aligned and, if necessary, repeat the adjustment procedure.

⚠ **Warning: At all times, avoid touching the HT leads, and keep loose clothing, long hair, etc, well away from the moving parts of the engine.**

8 When the timing is correctly set, increase the engine speed, and check that the pulley mark advances to beyond the beginning of the timing plate reference marks, returning to close to the specified mark when the engine is allowed to idle; this shows that the centrifugal advance mechanism is functioning, but a detailed check must be left to a Nissan dealer.

9 Reconnect the vacuum hose to the distributor (non-catalyst models) or boost pressure sensor (catalyst models). Check that the timing advances by the correct amount, so that the crankshaft pulley timing marks are correctly positioned (refer to the Specifications for the correct timing setting). If not, it is likely that the vacuum diaphragm unit/boost pressure sensor (as applicable) is faulty, or that the vacuum hose is leaking.

10 When the ignition timing is correct, stop the engine and disconnect the timing light.

Fuel-injected models

11 Disconnect the wiring connector from the throttle potentiometer (see the relevant Part of Chapter 4).

12 Check and adjust the ignition timing as described above in paragraphs 5 to 7.

13 When the ignition timing is correctly set, stop the engine and disconnect the timing light.

14 Reconnect the throttle potentiometer wiring connector.

7.2 Crankshaft pulley TDC notch aligned with timing chain cover pointer (arrowed)

Notes

Chapter 6
Clutch

Contents

Degrees of difficulty

Easy, suitable for novice with little experience	**Fairly easy,** suitable for beginner with some experience	**Fairly difficult,** suitable for competent DIY mechanic	**Difficult,** suitable for experienced DIY mechanic	**Very difficult,** suitable for expert DIY or professional

Specifications

Type . . . . Single dry plate with diaphragm spring. Cable-operated release mechanism

Adjustment data
Clutch pedal height:
  Right-hand drive models . . . . 178 to 188 mm
  Left-hand drive models . . . . 166 to 176 mm
Clutch pedal free play:
  At transmission lever . . . . 2.5 to 3.5 mm
  At pedal pad . . . . 13 to 17 mm

Friction plate
Diameter:
  1.4 litre models . . . . 180 mm
  1.6 litre models . . . . 190 mm
Friction material thickness (new) . . . . 8.0 to 8.4 mm
Minimum friction material-to-rivet head depth . . . . 0.3 mm
Maximum friction plate run-out:
  1.4 litre models (measured 85 mm out from plate centre) . . . . 1.0 mm
  1.6 litre models (measured 90 mm out from plate centre) . . . . 1.0 mm

Torque wrench settings

	Nm	lbf ft
Clutch pedal height adjustment bolt locknut	19	14
Clutch cable retainer-to-bulkhead nuts	10	7
Clutch pedal pivot bolt	19	14
Pressure plate retaining bolts	25	18

6

1 General information

The clutch consists of a friction plate, a pressure plate assembly, a release bearing and the release mechanism. All of these components are contained in the transmission bellhousing. The release mechanism is mechanical, being operated by a cable.

The friction plate is fitted between the engine flywheel and the clutch pressure plate, and is allowed to slide on the transmission input shaft splines. It consists of two circular facings of friction material riveted in position to provide the clutch bearing surface, and a spring-cushioned hub to damp out transmission shocks.

The pressure plate assembly is bolted to the engine flywheel, and is located by three dowel pins. When the engine is running, drive is transmitted from the crankshaft via the flywheel to the friction plate (these components being clamped securely together by the pressure plate assembly), and from the friction plate to the transmission input shaft.

To interrupt the drive, the spring pressure must be relaxed. This is achieved by a sealed release bearing fitted concentrically around the transmission input shaft; when the driver depresses the clutch pedal, the release bearing is pressed against the fingers at the centre of the diaphragm spring. Since the spring is held by rivets between two annular fulcrum rings, the pressure at its centre causes it to deform, so that it flattens and thus releases the clamping force it exerts, at its periphery, on the pressure plate.

Depressing the clutch pedal pulls the control cable inner wire, and this in turn rotates the release fork by acting on the lever at the fork's upper end, above the bellhousing. The release bearing is clipped to the ends of the fork.

As the friction plate facings wear, the pressure plate moves towards the flywheel and this causes the diaphragm spring fingers to move outwards. To ensure correct operation, the clutch cable must be regularly adjusted.

2 Clutch - adjustment

1 The clutch adjustment is checked by first setting the clutch pedal height, and then adjusting the pedal free play.

2 Peel back the carpet from under the clutch pedal, and ensure that there are no obstructions between the pedal and floor panel. Measure the distance from the centre of the clutch pedal pad to the floor **(see illustration)**. Note: *This measurement can be taken with the carpet in position, so long as the thickness of the carpet is added onto the pedal height measurement.* The pedal height should be within the range given in the Specifications at the start of this Chapter.

3 If height adjustment is necessary, reach up behind the facia, and slacken the pedal height adjusting bolt (or clutch switch where fitted) locknut. If necessary, remove the lower facia panel (see Chapter 11) to improve access to the bolt. Position the bolt/switch as required, so that the pedal height is correctly set, then tighten the locknut to the specified torque.

4 With the pedal height correctly set, check the pedal free play as follows:

5 Slowly depress the clutch pedal, and measure the distance that the clutch pedal pad travels from the at-rest position to the point where resistance is felt (see illustration 2.2). This is the pedal free play, and should be within the range given in the Specifications.

6 If free play adjustment is necessary, working within the engine compartment, locate the clutch release lever, which is situated on the top of the transmission. Slacken the cable locknut, then rotate the knurled adjusting nut until the release lever travel from the at-rest position to the position where resistance is felt is approximately 2.5 to 3.5 mm **(see illustration)**. Recheck the clutch pedal free play as described in paragraph 5, and readjust if necessary. Once the pedal free play is correctly set, securely tighten the cable locknut.

7 With the pedal height and free play correctly adjusted, refit all components removed for access.

2.2 Clutch pedal height adjustment details

Dimension "H" - pedal height measurement
Dimension "A" - pedal free play measurement

1 Pedal mounting bracket
2 Locknut
3 Pedal height adjustment bolt
4 Carpet
5 Insulator sheet
6 Insulator sheet
7 Floor panel

3 Clutch cable - removal and refitting

Removal

1 Working in the engine compartment, locate the clutch release lever which is situated on the top of the transmission, then slacken the locknut and knurled adjuster nut situated on the cable end fitting.

2 Release the inner cable end fitting from the release lever, and the outer cable fitting from its mounting bracket on the transmission **(see illustration)**.

3 Working inside the vehicle, remove the lower facia panel from the driver's side of the facia as described in Chapter 11. Unhook the clutch inner cable from the top of the clutch pedal. Note that access to the top of the pedal is very poor, but can only be significantly improved by removing the complete facia.

4 Return to the engine compartment, and withdraw the cable from the engine compartment bulkhead. If necessary, undo the two nuts securing the cable retainer to the bulkhead, and remove the retainer along with the cable.

5 Work back along the cable, releasing it from any relevant retaining clips and guides, and noting its correct routing, and remove it from the vehicle.

6 Examine the cable, looking for worn end fittings or a damaged outer casing, and for signs of fraying of the inner wire. Check the cable's operation; the inner wire should move smoothly and easily through the outer casing. Remember that a cable that appears serviceable when tested off the car may well be much heavier in operation, when compressed into its working position. Renew the cable if it shows any signs of excessive wear or damage.

Refitting

7 Apply a thin smear of multi-purpose grease to the cable end fittings, then pass the cable through the engine compartment bulkhead. Locate the cable retainer on its studs (where removed), and tighten its retaining nuts to the specified torque.

8 From inside the vehicle, hook the inner cable over the clutch pedal end, and check that it is securely retained.

9 Work along the cable, ensuring that it is correctly routed, and retained by all the relevant retaining clips and guides. Clip the outer cable into its mounting bracket on the transmission.

10 Hook the inner cable end fitting over the end of the clutch release lever, and adjust the clutch pedal settings as described in Section 2.

4 Clutch pedal - removal and refitting

Note: *Access to the pedal and spring is very poor, and can only be significantly improved by removing the facia as described in Chapter 11.*

Removal

1 Working as described in Section 2, slacken the clutch cable locknut and knurled adjuster nut, to obtain maximum free play in the cable.

2 Working inside the vehicle, remove the lower facia panel from the driver's side of the facia (see Chapter 11). Unhook the clutch inner cable from the top of the clutch pedal; access to the top of the pedal is very poor.

2.6 Slacken the locknut, and adjust the clutch cable by rotating the knurled adjusting nut (arrowed)

3.2 Detach the clutch inner cable from the release lever, then free the outer cable from its mounting bracket

3 Carefully unhook the ends of the clutch pedal assist spring from its locations in the pedal mounting bracket, and recover the spring seats.

4 Slacken and remove the nut and pivot bolt, then withdraw the clutch pedal and assist spring from the mounting bracket. If necessary, the pedal and spring can then be separated.

5 Carefully clean all components, and renew any that are worn or damaged. Check the bearing surfaces of the pivot bushes and bolt with particular care; the bushes can be renewed separately if worn.

Refitting

6 Press the pivot bushes into the pedal bore, then apply a smear of multi-purpose grease to their bearing surfaces. Ensure that the clutch pedal and assist spring are correctly mated.

7 Refit the spring seats to the pedal mounting bracket, and install the pedal assembly. Refit the pivot bolt and nut, and tighten it to the specified torque setting.

8 Locate each end of the assist spring in its relevant seat.

9 Hook the clutch cable onto the end of the pedal, then adjust the clutch pedal settings as described in Section 2.

5 Clutch assembly - removal, inspection and refitting

Warning: Dust created by clutch wear and deposited on the clutch components may contain asbestos, which is a health hazard. DO NOT blow it out with compressed air, or inhale any of it. DO NOT use petrol or petroleum-based solvents to clean off the dust. Brake system cleaner or methylated spirit should be used to flush the dust into a suitable receptacle. After the clutch components are wiped clean with rags, dispose of the contaminated rags and cleaner in a sealed, marked container.

Note: *Although some friction materials may no longer contain asbestos, it is safest to assume that they DO, and to take precautions accordingly*

Removal

1 Unless the complete engine/transmission is to be removed from the car, and separated for major overhaul (see Chapter 2B), the clutch can be reached by removing the transmission as described in Chapter 7A.

2 Before disturbing the clutch, use chalk or a marker pen to mark the relationship of the pressure plate assembly to the flywheel **(see illustration)**.

3 Working in a diagonal sequence, slacken the pressure plate bolts by half a turn at a time, until the spring pressure is released and the bolts can be unscrewed by hand.

4 Prise the pressure plate assembly off its locating dowels, and collect the friction plate, noting which way round the friction plate is fitted.

Inspection

Note: *Due to the amount of work necessary to remove and refit clutch components, it is usually considered good practice to renew the clutch friction plate, pressure plate assembly and release bearing as a matched set, even if only one of these is actually worn enough to require renewal.*

5 When cleaning clutch components, first read the warning at the beginning of this Section. Remove the dust only as described - working with dampened cloths will help to keep dust levels to a minimum. Wherever possible, work in a well-ventilated atmosphere.

6 Check the friction plate facings for signs of wear, damage or oil contamination. If the friction material is cracked, burnt, scored or damaged, or if it is contaminated with oil or grease (shown by shiny black patches), the friction plate must be renewed. Measure the depth of the rivets below the friction material surface. If the depth of any rivet is equal to, or less than, the service limit given in the Specifications, then the friction plate must be renewed.

7 If the friction material is still serviceable, check that the centre boss splines are unworn, that the torsion springs are in good condition and securely fastened, and that all the rivets are tightly fastened. If excessive wear or damage is found, the friction plate must be renewed.

8 If the friction material is fouled with oil, this must be due to an oil leak from the crankshaft oil seal, from the sump-to-cylinder block joint, or from the transmission input shaft. Make the necessary repairs before fitting the new components.

9 Check the pressure plate assembly for obvious signs of wear or damage; shake it to check for loose rivets, or worn or damaged fulcrum rings. Check that the drive straps securing the pressure plate to the cover do not show signs (such as a deep yellow or blue discoloration) of overheating. If the diaphragm spring is worn or damaged, or if its pressure is in any way suspect, the pressure plate assembly should be renewed.

10 Examine the machined bearing surfaces of the pressure plate and of the flywheel; they should be clean, completely flat, and free from scratches or scoring. If either is discoloured from excessive heat, or shows signs of cracks, it should be renewed; however, minor damage of this nature can sometimes be polished away using emery paper.

11 Check that the release bearing contact surface rotates smoothly and easily, with no sign of noise or roughness, and that the surface itself is smooth and unworn, with no signs of cracks, pitting or scoring. If there is any doubt about its condition, the bearing must be renewed

Refitting

12 On reassembly, ensure that the bearing surfaces of the flywheel and pressure plate are completely clean, smooth, and free from oil or grease.

13 Fit the friction plate so that its spring hub assembly faces away from the flywheel; there may also be a marking showing which way round the plate is to be refitted **(see illustration)**.

14 Refit the pressure plate assembly, aligning the marks made on dismantling (if the original pressure plate is re-used), and locating the pressure plate on its three locating dowels. Fit the pressure plate bolts, but tighten them only finger-tight so that the friction plate can still be moved.

15 The friction plate must now be centralised, so that when the transmission is refitted, its input shaft will pass through the splines at the centre of the friction plate.

16 Centralisation can be achieved by passing a screwdriver or other long bar through the friction plate, and into the hole in the crankshaft. The friction plate can then be moved around until it is centred on the crankshaft hole. Alternatively, a clutch-aligning tool can be used to eliminate the

5.2 Prior to removal, make alignment marks between the clutch pressure plate and flywheel

5.13 Fit the friction plate with its spring hub assembly facing away from the flywheel, and install the pressure plate

5.16 Using a clutch-aligning tool to centralise the friction plate

6.3 Clutch release fork is secured to the release lever shaft by two dual-roll pin arrangements (arrowed)

guesswork. These can be obtained from most accessory shops, or can be made up from a length of metal rod or wooden dowel which fits closely inside the crankshaft hole, and has insulating tape wound around it to match the diameter of the friction plate splined hole **(see illustration)**.

17 When the friction plate is centralised, tighten the pressure plate bolts evenly and in a diagonal sequence to the specified torque setting.

18 Apply a thin smear of high-melting point grease to the splines of the friction plate and the transmission input shaft, also to the release bearing bore and release fork shaft.

19 Refit the transmission as described in Chapter 7A.

| 6 | **Clutch release mechanism -** removal, inspection and refitting |

Note: *Refer to the warning concerning the dangers of asbestos dust at the beginning of Section 5*

Removal

1 Unless the complete engine/transmission is to be removed from the car, and separated for major overhaul (see Chapter 2B), the clutch release mechanism can be reached by removing the transmission as described in Chapter 7A.

2 Lift the retaining clips, then slide the release bearing from the fork and remove it from the transmission. Note the correct fitted direction of each clip on the bearing.

3 Rotate the release fork then, using a hammer and suitable punch, drive out the roll pins securing the release fork to the shaft (drive out the small inner pins first, then remove the outer pins) **(see illustration)**. Discard the roll pins; new ones should be used on refitting.

4 Note the correct fitted position of the return spring, then withdraw the release lever; recover the release fork and spring from the transmission housing.

Inspection

5 Check the release mechanism, renewing any component which is worn or damaged. Carefully check all bearing surfaces and points of contact.

6 Inspect the bush and dust seal fitted to the transmission housing for signs of damage and deterioration, and renew if necessary. The old bush can be tapped out of position, and the new one installed using a hammer and suitable tubular socket.

7 When checking the release bearing itself, note that it is often considered worthwhile to renew it as a matter of course, given that a significant amount of work is required to gain access to it. Check that the contact surface rotates smoothly and easily, with no sign of noise or roughness. Also check that the surface itself is smooth and unworn, with no signs of cracks, pitting or scoring. If there is any doubt about its condition, the bearing must be renewed.

Refitting

8 Apply a smear of high-melting point grease to the shaft pivot points and the contact surfaces of the release fork.

9 Slide the release lever partially into position in the transmission.

10 Offer up the release fork and spring, aligning them with the lever shaft, and push the release lever fully into position.

11 Align the release fork holes with the holes in the lever shaft, and drive the two new roll pins into position.

12 Fit the retaining clips (where removed) to the release bearing, making sure that they are fitted the correct way round. Apply a smear of high-melting point grease to the contact surfaces of the bearing and input shaft, then slide the bearing along the shaft and clip it onto the release fork **(see illustrations)**.

13 Check the operation of the release mechanism, ensuring that it moves smoothly, and returns easily under the pressure of the return spring, then refit the transmission as described in Chapter 7A.

6.12a Ensure that the retaining clips (arrowed) are correctly fitted to the release bearing . . .

6.12b . . . then fit the bearing to the transmission, making sure the clips are correctly engaged with the release fork ends

Chapter 7 Part A:
Manual transmission

Contents

Degrees of difficulty

| Easy, suitable for novice with little experience | | Fairly easy, suitable for beginner with some experience | Fairly difficult, suitable for competent DIY mechanic | Difficult, suitable for experienced DIY mechanic | Very difficult, suitable for expert DIY or professional | |

Specifications

General
Type . . . . Manual, five forward speeds and reverse. Synchromesh on all forward speeds

Designation:
1.4 litre models RS5F30A
1.6 litre models RS5F31A

Gear ratios
1.4 litre models:
1st . . . . 3.333 : 1
2nd . . . . 1.955 : 1
3rd . . . . 1.286 : 1
4th . . . . 0.902 : 1
5th . . . . 0.733 : 1
Reverse . . . . 3.417 : 1
Final drive . . . . 4.167 : 1
1.6 litre carburettor models:
1st . . . . 3.063 : 1
2nd . . . . 1.826 : 1
3rd . . . . 1.207 : 1
4th . . . . 0.902 : 1
5th . . . . 0.756 : 1
Reverse . . . . 3.417 : 1
Final drive . . . . 4.167 : 1
1.6 litre fuel injection models:
1st . . . . 3.063 : 1
2nd . . . . 1.826 : 1
3rd . . . . 1.286 : 1
4th . . . . 0.975 : 1
5th . . . . 0.810 : 1
Reverse . . . . 3.417 : 1
Final drive . . . . 4.167 : 1

Torque wrench settings

	Nm	lbf ft
Oil filler/level plug	29	22
Oil drain plug	29	22
Gearchange linkage components:		
Selector rod front pivot bolt	16	12
Selector rod rear pivot bolt	21	15
Support rod-to-transmission bolt	41	30
Support rod-to-gear lever retaining plate nuts	14	10
Support rod rear mounting bracket to body nuts	14	10
Support rod-to-rear mounting bracket nut	25	18
Gaiter retaining plate nuts	5	4
Neutral switch	25	19
Reversing light switch	25	19
Engine-to-transmission fixing bolts:		
Bolts less than 30 mm long	19	14
Bolts 30 mm long, and longer	35	26
Left-hand engine/transmission mounting:		
Through-bolt	49	37
Mounting-to-transmission bolts	49	37
Rear engine/transmission mounting:		
Through-bolt	49	37
Mounting bracket retaining bolts	49	37

1 General information

The manual transmission is mounted transversely in the engine compartment, bolted directly to the left-hand end of the engine. The cast-aluminium alloy casing includes the gears and final drive differential.

Drive is transmitted from the crankshaft via the clutch to the input shaft, which has a splined extension to accept the clutch friction plate, and rotates in sealed ball-bearings. From the input shaft, drive is transmitted to the output shaft, which rotates in tapered roller bearings. From the output shaft, the drive is transmitted to the differential crownwheel, which rotates with the differential case and planetary gears, driving the sun gears and driveshafts. The rotation of the planetary gears on their shaft allows the inner roadwheel to rotate at a slower speed than the outer roadwheel when the car is cornering.

The input and output shafts are arranged side by side, parallel to the crankshaft and driveshafts, so that their gear pinion teeth are in constant mesh. In the neutral position, the output shaft gear pinions rotate freely, so that drive cannot be transmitted to the crownwheel.

Gear selection is via a floor-mounted lever and selector rod mechanism. The selector rod causes the appropriate selector fork to move its respective synchro-sleeve along the shaft, to lock the gear pinion to the synchro-hub. Since the synchro-hubs are splined to the output shaft, this locks the pinion to the shaft so that drive can be transmitted. To ensure that gearchanging can be made quickly and quietly, a synchromesh system is fitted to all forward gears, consisting of baulk rings and spring-loaded fingers, as well as the gear pinions and synchro-hubs; the synchromesh cones are formed on the mating faces of the baulk rings and gear pinions.

2 Gearchange linkage - removal and refitting

Removal

1 Remove the centre console as described in Chapter 11.

2 Firmly apply the handbrake, then jack up the front of the vehicle and support it on axle stands (see "*Jacking and Vehicle Support*").

3 From underneath the vehicle, using a pair of pliers, unhook the spring securing the rear of the selector rod to the support rod.

4 Slacken and remove the nuts, and withdraw the pivot bolts securing the selector rod to the gear lever and transmission. Remove the selector rod from underneath the vehicle, and recover the O-rings and bushes from the base of the gear lever.

5 Unscrew the nut and washer securing the support rod to the bracket on the transmission housing. Slacken and remove the nuts securing the rear of the support rod and the support rod bracket to the underside of the vehicle, and manoeuvre the rod and bracket assembly out of position. If necessary, undo the retaining nut, and separate the support rod and mounting bracket.

6 From inside the vehicle, lift out the gear lever and retaining plate, and recover the small rubber gaiter from the base of the lever.

7 If necessary, slacken and remove the retaining nuts, then lift off the retaining plate and remove the main gear lever gaiter from the vehicle.

8 Inspect all the linkage components for signs of wear or damage, paying particular attention to the pivot bushes and selector rod universal joint, and renew worn components as necessary. Renew the rubber gaiters if they are split or badly perished.

Refitting

9 Refitting is a reversal of the removal procedure, applying a smear of multi-purpose grease to the gear lever pivot ball and bushes, and to the selector rod rear pivot bolt. Tighten all the linkage nuts and bolts to their specified torque settings (where given).

3 Oil seals - renewal

Driveshaft oil seal

1 Chock the rear wheels of the car, firmly apply the handbrake, then jack up the front of the car and support it on axle stands (see "*Jacking and Vehicle Support*"). Remove the appropriate front roadwheel.

2 Drain the transmission oil (Chapter 1).

3 With reference to Chapter 8, free the inner end of the driveshaft from the transmission, and place it clear of the seal, noting that there is no need to unscrew the driveshaft retaining nut; the driveshaft can be left secured to the hub. Support the driveshaft, to avoid placing any strain on the joints or gaiters.

4 Carefully prise the oil seal out of the transmission using a large flat-bladed screwdriver **(see illustration)**.

3.4 Using a large flat-bladed screwdriver to lever out a driveshaft oil seal

3.11 Selector rod end fitting is retained by a dual-roll pin arrangement (arrowed)

5 Remove all traces of dirt from the area around the oil seal aperture, then apply a smear of grease to the outer lip of the new oil seal, and locate it in its aperture. Drive the seal squarely into position, using a tubular drift which bears only on the hard outer edge of the seal. Drive the seal into position until it seats against its locating shoulder.
6 Refit the driveshaft (Chapter 8).
7 Refill the transmission with the specified type and amount of oil, as described in Chapter 1.

Input shaft oil seal

8 To renew the input shaft seal, the transmission must be dismantled. This task should therefore be entrusted to a Nissan dealer.

Selector shaft oil seal

9 Chock the rear wheels of the car, firmly apply the handbrake, then jack up the front of the car and support it on axle stands (see *"Jacking and Vehicle Support"*). Drain the transmission oil as described in Chapter 1, or be prepared for some oil loss as the seal is removed.
10 Unscrew and remove the pivot bolt and disconnect the gearchange rod from the transmission.
11 Slide back the transmission selector rod rubber gaiter, to reveal the roll pin **(see illustration)**.
12 Using a hammer and punch, tap out the roll pin (tap out the small inner pin first, followed by the larger outer pin) then remove the yoke from the selector rod. Discard the roll pin; a new one should be used on refitting.
13 Remove the rubber gaiter, then carefully lever or drive the selector shaft oil seal out of position and slide it off the shaft.
14 Before fitting a new seal, check the selector shaft's seal rubbing surface for signs of burrs, scratches or other damage. It may be possible to polish away minor faults of this sort using fine abrasive paper.
15 Apply a smear of grease to the new seal's outer edge and sealing lip, then carefully slide the seal along the selector rod. Using a metal tube or socket, drive the seal fully into position in the transmission housing.
16 Refit the rubber gaiter, making sure that it is correctly seated on the seal, then locate the yoke on the selector rod. Align the pin holes, and tap the new roll pins into position.

17 Refit the gearchange rod and tighten the pivot bolt.
18 Lower the vehicle to the ground, and top-up/refill (as applicable) the transmission oil as described in Chapter 1.

4 Neutral switch - testing, removal and refitting

Testing

1 A neutral switch is fitted to manual transmission models with a catalytic converter. The switch is one of the many fuel system switches/sender units (see Chapter 4), and is screwed into the base of the transmission on its right-hand side **(see illustration)**. **Note:** *Do not confuse the neutral switch with the reversing light switch, which is screwed in to the left-hand side of the transmission.*
2 To test the switch, trace the wiring back from the switch to its connector, which is on top of the transmission. Disconnect the wiring connector, and use a multi-meter (set to the resistance function) or a battery-and-bulb test circuit to check that there is continuity between the switch terminals only when the transmission is in neutral. If this is not the case, and there are no obvious breaks or other damage to the wires, the switch is faulty and must be renewed.

Removal

3 Chock the rear wheels of the car, firmly apply the handbrake, then jack up the front of the car and support it on axle stands (see *"Jacking and Vehicle Support"*). Drain the transmission oil as described in Chapter 1, or be prepared for some oil loss as the switch is removed.
4 Trace the switch wiring back to its connector, and disconnect it from the main harness.
5 Unscrew the switch from the transmission, and remove it. Plug the transmission housing aperture, to minimise oil loss (if the transmission has not been drained) and to prevent dirt entry.

4.1 The neutral switch (where fitted) is screwed into the right-hand side of the transmission (arrowed)

Refitting

6 Remove all traces of sealant from the threads of the switch, and apply a smear of fresh sealant to them.
7 Remove the plug from the switch aperture in the transmission, and screw the switch into position.
8 Tighten the switch to the specified torque, and reconnect the wiring connector.
9 Lower the vehicle to the ground, and top-up/refill the transmission oil (as applicable) as described in Chapter 1.

5 Reversing light switch - testing, removal and refitting

Testing

1 The reversing light circuit is controlled by a plunger-type switch that is screwed into the base of the transmission on its left-hand side **(see illustration)**. **Note:** *Do not confuse the reversing light switch with the neutral switch, which is screwed in to the right-hand side of the transmission.* If a fault develops in the circuit, first ensure that the circuit fuse has not blown.
2 To test the switch, trace the wiring back from the switch to its connector, which is on top of the transmission. Disconnect the wiring connector, and use a multi-meter (set to the resistance function) or a battery-and-bulb test circuit to check that there is continuity between the switch terminals only when reverse gear is selected. If this is not the case, and there are no obvious breaks or other damage to the wires, the switch is faulty and must be renewed.

Removal

3 Chock the rear wheels of the car, firmly apply the handbrake, then jack up the front of the car and support it on axle stands (see *"Jacking and Vehicle Support"*). Drain the transmission oil as described in Chapter 1, or be prepared for some oil loss as the switch is removed.
4 Trace the switch wiring back to its connector, and disconnect it from the main harness.

7A

5.1 The reversing light switch (arrowed) is screwed into the left-hand side of the transmission

6.3a Unscrew the retaining bolt . . .

6.3b . . . and withdraw the speedometer drive assembly (shown with transmission removed for clarity)

5 Unscrew the switch from the transmission, and remove it. Plug the transmission housing aperture, to minimise oil loss (if the transmission has not been drained), and to prevent dirt entry.

Refitting

6 Remove all traces of sealant from the threads of the switch, and apply a smear of fresh sealant to them.
7 Remove the plug from the switch aperture in the transmission, and screw the switch into position.
8 Tighten the switch to the specified torque, then reconnect the wiring connector and check the operation of the circuit.
9 Lower the vehicle to the ground, and top-up/refill the transmission oil (as applicable) as described in Chapter 1.

6 Speedometer drive - removal and refitting

Removal

1 Chock the rear wheels of the car, firmly apply the handbrake, then jack up the front of the car and support it on axle stands (see

"*Jacking and Vehicle Support*"). The speedometer drive is situated on the rear of the transmission housing, next to the inner end of the right-hand driveshaft.
2 Unscrew the knurled retaining ring, and disconnect the speedometer cable from the speedometer drive.
3 Slacken and remove the retaining bolt, and withdraw the speedometer drive and driven pinion assembly from the transmission housing, along with its O-ring **(see illustrations)**. Remove the O-ring.
4 If necessary, tap out the roll pin, then remove the pinion and recover the thrustwasher **(see illustration)**.
5 Examine all components for signs of damage, and renew if necessary. Renew the housing O-ring as a matter of course. Note that the thrustwasher is available in various thicknesses - measure the thickness of the original, and quote this when ordering a new one.
6 If the driven pinion is worn or damaged, also examine the drive pinion in the transmission housing for signs of wear or damage. To renew the drive pinion, the transmission must be dismantled and the differential gear removed. This task should therefore be entrusted to a Nissan dealer.

Refitting

7 Refit the pinion and thrustwasher and secure using a new roll pin.
8 Fit a new O-ring to the housing then refit it to the transmission, ensuring that the drive and driven pinions are correctly engaged. Securely tighten the retaining bolt.
9 Reconnect the speedometer cable, and securely tighten its retaining ring. Lower the vehicle to the ground.

7 Manual transmission - removal and refitting

Removal

1 Chock the rear wheels, then firmly apply the handbrake. Apply the handbrake, then jack up the front of the vehicle and securely support it on axle stands (see "*Jacking and Vehicle Support*"). Remove both front roadwheels. Where necessary, undo the retaining screws, and remove the plastic undershields from beneath the engine/transmission, and the covers from underneath both wheel arches.
2 Drain the transmission oil as described in Chapter 1, then refit the drain and filler/level plugs and tighten them to their specified torque settings.
3 Remove the battery as described in Chapter 5.
4 If necessary, to improve access to the top of the transmission, remove the air cleaner housing inlet duct as described in the relevant Part of Chapter 4.
5 Remove the starter motor as described in Chapter 5.
6 Slacken the clutch cable locknut and knurled adjuster nut, then free the cable end fitting from the release lever, and the outer cable fitting from its mounting bracket **(see illustration)**.

6.4 Speedometer drive pinion roll pin and housing O-ring (arrowed)

7.6 Free the clutch cable from the release lever

7.7a Disconnect the reversing light switch wiring connector . . .

7.7b . . . and neutral switch connector (where fitted) then detach the earth lead(s) from the transmission housing (arrowed)

7 Disconnect the wiring connectors from the reversing light switch and, where applicable, from the neutral switch. Disconnect the earth lead(s) from the top of the transmission housing (see illustrations). Free the wiring from any relevant retaining clips, and position it clear of the transmission.

8 Unscrew and remove the nut and pivot bolt securing the gearchange linkage selector rod to the yoke on the transmission, and the nut and washer securing the support rod to the stud on the transmission. Free both rods, and position them clear of the transmission (see illustrations).

9 Disconnect the breather pipe from the top of the transmission housing (see illustration).

10 Unscrew the knurled retaining ring, and disconnect the speedometer cable from the transmission.

11 Working as described in Chapter 8, free the inner end of each driveshaft from the transmission, and place the ends clear of the transmission. Note that there is no need to unscrew the driveshaft retaining nuts - each driveshaft can be left secured to the hub. Support the driveshafts, to avoid placing any strain on the driveshaft joints or gaiters.

12 Place a jack with interposed block of wood beneath the engine, or alternatively attach a hoist or support bar to the engine. Raise the engine/transmission slightly and position a block of wood between the engine compartment centre member and the sump. Lower the engine onto the block of wood.

13 Place a jack and block of wood beneath the transmission, and raise the jack to take the weight of the transmission.

14 Slacken and remove the through-bolt from the left-hand engine/transmission mounting. Undo the three bolts securing the mounting to the transmission, and manoeuvre the mounting out of position. Recover the rubbers from each side of the mounting bracket, if they are loose.

15 Slacken and remove the through-bolt from the rear engine/transmission mounting. Undo the bolts securing the mounting bracket in position, and manoeuvre it away from the engine/transmission.

16 With the jack positioned beneath the transmission taking the weight, slacken and remove the remaining bolts securing the transmission housing to the engine. Note the correct fitted positions of each bolt (and the relevant brackets) as they are removed, to use as a reference on refitting - the bolts are of different lengths. Note that it may be necessary to raise the transmission slightly to gain access to the lower bolts.

17 Make a final check that all necessary components have been disconnected, and are positioned clear of the transmission so that they will not hinder the removal procedure.

18 Move the trolley jack and transmission to the left to free it from its locating dowels. Keep the transmission fully supported until the input shaft is free of the engine.

19 Once the transmission is free, lower the jack and manoeuvre the unit out from under the car (see illustration). If they are loose, remove the locating dowels from the transmission or engine, and keep them in a safe place.

Refitting

20 The transmission is refitted by a reversal of the removal procedure, bearing in mind the following points:

a) *Apply a little high-melting point grease to the splines of the transmission input shaft. Do not apply too much, otherwise there is a possibility of the grease contaminating the clutch friction plate.*

b) *Ensure that the locating dowels are correctly positioned prior to installation.*

c) *Insert the transmission-to-engine bolts into their original locations, as noted on removal. Tighten all nuts and bolts to the specified torque (where given).*

7A

7.8a Unscrew the nut, then withdraw the pivot bolt . . .

7.8b . . . and free the selector rod from the transmission

7.8c Recover the washer securing the gearchange linkage support rod to the stud on the transmission

7.9 Disconnect the breather hose from the top of the transmission

7.19 Removing the transmission from underneath the vehicle

d) *Renew the driveshaft oil seals using the information given in Section 3.*

e) *On completion, refill the transmission with the specified type and quantity of lubricant as described in Chapter 1.*

8 Manual transmission overhaul - general information

Overhauling a manual transmission is a difficult and involved job for the DIY home mechanic. In addition to dismantling and reassembling many small parts, clearances must be precisely measured and, if necessary, changed by selecting shims and spacers. Internal transmission components are also often difficult to obtain, and in many instances, extremely expensive. Because of this, if the transmission develops a fault or becomes noisy, the best course of action is to have the unit overhauled by a specialist repairer, or to obtain an exchange reconditioned unit.

Nevertheless, it is not impossible for the more experienced mechanic to overhaul the transmission, if the special tools are available, and the job is done in a deliberate step-by-step manner so that nothing is overlooked.

The tools necessary for an overhaul include internal and external circlip pliers, bearing pullers, a slide hammer, a set of pin punches, a dial test indicator, and possibly a hydraulic press. In addition, a large, sturdy workbench and a vice will be required.

During dismantling of the transmission, make careful notes of how each component is fitted, to make reassembly easier and accurate.

Before dismantling the transmission, it will help if you have some idea which area is malfunctioning. Certain problems can be closely related to specific areas in the transmission, which can make component examination and replacement easier. Refer to the *"Fault Finding"* Section at the end of this manual for more information.

Chapter 7 Part B:
Automatic transmission

Contents

Degrees of difficulty

| Easy, suitable for novice with little experience | 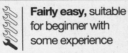 | Fairly easy, suitable for beginner with some experience | | Fairly difficult, suitable for competent DIY mechanic | | Difficult, suitable for experienced DIY mechanic | | Very difficult, suitable for expert DIY or professional | |

Specifications

General
Type . . . . Automatic, four forward speeds and reverse
Designation RL4F03A

Gear ratios
1st 2.861
2nd 1.562
3rd 1.000
4th 0.697
Reverse 2.310
Final drive 4.072

Torque wrench settings

	Nm	lbf ft
Drain plug	34	26
Selector cable fixings:		
Cable-to-transmission lever nut	21	15
Outer cable-to-floor mounting	5	4
Outer cable-to-transmission mounting	15	11
Engine-to-transmission fixing bolts:		
Bolts less than 30 mm long	19	14
Bolts 30 mm long, and longer	35	26
Left-hand engine/transmission mounting:		
Through-bolt	49	37
Mounting-to-transmission bolts	49	37
Rear engine/transmission mounting:		
Through-bolt	49	37
Mounting bracket retaining bolts	49	37
Torque converter-to-driveplate bolts:		
Bolts with flange	51	38
Bolts without flange	44	33

7B

1 General information

A four-speed fully automatic transmission is available on both 1.4 and 1.6 litre models. The transmission consists of a torque converter, an epicyclic geartrain, and hydraulically-operated clutches and brakes.

The torque converter provides a fluid coupling between engine and transmission which acts as an automatic clutch, and also provides a degree of torque multiplication when accelerating.

The epicyclic geartrain provides either of the four forward or one reverse gear ratios, according to which of its component parts are held stationary, or are allowed to turn. The components of the geartrain are held or released by brakes and clutches which are activated by a hydraulic control unit. A fluid pump within the transmission provides the necessary hydraulic pressure to operate the brakes and clutches.

Driver control of the transmission is by a six-position selector lever. The transmission has a "drive" option, and a "hold" facility on the first two gear ratios. The drive option "D" provides automatic changing throughout the range of all four gear ratios, and is the one to select for normal driving. An automatic kickdown facility will automatically shift the transmission down a gear if the accelerator

pedal is fully depressed. The first and second gear "hold" options are very similar, but they limit the gear ratios available - ie, when the selector lever is in the "2" position, only the first two ratios can be selected, and in the "1" position, only the first ratio can be selected. The lower ratios can be used to provide engine braking whilst travelling down steep gradients. Note, however, that the transmission should **never** be shifted down into positions "1" or "2" whilst the vehicle is travelling at 68 mph (110 km/h) or more. An overdrive switch button is also provided on the shift lever. For normal driving the switch should be in the ON position, however if engine braking is required when driving up and down long slopes the switch should be OFF.

Due to the complexity of the automatic transmission, any repair or overhaul work must be left to a Nissan dealer with the necessary special equipment for fault diagnosis and repair. The contents of the following Sections are therefore confined to supplying general information, and any service information and instructions that can be used by the owner.

2 Selector cable - adjustment

1 Position the selector lever in the "P" position.

2.4 Selector cable adjustment details. Pull cable end fitting in the direction of the arrow with the specified force

1 Transmission selector lever
2 Selector cable
3 Cable retaining nut
4 Starter/inhibitor switch

2 Apply the handbrake, then jack up the front of the vehicle and support it on axle stands (see "Jacking and Vehicle Support"). Check that the lever on the transmission is also in the "P" position.
3 Working underneath the vehicle, slacken the locknut securing the cable end fitting to the transmission selector lever. Note that the end fitting has an elongated hole for adjustment purposes.
4 Hook a spring balance onto the end of the cable, and pull the cable with a force of 6.9 N (0.7 kg, or 1.5 lbs) (see illustration).
5 From this position, remove the spring balance, and move the cable end fitting backwards by 1.0 mm. Hold the cable in this position, and tighten the locknut to the specified torque setting.
6 Check the operation of the selector lever, ensuring that it moves smoothly and easily, without any sign of the cable binding. If not, repeat the operations in paragraphs 3 to 5.
7 Once the selector lever is operating correctly, apply multi-purpose grease to the contact surfaces of the transmission selector lever and cable, and lower the vehicle to the ground.

3 Selector cable - removal and refitting

Removal

1 Firmly apply the handbrake, then jack up the front of the vehicle and support it on axle stands (see "Jacking and Vehicle Support"). Position the selector lever in the "P" position.
2 Remove the centre console as described in Chapter 11.
3 Unscrew the nut securing the selector cable to the lever. Slide out the clip securing the outer cable to its mounting bracket, and free the selector cable from the selector lever (see illustration).
4 From underneath the vehicle, unbolt the outer cable support from the underbody, and pull out the rear end of the cable.
5 Unscrew and remove the nut and washer securing the cable to the transmission selector lever. Slide out the clip securing the outer cable to its mounting bracket, then remove the cable from the transmission mounting and remove it from underneath the vehicle. Note that the transmission selector lever must not be disturbed until the cable is refitted. As a precaution, mark the position of the lever in relation to the transmission housing.
6 Examine the cable, looking for worn end fittings or a damaged outer casing. Check the inner cable for damage. Check the cable's operation; the inner cable should move smoothly and easily through the outer casing. Remember, however, that a cable that appears serviceable when tested off the car may well be much heavier in operation, when

3.3 Selector cable fixing details

1 Selector lever
2 Selector cable-to-vehicle body fixing
3 Vehicle floorpan
4 Selector cable
5 Mounting bracket
6 Mounting bracket
7 Selector cable retaining nut
8 Transmission selector lever

compressed into its working position. Renew the cable if it shows any signs of excessive wear or of damage.

Refitting

7 Feed the cable up into position from underneath the vehicle. Refit the bolts securing the cable to the floor, and tighten them to the specified torque setting.

8 From inside the vehicle, connect the cable to the selector lever, and clip the outer cable into its mounting bracket. Tighten the cable retaining nut to the specified torque setting, and secure the outer cable in position with the retaining clip.

9 Move the selector lever to the "P" position and also check that the lever on the transmission is in the "P" position.

10 Hook the inner cable onto the transmission selector lever. Clip the outer cable into position in its mounting bracket, and secure it in position with the retaining clip.

11 Adjust the cable as described in Section 2.

12 Refit the centre console and lower the car to the ground.

4 Selector lever assembly - removal and refitting

Removal

1 Firmly apply the handbrake, then jack up the front of the vehicle and support it on axle stands (see "Jacking and Vehicle Support"). Position the selector lever in the "P" position.

2 Remove the centre console as described in Chapter 11.

3 Unscrew the nut securing the selector cable to the lever. Slide out the clip securing the outer cable to its mounting bracket, and free the selector cable from the selector lever (see illustration).

4.3 Selector lever components

1 Gear indicator panel
2 Detent button
3 Spring
4 Selector lever handle
5 Wiring connector
6 Gear indicator light bulb
7 Cable clip
8 Selector cable
9 Dust cover
10 Dust cover support
11 Selector lever assembly

4 Disconnect the wiring from the overdrive switch and gear indicator light bulb.

5 Undo the two retaining screws, depress the detent button, and slide the handle off the top of the selector lever. If necessary, the detent button and spring can then be withdrawn from the handle, as can the overdrive switch.

6 Undo the nuts, accessed both from inside and underneath the vehicle, securing the selector lever to the floor, and lift the lever assembly out of the vehicle. Do not attempt to dismantle the selector lever components; the lever assembly is a sealed unit, with no individual components being available separately.

Refitting

7 Refit the selector lever assembly to the vehicle, and securely tighten its retaining nuts.

8 Clip the overdrive switch, detent button and spring back into position in the selector lever handle (where removed).

9 Ensure that the switch wiring is correctly routed down through the handle, and refit the handle to the selector lever. Securely tighten its retaining screws, then check the operation of the lever detent mechanism.

10 Connect the overdrive switch and gear indicator light wiring connector.

11 Connect the cable to the selector lever, and locate the outer cable into its mounting bracket. Tighten the cable retaining nut to the specified torque setting, and secure the outer cable in position with the retaining clip.

12 Adjust the selector cable as described in Section 2, then refit the centre console as described in Chapter 11.

---

5 Kickdown cable - adjustment

1 Ensure that the accelerator cable is correctly adjusted as described in the relevant Part of Chapter 4.

2 Depress the adjuster to release the outer cable locking mechanism, and move the outer cable fully towards the mounting bracket. Release the adjuster, so that the outer cable is locked in position.

3 Using a dab of white paint or a suitable marker pen, make a mark on the kickdown inner cable. This mark can then be used for measuring the cable travel.

4 Position a ruler next to the mark on the inner cable, then quickly move the throttle cam from its fully closed position to its fully open position, whilst measuring the travel of the kickdown cable. This should be within the range quoted **(see illustration)**.

5 If adjustment is necessary, depress the adjuster, then reposition the outer cable and repeat the procedure described in paragraph 4.

6 Repeat the procedure as necessary, until the kickdown cable travel is within the specified range.

5.4 Adjust the kickdown cable so dimension "L" is as specified

1 Throttle cam	5 Kickdown cable
2 Mounting bracket	casing
3 Outer cable tube	L 40 to 42 mm
4 Adjuster	

---

6 Kickdown cable - removal and refitting

Renewal of the kickdown cable is complex task, which should be entrusted to a Nissan dealer. To detach the cable at the transmission end first requires the removal of the hydraulic control valve assembly, which is a task that should not be undertaken by the home mechanic.

---

7 Speedometer drive - removal and refitting

Refer to Chapter 7A, Section 6.

---

8 Oil seals - renewal

Driveshaft seals

Refer to the information given in Section 3 of Chapter 7A, noting that the seals must be positioned as shown **(see illustration)**.

Selector shaft seal

Renewal of the selector shaft seal is a complex task, requiring much dismantling of the transmission, and should therefore be entrusted to a Nissan dealer.

---

9 Starter inhibitor/reversing light switch - testing, removal and refitting

Testing

1 The starter inhibitor/reversing light switch is a dual-function switch which is screwed onto the front of the transmission housing. The inhibitor function of the switch ensures that the engine can only be started whilst the selector lever is in either the "N" or "P" positions, therefore preventing the engine being started whilst the transmission is in gear. If at any time it is noted that the engine can be started whilst the selector lever is in any position other than "P" or "N", then it is likely that the inhibitor function of the switch is incorrectly adjusted or faulty. The switch also performs the function of the reversing light switch, illuminating the reversing lights whenever the selector lever is in the "R" position. If either function of the switch is faulty, the switch must be tested as follows.

2 To improve access to the switch, firmly apply the handbrake, then jack up the front of the vehicle and support it on axle stands (see "Jacking and Vehicle Support").

8.1 Correct fitted positions of driveshaft seals
Right-hand side seal (dimension A) - 5.5 to 6.5 mm
Left-hand side seal (dimension B) - 0.5 mm or less

9.4 Starter/inhibitor switch terminal identification. Test switch as described in text

9.11 Adjust the switch using a drill/rod as described in text

1 *Starter/inhibitor switch*
2 *Transmission selector lever*
3 *Adjustment holes*
4 *4 mm diameter drill/rod*

3 Disconnect the wiring connector from the switch.

4 Measure the resistances between the various terminals of the switch (see illustration) with the selector lever in the "P", "N" and "R" positions. If the switch is functioning correctly, there should be continuity between terminals 1 and 2 in the "P" and "N" positions, and continuity between terminals 3 and 4 in the "R" position.

5 If this is not the case, slacken the switch retaining bolts, and adjust the switch as described in paragraphs 10 and 11. If the switch still fails to function properly after adjustment, it is faulty and must be renewed.

Removal

6 To improve access to the switch, firmly apply the handbrake, then jack up the front of the vehicle and support it on axle stands (see "*Jacking and Vehicle Support*").

7 Disconnect the wiring connector from the switch.

8 Slacken and remove the three retaining bolts, then free the switch from the transmission selector mechanism and remove it from the vehicle.

Refitting

9 Manoeuvre the switch into position, and engage it with the selector mechanism. Install the switch retaining bolts, tightening them loosely at this stage.

10 Position the selector lever in the "N" position, and obtain a 4 mm diameter twist drill or rod.

11 Insert the drill/rod through the hole in the top of the selector lever, and also through the hole in the top of the switch lever (see illustration). With the holes aligned, securely tighten the switch retaining bolts, then withdraw the drill/rod.

12 Reconnect the switch wiring, and check the operation of the switch.

10 Overdrive switch - testing, removal and refitting

Testing

1 Remove the centre console as described in Chapter 11.

2 Disconnect the wiring from the overdrive switch and gear indicator light.

3 Measure the resistance between terminals 1 and 2 of the connector (see illustration). If the switch is functioning correctly, there should be continuity between the terminals only when the switch is "off". If not, the switch must be renewed.

Removal

4 Remove the centre console (Chapter 11).

5 Disconnect the wiring from the overdrive switch and gear indicator light.

6 Undo the two retaining screws, depress the detent button, and slide the handle off the top of the selector lever.

7 Unclip the overdrive switch, and remove it from the handle.

Refitting

8 Clip the overdrive switch back into position in the selector lever handle.

9 Ensure that the switch wiring is correctly routed down through the handle, and refit the handle to the selector lever. Securely tighten its retaining screws, then check the operation of the lever detent mechanism.

10 Connect the overdrive switch and gear indicator light wiring, then refit the centre console as described in Chapter 11.

10.3 Overdrive switch terminal identification. Test switch as described in text

11 Automatic transmission - removal and refitting

Removal

1 Chock the rear wheels, then firmly apply the handbrake and position the selector lever in the "N" (neutral) position. Jack up the front of the vehicle, and securely support it on axle stands (see "*Jacking and Vehicle Support*"). Remove both front roadwheels.

2 Drain the transmission fluid as described in Chapter 1, then refit the drain plug and tighten it to the specified torque.

3 Remove the battery and battery tray as described in Chapter 5.

4 On the GE16DE engine, remove the air cleaner housing inlet duct as described in Chapter 4B.

5 Disconnect the wiring connectors from the starter inhibitor/reversing light switch and the transmission solenoid wiring.

6 Detach the kickdown inner cable from the throttle body cam. Slacken the outer cable locknuts, and unbolt the cable mounting bracket. Release the kickdown cable from any relevant retaining clips, so that it is free to be removed with the transmission.

7 Slacken and remove the nut and washer securing the selector cable to the transmission selector lever. Slide out the clip securing the outer cable to its mounting bracket, then free the cable from the transmission.

8 Using a hose clamp or similar, clamp both the fluid cooler hoses to minimise coolant loss. Slacken the retaining clips, and disconnect both hoses from the transmission - be prepared for some spillage. Wipe up any spilt fluid immediately.

9 Remove the driveshafts as described in Chapter 8.

10 Remove the exhaust front downpipe with reference to Chapter 4A or 4B.

11 Remove the starter motor as described in Chapter 5.

12 Undo the retaining bolts, and remove the cover plate from the sump flange to gain access to the torque converter retaining bolts. Slacken and remove the visible bolt then, using a socket and extension bar to rotate the crankshaft pulley, undo the remaining bolts securing the torque converter to the driveplate as they become accessible. There are four bolts in total.

13 Place a jack with interposed block of wood beneath the engine, to take the weight of the engine. Alternatively, attach a hoist or support bar to the engine lifting eyes, and take the weight of the engine.

14 Place a jack and block of wood beneath the transmission, and raise the jack to take the weight of the transmission.

15 Slacken and remove the through-bolt from the rear engine/transmission mounting. Undo the bolts securing the mounting bracket in position, and manoeuvre it away from the engine/transmission. Recover the stopper ring which is fitted between the mounting bracket and mounting.

16 Slacken and remove the through-bolt from the left-hand engine/transmission mounting. Undo the three bolts securing the mounting to the transmission, and manoeuvre the mounting out of position. Recover the rubbers from each side of the mounting bracket.

17 To ensure that the torque converter does not fall out as the transmission is removed, secure it in position using a length of metal strip bolted to one of the starter motor bolt holes.

18 With the jack positioned beneath the transmission taking the weight, slacken and remove the remaining bolts securing the transmission housing to the engine. Note the correct fitted positions of each bolt (and any relevant brackets) as they are removed, to use as a reference on refitting.

19 Make a final check that all necessary components have been disconnected, and are positioned clear of the transmission so that they will not hinder the removal procedure.

20 With the bolts removed, move the trolley jack and transmission to the left, to free it from its locating dowels.

21 Once the transmission is completely free from the engine, lower the jack and manoeuvre the unit out from under the car. If they are loose, remove the locating dowels from the transmission or engine, and keep them in a safe place.

Refitting

22 The transmission is refitted by a reversal of the removal procedure, bearing in mind the following points:

a) Prior to installing the transmission, ensure that the torque converter is correctly engaged with the transmission. This can be checked by measuring the distance from the converter mounting bolt holes to the transmission mating surface; if the converter is correctly seated, this distance will be at least 21.1 mm **(see illustration)**.

b) Ensure that the locating dowels are correctly positioned prior to installation.

c) Tighten all nuts and bolts to the specified torque (where given).

d) Inspect the mounting rubbers for signs of damage or deterioration, and renew if necessary.

e) Prior to refitting the driveshafts, renew the driveshaft seals using the information given in Section 8.

f) Adjust the selector cable and kickdown cable as described in Sections 2 and 5 of this Chapter.

g) On completion, refill the transmission with the specified type and quantity of lubricant, as described in Chapter 1.

12 Automatic transmission overhaul - general information

In the event of a fault occurring, it will be necessary to establish whether the fault is electrical, mechanical or hydraulic in nature, before repair work can be contemplated. Diagnosis requires detailed knowledge of the transmission operation and construction, as well as access to specialised test equipment, and so is deemed to be beyond the scope of this manual. It is therefore essential that problems with the automatic transmission are referred to a Nissan dealer for assessment.

Note that a faulty transmission should not be removed before the vehicle has been assessed by a dealer, as fault diagnosis must be carried out with the transmission in situ.

11.22 Prior to refitting, ensure that the distance (A) from the torque converter bolt holes to the transmission mating surface is at least 21.1 mm, indicating that the converter is correctly seated

Chapter 8
Driveshafts

Contents

Degrees of difficulty

| Easy, suitable for novice with little experience | | Fairly easy, suitable for beginner with some experience | | Fairly difficult, suitable for competent DIY mechanic | | Difficult, suitable for experienced DIY mechanic | | Very difficult, suitable for expert DIY or professional | |

Specifications

General
Type . . . . Unequal-length, solid steel shafts, splined to inner and outer constant velocity joints. Intermediate support bearing on later models with equal length driveshafts.

Lubrication
Lubricant type . . . . Nissan grease supplied with gaiter repair kit

Torque wrench settings

	Nm	lbf ft
Roadwheel nuts	110	82
Driveshaft nut*	250	185
Brake caliper guide pin bolts	25	19
Track-rod end-to-steering arm nut:		
Recommended torque	39	30
Maximum permissible torque	49	35
Lower arm balljoint-to-hub carrier nuts*	65	50
Intermediate bearing housing-to-support bracket bolts	15	12

*Use a new nut.

8

1.1 Exploded view of typical driveshaft assembly

1 Outer CV joint
2 Gaiter clips
3 Outer CV joint gaiter
4 Circlip
5 Driveshaft
6 Gaiter clips
7 Inner CV joint gaiter
8 Retaining ring
9 Snap-ring
10 Inner race
11 Cage
12 Ball
13 Snap-ring
14 Inner CV joint housing (left hand driveshaft)
15 Dust shield (left hand driveshaft)
16 Circlip (left hand driveshaft)
17 Inner CV joint housing and intermediate shaft (right hand driveshaft)
18 Snap-ring (right hand driveshaft)

19 Dust shield (right hand driveshaft)
20 Support bearing (right hand driveshaft)
21 Support bearing retainer (right hand driveshaft)
22 Bracket (right hand driveshaft)
23 Snap-ring
24 Dust shield

L.H. DRIVE SHAFT

R.H. DRIVE SHAFT

H28753

1 General information

Power is transmitted from the gearbox output shafts to the roadwheels by the driveshafts, via inboard and outboard constant velocity (CV) joints **(see illustration)**.

An intermediate drive shaft, with its own support bearing is fitted between the gearbox output and right hand drive shafts on certain models. This layout has the effect of equalising driveshaft angles at all suspension positions and reduces driveshaft flexing, improving directional stability.

The outer Rzeppa-type CV joints allow smooth transmission of drive to the wheels at all steering and suspension angles. Drive is transmitted by means of six radially static steel balls that run in grooves between the two halves of the joint. The joints are protected by rubber gaiters and are packed with grease, to provide permenant lubrication. In the event of wear being detected, the joint can be detached from the driveshaft and renewed. Normally, the CV joints do not require additional lubrication, unless they have been renovated or the rubber gaiters have been damaged, allowing the grease to become contaminated. Refer to Chapter 1 for guidance in checking the condition of the driveshaft gaiters.

The inboard CV joints on early models are of the plunge-cup type; drive is transmitted across the joint by means of three rollers, mounted on the driveshaft in a tripod arrangement, that are radially static but are free to slide in grooves. This arrangement permits axial movement of the driveshaft, which in turn allows the effective length of the driveshaft to alter with suspension travel, without the need for spline joints along the driveshaft itself. The plunge cup joints are permanently lubricated by grease, packed into the gaiters, which only requires renewal in the event of joint overhaul or gaiter repair.

On later models, the inboard joints are of the double-offset type, consisting of a set of ball-bearings housed in a cage and running between inner race and outer races.

2.3 Remove the split pin and castellated locking plate

Both driveshafts are splined at their outer ends, to accept the wheel hubs, and are threaded so that each hub can be fastened to the driveshaft by a large nut. The inner end of each driveshaft is splined, to accept the differential sun gear.

2 Driveshafts - removal and refitting

Note: *A balljoint separator tool will be required for this operation. A new driveshaft nut, driveshaft inner joint retaining clip, and and track-rod end nut split-pins (where applicable) must be used on refitting. In addition, new lower arm balljoint nuts should be used.*

Removal

1 Chock the rear wheels, apply the handbrake, then jack up the front of the vehicle and support on axle stands (see *"Jacking and Vehicle Support"*). Remove the appropriate roadwheel(s).

2 To reduce spillage when the inner end of the driveshaft is withdrawn from the transmission, drain the transmission oil/fluid as described in Chapter 7A or 7B, as applicable.

3 Remove the split-pin from the outer end of the driveshaft, then withdraw the castellated locking plate and the spacer. Discard the split-pin - a new one must be used on refitting **(see illustration)**.

2.4 Using a suitable tool to immobilise the hub whilst loosening the hub nut

4 The front hub must now be held stationary in order to loosen the driveshaft nut. Ideally, the hub should be held by a suitable tool bolted into place using two of the roadwheel nuts. Alternatively, have an assistant firmly apply the brake pedal to prevent the hub from rotating. Using a socket and extension bar, slacken and remove the driveshaft nut **(see illustration)**.

 Warning: Take care, the nut is very tight! Discard the nut - a new one must be used on refitting. Recover the washer.

5 Refer to Chapter 9 and remove the brake caliper from the hub carrier. Note that there is no need to disconnect the brake fluid hose - suspend the caliper from the suspension or body using wire or a cable-tie, to prevent the straining the brake hose. **Do not** depress the brake pedal whilst the caliper is removed, as this will cause the piston to be ejected.
6 Remove the split-pin (where fitted), then partially unscrew the castellated nut securing the track-rod end to the steering arm. Using a balljoint separator tool, separate the track-rod end from the steering arm (refer to Chapter 10 for details). Remove the nut. Discard the split-pin - a new one must be used on refitting.
7 With reference to Chapter 10, unscrew the nut from the hub carrier-to-suspension lower arm balljoint, then press the joint out of the hub carrier using a ball joint splitter - this frees the hub carrier from the suspension lower arm. **Note:** *Discard the balljoint nut - a new one should be used on refitting.*

2.13 Separate the bearing housing from the bracket - models with intermediate driveshaft

2.8 Extracting the outer driveshaft from the hub carrier

8 Temporarily refit the driveshaft nut to the end of the driveshaft, to prevent damage to the driveshaft threads, then using a soft-faced mallet, carefully tap the driveshaft from the hub carrier **(see illustration)**. If the shaft is a tight fit, a suitable hub puller can be used to force the end of the shaft from the hub. Support the end of the driveshaft - do not allow the end of the driveshaft to hang down as this will strain the joint components.
9 Proceed as follows, according to which driveshaft is to be removed.

Right-hand driveshaft - early models without intermediate shaft

10 Separate the driveshaft from the transmission, using a suitable lever inserted between the casing of the inner constant velocity joint and the transmission casing **(see illustration)**. Prise out the driveshaft until the retaining clip compresses into its groove, and is released from the differential sun gear. Discard the retaining clip - a new clip must be used on refitting.
11 Withdraw the driveshaft assembly.

Right-hand driveshaft - later models with intermediate shaft

12 Unscrew the three bolts securing the intermediate bearing housing to the support bracket.
13 Separate the housing from the bracket by rotating it (using both hands!) until a gap has opened into which a suitable lever can be inserted **(see illustration)**. **Do not** lever against the seal on the inner end of the driveshaft, or attempt to separate the intermediate bearing from its housing.
14 Withdraw the driveshaft assembly, complete with the intermediate bearing and housing.

Left-hand driveshaft - all except models with automatic transmission

15 The procedure is as described for the right-hand driveshaft earlier in this Section, but take care not to damage the oil seal when prising the driveshaft from the transmission.

Left-hand driveshaft - models with automatic transmission

16 To remove the left-hand driveshaft, the right-hand driveshaft must be removed first, as described earlier in this Section.

2.10 Extracting the inner driveshaft from the differential

17 Working through the aperture in the right-hand side of the differential created by removal of the right-hand driveshaft, pass a suitable long-bladed screwdriver or a similar drift into the differential until it rests against the inner end of the left-hand driveshaft. Take care not to damage the planet gear shaft or the sun gear **(see illustration)**.
18 Tap the end of the driveshaft until the retaining clip compressed into its groove, and is released from the differential sun gear.
19 Withdraw the driveshaft assembly. Discard the retaining clip - a new clip must be used on refitting.

Refitting

20 Before installing a driveshaft, examine the driveshaft oil seal in the transmission for signs of damage or deterioration and, if necessary, renew it, referring to Chapter 7A or 7B for further information (it is advisable to renew the seal as a matter of course).
21 Thoroughly clean the driveshaft splines, and the apertures in the transmission and hub assembly. Apply a thin film of grease to the oil

2.17 Using a screwdriver to release the inner end of the left hand driveshaft from the from the differential - models with automatic transmission

1 Screwdriver tip	3 Driveshaft
2 Sun gear	4 Planet gear shaft

8

seal lips, and to the driveshaft splines and shoulders. Check that all driveshaft gaiter clips are securely fastened.

22 Note that the retaining clip at the inner end of the driveshaft **must** be renewed on refitting.

23 When refitting a driveshaft, great care must be taken ·to prevent damage to the driveshaft oil seals. Nissan specify the use of special tools which guide the shafts through the seal lip on refitting. Provided that the seal lips and the shaft ends are lightly greased, and that care is taken on refitting, these tools should not be necessary.

Right-hand driveshaft - early models without intermediate shaft

24 Insert the inner end of the driveshaft into the transmission, taking care not to damage the oil seal.

25 Engage the driveshaft splines with those of the differential sun gear, and press the driveshaft into place until the retaining clip (a new clip should be fitted) engages correctly behind (inboard of) the sun gear.

26 Grasp the inner joint body firmly, and check that the clip is correctly engaged - it should not be possible to pull the driveshaft from the transmission.

Right-hand driveshaft - later models with intermediate shaft

27 Insert the inner end of the driveshaft through the intermediate bearing bracket, and engage the driveshaft splines with those of the differential sun gear, taking care not to damage the oil seal.

28 Manipulate the bearing housing into position in the bracket, ensuring that the bolt holes are aligned.

29 Refit the bolts securing the bearing housing to the support bracket, and tighten them to the specified torque.

Left-hand driveshaft - all except models with automatic transmission

30 Proceed as described for the right hand driveshaft, in paragraphs 24 to 26.

Left-hand driveshaft - models with automatic transmission

31 Proceed as described for the right hand driveshaft, in paragraphs 24 to 26. On completion, refit the right-hand driveshaft itself.

All models

32 Apply a thin film of grease to the outer driveshaft joint splines, then engage the outer end of the driveshaft with the hub, ensuring that the splines engage correctly.

33 Refit the washer and a new driveshaft nut, but do not tighten the nut at this stage.

34 Push the suspension lower arm balljoint up into the base of hub carrier and fit a new nut, tightening it to the specified torque.

35 Reconnect the track-rod end to the steering arm, then refit the castellated nut, and tighten to the specified torque.

36 If necessary, tighten the nut further (ensure that the maximum torque for the nut is not exceeded) until the nearest grooves in the nut are aligned with the split-pin hole in the track-rod end, then fit a new split-pin.

37 Refit the brake caliper (Chapter 9).

38 Hold the front hub stationary as during removal, then tighten the new driveshaft nut to the specified torque.

39 Fit the spacer and the castellated locking plate (ensure that the grooves in the locking plate are aligned with the split-pin hole in the end of the driveshaft, then fit a new split-pin.

40 Refit the roadwheel(s), and lower the vehicle to the ground.

41 Refill the transmission with oil/fluid as described in Chapter 1.

3 Driveshaft overhaul and rubber gaiter renewal

Outer joint

Note: *New gaiter securing clips and a new joint retaining clip must be used on refitting.*

1 Remove the driveshaft (Section 2).

2 Measure the length of the gaiter as fitted, so that the new gaiter can be set to the same length before securing it in position **(see illustration)**.

3 Remove the rubber gaiter securing clips, then slide the gaiter away from the joint towards the centre of the driveshaft.

4 If the original joint is to· be re-used, make alignment marks between the joint and the driveshaft.

5 The joint must now be pulled from the end of the driveshaft. Clamp the driveshaft in a vice.

6 To remove the joint, temporarily refit the driveshaft nut to the end of the driveshaft, then attach a slide hammer with a suitable puller adapter to act on the driveshaft nut **(see illustration)**. Take great care not to damage the threads on the end of the driveshaft. Alternatively, tap the driveshaft joint outwards using a mallet, to force the retaining clip to contract into its groove, thus releasing the joint from the shaft.

3.2 Measure the length of the gaiter as fitted, so that the new gaiter can be set to the same length on reassembly

7 Slide the gaiter from the end of the shaft, then remove the joint retaining clip. Discard the clip - a new clip must be used on refitting.

8 Thoroughly clean the outer constant velocity joint and the end of the driveshaft using paraffin, or a suitable solvent, and dry thoroughly. Carry out a visual inspection of the joint. If any of the joint components are worn, it will be necessary to renew the joint complete, as no spare parts are available.

9 Commence refitting by winding a thin layer of tape around the end of the shaft, to protect the gaiter from the shaft splines **(see illustration)**.

10 Slide the smaller gaiter securing clip onto the shaft, followed by the gaiter.

11 Remove the tape from the end of the shaft, then fit a new joint retaining clip to the end of the shaft.

12 Fit the outer joint to the shaft, and engage it with the shaft splines. If the original joint is re-used, align the marks made on the joint and the end of the driveshaft before dismantling.

13 Temporarily refit the driveshaft nut to protect the joint threaded end, then clamp the driveshaft in a vice, and use a mallet to tap the joint onto the shaft until the retaining clip engages correctly behind the joint cage.

14 Pack the joint with the correct amount of the specified grease (supplied with the gaiter kit), then twist the joint to ensure that all the recesses are filled. Pack any surplus grease into the gaiter.

3.6 Using a slide hammer to remove the outer driveshaft joint

1 Slide hammer   *2 Driveshaft nut*

3.9 Wrap tape (arrowed) around the shaft splines to protect the gaiter

3.15 Bend back the end of the gaiter clip, and secure it under the tags

15 Slide the gaiter onto the outer joint, then fit the new outer gaiter securing clip. Bend back the end of the clip, and secure it under the tags as shown (see illustration).

16 Set the gaiter so that the length is as measured earlier.

17 Check that the smaller end of the gaiter is located in the driveshaft groove, and ensure that the gaiter is not trapped or deformed.

18 Slide the smaller securing clip onto the gaiter, and tighten and secure it as described previously.

19 Refit the driveshaft as described in Section 2.

Inner joint

Ball-and-cage type joint

Note: *New gaiter securing clips and a new joint retaining clip must be used on refitting.*

20 The procedure is as described for the outer joint in paragraphs 1 to 18 inclusive, bearing in mind the following points (see illustration):

a) *Ignore the reference to refitting the driveshaft nut and using a slide hammer to remove the joint - the joint must be tapped off using a mallet and soft metal drift.*

b) *Measure the length of the gaiter at the points shown.*

Tripod joint

Note: *New gaiter securing clips and a new joint tripod circlip must be used on refitting.*

21 Remove the driveshaft as described in Section 2.

3.20 Measure the length of the gaiter at the points shown

22 Measure the length of the gaiter, so that the new gaiter can be set to the same length before securing it in position (see illustration).

23 Remove the gaiter securing clips, and slide the gaiter off the joint towards the middle of the driveshaft (see illustration).

24 If the original joint is to be re-used, make alignment marks between the joint and the driveshaft.

25 Pull the joint body from the tripod, ensuring that the rollers remain in place on the tripod (see illustration).

26 Mark the relationship bewteen the tripod and the driveshaft, then using circlip pliers, remove the circlip securing the tripod to the end of the shaft (see illustrations). Discard the circlip - a new one should be used on refitting.

27 Withdraw the tripod and the gaiter from the end of the shaft.

28 Thoroughly clean the constant velocity joint components and the end of the driveshaft using paraffin, or a suitable solvent (taking care not to obliterate the alignment markings made during removal) and dry thoroughly. Carry out a visual inspection of the joint

29 If any of the joint components are worn, the tripod assembly or the joint body can be renewed separately as complete units, but no other spare parts are available. Note the number stamped on the sides of the tripod rollers and ensure that only new components marked with the same number are purchased.

3.22 Measure the length of the gaiter, so that the new gaiter can be set to the same length on reassembly

3.23 Remove the gaiter securing clips

30 Commence refitting by winding a thin layer of tape around the end of the shaft, to protect the gaiter from the shaft splines.

31 Slide the smaller gaiter securing clip onto the shaft, followed by the gaiter.

32 Remove the tape from the end of the shaft, then refit the tripod. If the original tripod is being refitted, align the marks made on the tripod and the driveshaft before removal.

33 Fit a new circlip to secure the tripod.

34 Pack the correct amount of the specified grease (supplied with the gaiter kit), around the tripod rollers and into the joint body.

35 Fit the joint body over the tripod. If the original body is being refitted, align the marks made between the body and the driveshaft before removal.

3.25 Pull the joint body from the tripod, ensuring that the rollers remain in place on the tripod

3.26a If the original joint is to be re-used, make alignment marks (arrowed) between the joint and the driveshaft

3.26b Using circlip pliers, remove the circlip securing the tripod to the end of the shaft

8

36 Slide the gaiter onto the joint body, expelling any trapped air, then fit a new outer gaiter securing clip, and tighten it. Bend back the end of the clip, and secure it under the tags as shown in illustration 3.15.

37 Set the gaiter so that the length is as measured in paragraph 22, then check that the smaller end of the gaiter is located in the driveshaft groove, and that the gaiter is not stretched or deformed when at this length.

38 Locate the smaller gaiter securing clip on the end of the gaiter, and secure it as described previously.

39 Refit the driveshaft as described in Section 2.

4 Driveshaft overhaul - general information

1 If any of the checks described in Chapter 1 reveal wear in any driveshaft joint, first remove the roadwheel trim or centre cap (as appropriate).

2 Check that the driveshaft nut is correctly tightened; if in doubt, remove the split pin and the castellated locking plate and spacer. Check that the nut is tightened to the specified torque, then refit the spacer, the locking plate, and a new split-pin. Refit the roadwheel trim or centre cap (as applicable), and repeat the check on the remaining driveshaft nut.

3 Road test the vehicle, and listen for a metallic clicking from the front as the vehicle is driven slowly in a circle on full-lock. If a clicking noise is heard, this indicates wear in the outer constant velocity joint.

4 If vibration, consistent with road speed, is felt through the car when accelerating, there is a possibility of wear in the inner constant velocity joints.

5 To check the joints for wear, remove the driveshafts, then dismantle them as described in Section 3. If any wear or free play is found, the relevant joint must be renewed (no individual spare parts are available).

5 Right-hand driveshaft intermediate bearing - renewal

Note: *A suitable press will be required for this operation. New bearing circlips must be used on refitting.*

1 Remove the right-hand driveshaft as described in Section 2.

2 To ease the operation, remove the inner constant velocity joint, complete with the intermediate bearing and housing, from the driveshaft as described in Section 3.

3 Clamp the joint in a vice, then tap the dust shield from the inner end of the shaft, using a suitable drift.

4 Using a suitable screwdriver, prise the bearing dust shield from the inboard end of the bearing housing.

5 Using circlip pliers, remove the bearing circlip. Discard the circlip - a new one should be used on refitting.

6 Using a suitable press, remove the bearing/housing assembly from the end of the shaft. It should be possible to tap the bearing from the end of the shaft, if the bearing inner race is supported adequately, but this is not recommended if the bearing is to be re-used, as damage to the bearing is likely to result.

7 Invert the bearing/housing assembly, and use circlip pliers to remove the large circlip from the outboard end of the bearing. Discard the circlip - a new one should be used on refitting. Prise off the dust seal.

8 Support the bearing housing, then using a suitable tube or socket, which bears only on the bearing outer race, tap the bearing from the housing.

9 Commence refitting by packing the bearing with grease.

10 Using a suitable tube or socket which bears only on the bearing outer race, tap the bearing into the housing until the outboard dust shield and the large circlip can be refitted.

11 Ensure that the bearing inner race is adequately supported, then using a suitable tool (a block of wood should serve) to bear across the end of the driveshaft joint, press the shaft into the bearing until the inboard circlip can be refitted.

12 Carefully tap the bearing dust seal into position against the bearing, then tap the dust seal into position on the inboard end of the driveshaft.

13 Refit the inner constant velocity joint as described in Section 3.

14 Refit the driveshaft as described in Section 2.

Chapter 9
Braking system

Contents

Degrees of difficulty

Easy, suitable for novice with little experience		Fairly easy, suitable for beginner with some experience		Fairly difficult, suitable for competent DIY mechanic		Difficult, suitable for experienced DIY mechanic		Very difficult, suitable for expert DIY or professional	

Specifications

General

System type	Dual hydraulic circuit. Anti-lock braking system fitted to some models. Front disc brakes on all models. Rear drum brakes on models with conventional braking, rear disc brakes on models with ABS. Vacuum servo-assistance on all models. Cable-operated handbrake to rear wheels.

Front brakes

Type	Single-piston sliding caliper with solid discs on 1.4 litre models, ventilated discs on 1.6 models.
Type No.:	
1.4 litre models.	CL18C
1.6 litre models	CL18VD
Disc diameter (all models)	240.0 mm
Disc thickness:	
New:	
CL18C	12.0 mm
CL18VD	18.0 mm
Minimum:	
CL18C	10.0 mm*
CL18VD	16.0 mm*
*(0.02 mm maximum variation between sides)	
Maximum disc run-out	0.07 mm
Minimum pad friction material thickness	2.0 mm

9

Rear disc brakes

Type	Solid disc with single-piston sliding caliper
Type No.	AD7HA
Disc diameter	234.0 mm
Disc thickness:	
New	7.0 mm
Minimum thickness	6.0 mm*
*(0.02 mm maximum variation between sides)	
Maximum disc run-out	0.07 mm
Minimum pad friction material thickness	2.0 mm

Rear drum brakes

Type	Drum, with leading and trailing shoes operated by twin-piston wheel cylinder and handbrake cables.
Type No.	LT18C
Drum inner diameter:	
New	180.0 mm
Maximum diameter after machining	181.0 mm
Maximum out-of-round	0.03 mm
Minimum shoe lining thickness	1.5 mm

Brake pedal

Free height:	
Right-hand-drive models:	
Manual transmission	155.0 to 165.0 mm
Automatic transmission	164.0 to 174.0 mm
Left-hand-drive models:	
Manual transmission	148.0 to 158.0 mm
Automatic transmission	157.0 to 167.0 mm
Pedal free-play	1.0 to 3.0 mm

Vacuum servo

Diaphragm diameter:	
1.4 litre models	205 mm
1.6 litre models:	
Primary	180 mm
Secondary	155 mm
Output pushrod length*:	
C180 and S180 units	4.875 to 5.125 mm
M165T, M195T, S205 and C205 units	10.275 to 10.525 mm
*(measured from with a vacuum of 500 mmHg applied to vacuum hose port.)	

Rear brake pressure-regulating valve

1.4 litre and non-ABS 1.6 litre models:	
Right hand drive	Dual proportioning valve (separate from master cylinder)
Left hand drive	Dual proportioning valve (built into master cylinder)
1.6 litre models with ABS	Twin load sensing valve; variable pressure split point and reduction ratio

Master cylinder

Cylinder bore diameter	20.64 mm

Handbrake

Number of notches required to operate handbrake:	
Drum brake models	5 to 6 notches
Disc brake models	7 to 8 notches
Number of notches required to operate handbrake warning light	1 or less

Torque wrench settings

	Nm	lbf ft
Brake hydraulic system bleed screws	10	7
Brake fluid pipe union nuts	16	12
Brake fluid hose union banjo bolts	18	14
Front brake caliper guide pin bolts*	25	18
Front brake caliper mounting bracket bolts	60	45
Rear brake caliper guide pin bolts*	35	27
Rear brake caliper mounting bracket bolts	45	33
Rear brake caliper handbrake lever cam nut	40	30
Rear wheel cylinder mounting bolts	8	6
Rear brake backplate bolts (drum brake models)	45	33
Master cylinder securing nuts	10	7
Brake servo/pedal bracket securing bolts/nuts	15	11
Handbrake lever mounting bolts	10	7

*Apply locking compound to the bolt threads.

1 General information

The braking system is of the servo-assisted, dual-circuit hydraulic type. The arrangement of the hydraulic system is such that each circuit operates one front and one rear brake from a tandem master cylinder. Under normal circumstances, both circuits operate in unison. However, in the event of hydraulic failure in one circuit, full braking force will still be available at two diagonally-opposite wheels.

All models covered in this manual are fitted with front disc brakes and either rear drum or disc brakes.

The front disc brakes are actuated by single-piston sliding type calipers, which ensure that equal pressure is applied to each disc pad.

The rear drum brakes incorporate leading and trailing shoes, which are actuated by twin-piston wheel cylinders. A self-adjust mechanism is incorporated, to automatically compensate for brake shoe wear. As the brake shoe linings wear, the footbrake operation automatically operates the adjuster mechanism, which effectively lengthens the shoe strut and repositions the brake shoes, to remove the lining-to-drum clearance.

The mechanical handbrake linkage operates the brake shoes via a lever attached to the trailing brake shoe.

Models with conventional (non-ABS) braking systems are fitted with a rear brake pressure-proportioning valve, to prevent the possibility of the rear wheels locking before the front wheels under heavy braking. Models with ABS are fitted with dual rear brake pressure regulating valves, which are load sensitive.

Note: *When servicing any part of the system, work carefully and methodically; also observe scrupulous cleanliness when overhauling any part of the hydraulic system. Always renew components (in axle sets, where applicable) if in doubt about their condition, and use only genuine Nissan replacement parts, or at least those of known good quality. Note the warnings given in "Safety first" and at relevant points in this Chapter concerning the dangers of asbestos dust and hydraulic fluid.*

2.14a Bleed screw dust cap (arrowed) - rear brake drum shown

2 Hydraulic system - bleeding

⚠️ *Warning: Hydraulic fluid is poisonous; wash off immediately and thoroughly in the case of skin contact, and seek immediate medical advice if any fluid is swallowed, or gets into the eyes. Certain types of hydraulic fluid are inflammable, and may ignite when allowed into contact with hot components. When servicing any hydraulic system, it is safest to assume that the fluid IS inflammable, and to take precautions against the risk of fire as though it is petrol that is being handled. Hydraulic fluid is also an effective paint stripper, and will attack plastics; if any is spilt, it should be washed off immediately, using copious quantities of fresh water. Finally, it is hygroscopic (it absorbs moisture from the air) - old fluid may be contaminated and unfit for further use. When topping-up or renewing the fluid, always use the recommended type, and ensure that it comes from a freshly-opened sealed container.*

General

1 The correct operation of any hydraulic system is only possible after removing all air from the components and circuit; and this is achieved by bleeding the system.

2 During the bleeding procedure, add only clean, unused hydraulic fluid of the recommended type; never re-use fluid that has already been bled from the system. Ensure that sufficient fluid is available before starting work.

3 If there is any possibility of incorrect fluid being already in the system, the brake components and circuit must be flushed completely with uncontaminated, correct fluid, and new seals should be fitted throughout the system.

4 If hydraulic fluid has been lost from the system, or air has entered because of a leak, ensure that the fault is cured before proceeding further.

2.14b Removing the dust cap from the bleed screw - front disc brake shown

5 Park the vehicle on level ground, switch off the engine and select first or reverse gear (or "P"), then chock the wheels and release the handbrake.

6 Check that all pipes and hoses are secure, unions tight and bleed screws closed. Remove the dust caps (where applicable), and clean any dirt from around the bleed screws.

7 Unscrew the master cylinder reservoir cap, and top the master cylinder reservoir up to the "MAX" level line; refit the cap loosely. Remember to maintain the fluid level at least above the "MIN" level line throughout the procedure, otherwise there is a risk of further air entering the system.

8 There are a number of one-man, do-it-yourself brake bleeding kits currently available from motor accessory shops. It is recommended that one of these kits is used whenever possible, as they greatly simplify the bleeding operation, and also reduce the risk of expelled air and fluid being drawn back into the system. If such a kit is not available, the basic (two-man) method must be used, which is described in detail below.

9 If a kit is to be used, prepare the vehicle as described previously, and follow the kit manufacturer's instructions, as the procedure may vary slightly according to the type being used; generally, they are as outlined below in the relevant sub-section.

10 Whichever method is used, the same sequence must be followed (paragraphs 11 and 12) to ensure that the removal of all air from the system.

Bleeding sequence

11 If the system has been only partially disconnected, and suitable precautions were taken to minimise fluid loss, it should be necessary to bleed only that part of the system (ie the primary or secondary circuit).

12 If the complete system is to be bled, then it should be done working in the following sequence:

   a) *Left-hand rear wheel.*
   b) *Right-hand front wheel.*
   c) *Right-hand rear wheel.*
   d) *Left-hand front wheel.*

Bleeding - basic (two-man) method

13 Collect a clean glass jar, a suitable length of plastic or rubber tubing which is a tight fit over the bleed screw, and a ring spanner to fit the screw. The help of an assistant will also be required.

14 Remove the dust cap from the first screw in the sequence if not already done. Fit a suitable spanner and tube to the screw, place the other end of the tube in the jar, and pour in sufficient fluid to cover the end of the tube **(see illustrations)**.

15 Ensure that the master cylinder reservoir fluid level is maintained at least above the "MIN" level line throughout the procedure.

16 Have the assistant fully depress the brake pedal several times to build up pressure, then maintain it on the final downstroke.

9

17 While pedal pressure is maintained, unscrew the bleed screw (approximately one turn) and allow the compressed fluid and air to flow into the jar. The assistant should maintain pedal pressure, following the pedal down to the floor if necessary, and should not release the pedal until instructed to do so. When the flow stops, tighten the bleed screw again, have the assistant release the pedal slowly, and recheck the reservoir fluid level.

18 Repeat the steps given in paragraphs 16 and 17 until the fluid emerging from the bleed screw is free from air bubbles. If the master cylinder has been drained and refilled, and air is being bled from the first screw in the sequence, allow approximately five seconds between cycles for the master cylinder passages to refill.

19 When no more air bubbles appear, tighten the bleed screw securely, remove the tube and spanner, and refit the dust cap (where applicable). Do not overtighten the bleed screw.

20 Repeat the procedure on the remaining screws in the sequence, until all air is removed from the system, and the brake pedal feels firm again.

Bleeding - using a one-way valve kit

21 As their name implies, these kits consist of a length of tubing with a one-way valve fitted, to prevent expelled air and fluid being drawn back into the system; some kits include a translucent container, which can be positioned so that the air bubbles can be more easily seen flowing from the end of the tube.

22 The kit is connected to the bleed screw, which is then opened. The user returns to the driver's seat, depresses the brake pedal with a smooth, steady stroke, and slowly releases it; this is repeated until the expelled fluid is clear of air bubbles **(see illustration).**

23 Note that these kits simplify work so much that it is easy to forget the master cylinder reservoir fluid level; ensure that this is maintained at least above the "MIN" level line at all times.

Bleeding - using a pressure-bleeding kit

24 These kits are usually operated by the reservoir of pressurised air contained in the

2.22 One-way bleed kit connected to the front brake caliper

spare tyre. However, note that it will probably be necessary to reduce the pressure to a lower level than normal; refer to the instructions supplied with the kit.

25 By connecting a pressurised, fluid-filled container to the master cylinder reservoir, bleeding can be carried out simply by opening each screw in turn (in the specified sequence), and allowing the fluid to flow out until no more air bubbles can be seen in the expelled fluid.

26 This method has the advantage that the large reservoir of fluid provides an additional safeguard against air being drawn into the system during bleeding.

27 Pressure-bleeding is particularly effective when bleeding "difficult" systems, or when bleeding the complete system at the time of routine fluid renewal.

All methods

28 When bleeding is complete, and firm pedal feel is restored, wash off any spilt fluid, tighten the bleed screws securely, and refit their dust caps (where applicable).

29 Check the hydraulic fluid level in the master cylinder reservoir, and top-up if necessary (Chapter 1).

30 Discard any hydraulic fluid that has been bled from the system; it will not be fit for re-use.

31 Check the feel of the brake pedal. If it feels at all spongy, air must still be present in the system, and further bleeding is required. Failure to bleed satisfactorily after a reasonable repetition of the bleeding procedure may be due to worn master cylinder seals.

3 Hydraulic pipes and hoses - renewal

Note: *Before starting work, refer to the note at the beginning of Section 2 concerning the dangers of hydraulic fluid.*

1 If any pipe or hose is to be renewed, minimise fluid loss by first removing the master cylinder reservoir cap, then tighten the cap down onto a piece of polythene to obtain an airtight seal. Alternatively, flexible hoses can be sealed, if required, using a proprietary brake hose clamp; metal brake pipe unions can be plugged (if care is taken not to allow dirt into the system) or capped immediately they are disconnected. Place a wad of rag under any union that is to be disconnected, to catch any spilt fluid.

2 If a flexible hose is to be disconnected, unscrew the brake pipe union nut before removing the spring clip which secures the hose to its mounting bracket.

3 To unscrew the union nuts, it is preferable to obtain a brake pipe spanner of the correct size; these are available from most large motor accessory shops. Failing this, a close-fitting open-ended spanner will be required, though if the nuts are tight or corroded, their flats may be

rounded-off if the spanner slips. In such a case, a self-locking wrench is often the only way to unscrew a stubborn union, but it follows that the pipe and the damaged nuts must be renewed on reassembly. Always clean a union and surrounding area before disconnecting it. If disconnecting a component with more than one union, make a careful note of the connections before disturbing any of them.

4 If a brake pipe is to be renewed, it can be obtained, cut to length and with the union nuts and end flares in place, from Nissan dealers. All that is then necessary is to bend it to shape, following the line of the original, before fitting it to the vehicle. Alternatively, most motor accessory shops can make up brake pipes from kits, but this requires very careful measurement of the original, to ensure that the replacement is of the correct length. The safest answer is usually to take the original to the shop as a pattern.

5 On refitting, do not overtighten the union nuts. It is not necessary to exercise brute force to obtain a sound joint.

6 Ensure that the pipes and hoses are correctly routed, with no kinks, and that they are secured in the clips or brackets provided. After fitting, remove the polythene from the reservoir, and bleed the hydraulic system as described in Section 2. Wash off any spilt fluid, and check carefully for fluid leaks.

4 Front brake pads - renewal

> *Warning: Renew BOTH sets of front brake pads at the same time - NEVER renew the pads on only one wheel, as uneven braking may result.*

> *Warning: Note that the dust created by wear of the pads may contain asbestos, which is a health hazard. Never blow it out with compressed air, and don't inhale any of it. An approved filtering mask should be worn when working on the brakes. DO NOT use petrol or petroleum-based solvents to clean brake parts; use brake cleaner or methylated spirit only.*

Note: *Suitable locking compound will be required to coat the threads of the caliper guide pin bolt(s) on refitting.*

1 Chock the rear wheels, apply the handbrake, then jack up the front of the vehicle and support it on axle stands (see *"Jacking and Vehicle Support"*). Remove the front roadwheels. (Note the white paint blob on one of the roadwheel studs - for wheel alignment on refitting.)

2 Working on one side of the vehicle, push the caliper piston into its bore by pulling the caliper outwards. If necessary, press the piston back into its bore using a large G-

4.2 Pressing the caliper piston back into its bore using a G-clamp

4.3a Unscrew the upper and lower caliper guide pin bolts (arrowed) . . .

4.3b . . . then lift the caliper body away from the pads

clamp or similar **(see illustration)**. Keep a careful eye on the level of brake fluid in the reservoir as you do this - ensure that the level does not rise above the 'MAX' mark.

3 Unscrew the upper and lower caliper guide pin bolts (if necessary, use a slim open-ended spanner to counterhold the head of the guide pin), then lift the caliper from the hub/disc assembly. Note that the outboard pad may be retained in the caliper bracket. **Do not** depress the brake pedal until the caliper is refitted, or the piston will be pushed out of its bore **(see illustrations)**.

4 Ensure that the caliper is adequately supported to avoid straining the brake hose, then withdraw the brake pads. Note that the inboard pad is clipped into the caliper piston. Where applicable, recover the shims from the rear of the pads and the pad retainers **(see illustrations)**.

4.4a Ensure that the caliper is adequately supported to avoid straining the brake hose . . .

5 First measure the thickness of each brake pad's friction material. If either pad is worn at any point to the specified minimum thickness or less, all four pads must be renewed. Also, the pads should be renewed if any are fouled with oil or grease; there is no satisfactory way of degreasing friction material, once contaminated. If any of the brake pads are worn unevenly, or are fouled with oil or grease, trace and rectify the cause before reassembly.

6 New brake pads and shim/clip kits are available from Nissan dealers. Do not be tempted to swap brake pads over to compensate for uneven wear.

7 If the brake pads are still serviceable, carefully clean them using a clean, fine wire brush or similar, paying particular attention to the sides and back of the metal backing. Where applicable, clean out the grooves in the friction material, and pick out any large embedded particles of dirt or debris.

8 Clean the surfaces of the bracket, clips, and the pad locations in the caliper body/mounting bracket.

9 Prior to fitting the pads, check that the guide pins are free to slide easily in the caliper body/mounting bracket, and check that the rubber guide pin gaiters are undamaged. Brush the dust and dirt from the caliper and piston, but *do not* inhale it, as it is a health hazard. Inspect the dust seal around the piston for damage, and the piston for evidence of fluid leaks, corrosion or damage. If attention to any of these components is necessary, refer to Section 9.

10 If new brake pads are to be fitted, the caliper piston must be pushed back into the cylinder, to make room for them. Either use a G-clamp or similar tool, or use suitable pieces of wood as levers. Provided that the master cylinder reservoir has not been overfilled with hydraulic fluid, there should be no spillage, but keep a careful watch on the fluid level while retracting the piston. If the fluid level rises above the "MAX" level line at any time, the surplus should be siphoned off or ejected via a plastic tube connected to the bleed screw (see Section 2).

Caution: Do not syphon the fluid by mouth, as it is poisonous; use a syringe or an old poultry baster.

11 Apply a little anti-squeal brake grease to the contact surfaces of the pad backing plates and the shims (where applicable), but take great care not to allow any grease onto the pad friction linings. Similarly, apply brake grease to the contact surfaces of the anti-rattle clips - again take care not to apply excess grease, which may contaminate the pads.

12 Refit the anti-rattle clips to the caliper mounting bracket, then refit the pads and shims (where applicable), in the positions noted before removal, ensuring that the pad friction material is against the disc. Note that the outboard pad should be fitted to the caliper mounting bracket, and the inboard pad should be fitted to the caliper. Ensure that the inboard pad retaining clip is securely engaged with the caliper piston.

9

4.4b . . . then remove the shims . . .

4.4c . . . and withdraw the brake pads . . .

4.4d . . . and pad retainer(s)

5.3 Unscrewing the caliper guide pin bolts (arrowed)

13 Slide the caliper into position on the mounting bracket, then apply a little locking fluid to the threads of the caliper guide pin bolts, and refit the bolts. Tighten the bolts to the specified torque wrench setting.
14 Check that the caliper body slides smoothly on the guide pins.
15 Repeat the procedure on the remaining front caliper.
16 With both sets of front brake pads refitted, depress the brake pedal repeatedly until the pads are pressed into firm contact with the brake disc, and normal pedal pressure is restored.
17 Refit the roadwheels, and lower the vehicle to the ground.
18 Finally, check the hydraulic fluid level as described in Chapter 1.
19 Check the operation of the braking system thoroughly before bringing the vehicle back into service on the public highway.

5.6a Remove the pad shims . . .

5.4 Lift the caliper body away from the carrier to expose the brake pads

5 Rear brake pads - renewal

Note: *Suitable locking compound will be required to coat the threads of the caliper guide pin bolt(s) on refitting.*

 Warning: Renew BOTH sets of rear brake pads at the same time - NEVER renew the pads on only one wheel, as uneven braking may result.

 Warning: Before starting work, refer to the warning given at the beginning of Section 4, concerning the dangers of asbestos dust.

1 Chock the front wheels, then jack up the rear of the vehicle, and support on axle stands (see *"Jacking and Vehicle Support"*). Remove the rear roadwheels, and release the handbrake.
2 Working on one side of the vehicle, release the spring clip securing the handbrake cable to the bracket on the brake caliper, then release the cable from the bracket, and disconnect the end of the cable from the lever on the caliper (refer to Section 17).
3 Unscrew the caliper upper and lower guide pin bolts **(see illustration)**. If necessary, use a slim open-ended spanner to counterhold the head of the guide pin.
4 Lift the caliper body away from the carrier to expose the brake pads **(see illustration)**.

Do not depress the brake pedal until the caliper is refitted. Take care not to strain the brake fluid hose - suspend the caliper from a suitable point on the suspension using a length of wire.
5 Where applicable, note the locations and orientation of the shims fitted to the rear of each pad and, where applicable, the anti-rattle shims fitted to the top and bottom of the pads.
6 Withdraw the pads, and where applicable, the shims and the anti-rattle springs **(see illustrations)**
7 First measure the thickness of each brake pad's friction material. If either pad is worn at any point to the specified minimum thickness or less, all four pads must be renewed. Also, the pads should be renewed if any are fouled with oil or grease; there is no satisfactory way of degreasing friction material, once contaminated. If any of the brake pads are worn unevenly, or are fouled with oil or grease, trace and rectify the cause before reassembly. New brake pads and shim/spring kits are available from Nissan dealers. Do not be tempted to swap brake pads over to compensate for uneven wear.
8 If the brake pads are still serviceable, carefully clean them using a clean, fine wire brush or similar, paying particular attention to the sides and back of the metal backing. Where applicable, clean out the grooves in the friction material, and pick out any large embedded particles of dirt or debris. Carefully clean the pad locations in the caliper body/mounting bracket.
9 Prior to fitting the pads, check that the guide pins are free to slide easily in the caliper body/mounting bracket, and check that the rubber guide pin gaiters are undamaged. Brush the dust and dirt from the caliper and piston, but *do not* inhale it, as it is a health hazard. Inspect the dust seal around the piston for damage, and the piston for evidence of fluid leaks, corrosion or damage. If attention to any of these components is necessary, refer to Section 10.
10 If new brake pads are to be fitted, the caliper piston must be pushed back into the cylinder, to make room for them. To retract the piston, ideally a suitable retractor tool should be used (available from motor factors).

5.6b . . . pads . . .

5.6c . . . and anti-rattle springs from the carrier bracket

5.10 Using a pair of long nosed pliers to retract the caliper piston

Alternatively, engage a suitable pair of long-nosed pliers with the notches in the piston, then turn the piston clockwise (viewed from the outboard end of the caliper), whilst simultaneously pushing it into the caliper **(see illustration)**. Take care not to damage the surface of the piston, or twist the dust seal. Provided that the master cylinder reservoir has not been overfilled with hydraulic fluid, there should be no spillage, but keep a careful watch on the fluid level while retracting the piston. If the fluid level rises above the "MAX" level line at any time, the surplus should be siphoned off or ejected via a plastic tube connected to the bleed screw (see Section 2). *Caution: Do not syphon the fluid by mouth, as it is poisonous; use a syringe or an old poultry baster.*

11 Apply a little anti-squeal brake grease to the contact surfaces of the pad backing plates and the shims (where applicable), but take great care not to allow any grease onto the pad friction linings. Similarly, where applicable, apply brake grease to the contact surfaces of the anti-rattle springs - again take care not to apply excess grease, which may contaminate the pads. Note that new pads may be supplied with an anti-squeal coating on their contact faces, in which case there is no need to apply brake grease.

12 Where applicable, refit the anti-rattle springs to the caliper mounting bracket, then refit the pads and the shims (where applicable), in the positions noted before removal. Ensure that the pad friction material is against the disc.

13 Fit the caliper body over the brake pads. Ensure that the peg on the back of the inboard pad engages with the nearest notch in the piston. It may be necessary to rotate the piston slightly (as described in earlier) to align the nearest notch with the peg.

14 Coat the threads of the caliper lower guide pin bolt with locking fluid, then refit the bolt, and tighten it to the specified torque.

15 Check that the caliper body slides smoothly on the guide pins.

16 Reconnect the end of the handbrake cable to the lever with reference to Section 17. Refit the cable mounting bracket, and where applicable, the spring clip. Where applicable, ensure that the locating peg on the mounting

6.4 Using a suitable tool to remove the outer spring cups

bracket engages with the corresponding hole in the caliper body.

17 Repeat the procedure on the remaining rear caliper.

18 With both sets of rear brake pads refitted, check and if necessary adjust the operation of the handbrake as described in Section 17.

19 Depress the brake pedal repeatedly to ensure that normal pedal pressure is restored.

20 Refit the roadwheels, and lower the vehicle to the ground.

21 Finally check the hydraulic fluid level as described in Chapter 1.

22 Check the operation of the braking system thoroughly before bringing the vehicle back into service on the public highway.

6 Rear brake shoes - renewal

> ⚠️ *Warning: Renew BOTH sets of rear brake shoes at the same time - NEVER renew the shoes on only one wheel, as uneven braking may result.*

> ⚠️ *Warning: Before starting work, refer to the warning given at the beginning of Section 4, concerning the dangers of asbestos dust.*

1 Remove the rear brake drums, as described in Section 8.

6.6 Carefully pull both brake shoes forwards from the backplate complete with the adjuster and handbrake operating components

2 Working on one side of the vehicle, brush the dirt and dust from the brake backplate and drum. **Do not** inhale the dust, as it may be a health hazard.

3 Note the position of each shoe, and the location of the return and steady springs. Also make a note of the adjuster component locations, to aid refitting later.

4 Remove the shoe hold-down springs **(see illustration)**. Use a suitable tool to depress the outer spring cups, and turn them through 90°

5 Recover the springs and cups (and where applicable, the spring seats), and remove the spring retainer pins from the rear of the backplate.

6 Carefully pull both brake shoes forwards from the backplate complete with the adjuster and handbrake operating components **(see illustration)**. Using a suitable pair of pliers, unhook and remove the upper and lower return springs.

7 If necessary, position a rubber band or a cable-tie over the wheel cylinder, to prevent the pistons from being ejected. If there is any evidence of fluid leakage from the wheel cylinder, renew it or overhaul it as described in Section 11.

8 Separate the adjuster and adjuster spring from the leading and trailing shoes **(see illustrations)**.

9 Remove the adjuster lever from the trailing shoe **(see illustration)**.

6.8a Separate the adjuster and adjuster spring from the leading . . .

6.8b . . . and trailing shoes

6.9 Remove the adjuster lever from the trailing shoe

9

6.10a Unhook the handbrake cable from the handbrake operating lever

6.10b Prise off the retaining clip to remove the handbrake operating lever from the trailing brake shoe

6.13a Manipulate the trailing shoe into position and secure with the hold-down pin, spring and cup

6.13b Ensure that the upper edge of the shoe engages with the recess in the end of the wheel cylinder piston (arrowed)

6.14 Attach the adjuster spring to the upper edge trailing shoe

6.15 Attach the lower return spring to the trailing shoe

10 Unhook the handbrake cable from the handbrake operating lever. Prise off the retaining clip, then remove the pivot pin and withdraw the handbrake operating lever from the trailing brake shoe (see illustrations).

11 Transfer the handbrake operating lever to the new trailing shoe as required, and secure with a new retaining clip. Note: The levers are different on each side of the vehicle - take care not to mix up the components.

12 Apply brake grease sparingly to the shoe contact surfaces of the brake backplate.

13 Offer up the trailing shoe to the backplate, then engage the handbrake cable with the operating lever on the shoe, ensuring that the operating lever spring is correctly located. Manipulate the shoe into position, and secure

with the hold-down pin, spring and cup. Ensure that the upper edge of the shoe engages with the recess in the end of the wheel cylinder piston (see illustrations).

14 Attach the adjuster spring to the upper edge trailing shoe (see illustration), noting that the end of the spring is hooked into the hole from the rear.

15 Attach the lower return spring to the trailing shoe (see illustration), noting that the end of the spring is hooked into the hole from the front.

16 Offer the leading shoe up to the backplate, then hook the adjuster spring over the stud on the rear surface of the shoe (see illustration). Engage the lower return spring with the base of the leading shoe.

17 Shorten the adjuster strut to its minimum length by turning the toothed wheel, and apply a small amount of brake grease to the contact faces of the adjuster strut and handbrake operating lever/adjuster operating lever, as applicable.

18 Insert the adjuster between the trailing and leading shoes (see illustrations), engaging the end of the adjuster with the relevant cut-outs in the shoes. Ensure that the adjuster is fitted the correct way round.

19 Manipulate the leading shoe into position against the lower anchor and engage the upper edge of the shoe with the recess in the end of the wheel cylinder piston. Fit the hold-down pin, spring and cup to secure the leading shoe in position on the backplate (see illustration).

6.16 Hook the adjuster spring over the stud on the rear surface of the shoe

6.18a Insert the adjuster between the trailing and leading shoes

6.18b Ensure that the adjuster is fitted the correct way round and is engaged with the relevant cut-outs in the shoes

6.19 Manipulate the leading shoe into position, then fit the hold-down pin, spring and cup

6.20 Fit the adjuster lever to the trailing shoe

6.21 Refitting the upper return spring

20 Fit the adjuster lever to the trailing shoe **(see illustration)**, ensuring that it engages with the adjuster toothed wheel and pivot pin.

21 Hook the front end of the upper return spring into the hole in the adjuster lever, and the rear end over the stud on the leading shoe **(see illustration)**.

22 Check that all components have been correctly refitted, and check that the adjuster mechanism operates correctly.

23 Turn the adjuster wheel to ensure that the overall diameter of the shoes is less than that of the drum.

24 Repeat the procedure on the remaining side of the vehicle, then refit the brake drums as described in Section 8.

25 Check the operation of the braking system thoroughly before bringing the vehicle back into service on the public highway.

7 Brake disc - inspection, removal and refitting

Warning: Before starting work, refer to the warning at the beginning of Section 4 concerning the dangers of asbestos dust.

Front disc

Inspection

Note: *If either disc requires renewal, BOTH should be renewed at the same time, to ensure even and consistent braking. New brake pads should also be fitted.*

1 Chock the rear wheels, apply the handbrake, then jack up the front of the vehicle and support it on axle stands (see *"Jacking and Vehicle Support"*). Remove the appropriate front roadwheel.

2 Slowly rotate the brake disc so that the full area of both sides can be checked; remove the brake pads (see Section 4) if better access is required to the inboard surface. Light scoring is normal in the area swept by the brake pads, but if heavy scoring or cracks are found, the disc must be renewed.

3 It is normal to find a lip of rust and brake dust around the disc's perimeter; this can be

scraped off if required. If, however, a lip has formed due to excessive wear of the brake pad swept area, then the disc's thickness must be measured using a micrometer. Take measurements at several places around the disc, at the inside and outside of the pad swept area; if the disc has worn at any point to the specified minimum thickness or less, the disc must be renewed.

4 If the disc is thought to be warped, it can be checked for run-out. Either use a dial gauge mounted on any convenient fixed point, while the disc is slowly rotated, or use feeler blades to measure (at several points all around the disc) the clearance between the disc and a fixed point, such as the caliper mounting bracket. If the measurements obtained are at the specified maximum or beyond, the disc is excessively warped, and must be renewed; however, it is worth checking first that the hub bearing is in good condition (Chapters 1 and/or 10). Also try the effect of removing the disc and turning it through 180°, to reposition it on the hub; if the run-out is still excessive, the disc must be renewed.

5 Check the disc for cracks, especially around the wheel stud holes, and any other wear or damage, and renew if necessary.

Removal

6 If not already done, chock the rear wheels, apply the handbrake, then jack up the front of the vehicle and support it on axle stands (see *"Jacking and Vehicle Support"*). Remove the appropriate front roadwheel.

7 Unscrew the two bolts securing the caliper mounting bracket to the hub carrier. Withdraw the caliper assembly, and suspend it using wire or string. Take care not to strain the brake fluid hose - if necessary release the hose from the securing clip(s).

Place a clean spacer (of the same thickness as the disc) between the pads, to prevent them from being dislodged.

8 If the original disc is to be refitted, mark the relationship between the disc and the hub, then pull the disc from the roadwheel studs.

9 If the disc is stuck, it can be pushed off by screwing two M8 bolts into the holes provided in the disc, and evenly tightening the bolts to push the disc from the hub.

Refitting

10 Ensure that the mating faces of the disc and the hub are clean and flat. If necessary, wipe the mating surfaces clean.

11 If the original disc is being refitted, align the marks made on the disc and hub before removal, then refit the disc.

12 If a new disc has been fitted, use a suitable solvent to wipe any preservative coating from the disc.

13 Refit the caliper, ensuring that the pads locate correctly over the disc, then tighten the caliper bracket securing bolts to the specified torque. Where applicable, refit the brake fluid hose to the clip(s).

14 Depress the brake pedal repeatedly until the pads are pressed into contact with the brake disc, and normal pedal pressure is restored.

15 Refit the roadwheel, and lower the vehicle to the ground. Check the operation of the braking system thoroughly before bringing the vehicle back into service on the public highway.

Rear disc

Inspection

Note: *If either disc requires renewal, BOTH should be renewed at the same time, to ensure even and consistent braking. New brake pads should also be fitted.*

16 Chock the front wheels, then jack up the rear of the vehicle and support it on axle stands. Remove the rear roadwheel

17 Fully release the handbrake.

18 Proceed as described for the front disc in paragraphs 2 to 5, but refer to Section 5 if the brake pads are to be removed.

Removal

19 If not already done, chock the front wheels, then jack up the rear of the vehicle, and support securely on axle stands (see *"Jacking and Vehicle Support"*). Remove the appropriate rear roadwheel.

20 Unbolt the handbrake cable mounting bracket from the caliper, then disconnect the end of the cable from the lever on the caliper. It may be necessary to release the spring clip securing the cable to the mounting bracket to enable the cable to be disconnected.

21 Proceed as described for the front brake disc in paragraphs 7 to 9.

9

Refitting

22 Proceed as described for the front brake disc in paragraphs 10 to 13.

23 Reconnect the handbrake cable to the lever on the caliper, then refit the cable mounting bracket, and where applicable, the spring clip. Where applicable, ensure that the locating peg on the mounting bracket engages with the corresponding hole in the caliper body.

24 Operate the handbrake repeatedly until the correct brake pad-to-disc clearance is established (adjustment occurs automatically when the handbrake is operated).

25 Depress the brake pedal repeatedly to ensure that normal pedal pressure is restored.

26 Refit the roadwheel, and lower the vehicle to the ground. Check the operation of the braking system thoroughly before bringing the vehicle back into service on the public highway.

8 Rear brake drum - removal, inspection and refitting

> **Warning: Before starting work, refer to the warning at the beginning of Section 4 concerning the dangers of asbestos dust.**

Removal

1 Chock the front wheels, then jack up the rear of the vehicle and support it on axle stands (see *"Jacking and Vehicle Support"*). Remove the appropriate rear roadwheel.

2 Fully release the handbrake.

3 If the drum cannot easily be pulled from the wheel studs, retract the brake shoes as follows.

4 Remove the blanking plug from the rear of the brake backplate. Insert a suitable tool through the hole in the backplate and through the hole in the shoe, until the tool contacts the handbrake operating lever. Lightly tap the tool in order to free the adjuster mechanism and retract the shoes **(see illustrations)**.

5 If the original drum is to be refitted, mark the relationship between the drum and the hub, then pull the drum from the roadwheel studs.

6 If the drum is still tight, it can be pushed off by screwing two M8 bolts into the holes provided in the drum, and evenly tightening the bolts to push the drum from the hub **(see illustration)**.

Inspection

Note: *If either drum requires renewal, BOTH should be renewed at the same time, to ensure even and consistent braking. New brake shoes should also be fitted.*

7 Working carefully, remove all traces of brake dust from the drum, but *avoid inhaling the dust, as it is a health hazard*.

8.4a Removing a blanking plug from the brake backplate

8 Clean the outside of the drum, and check it for obvious signs of wear or damage, such as cracks around the roadwheel stud holes; renew the drum if necessary.

9 Carefully examine the inside of the drum. Light scoring of the friction surface is normal, but if heavy scoring is found, the drum must be renewed.

10 It is usual to find a lip on the drum's inboard edge which consists of a mixture of rust and brake dust; this should be carefully scraped away, to leave a smooth surface which can be polished with fine (120- to 150- grade) emery paper. If, however, the lip is due to the friction surface being recessed by excessive wear, then the drum must be renewed.

11 If the drum is thought to be excessively worn, or oval, its internal diameter must be measured at several points using an internal micrometer. Take measurements in pairs, the second at right-angles to the first, and compare the two, to check for signs of ovality. Provided that it does not enlarge the drum to beyond the specified maximum diameter, it may be possible to have the drum refinished by skimming or grinding; if this is not possible, the drums on both sides must be renewed. Note that if the drum is to be skimmed, BOTH drums must be refinished, to maintain a consistent internal diameter on both sides.

Refitting

12 If a new brake drum is to be installed, use a suitable solvent to remove any preservative coating that may have been applied to its internal friction surfaces. Note that it may also

8.6 Using two M8 bolts to remove a brake drum

8.4b Using a screwdriver to release the handbrake adjuster mechanism

be necessary to shorten the adjuster strut length, by rotating the strut wheel, to allow the drum to pass over the brake shoes.

13 If the original drum is being refitted, align the marks made on the drum and hub before removal, then fit the drum over the wheel studs.

14 Depress the footbrake repeatedly to expand the brake shoes against the drum, and ensure that normal pedal pressure is restored.

15 Check and if necessary adjust the handbrake cable as described in Chapter 1.

16 Refit the roadwheel, and lower the vehicle to the ground.

17 Check the operation of the braking system thoroughly before bringing the vehicle back into service on the public highway.

9 Front brake caliper - removal, overhaul and refitting

> **Warning: Before starting work, refer to the note at the beginning of Section 2 concerning the dangers of hydraulic fluid, and to the warning at the beginning of Section 4 concerning the dangers of asbestos dust.**

Note: *Suitable locking compound will be required to coat the threads of the caliper guide pin bolts on refitting.*

Removal

1 Chock the rear wheels, apply the handbrake, then jack up the front of the vehicle and support it on axle stands (see *"Jacking and Vehicle Support"*). Remove the appropriate front roadwheel.

2 To minimise fluid loss during the following operations, remove the master cylinder reservoir cap, then tighten it down onto a piece of polythene, to obtain an airtight seal. Alternatively, use a brake hose clamp, a G-clamp or a similar tool to clamp the flexible hose running to the caliper.

3 Clean the area around the fluid hose union on the caliper, then unscrew the hose union banjo bolt. Recover the two sealing washers.

HAYNES HiNT

Plug the brake line union with a length of rubber hose to prevent fluid loss and dirt ingress

4 Remove the brake pads as described in Section 4.

5 Where applicable, unscrew the caliper upper guide pin bolt. If necessary, use a slim open-ended spanner to counterhold the head of the guide pin.

6 Withdraw the caliper.

7 If desired, the caliper mounting bracket can be unbolted from the hub carrier.

Overhaul

Note: *Before commencing work, ensure that the appropriate caliper overhaul kit is obtained.*

8 With the caliper on the bench, wipe away all traces of dust and dirt, but *avoid inhaling the dust, as it is a health hazard.*

9 Extract the caliper guide pins, if necessary by screwing the bolts into the pins, and pulling on the bolts to withdraw the pins. Peel off the rubber dust cover from each guide pin.

10 Remove the retaining ring (where applicable) and peel the dust seal off the piston **(see illustration)**.

11 Place a small block of wood between the caliper body and the piston. Remove the piston by applying a jet of compressed air, such as that from a tyre pump, to the fluid inlet port. Use a blunt wooden instrument (**not** a screwdriver) to extract the piston seal from the caliper cylinder bore **(see illustrations)**.

12 Thoroughly clean all components, using only methylated spirit or clean hydraulic fluid.

9.10 Remove the dust seal retaining ring

Never use mineral-based solvents such as petrol or paraffin, which will attack the hydraulic system rubber components.

13 The caliper piston seal and the dust seal, the guide pin dust covers, and the bleed nipple dust cap, are only available as part of a seal kit. Since the manufacturers recommend that the piston seal and dust seal are renewed whenever they are disturbed, all of these components should be discarded, and new ones fitted on reassembly as a matter of course.

14 Carefully examine all parts of the caliper assembly, looking for signs of wear or damage. In particular, the cylinder bore and piston must be free from any signs of scratches, corrosion or wear. If there is any doubt about the condition of any part of the caliper, the relevant part should be renewed; note that if the caliper body or the mounting bracket are to be renewed, they are available only as part of the complete assembly.

15 The manufacturers recommend that minor scratches, rust, etc, may be polished away from the cylinder bore using fine emery paper, but the piston must be renewed to cure such defects. The piston surface is plated, and **must not** be polished with emery or similar abrasives.

16 Check that the threads in the caliper body and the mounting bracket are in good condition. Check that both guide pins are undamaged, and (when cleaned) a reasonably tight sliding fit in the mounting bracket bores.

17 Use compressed air to blow clear the fluid passages.

 Warning: **Wear eye protection when using compressed air.**

18 Before commencing reassembly, ensure that all components are spotlessly-clean and dry.

19 Soak the new piston seal in clean hydraulic fluid, and fit it to the groove in the cylinder bore, using your fingers only (no tools) to manipulate it into place.

20 Fit the new dust seal inner lip to the cylinder groove, smear clean hydraulic fluid over the piston and caliper cylinder bore, and twist the piston into the dust seal. Press the piston squarely into the cylinder, then slide the dust seal outer lip to the groove in the piston **(see illustration)**.

21 Fit a new rubber dust cover to each guide pin, and apply a smear of brake grease to the guide pins before refitting them to their bores.

Refitting

22 Where applicable, refit the caliper mounting bracket to the hub carrier, and tighten the mounting bolts to the specified torque.

23 Place the caliper in position, then coat the threads of the caliper upper guide pin bolt with locking compound, refit the bolt, and tighten it to the specified torque.

24 Refit the brake pads (Section 4).

25 Check that the caliper slides smoothly on the mounting bracket.

26 Check that the brake fluid hose is correctly routed, without being twisted, then reconnect the union to the caliper, using two new sealing washers. Refit the union banjo bolt, and tighten to the specified torque.

27 Remove the polythene from the master cylinder reservoir cap, or remove the clamp from the fluid hose, as applicable.

28 Bleed the hydraulic fluid circuit (Section 2). Note that if no other part of the system has been disturbed, it should only be necessary to bleed the relevant front circuit.

29 Depress the brake pedal repeatedly to bring the pads into contact with the brake disc, and ensure that normal pedal pressure is restored.

30 Refit the roadwheel, and lower the vehicle to the ground.

9.11a Remove the piston by applying a jet of compressed air, such as that from a tyre pump, to the fluid inlet port

9.11b Use a blunt instrument to extract the piston seal from the caliper cylinder bore

9.20 Smear clean hydraulic fluid over the piston and cylinder bore, then twist the piston into the dust seal

9

10 Rear brake caliper - removal, overhaul and refitting

Note: *Suitable locking compound will be required to coat the threads of the caliper guide pin bolts on refitting.*

⚠️ **Warning: Before starting work, refer to the note at the beginning of Section 2 concerning the dangers of hydraulic fluid, and to the warning at the beginning of Section 4 concerning the dangers of asbestos dust.**

Removal

1 Chock the front wheels, then jack up the rear of the vehicle and support securely on axle stands (see *"Jacking and Vehicle Support"*). Remove the appropriate rear wheel.
2 Release the spring clip securing the handbrake cable to the mounting bracket, then disconnect the end of the cable from the lever on the caliper (see Section 17 for details).
3 To minimise fluid loss during the following operations, remove the master cylinder reservoir cap, then tighten it down onto a piece of polythene, to obtain an airtight seal. Alternatively, use a brake hose clamp to seal off the flexible hose running to the caliper.
4 Clean the area around the fluid hose union on the caliper, then unscrew the hose union banjo bolt. Recover the two sealing washers. Cover the open ends of the banjo and the caliper, to prevent dirt ingress.
5 Remove the brake pads (Section 5).
6 Unscrew the caliper upper guide pin bolt. If necessary, use a slim open-ended spanner to counterhold the head of the guide pin.
7 Withdraw the caliper from the mounting bracket.
8 If desired, the caliper mounting bracket can be unbolted from the hub carrier.

Overhaul

Note: *Before commencing work, ensure that the appropriate caliper overhaul kit is obtained.*

9 With the caliper on the bench, wipe away all traces of dust and dirt, but *avoid inhaling the dust, as it is a health hazard.*
10 Extract the caliper guide pins, if necessary by screwing the bolts into the pins, and pulling on the bolts to withdraw the pins. Peel off the rubber dust cover from each guide pin, and the rubber sleeve which may be fitted to the upper guide pin of some models.
11 Engage a suitable pair of long-nosed pliers with the notches in the piston, then turn the piston anti-clockwise (viewed from the outboard end of the caliper), to unscrew it from the caliper. Withdraw the piston from the caliper body, and peel off the dust seal.
12 Working inside the caliper cylinder bore, use circlip pliers to extract the circlip, whilst using a suitable length of tubing to compress the spring cap against the spring pressure.

13 With the circlip removed from its groove, allow the spring to push out the components until pressure is relaxed, then withdraw the circlip, spring cap, spring, key plate, pushrod and strut. Prise the sealing O-ring off the pushrod, then discard it - a new seal must be fitted on reassembly.
14 Using a blunt instrument such as a knitting needle, extract the piston seal from the caliper cylinder bore.
15 Unhook the return spring from the handbrake lever, then unscrew the nut and remove the lever assembly from the caliper body.
16 Thoroughly clean all components, using only methylated spirit or clean hydraulic fluid. Never use mineral-based solvents such as petrol or paraffin, which will attack the hydraulic system rubber components.
17 Discard all seals, cups, dust covers and other rubber components. These are available as part of a caliper seal kit, and should be renewed as a matter of course whenever they are disturbed.
18 Carefully examine all parts of the caliper assembly, looking for signs of wear or damage. In particular, the cylinder bore and piston must be free from any signs of scratches, corrosion or wear. If there is any doubt about the condition of any part of the caliper, the relevant part should be renewed. Note that if the caliper body or the mounting bracket are to be renewed, they are available only as part of the complete assembly.
19 The manufacturers recommend that minor scratches, rust, etc, may be polished away from the cylinder bore using fine emery paper, but the piston must be renewed to cure such defects. The piston surface is plated, and **must not** be polished with emery or similar abrasives.
20 Check that the threads in the caliper body and the mounting bracket are in good condition. Check that both guide pins are undamaged, and (when cleaned) a reasonably tight sliding fit in the mounting bracket bores.
21 Use compressed air to blow clear the fluid passages.

⚠️ **Warning: Wear eye protection when using compressed air.**

22 Before reassembling, ensure that all components are spotlessly-clean and dry.
23 Fit the new dust seal to the handbrake lever cam, and locate the lever on the cam flats. Refit the return spring, spring washer, and nut. Tighten the nut securely, observing the specified torque. Apply a smear of brake grease to the cam, then slide the cam into the caliper body. Check that the assembly is correctly installed, and that the cam cut-out aligns with the pushrod aperture when the lever is rotated. Hook the return spring over its stop and into the lever.
24 Soak the new piston seal in clean hydraulic fluid, and fit it to the groove in the cylinder bore, using your fingers only (no tools) to manipulate it into position.

25 Fit a new O-ring to the pushrod, and apply a smear of rubber grease to the strut and the pushrod. Assemble the strut and pushrod, and fit them to the caliper body.
26 Refit the key plate so that its cut-out fits over the squared section of the pushrod, and its convex locating pip matches the concave depression in the caliper body. Secure the assembly by refitting the circlip.
27 Refit the spring and the spring cap, then compress the spring cap while refitting the securing circlip. Check that the circlip is correctly seated in its groove.
28 Apply a smear of rubber grease to the inner and outer lip of the new dust seal, then fit it to the piston.
29 Smear clean hydraulic fluid over the piston and the caliper cylinder bore, then refit the piston assembly, and screw it in clockwise (using a retractor tool or long-nosed pliers if necessary - see Section 5) until it seats.
30 Engage the dust seal with the caliper body.
31 Fit a new rubber dust cover to each guide pin (also fit a new rubber sleeve to the upper guide pin, where applicable). Apply a smear of brake grease to the guide pins before refitting them to their bores.

Refitting

32 Where applicable, refit the caliper mounting bracket to the hub carrier, and tighten the mounting bolts to the specified torque.
33 Place the caliper in position, coat the threads of the caliper upper guide pin bolt with locking compound, refit the bolt, and tighten it to the specified torque.
34 Refit the brake pads (Section 5).
35 Check that the caliper slides smoothly on the mounting bracket.
36 Check that the brake fluid hose is correctly routed, without being twisted, then reconnect the union to the caliper, using two new sealing washers. Refit the union banjo bolt, and tighten to the specified torque.
37 Reconnect the end of the handbrake cable to the lever. Refit the cable mounting bracket, and where applicable, the spring clip. Where applicable, ensure that the locating peg on the mounting bracket engages with the corresponding hole in the caliper body.
38 Remove the polythene from the master cylinder reservoir cap, or remove the clamp from the fluid hose, as applicable.
39 Bleed the hydraulic fluid circuit as described in Section 2. Note that if no other part of the system has been disturbed, it should only be necessary to bleed the relevant rear circuit.
40 Depress the brake pedal repeatedly to bring the pads into contact with the brake disc, and ensure that normal pedal pressure is restored.
41 Refit the roadwheel, and lower the vehicle to the ground.
42 Check the operation of the braking system thoroughly before bringing the vehicle back into service on the public highway.

11.5 Rear wheel cylinder bolts and hydraulic pipe union

11.10 Exploded view of a rear wheel cylinder -
models with brake drum

A Securing bolts

B Union

1 Dust cover
2 Piston head
3 Piston
4 Piston cup

5 Wheel cylinder housing
6 Bleed screw
7 Bleed screw cap

11 Rear wheel cylinder - removal, overhaul and refitting

 Warning: Before starting work, refer to the note at the beginning of Section 2 concerning the dangers of hydraulic fluid, and to the warning at the beginning of Section 4 concerning the dangers of asbestos dust.

Removal

1 Remove the brake drum (Section 8).
2 Remove the brake shoes (Section 6).
3 To minimise fluid loss during the following operations, remove the master cylinder reservoir cap, then tighten it down onto a piece of polythene, to obtain an airtight seal.
4 Clean the brake backplate around the wheel cylinder mounting bolts and the hydraulic pipe union, then unscrew the union nut and disconnect the hydraulic pipe. Cover the open ends of the pipe and the master cylinder to prevent dirt ingress.
5 Remove the securing bolts **(see illustration)** then withdraw the wheel cylinder from the backplate.

Overhaul

Note: *Before commencing work, ensure that the appropriate wheel cylinder overhaul kit is obtained.*

6 Clean the assembly thoroughly, using only methylated spirit or clean brake fluid.
7 Peel off both rubber dust covers, then use paint or similar to mark one of the pistons so that the pistons are not interchanged on reassembly.

8 Withdraw both pistons and the spring.
9 Discard the rubber piston cups and the dust covers. These components should be renewed as a matter of course, and are available as part of an overhaul kit, which also includes the bleed nipple dust cap.
10 Check the condition of the cylinder bore and the piston - the surfaces must be perfect and free from scratches, scoring and corrosion. It is advisable to renew the complete wheel cylinder if there is any doubt as to the condition of the cylinder bore or piston **(see illustration)**.
11 Ensure that all components are clean and dry. The pistons, spring and cups should be fitted wet, using hydraulic fluid as a lubricant - soak them in clean fluid before installation.
12 Fit the cups to the pistons, ensuring that they are the correct way round. Use only your fingers (no tools) to manipulate the cups into position.
13 Fit the first piston to the cylinder, taking care not to distort the cup. If the original pistons are being re-used, the marks made on dismantling should be used to ensure that the pistons are refitted to their original bores.
14 Refit the spring and the second piston.
15 Apply a smear of rubber grease to the exposed end of each piston and to the dust cover sealing lips, then fit the dust covers to each end of the wheel cylinder.

Refitting

16 Refitting is a reversal of removal, bearing in mind the following points:
a) Tighten the mounting bolts to the specified torque.
b) Refit the brake shoes as described in Section 6, and refit the brake drum as described in Section 8.
c) Before refitting the roadwheel and lowering the vehicle to the ground,

remove the polythene from the fluid reservoir, and bleed the hydraulic system as described in Section 2. Note that if no other part of the system has been disturbed, it should only be necessary to bleed the relevant rear circuit.

12 Master cylinder - removal, overhaul and refitting

Note: *Before starting work, refer to the warning at the beginning of Section 2 concerning the dangers of hydraulic fluid.*

Removal

 Warning: Do not syphon the fluid by mouth, as it is poisonous; use a syringe or an old poultry baster

1 Remove the master cylinder fluid reservoir cap, and syphon the hydraulic fluid from the reservoir. Alternatively, open any convenient bleed screw in the system, and gently pump the brake pedal to expel the fluid through a tube connected to the screw (see Section 2). Disconnect the wiring connector from the brake fluid level sender unit.
2 Wipe clean the area around the brake pipe unions on the side of the master cylinder, and place absorbent rags beneath the pipe unions to catch any surplus fluid. Make a note of the correct fitted positions of the unions, then unscrew the union nuts and carefully withdraw the pipes. Plug or tape over the pipe ends and master cylinder orifices, to minimise the loss of brake fluid, and to prevent the entry of dirt into the system. Wash off any spilt fluid immediately with cold water.

9

Cut the finger tips from an old rubber glove and secure them over the open ends of the brake pipes with elastic bands - this will help to minimise fluid loss and prevent the ingress of contaminants.

3 Slacken and remove the nuts securing the master cylinder to the vacuum servo unit, then withdraw the unit from the engine compartment.

4 Where applicable, recover the seal from the rear of the master cylinder, and discard it.

Overhaul

Note: Before attempting overhaul of the master cylinder, ensure that the appropriate overhaul kit is obtained - a number of different master cylinder assemblies may be fitted, depending on model.

5 Pull the fluid reservoir from the top of the master cylinder. Prise the reservoir seals from the reservoir or the master cylinder, as applicable.

6 Using a suitable screwdriver, bend back the tangs securing the master cylinder end cap, then withdraw the end cap.

7 On models with ABS, push on the end of the primary piston assembly using a suitable wooden dowel to compress the primary and secondary piston assemblies, then unscrew the stop-bolt from the side of the master cylinder. Where applicable, remove the circlip (see illustration).

8 Noting the order of removal, and the direction of fitting of each component, withdraw the washer and the piston assemblies with their springs and seals, tapping the body onto a clean wooden surface to dislodge them (see illustration). If necessary, clamp the master cylinder body in a vice (fitted with soft jaw covers) and gradually apply compressed air (applied through the secondary circuit fluid port) to assist the removal of the secondary piston assembly.

Warning: Wear eye protection when working with compressed air.

9 Thoroughly clean all components, using only methylated spirit, isopropyl alcohol or clean hydraulic fluid as a cleaning medium. Never use mineral-based solvents such as petrol or paraffin, as they will attack the hydraulic system rubber components. Dry the components immediately, using compressed air or a clean, lint-free cloth.

10 Check all components, and renew any that are worn or damaged (note that individual seal components are not available - the overhaul kit will contain complete primary and secondary piston assemblies, complete with all seals, washers, etc). Check particularly the cylinder bores and pistons; the complete assembly should be renewed if these are scratched, worn or corroded. If there is any doubt about the condition of the assembly or

12.7 Compress the piston assembly and remove the circlip

of any of its components, renew it. Check that the cylinder body fluid passages are clear.

11 Before reassembly, soak the pistons and the new seals in clean hydraulic fluid. Smear clean fluid into the cylinder bore.

12 Insert the piston assemblies into the cylinder bore (make sure that the assemblies are inserted squarely), using a twisting motion to avoid trapping the seal lips. Ensure that all components are refitted in the correct order and the right way round, then fit the washer to the end of the primary piston. Where applicable, follow the assembly instructions supplied with the repair kit. On models with ABS, ensure that the slot in the secondary piston assembly aligns with the stop-bolt hole in the side of the master cylinder.

13 On models with ABS, compress the piston assemblies into the cylinder bore, using a clean wooden dowel as during removal, then refit the stop-bolt, ensuring that it engages with the slot in the secondary piston assembly.

14 Press the piston assemblies fully into the bore using a clean wooden dowel, and secure them in position with the new end cap (supplied in the overhaul kit). Bend the tangs into position to secure the end cap.

15 Examine the fluid reservoir seals, and if necessary renew them. Fit the reservoir seals to the master cylinder body, then refit the reservoir.

Refitting

16 Remove all traces of dirt from the master cylinder and servo unit mating surfaces, and where applicable, fit a new seal between the master cylinder body and the servo.

17 Fit the master cylinder to the servo unit, ensuring that the servo unit pushrod enters the master cylinder bore centrally. Refit the master cylinder mounting nuts, and tighten them to the specified torque.

18 Wipe clean the brake pipe unions, then refit them to the correct master cylinder ports, as noted before removal, and tighten the union nuts securely.

19 Refill the master cylinder reservoir with new fluid, and bleed the complete hydraulic system as described in Section 2.

20 Check the operation of the braking system thoroughly before bringing the vehicle back into service on the public highway.

12.8 Removing the primary piston from the master cylinder bore

13 Brake pedal - adjustment, removal and refitting

Adjustment

1 The pedal free height should be measured from the top face of the pedal to the floor reinforcement panel.

2 If desired, to improve access, remove the driver's side lower facia panel, (Chapter 11).

3 To take the measurement, remove the driver's side footwell trim panel, with reference to Chapter 11 if necessary, then release the securing clip(s) and lift the carpet trim panel to expose the flap in the floor insulation.

4 Lift the flap in the floor insulation, and measure the pedal free height as shown (see illustration). Check the measured height against the value given in the Specifications.

5 If the height of the pedal requires adjustment, proceed as follows.

6 Loosen the locknut on the servo pushrod, and turn the pushrod as required until the specified height is achieved. Retighten the locknut to the specified torque on completion.

13.4 Brake pedal height measurements

A Free play   H Free height
D Depressed height

7 Check the free play of the pedal by pressing the pedal slowly until resistance is felt. The free play should be as specified.
8 Check that the stop-lights go out when the pedal is released. Note that the switch (a bayonet fit in the pedal bracket) cannot be adjusted, and if faulty must be renewed.
9 Start the engine and allow it to idle for a few minutes. Depress the brake pedal to simulate normal, firm braking and measure the depressed height of the brake pedal as shown. Compare the measurement with the Specifications - if the pedal height is too low, there may be a fault within the braking system. Refer initially to Section 2 and bleed the braking system to expel any trapped air or contaminated/old brake fluid. Repeat the test and if there is no improvement, refer to Sections 12, 9, 10 and 11 and check the condition of the master cylinder, brake calipers/wheel cylinders.
10 On completion, refit the carpet and the trim panel(s).

Removal

11 To improve access, if not already done, remove the driver's side lower facia panel as described in Chapter 11.
12 Working in the driver's footwell, remove the split-pin from the end of the servo pushrod clevis pin, then withdraw the clevis pin. Examine the clevis pin carefully for signs of cracking or wear; renew it if necessary.
13 Disconnect the wiring plug from the stop-light switch.
14 Unscrew the four nuts securing the pedal bracket to the bulkhead (note that these nuts also secure the vacuum servo to the engine bay-side of the bulkhead).
15 Unscrew the pedal bracket upper securing bolt, then withdraw the pedal/bracket assembly from the footwell.
16 The brake pedal is integral with the bracket assembly, and cannot be renewed individually.

Refitting

17 Refitting is a reversal of removal but:
18 On completion, check the pedal free and depressed height as described earlier.

14 Vacuum servo unit - removal and refitting

Removal

1 Disconnect the battery negative lead.
2 On carburetted models, it should be possible to remove the servo unit without removing the inlet manifold or the master cylinder.
3 On fuel-injected models, it may be necessary to remove the inlet manifold (see the relevant Part of Chapter 4) to gain sufficient clearance to remove the servo unit.
4 On carburettor models, to improve access, remove the air cleaner as described in Chapter 4.

5 Where applicable, disconnect the power steering fluid pressure switch wiring plug, and/or unbolt the power steering fluid hose bracket from the body for improved access.
6 Remove the master cylinder from the vacuum servo unit, with reference to Section 12.
7 Disconnect the vacuum hose from the servo.
8 With reference to the relevant paragraphs of Section 13, disconnect the servo pushrod from the brake pedal, then unscrew the four nuts securing the brake pedal mounting bracket to the servo mounting studs.
9 Working in the engine compartment, withdraw the servo.
Caution: Take care to avoid damaging the threads of the vacuum unit studs.

Refitting

10 Refitting is a reversal of removal, bearing in mind the following points:
a) Before refitting the servo, check that the distance measured from the end of the pushrod to the master cylinder mating surface is as specified (see Specifications).
b) On non-ABS vehicles, initially set the brake pedal pushrod to the dimension shown in the illustration.
c) Tighten all fixings to the specified torque.
d) Where applicable, refit the master cylinder as described in Section 12.
e) Where applicable, refit the inlet manifold as described in the relevant Part of Chapter 4.
f) On completion, check the brake pedal height as described in Section 13.

15 Vacuum servo unit check valve - removal, testing and refitting

Models with servo-mounted valve

Removal

1 The valve is a push-fit in the front of the servo unit.
2 Release the securing clip, and disconnect the vacuum hose from the valve.
3 Withdraw the valve from its rubber sealing grommet, using a pulling and twisting motion. Remove the grommet from the servo.

Testing

4 Examine the check valve for signs of damage, and renew if necessary. The valve may be tested by blowing through it in both directions. Air should flow through the valve in one direction only - when blown through from the servo unit end of the valve. Renew the valve if this is not the case.
5 Examine the rubber sealing grommet and flexible vacuum hose for signs of damage or deterioration, and renew as necessary.

Refitting

6 Fit the sealing grommet into position in the servo unit.

7 Carefully ease the check valve into position, taking great care not to displace or damage the grommet - do not use any lubricants. Reconnect the vacuum hose to the valve and, where necessary, securely tighten its retaining clip.
8 On completion, start the engine, and check the check valve-to-servo unit connection for signs of air leaks.

Models with vacuum-hose mounted valve

Removal

9 The valve is located in the vacuum hose leading to the servo, and is secured to the body panel by a clip.
10 Release the valve from the securing clip. Take note of the direction of the arrow on the valve body, which should point in the direction of the hose connected to the engine.
11 Release the retaining clips (where fitted), and disconnect the vacuum hoses from the valve, then withdraw the valve.

Testing

12 Proceed as described in paragraph 4.

Refitting

13 Refitting is a reversal of removal, ensuring that the arrow on the valve body points towards the engine.
14 On completion, start the engine and check the hose connections to the valve for air leaks.

16 Handbrake lever - removal and refitting

Removal

1 Disconnect the battery negative lead.
2 Remove the centre console as described in Chapter 11.
3 Chock the wheels, and fully release the handbrake.
4 Disconnect the wiring plug from the handbrake "on" warning light switch.
5 Count the number of exposed threads on the cable adjuster rod (to ease adjustment on refitting), then unscrew the adjuster nut, and disconnect adjuster rod from the handbrake lever.
6 Remove the two securing bolts, and withdraw the handbrake lever assembly.

Refitting

7 Refitting is a reversal of removal, bearing in mind the following point:
a) Screw the adjuster nut onto the cable adjuster rod to give the number of exposed threads noted before removal, then check the handbrake operation, and adjust if necessary, as described in Section 17.
b) Before refitting the centre console, check the operation of the handbrake "on" warning light.

9

17.3 Handbrake cable bracket nuts (arrowed) - models with rear drum brakes

17 Handbrake cables - removal and refitting

Rear cables

Removal

1 There are two rear handbrake cables, one on each side of the vehicle. To renew either rear cable, proceed as follows.

2 Chock the front wheels, then jack up the front of the vehicle and support securely on axle stands (see *"Jacking and Vehicle Support"*). Release the handbrake fully.

3 On models with rear drum brakes, remove the brake shoes, and disconnect the end of the handbrake cable from the lever on the trailing shoe, as described in Section 6. Recover the return spring from the end of the cable, then unbolt the cable bracket from the brake backplate **(see illustration)**.

4 On models with rear disc brakes, release the spring clip securing the cable to the mounting bracket, then disconnect the end of the cable from the lever on the caliper **(see illustrations)**.

5 Unscrew the nuts and bolts securing the handbrake cable brackets to the underbody, and to the suspension, where applicable.

6 Disconnect the front of the cable from the cable equaliser at the front of the vehicle, then withdraw the cable. Note that on certain models, it will be necessary to remove the exhaust heat shield for access to the handbrake cable equaliser.

Refitting

7 Refitting is a reversal of removal, bearing in mind the following points:
a) *On models with rear disc brakes, where applicable, when refitting the cable mounting bracket to the caliper, ensure that the locating peg on the bracket engages with the corresponding hole in the caliper body.*
b) *On models with rear drum brakes, reconnect the cable end to the lever on the trailing shoe, and refit the brake shoes, as described in Section 6.*
c) *On completion, check the handbrake adjustment, as described at the end of this Section.*

Front cable

Removal

8 Disconnect the battery negative lead.

9 Chock the rear wheels and fully release the handbrake.

10 Working inside the vehicle, remove the centre console as described in Chapter 11.

11 Disconnect the wiring plug from the handbrake "on" warning light switch.

12 Count the number of exposed threads on the cable adjuster rod (to ease adjustment on refitting), then unscrew the adjuster nut, and disconnect adjuster rod from the handbrake lever.

13 For improved access, ensure that the rear wheels are chocked, then jack up the front of the vehicle and support securely on axle stands (see *"Jacking and Vehicle Support"*).

14 Working under the vehicle, disconnect the two rear cables from the cable equaliser, then withdraw the front section of the cable (which includes the cable equaliser and the adjuster rod) down through the floor panel. Note that on certain models, it will be necessary to remove the exhaust heat shield for access to the handbrake cable equaliser.

Refitting

15 Refitting is a reversal of removal, bearing in mind the following points.
a) *Screw the adjuster nut onto the cable adjuster rod to give the number of exposed threads noted before removal, then check the handbrake adjustment as described in following sub-Section.*
b) *Before refitting the centre console, check the operation of the handbrake "on" warning light.*

Handbrake adjustment

16 Before attempting to adjust the handbrake cables, check first that the brake shoe to drum/pad to disc clearance is correct by depressing the brake pedal several times.

17 Chock the front roadwheels, then raise the rear of the vehicle and rest it securely on axle stands (see *"Jacking and Vehicle Support"*). Remove the rear roadwheels.

18 On vehicles with rear disc brakes, check that the caliper handbrake operating lever rests against its stop when both the handbrake lever and the brake pedal are released.

19 Remove the centre console as described in Chapter 11.

20 Apply the handbrake and count the number of ratchet 'clicks' the lever has to be pulled through before normal resistance is felt.

21 Adjust the cable adjuster locknut **(see illustration)** to achieve the correct handbrake lever travel (see Specifications). Verify that the rear wheels are fully locked when the handbrake is applied, and rotate without binding when the handbrake is released.

17.4a Release the spring clip securing the cable to the mounting bracket . . .

17.4b . . . then disconnect the end of the cable from the lever on the caliper (arrowed) - models with rear disc brakes

17.21 Handbrake cable adjuster locknut (arrowed)

22 Check that the handbrake 'on' warning lamp illuminates after the specified number of 'clicks' (see Specifications). If necessary adjust it with reference to Section 19.
23 On completion, refit the centre console, then lower the vehicle to the ground.
24 Check the operation of the handbrake before bringing the vehicle back into service on the public highway.

18 Stop-light switch - adjustment, removal and refitting

Adjustment

1 The switch plunger operates on a ratchet.
2 If adjustment is required, pull the plunger fully out - the switch is then self-adjusting.

Removal

3 Disconnect the battery negative lead.
4 For improved access, remove the driver's side lower facia panel, as described in Chapter 11.
5 Disconnect the wiring plug from the switch.
6 Twist the switch anti-clockwise, and withdraw the switch from the pedal bracket.

Refitting

7 Refitting is a reversal of removal, but pull the switch plunger fully out before refitting (see paragraph 2).

19 Handbrake "on" warning light switch - removal and refitting

Removal

1 Disconnect the battery negative lead.
2 Remove the centre console as described in Chapter 11.
3 Disconnect the wiring plug from the switch.
4 Remove the securing screw, and withdraw the switch.

Refitting

5 Refitting is a reversal of removal, but before refitting the centre console, check that the warning light comes on after the specified number of handbrake clicks (see Specifications). If necessary, bend the switch bracket to give the correct adjustment.

20 Anti-lock braking system (ABS) - general information

The Anti-lock Braking System (ABS) is managed by an Electronic Control Unit (ECU), which has the capacity to monitor the status and condition of all the components in the system, including itself. If the ECU detects a fault, it responds by shutting down the ABS and illuminating the dashboard mounted ABS warning lamp. Under these circumstances, conventional non-ABS braking is maintained.

If the ABS develops a fault, the vehicle must be examined by a Nissan dealer, who will have the dedicated test equipment required for fault diagnosis. For safety reasons, owners are strongly advised against attempting to diagnose complex problems with the ABS using standard workshop equipment.

Chapter 10
Suspension and steering

Contents

Degrees of difficulty

Easy, suitable for novice with little experience	Fairly easy, suitable for beginner with some experience	Fairly difficult, suitable for competent DIY mechanic	Difficult, suitable for experienced DIY mechanic	Very difficult, suitable for expert DIY or professional

Specifications

Front suspension

Type .... Independent multi-link, incorporating transverse lower arms and coil spring-over-damper strut units. Anti-roll bar fitted to all models.

Rear suspension

Type .... Independent incorporating trailing radius rods, parallel transverse lower arms and coil spring-over-damper strut units. Anti-roll bar fitted on certain models.

Wheel bearings

Maximum endfloat at hub (front and rear) .... 0.05 mm

Steering

Type .... Rack-and-pinion, manual or power-assisted, depending on model
Maximum steering wheel rotational free play .... 35.0 mm
Steering column length .... 536.2 to 537.8 mm

Roadwheels and tyres

See "Weekly Checks"

Torque wrench settings	Nm	lbf ft
Front suspension		
Driveshaft nut	250	185
Hub carrier-to-suspension strut nuts and bolts*	120	90
Suspension strut damper rod top nut	70	52
Suspension strut upper mounting nuts	27	20
Lower arm front mounting nut	115	85
Lower arm rear mounting clamp bolts	85	60
Lower arm balljoint-to-hub carrier nut	65	50
Anti-roll bar drop link-to-lower arm nuts*	20	15
Anti-roll bar drop link-to-anti-roll bar nuts*	50	35
Anti-roll bar mounting clamp bolts	35	25
Track-rod end-to-steering arm nut:		
Recommended torque	39	30
Maximum permissible torque	49	36

10

Torque wrench settings (continued)

	Nm	lbf ft
Rear suspension		
Rear hub nut	230	170
Suspension strut damper rod top nut	65	50
Suspension strut upper mounting nuts*	27	20
Suspension strut-to-hub carrier nuts*	120	90
Parallel link mounting nuts*	110	80
Radius rod front mounting nut*	110	80
Radius rod-to-hub carrier nut*	110	80
Anti-roll bar drop link-to-anti-roll bar nuts*	50	35
Anti-roll bar drop link-to-suspension strut nuts*	25	20
Anti-roll bar mounting bracket-to-body bolts	35	25
Steering		
Steering wheel securing nut	35	25
Steering column securing nuts and bolts	17	15
Steering column universal joint clamp bolts	27	20
Steering gear mounting clamp bolts	85	65
Track-rod end locknut	40	30
Track-rod end-to-steering arm nut:		
Minimum torque	39	30
Maximum permissible torque	49	35
Power steering pump-to-bracket bolts	30	22
Power steering fluid pipe-to-steering gear unions	22	15
Power steering fluid pipe union banjo-to-pump bolt	55	40
Roadwheels		
Roadwheel nuts	110	82

Use new nut(s)/bolt(s).

---

1 General information

Front suspension

The front suspension is independent, comprising transverse lower arms, coil spring-over-damper strut units and an anti-roll bar. The hub carriers are bolted to the base of the strut units and are linked to the lower arms by means of balljoints. The entire front suspension assembly is mounted on a subframe, which is in turn bolted to the vehicle body.

Rear suspension

The independent rear suspension is of the MacPherson strut type, incorporating coil springs and integral telescopic shock absorbers. The upper ends of the struts are connected to the bodyshell front suspension turrets, and the lower ends are bolted to the hub carriers, which carry the wheel bearings, brake calipers/backplates and hub/disc/drum assemblies. The hub carriers are located at their lower ends by transverse parallel links and trailing radius rods. A rear anti-roll bar is fitted to all models, bracketed to the vehicles underside and connected to the base of the suspension struts by drop-links.

Steering

The one-piece steering shaft runs in a tubular column assembly, which is bolted to a bracket mounted on the vehicles bulkhead. The shaft is articulated at its lower end by means of a universal joint, which is clamped to the steering shaft and the steering gear pinion by means of clamp bolts.

The steering gear is mounted on the engine compartment bulkhead, and is connected to the steering arms projecting rearwards from the hub carriers. The track-rods are fitted with balljoints at their inner and outer ends, to allow for suspension movement, and are threaded to facilitate adjustment.

Power steering is fitted as standard on some models. The hydraulic system is powered by a belt-driven pump, which is driven from the crankshaft pulley.

Certain post-1994 models are fitted with a Supplementary Restraint System (SRS). Sensors built into the vehicle body are triggered in the event of a front end collision and prompt an Electronic Control Unit (ECU) to activate the airbag, mounted in the centre of the steering wheel. This reduces the risk of the driver striking the steering wheel, windscreen or facia during an accident.

 Warning: For safety reasons, owners are strongly advised to entrust to an authorised Nissan dealer any work which involves disturbing the SRS components. Specialised test equipment is needed to check that the SRS is fully operational following reassembly.

2 Front hub bearings - renewal

Note: *A balljoint separator tool, and a press or suitable alternative tools (see text) will be required for this operation. The bearing will be destroyed during the removal procedure.*

Removal

1 Chock the rear wheels, apply the handbrake, then jack up the front of the vehicle and support on axle stands (see *"Jacking and Vehicle Support"*). Remove the appropriate roadwheel.

2 Remove the brake disc and caliper, with reference to Chapter 9.

3 On models with ABS, unbolt the ABS wheel sensor, and remove the screw securing the ABS sensor wiring to the hub carrier. Suspend the sensor away from the working area, to avoid the possibility of damage.

4 Disconnect the outboard end of the driveshaft from the hub, as described during the driveshaft removal and refitting procedure in Chapter 8. Note that there is no need to disconnect the inboard end of the driveshaft from the transmission. **Do not** allow the end of the driveshaft to hang down under its own weight - support the end of the driveshaft using wire or string.

5 Remove the two nuts from the bolts securing the hub carrier to the suspension strut (refer to Section 3). Withdraw the bolts

3.3 Front suspension strut-to-hub carrier nuts and bolts (arrowed)

3.4 Front suspension strut upper mounting nuts (arrowed) - DO NOT UNSCREW THE CENTRE DAMPER ROD NUT AT THIS STAGE

and separate the top of hub carrier from the base of the strut. Discard the nuts and bolts - new ones must be used on refitting.

6 Remove the split pin and slacken the nut, then separate the hub carrier from the lower arm balljoint. If necessary, use a balljoint separator tool (refer to Section 4). Remove the nut, then lower the ball joint away from the hub carrier. Separate the track-rod end from the hub carrier steering arm in a similar manner.

7 Support the outer face of the hub carrier on two metal bars, or across the open jaws of a bench vice, ensuring that the hub is free (take care not to damage the brake disc shield). Using a metal bar or tube of suitable diameter, press or drive the hub from the wheel bearing. Note that one half of the inner bearing race will remain on the hub.

8 Support the inner bearing race which is still attached to the hub, then press or drive the hub from the race. Alternatively, pull the bearing race from the hub using a suitable puller.

9 Recover the outer oil seal from the hub.

10 Working at the rear of the hub carrier, prise out the inner oil seal.

11 Using a pair of circlip pliers, extract the bearing retaining circlip from the hub carrier. Recover the remaining inner bearing race if it is loose.

12 Support the inner face of the hub carrier, then using a suitable metal tube which bears only on the outer bearing race, press or drive the bearing from the hub carrier. Alternatively, temporarily refit the bearing inner race, and drive out the bearing using a tube or bar bearing on the inner race.

Refitting

13 Before installing the new bearing, thoroughly clean the bearing location in the hub carrier.

14 Fit the new bearing from the rear of the hub, and press or drive the bearing into position, applying pressure only to the bearing

outer race. **Do not** lubricate the mating surface of the bearing in an attempt to ease installation.

15 Fit the bearing retaining circlip to its groove in the hub carrier.

16 Pack the lips of the new outer oil seal with grease then, using a tube of suitable diameter, carefully press or tap the seal into position in the outer face of the hub carrier.

17 Support the outer face of the hub carrier on its periphery, taking care not to damage the outer oil seal.

18 Pack the lips of the new inner oil seal with grease then, using a tube of suitable diameter, carefully press or tap the seal into position in the inner face of the hub carrier.

19 Support the inner face of the hub carrier, using a suitable diameter metal bar or tube, which will just pass through the inner oil seal to support the wheel bearing inner race. Carefully press or draw the hub into the bearing, noting that the bearing inner race **must** be supported during this operation, as described previously. This can be achieved using a suitable socket, threaded rod, washers and a length of bar. Check that the hub rotates freely in the hub carrier.

20 Reconnect the outboard end of the driveshaft to the hub as described in Chapter 8. Ensure that the driveshaft nut is tightened to the correct torque noting that the brake disc must be refitted before refitting the brake caliper (see Chapter 9).

21 Reconnect the hub carrier to the lower arm balljoint, then fit a new balljoint nut. Tighten the nut to the specified torque, then fit a new split pin.

22 Engage the hub carrier with the suspension strut, then refit the new securing bolts and nuts, tightening them to the specified torque.

23 Reconnect the steering track rod ball joint to the hub carrier steering arm. Use a new nut and split pin - tighten the nut to the specified torque.

24 Refit the roadwheel, and lower the vehicle to the ground.

3 Front suspension strut - removal, overhaul and refitting

 Warning: If renewing the strut damper during overhaul, both the left and right hand dampers should be renewed as a pair, to preserve the handling characteristics of the vehicle.

Estate models

Removal

Note: *The manufacturers recommend that the suspension strut-to-hub carrier bolts and nuts, and the suspension strut top mounting nuts and gasket, are renewed on refitting.*

1 Chock the rear wheels, apply the handbrake, then jack up the front of the vehicle and support securely on axle stands (see *"Jacking and Vehicle Support"*). Remove the relevant roadwheel.

2 Release the brake fluid line from the bracket on the hub carrier.

3 Remove the two nuts from the bolts securing the lower end of the strut to the hub carrier, noting that the nuts fit on the front side of the strut **(see illustration)**. Withdraw the bolts, and support the hub carrier. Discard the bolts and nuts - new ones should be used on refitting.

4 Have an assistant support the strut from underneath the wheel arch then, working in the engine compartment, unscrew the three nuts securing the top of the strut to the suspension turret **(see illustration)**.

 Warning: Do not unscrew the centre damper rod nut yet. Release the lower end of the strut from the hub carrier, then withdraw the assembly from under the wheel arch.

10

3.7 Fit suitable spring compressors and compress the coil spring

3.8 Removing the damper rod nut - do not allow the damper rod to rotate

3.9a Removing the top mounting plate . . .

Overhaul

Note: *Suitable coil spring compressor tools will be required for this operation, and a new damper rod top nut must be used on reassembly.*

5 Clamp the lower end of the strut in a vice fitted with jaw protectors.

6 Temporarily refit two of the strut upper securing nuts to their studs. Using a suitable bar inserted between the upper mounting studs, counterhold the upper strut mounting whilst loosening the damper rod top nut. **Do not** remove the nut completely at this point.

7 Fit suitable spring compressors to the spring, and compress the spring sufficiently to enable the upper spring seat to be turned by hand **(see illustration)**.

8 Fully unscrew and remove the damper rod top nut. Counterhold the damper rod, using a suitable spanner, as the nut is unscrewed - do not allow the rod to rotate inside the damper **(see illustration)**. Discard the nut - a new one must be used on reassembly.

9 Withdraw the washer, gasket, top mounting plate, insulator, bearing, upper spring seat, and upper spring seat rubber - making a careful note of the order of assembly **(see illustrations)**.

10 Withdraw the spring, complete with the compressors, then withdraw the dust cover, bump rubber and the lower spring seat rubber **(see illustration)**.

11 With the strut assembly now dismantled, examine all the components for wear, damage or deformation. Check the rubber components

for deterioration. Renew any of the components as necessary.

12 Examine the damper for signs of fluid leakage. Check the damper rod for signs of pitting along its entire length, and check the strut body for signs of damage. While holding it in an upright position, test the operation of the strut by moving the damper rod through a full stroke, and then through short strokes of 50 to 100 mm. In both cases, the resistance felt should be smooth and continuous. If the resistance is jerky, or uneven, or if there is any visible sign of wear or damage to the strut, renewal is necessary. Note that the damper cannot be renewed independently, and if leakage or damage is evident, the complete strut/damper assembly must be renewed (in which case, the spring, upper mounting components, bushes, and associated components can be transferred to the new strut).

13 If any doubt exists about the condition of the coil spring, carefully remove the spring compressors, and check the spring for distortion and signs of cracking. Renew the spring if it is damaged or distorted, or if there is any doubt as to its condition.

14 Clamp the strut body in a vice, as during dismantling, then refit the lower spring seat rubber, bump rubber and dust cover.

15 Ensure that the coil spring is compressed sufficiently to enable the upper mounting components to be fitted, then fit the spring over the damper rod, ensuring that the lower end of the spring is correctly located on the lower spring seat **(see illustration)**.

3.9b . . . and upper spring seat

16 Refit the upper spring seat rubber, and the upper spring seat, ensuring that the top end of the spring is correctly located on the upper spring seat. Note that when the strut is refitted, the arrow on the upper spring seat must be positioned nearest the outer edge of the suspension turret (ie, the side nearest the roadwheel) **(see illustration)**.

17 Refit the bearing, insulator and top mounting plate. Fit the new damper rod top nut together with its washer, then tighten the nut to the specified torque, counterholding the damper rod in a manner similar to that used during dismantling. Note that a suitable crows-foot adapter will be required to tighten the damper rod top nut to the specified torque.

18 Remove the spring compressors.

3.10 Withdraw the spring, complete with the compressors

3.15 On reassembly, ensure that the lower end of the spring engages with the recess in the lower spring seat (arrowed)

3.16 Front suspension strut upper spring seat alignment

A Front of vehicle
B Outside of vehicle

19 Where applicable, refit the plastic cap to the damper rod top nut.

Refitting

20 Fit a new gasket to the top mounting, then manoeuvre the strut assembly into position under the wheel arch, passing the mounting studs through the holes in the body turret. Note that the cut-out and arrow on the upper spring seat must be positioned nearest the outer edge of the suspension turret (ie, the side nearest the roadwheel) (refer to illustration 3.16). Fit the new upper mounting nuts, and tighten them to the specified torque.

21 Engage the lower end of the strut with the hub carrier, then fit the new securing bolts and nuts, noting that the nuts fit on the front side of the strut, and tighten to the specified torque.

22 Refit the brake fluid line to the bracket on the hub carrier.

23 On models with ABS, refit the ABS wheel sensor wiring bracket to the inner wing panel.

24 Refit the roadwheel, and lower the vehicle to the ground.

4 Front suspension lower arm - removal, overhaul and refitting

Removal

Note: *A balljoint separator tool may be required for this operation. The lower arm balljoint split pin, lower arm front mounting nut, and the anti-roll bar drop link nut, should be renewed on reassembly.*

1 Chock the rear wheels, apply the handbrake, then jack up the front of the vehicle and support securely on axle stands (see *"Jacking and Vehicle Support"*). Remove the relevant roadwheel.

2 Unscrew the nut securing the anti-roll bar drop link to the lower arm, and recover the washer and bushes (refer to Section 6) Note that it may be necessary to counterhold the drop link pin in order to unscrew the nut. Discard the nut - a new one should be used on refitting.

3 Unscrew the two bolts securing the lower arm rear mounting clamp to the vehicle suspension subframe, and remove the clamp **(see illustration)**.

4.3 Unscrew the two bolts (arrowed) securing the lower arm rear mounting clamp to the vehicle suspension subframe

4 Slacken the nut securing the front of the lower arm to the mounting pin. Do not remove the nut at this stage **(see illustration)**.

5 Remove the split pin, then unscrew the nut securing the lower end of the hub carrier to the lower arm balljoint **(see illustrations)**. Discard the split pin - a new one must be used.

6 Separate the hub carrier from the lower arm. If necessary, use a balljoint separator tool. Remove the nut, and lever the end of the lower arm down to release it from the hub carrier **(see illustration)**.

7 Remove the nut securing the front of the lower arm to the mounting pin, and recover the washer. Discard the nut - a new one must be used on refitting.

8 Pivot the lower arm down to release it from the anti-roll bar drop, then recover the remaining bush and washer from the drop link. Slide the lower arm forwards from the front mounting pin, and withdraw the lower arm from under the vehicle.

Overhaul

9 With the lower arm removed, examine the lower arm itself, and the mounting bushes, for wear, cracks or damage.

10 Check the balljoint for wear, excessive play, or stiffness. Also check the balljoint dust boot for cracks or damage.

11 The mounting bushes and balljoint assembly are integral with the lower arm, and cannot be renewed independently. If either the bushes or the balljoint are worn or damaged, the complete lower arm assembly must be renewed.

4.4 Slacken the nut securing the front of the lower arm to the mounting pin

Refitting

Note: *Final tightening of all fixings must be carried out with the vehicle resting on its wheels.*

12 Slide the lower arm into position on the front mounting pin. Engage the lower arm with the anti-roll bar drop link (ensure that the upper washer and bush are fitted to the drop link - the concave side of the washer should be against the bush). Refit the washer and the new nut to the front mounting pin. Do not fully tighten the nut at this stage.

13 Engage the lower arm balljoint with the hub carrier, then refit the balljoint nut. Do not fully tighten the nut at this stage.

14 Refit the lower arm rear mounting clamp, and refit the securing bolts. Do not fully tighten the bolts at this stage.

15 Refit the lower bush and washer to the anti-roll bar drop link (the concave side of the washer should be against the bush), then fit a new securing nut. Again, do not fully tighten the nut at this stage.

16 Refit the roadwheel, and lower the vehicle to the ground.

17 Make sure that the vehicle is parked on level ground, then release the handbrake. Roll the vehicle backwards and forwards, and bounce the front of the vehicle to settle the suspension components.

18 Chock the wheels, then tighten all relevant nuts and bolts to the specified torque. After tightening, fit a new split pin to the lower arm balljoint nut.

19 On completion the front wheel alignment should be checked, with reference to Chapter 1.

4.5a Remove the split pin . . .

4.5b . . . then unscrew the nut securing the lower end of the hub carrier to the lower arm balljoint

4.6 Separating the lower arm balljoint from the hub carrier

5 Front suspension lower arm balljoint - renewal

The balljoint is integral with the suspension lower arm. If the balljoint is worn or damaged, the complete lower arm must be renewed as described in Section 4.

6 Front suspension anti-roll bar - removal and refitting

Anti-roll bar

Removal

Note: *New anti-roll bar-to-drop link nuts should be used on refitting.*

1 Chock the rear wheels, apply the handbrake, then jack up the front of the vehicle and support on axle stands (see *"Jacking and Vehicle Support"*). Remove the front roadwheels.

2 Working at one side of the anti-roll bar, where necessary counterhold the drop link pin, then unscrew the nut securing the end of the anti-roll bar to the drop link **(see illustration)**. Recover the washer. Discard the nut - a new one should be used on refitting.

3 Repeat the operation on the remaining side of the anti-roll bar.

4 Unscrew the bolts, and withdraw the clamps securing the anti-roll bar to the vehicle floor **(see illustration)**.

5 Manipulate the anti-roll bar out from under the vehicle.

Refitting

6 Inspect the mounting clamp rubbers for cracks or deterioration. If renewal is necessary, slide the old rubbers from the bar, and fit the new rubbers. Note that the rubbers should be positioned with the paint marks on the bar against their inner edges.

7 Refitting is a reversal of removal, bearing in mind the following points **(see illustrations)**:

a) When refitting the clamps, make sure that the clamps are positioned with the paint

6.2 Unscrew the nut securing the end of the anti-roll bar to the drop link

A *Anti roll bar drop link-to-suspension lower arm nut*
B *Anti roll bar-to-drop link nut*

marks on the anti-roll bar against the inner edges of the clamps, and that the cut-out bolt holes in the clamps are positioned towards the rear of the vehicle.

b) When reconnecting the drop links to the anti-roll bar, make sure that the drop link balljoint is positioned centrally in its arc of movement, and is not under strain; use new nuts.

c) Do not fully tighten the clamp bolts until the vehicle is resting on its roadwheels, and the suspension has been settled.

Drop link

Removal

Note: *New securing nuts should be used on refitting.*

8 To improve access, chock the rear wheels, apply the handbrake, then jack up the front of the vehicle and support securely on axle stands (see *"Jacking and Vehicle Support"*). Remove the relevant front roadwheel.

9 Counterhold the drop link pin, then unscrew the nut securing the end of the anti-roll bar to the drop link. Recover the washer. Discard the nut - a new one should be used on refitting.

10 Again, counterhold the drop link pin, then unscrew the nut securing the anti-roll bar drop link to the lower arm (refer to illustration 6.2). Recover the washer and bush. Again, discard the nut - a new one should be used on refitting.

6.4 Unscrew the bolts (arrowed), and withdraw the clamps securing the anti-roll bar to the vehicle floor

11 Lift out the drop link, and recover the remaining bush and washer.

Refitting

12 Check the condition of the drop link bushes, and renew if necessary.

13 Refitting is a reversal of removal, bearing in mind the following points:

a) Note that the concave sides of the washers should be positioned against the bushes.

b) When reconnecting the drop links to the anti-roll bar, make sure that the drop link balljoint is positioned centrally in its arc of movement, and is not under strain.

c) Use new drop link securing nuts, and tighten them to the specified torque.

7 Rear hub bearings - renewal

Note: *The bearing will be destroyed during the removal operation, and a new rear hub/bearing assembly must be used on refitting - the old assembly cannot be re-used. A new rear hub nut and split pin must be used on refitting.*

1 The rear hub bearings are integral with the rear hubs, and cannot be renewed independently. If the bearings require renewal, the complete hub assembly must be renewed as follows.

2 Chock the front wheels, then jack up the rear of the vehicle and support securely on axle stands (see *"Jacking and Vehicle Support"*). Remove the appropriate rear roadwheel.

3 On models with rear disc brakes, remove the brake caliper and the brake disc, as described in Chapter 9. Note that there is no need to disconnect the brake fluid hose from the caliper - suspend the caliper with wire or string, to avoid straining the hose. **Do not** depress the brake pedal whilst the caliper is removed.

4 On models with rear drum brakes, remove the brake drum as described in Chapter 9. **Do not** depress the brake pedal whilst the brake drum is removed.

6.7a Correct positioning of anti roll bar clamps

1 Anti roll bar   *2 Paint mark*

6.7b Correct positioning of anti roll bar drop link balljoint

7.5 Prise off the dust cap, then remove the split pin from the end of the stub axle

7.6 Slacken and remove the hub nut and washer

7.7 Withdraw the hub assembly from the stub axle

5 Prise the dust cap from the hub, then remove the split pin from the end of the stub axle **(see illustration)**. Discard the split pin - a new one should be used on refitting.
6 The rear hub nut must now be loosened, using a suitable socket and extension bar **(see illustration)**.

 Warning: Take care, the nut is very tight! Do not remove the nut at this stage.

7 Remove the hub nut and washer, then withdraw the hub assembly from the stub axle **(see illustration)**. Discard the hub nut - a new one should be used on refitting.
8 Thoroughly clean the stub axle, then slide the new hub assembly into position.
9 Fit the washer, then fit a new hub nut - do not fully tighten the nut at this stage.
10 On models with rear drum brakes, refit the brake drum as described in Chapter 9.
11 On models with rear disc brakes, refit the brake disc and the caliper (Chapter 9).
12 Hold the hub stationary as during removal, then tighten the hub nut to the specified torque.
13 Check that the hub spins smoothly and freely, then fit a new split pin and tap the dust cap into position.
14 Refit the roadwheel, then lower the vehicle to the ground.

8 Rear suspension components - removal, overhaul and refitting

Suspension strut

Removal

Note: *New suspension strut upper and lower securing nuts, a new top mounting gasket, and a new anti-roll bar drop link securing nut should be used on refitting.*
1 Chock the front wheels, then jack up the rear of the vehicle and support on axle stands (see *"Jacking and Vehicle Support"*). Remove the relevant rear roadwheel.
2 Unscrew the nut securing the upper end of the anti-roll bar drop link to the lower end of the suspension strut (refer to the relevant sub-Section). Discard the nut - a new one should

be used on refitting. Separate the drop link from the strut.
3 Where applicable, unbolt ABS wiring from lower end of strut.
4 Pull out the securing clip, and disconnect the brake fluid hose from the bracket at the lower end of the suspension strut.
5 Unscrew the nuts from the bolts securing the lower end of the suspension strut to the hub carrier, then withdraw the bolts **(see illustration)**. Discard the nuts - new ones must be used on refitting.
6 Remove the rear seat back side bolster as described in Chapter 11. On Saloon models, remove the rear parcel shelf (see Chapter 11). Unclip the carpet trim panel to expose the suspension strut top mounting cover.
7 Prise the plastic cover from the top of the suspension strut top mounting, to expose the three securing nuts **(see illustration)**.
8 Have an assistant support the suspension strut from under the wheel arch, then unscrew the three top securing nuts, and lower the strut assembly from the vehicle. Discard the nuts - new ones must be used on refitting.

Overhaul

Note: *Suitable coil spring compressor tools will be required for this operation.*
9 Clamp the lower end of the strut in a vice fitted with jaw protectors.
10 Temporarily refit two of the strut upper securing nuts to their studs then, using a bar inserted between the upper mounting studs, counterhold the upper strut mounting whilst loosening the damper rod top nut. **Do not** remove the nut completely at this stage.

8.5 Unscrew the nuts (arrowed) securing the lower end of the suspension strut

HAYNES HINT *Temporarily fit the strut upper securing nuts upside-down (flanges facing upwards), to help prevent the bar from slipping off the studs.*

11 Fit suitable spring compressors to the spring, and compress the spring sufficiently to enable the upper spring seat to be turned by hand.

 Warning: Do not use makeshift or improvised tools to compress the spring, as there is a danger of serious injury if the spring is not retained properly and released slowly.

12 Fully unscrew and remove the damper rod top nut. Note that it will be necessary to counterhold the damper rod, using a suitable spanner, as the nut is unscrewed.
13 Withdraw the washers, gasket, top mounting, and upper spring seat.
14 Withdraw the spring, complete with compressors, then lift the rubber gaiter and the bump rubber from the damper rod.
15 With the strut assembly now dismantled, examine all the components for wear, damage or deformation. Renew any of the components as necessary.
16 Examine the damper for signs of fluid leakage. Check the damper rod for signs of pitting along its entire length, and check the strut body for signs of damage. While holding it in an upright position, test the operation of the strut by moving the damper rod through a full stroke, and then through short strokes of

8.7 Rear suspension strut top mounting nuts

10

8.20 Rear suspension strut upper spring seat orientation

A Outside of vehicle   B Front of vehicle

50 to 100 mm. In both cases, the resistance felt should be smooth and continuous. If the resistance is jerky, or uneven, or if there is any visible sign of wear or damage to the strut, renewal is necessary. Note that the damper cannot be renewed independently, and if leakage or damage is evident, the complete strut/damper assembly must be renewed (in which case, the spring, upper mounting components, bushes, and associated components can be transferred to the new strut).

17 If any doubt exists about the condition of the coil spring, carefully remove the spring compressors, and check the spring for distortion and signs of cracking. Renew the spring if it is damaged or distorted, or if there is any doubt as to its condition.

18 Clamp the strut body in a vice, as during dismantling, then refit the bump rubber and the rubber gaiter.

19 Ensure that the coil spring is compressed sufficiently to enable the upper mounting components to be fitted, then fit the spring over the damper rod, noting that two paint marks on the spring coils must be positioned towards the bottom of the strut. Make sure that the lower end of the spring is correctly located on the lower spring seat.

20 Refit the upper spring seat, noting that the seat must be positioned as shown, so that the arrow marking points to the outside of the vehicle **(see illustration)**. Ensure that the top end of the spring is correctly located on the upper spring seat.

21 Refit the top mounting, then refit the washers and the damper rod top nut. Tighten the top nut to the specified torque, counter-holding the damper rod in a manner similar to that used during removal.

22 Progressively release the spring compressors.

Refitting

23 Fit a new gasket to the top mounting, then manoeuvre the strut assembly into position under the wheel arch, passing the mounting studs through the holes in the body turret. Note that the cut-out in the upper spring seat must be positioned nearest the outer edge of the suspension turret - ie, the side nearest the roadwheel (refer to illustration 8.20). Fit the new upper mounting nuts, and tighten them to the specified torque.

24 Engage the lower end of the strut with the hub carrier, then refit the bolts and fit the new nuts, noting that the nuts fit on the front side of the strut, and tighten to the specified torque.

25 Reconnect the anti-roll bar drop link to the suspension strut, and secure with a new nut. Ensure that the balljoint is positioned in the centre of its arc of movement, and is not under strain, then tighten the nut to the specified torque.

26 Refit the roadwheel, and lower the vehicle to the ground.

Parallel links

Removal

Note: *New parallel link mounting nuts should be used on refitting. On completion of refitting, the rear wheel alignment must be checked with reference to Chapter 1.*

27 Chock the front wheels, then jack up the rear of the vehicle and support securely on axle stands (see *"Jacking and Vehicle Support"*). Remove the relevant rear roadwheel.

28 Unscrew the nut from the through-bolt securing the outboard ends of the two parallel links to the hub carrier. Recover the washer and withdraw the bolt **(see illustration)**. Discard the nut - a new one must be used on refitting.

29 If the rear parallel link is being removed, make a careful note of the position of the eccentrics on the inboard securing bolt. The eccentrics have graduations on the outer edges, and the position of the eccentrics determines the rear wheel toe-setting. Note that one eccentric is integral with the bolt head, and the other locates in a groove in the shank of the bolt, under the nut. Make alignment marks between the eccentric and the body bracket.

30 Unscrew the nut from the bolt securing the inboard end of the parallel link to the bracket on the body. Note that it will be necessary to counterhold the bolt. Recover the eccentric, then withdraw the bolt, and lower the parallel link from under the vehicle. Discard the nut - a new one must be used on refitting **(see illustration)**.

Overhaul

31 Inspect the parallel link for cracks or other signs of damage, and examine the bushes for wear and deterioration.

32 The bushes are integral with the parallel links, and if worn or damaged, the complete link assembly must be renewed.

Refitting

33 Manoeuvre the link into position beneath the vehicle, then refit the bolt securing the inboard end of the link to the bracket on the body (note that the bolt fits from the front of the vehicle). Where applicable, refit the washer, then fit a new securing nut, but do not tighten it fully at this stage.

8.28 Remove the through-bolt (arrowed) securing the outboard ends of the two parallel links to the hub carrier

8.30 Unscrew the nuts (arrowed) from the bolts (arrowed) securing the inboard ends of the parallel links to the bracket on the body

**8.38 Rear parallel link toe adjustment -
viewed from rear of vehicle**

A Toe-in   *B Toe-out*   *C Parallel link*

**8.41 Unscrew the nut from the bolt (arrowed) securing the front of
the radius rod to the bracket on the vehicle body**

34 Refit the through-bolt securing the outboard ends of the parallel links to the hub carrier (note that the bolt fits from the rear of the vehicle), then refit the washer, and a new nut, but do not fully tighten the nut at this stage.

35 Refit the roadwheel, and lower the vehicle to the ground.

36 Make sure that the vehicle is parked on level ground, then release the handbrake. Roll the vehicle backwards and forwards, and bounce the front of the vehicle to settle the suspension components.

37 Chock the wheels, then tighten the outboard parallel link securing nut to the specified torque.

38 Set the eccentric on the inboard parallel link securing bolt to the position noted before removal, then arrange to have the rear wheel alignment checked, before tightening the nut to the specified torque **(see illustration)**. If no suitable equipment is available to check the wheel alignment, tighten the nut with the eccentric positioned as noted before removal, then have the rear wheel alignment checked at the earliest opportunity by a Nissan dealer or a suitably-qualified tyre specialist.

Radius rod

Removal

Note: *A new radius rod front mounting nut should be used on refitting.*

39 Chock the front wheels, then jack up the rear of the vehicle and support securely on axle stands (see *"Jacking and Vehicle Support"*). To improve access, remove the relevant rear roadwheel.

40 Where applicable, remove the cover from the nut securing the rear end of the radius rod to the hub carrier, then unscrew the nut and recover the washer.

41 Unscrew the nut from the bolt securing the front of the radius rod to the bracket on the vehicle body, then remove the bolt, and withdraw the radius rod from under the vehicle **(see illustration)**. Discard the nut - a new one should be used on refitting.

Overhaul

42 Inspect the radius rod for cracks or other signs of damage, and examine the bushes for wear and deterioration.

43 The bushes are integral with the radius rods, and if worn or damaged, the complete assembly must be renewed.

Refitting

44 Manoeuvre the radius rod into position under the vehicle, and position the rear of the rod on the hub carrier stud. Refit the washer and nut, but do not fully tighten the nut at this stage.

45 Move the front of the rod into position in the front mounting bracket, then refit the front securing bolt, noting that the bolt fits from the inboard edge of the bracket. Fit a new nut, but do not fully tighten the nut at this stage.

46 Refit the roadwheel, and lower the vehicle to the ground.

47 Make sure that the vehicle is parked on level ground, then release the handbrake. Roll the vehicle backwards and forwards, and repeatedly press down on the vehicle to settle the suspension components.

48 Chock the wheels, then tighten the radius rod securing nuts to the specified torque. On completion, where applicable, refit the cover to the rear radius rod securing nut.

Hub carrier

Removal

Note: *A new parallel link outboard mounting nut, and new suspension strut-to-hub carrier nuts, should be used on refitting.*

49 Chock the front wheels, then jack up the rear of the vehicle and support securely on axle stands (see *"Jacking and Vehicle Support"*). Remove the relevant rear roadwheel.

50 On models with rear disc brakes, unbolt the brake caliper from the hub carrier as described in Chapter 9. Note that there is no need to disconnect the brake fluid hose - suspend the caliper using wire or string.

51 On models with rear drum brakes, remove the brake shoes, and disconnect the brake fluid pipe from the rear wheel cylinder, as described in Chapter 9 - be prepared for an amount of brake fluid spillage. Plug the open ends of the pipe and wheel cylinder, to reduce fluid spillage and to prevent dirt ingress.

52 Where applicable, remove the cover from the nut securing the rear end of the radius rod to the hub carrier, then unscrew the nut and recover the washer.

53 Unscrew the nut from the through-bolt securing the outboard ends of the two parallel links to the hub carrier. Recover the washer and withdraw the bolt. Discard the nut - a new one must be used on refitting.

54 Unscrew the nuts from the bolts securing the lower end of the suspension strut to the hub carrier, then withdraw the bolts, and remove the hub carrier from under the vehicle. Discard the nuts - new ones must be used on refitting.

Overhaul

55 Examine the hub carrier for signs of cracking or damage. If desired, the hub bearings can be renewed as described in Section 7.

Refitting

56 Lift the hub carrier into position, engaging the radius rod with the hub carrier stud, then fit the two bolts securing the hub carrier to the lower end of the suspension strut, noting that the bolts fit from the rear of the hub carrier. Fit new nuts to the bolts, and tighten them to the specified torque.

57 Reconnect the parallel links to the hub carrier, then refit the through-bolt, noting that the bolt fits from the rear of the hub carrier. Refit the washer and a new securing nut, but do not fully tighten the nut at this stage.

58 Refit the radius rod-to-hub carrier securing nut, ensuring that the washer is in place, but do not fully tighten the nut at this stage.

10

8.66 Unscrew the nuts (arrowed) securing the upper ends of the drop links to the suspension strut

8.67 Unscrew the nuts and bolts securing the anti-roll bar mounting clamps to the brackets on the body

59 On models with rear drum brakes, refit the brake shoes, and reconnect the brake fluid pipe to the wheel cylinder, then bleed the brake hydraulic circuit, as described in Chapter 9.

60 On models with rear disc brakes, refit the brake caliper as described in Chapter 9.

61 Refit the roadwheel, and lower the vehicle to the ground.

62 Make sure that the vehicle is parked on level ground, then release the handbrake. Roll the vehicle backwards and forwards, and repeatedly press down on the vehicle to settle the suspension components.

63 Chock the wheels, then tighten the radius rod securing nut, and the parallel link outboard securing nut, to the specified torque. On completion, where applicable, refit the cover to the rear radius rod securing nut.

64 Have the rear wheel alignment checked at the earliest opportunity (see Chapter 1).

Anti-roll bar

Removal

Note: *New anti-roll bar clamp nuts, and new anti-roll bar-to-drop link nuts, should be used on refitting.*

65 Chock the front wheels, then jack up the rear of the vehicle and support securely on axle stands (see *"Jacking and Vehicle Support"*). To improve access, remove the rear roadwheels.

66 Unscrew the nuts securing the upper ends of the drop links to the suspension strut **(see illustration)**. Discard the nuts - new ones should be used on refitting.

67 Unscrew the nuts and bolts securing the anti-roll bar mounting clamps to the brackets on the body **(see illustration)**, then withdraw the clamps, and manipulate the anti-roll bar out from under the vehicle. Discard the clamp nuts - new ones should be used on refitting.

Overhaul

68 Inspect the mounting clamp rubbers for cracks or deterioration. If renewal is

necessary, slide the old rubbers from the bar, and fit the new rubbers. Note that the rubbers should be positioned with their slits at the top of the bar.

Refitting

69 Refitting is a reversal of removal, bearing in mind the following points **(see illustration)**:
  a) *When refitting the anti-roll bar clamps, note that the elongated bolt holes should be positioned at the bottom.*
  b) *When refitting the clamp bushes, ensure that the slit is facing upwards.*
  c) *When reconnecting the drop links to the suspension strut, make sure that the drop link balljoint is positioned centrally in its arc of movement, and is not under strain, and use new nuts.*
  d) *Use new clamp nuts, and new anti-roll bar-to-drop link nuts.*

Anti-roll bar drop link

Removal

Note: *New anti-roll bar-to-drop link nuts should be used on refitting.*

70 Chock the front wheels, then jack up the rear of the vehicle and support securely on axle stands (see *"Jacking and Vehicle Support"*). Remove the relevant rear wheel.

71 If necessary, counterhold the drop link pin, then unscrew the nut securing the end of the anti-roll bar to the drop link. Discard the nut - a new one should be used on refitting.

72 Again, if necessary counterhold the drop link pin, then unscrew the nut securing the drop link to the lower end of the suspension strut, and withdraw the drop link. Discard the nut - a new one should be used on refitting.

Overhaul

73 Check the drop link balljoints for wear and damage, and if necessary renew the drop link.

Refitting

74 Refitting is a reversal of removal, bearing in mind the following points:
  a) *Make sure that the drop link balljoints are positioned centrally in their arcs of movement, and are not under strain.*
  b) *Use new drop link securing nuts, and tighten them to the specified torque.*

8.69 Orientation of rear anti roll bar mountings

A Slit
B Elongated hole
C Anti roll bat
D Drop link

H28757

9.6 Unplug the horn wiring from the centre pad at the connectors

9.8 Make alignment marks (arrowed) between the steering wheel and the end of the steering column shaft

9 Steering wheel - removal and refitting

Note: *This section does not include models fitted with a Supplementary Restraint System (SRS).*

 Warning: For safety reasons, owners are strongly advised to entrust to an authorised Nissan dealer any work which involves disturbing the SRS components. Specialised test equipment is needed to check that the SRS is fully operational following reassembly.

Removal

1 Disconnect the battery negative lead.
2 Set the front wheels in the straight-ahead position, then release the steering lock by inserting the ignition key.

Models with two spoke steering wheels

3 Carefully prise the centre pad away from steering wheel to release the pawls, then insert a flat bladed screwdriver into the gap between the pad and the steering wheel and release the clamps. Lift the pad away from the steering wheel.

Models with three spoke steering wheels

4 Insert a flat bladed screwdriver into the recess on the reverse of the lower spoke and release the clamp. Carefully prise off the lower end of the pad, then release remaining clips and lift off the pad.

Models with four spoke steering wheels

5 Insert a crosshead screwdriver into the recess in the base of the steering wheel hub, slacken the screw and release the clamps. Lift off the steering wheel pad.

All models

6 Unplug the horn wiring from the centre pad at the connectors (see illustration).

7 Where applicable, remove the screw securing the horn wiring bracket to the steering wheel.
8 Make alignment marks between the steering wheel and the end of the steering column shaft (see illustration).
9 Slacken and remove the steering wheel securing nut.
10 Lift the steering wheel off the column splines. If it is tight, tap it near the centre, using the palm of your hand, or twist it from side to side, whilst pulling upwards to release it from the shaft splines. If the wheel is particularly tight, a suitable puller should be used. Make alignment marks between the steering wheel and the end of the steering column shaft (see illustration).

Refitting

11 Before commencing refitting, lightly coat the surfaces of the direction indicator cancelling mechanism components and the horn contact slip ring components with grease.
12 Refitting is a reversal of removal, bearing in mind the following points:
   a) *Ensure that the direction indicator switch is in the central (cancelled/off) position, otherwise the switch may be damaged as the wheel is refitted.*
   b) *Align the marks made on the wheel and the steering column shaft during removal.*

   c) *Tighten the securing nut to the specified torque.*
13 Note that if necessary, the position of the steering wheel on the column shaft can be altered in order to centralise the wheel (ensure that the front roadwheels are pointing in the straight-ahead position), by moving the wheel the required number of splines on the shaft.

10 Ignition switch/steering column lock - removal and refitting

Removal

Note: *New shear-screws must be used when refitting the lock assembly.*
1 Disconnect the battery negative lead.
2 Remove the steering column shrouds as described in Chapter 11.
3 To remove the ignition switch, disconnect the wiring plug from the switch, then remove the grub screw from the rear of the lock (using a suitable cranked key), and withdraw the switch.
4 To remove the lock assembly, drill out and remove the two shear-bolts, then withdraw the two sections of the lock casting from the steering column (see illustration). Note that the lock assembly cannot be removed from the casting.

 10

9.10 Using a suitable puller to remove the steering wheel

10.4 To remove the ignition lock cylinder assembly, drill out the two bolts (arrowed)

Refitting

5 Refitting is a reversal of removal, but when refitting the lock assembly, use new shear-bolts, and tighten the screws until the heads break off.

11 Steering column - removal, inspection and refitting

Note: *This section does not include models fitted with a Supplementary Restraint System (SRS).*

 Warning: For safety reasons, owners are strongly advised to entrust to an authorised Nissan dealer any work which involves disturbing the SRS components. Specialised test equipment is needed to check that the SRS is fully operational following reassembly.

Removal

1 Disconnect the battery negative lead.
2 Remove the steering wheel as described in Section 9.
3 Remove the steering column stalk switches with reference to Chapter 12.
4 Disconnect the wiring plug from the ignition switch.
5 To improve access, remove the driver's side lower facia panel as described in Chapter 11.
6 Working in the driver's footwell, release the steering shaft boot from the bulkhead, then peel it back to expose the lower end of the shaft.
7 Where applicable, unscrew the three securing nuts and withdraw the metal cover from the studs on the bulkhead. Slide the cover up the steering column to gain access the lower universal joint.
8 Temporarily refit the steering wheel, and turn the steering column as necessary for access to the universal joint clamp bolt.
9 Unscrew and remove the universal joint clamp bolt.
10 Unscrew the two steering column upper securing bolts, and the two lower nuts, and withdraw the steering column.

Inspection

11 The steering column incorporates a telescopic safety feature. In the event of a front-end crash, the shaft collapses and prevents the steering wheel injuring the driver. Before refitting the steering column, examine the column and mountings for signs of damage and deformation, and renew as necessary.
12 Check the steering shaft for signs of free play in the column bushes, and check the universal joints for signs of damage or roughness in the joint bearings. If any damage or wear is found in the steering column universal joints or shaft bushes, the column must be renewed as an assembly.

12.3a Remove the split pin . . .

13 Measure the length of the steering column from the centre of the universal joint pin to the top of the column shaft. If the measurement is outside the specified limits, this is probably due to accident damage, and the complete column assembly should be renewed.

Refitting

14 Commence refitting by sliding the rubber gaiter (where applicable), and the metal cover onto the lower end of the shaft. Where applicable, refit and tighten the clip securing the upper end of the gaiter to the steering column.
15 Offer the steering column into position, and engage the lower end of the column shaft with the universal joint. Note the cut-out in the splined section at the end of the steering shaft - the joint must be reassembled such that the clamp bolt bears on this cut-out when it is tightened.
16 Refit the steering column lower securing nuts and the upper bolts, then tighten them to the specified torque.
17 At the steering shaft universal joint, tighten the clamp bolt to the specified torque.
18 Position the metal cover over the universal joint, then refit and tighten the securing nuts.
19 Clip the lower end of the rubber gaiter into position in the metal cover, then fit a new lower gaiter securing clip.
20 Where applicable, refit the driver's side lower facia panel.
21 Reconnect the ignition switch wiring plug.
22 Refit the steering column stalk switches.
23 Refit the steering wheel, (Section 9).
24 Reconnect the battery negative lead.

12.5 Remove the nuts (arrowed) and peel back the steering shaft-to-steering gear pinion gaiter

12.3b . . .then use a balljoint splitter to separate the track-rod end from the arm

12 Steering gear assembly - removal, inspection and refitting

Note: *This section does not include models fitted with a Supplementary Restraint System (SRS).*

 Warning: For safety reasons, owners are strongly advised to entrust to an authorised Nissan dealer any work which involves disturbing the SRS components. Specialised test equipment is needed to check that the SRS is fully operational following reassembly.

Manual steering gear

Removal

Note: *A balljoint separator tool will be required for this operation. A new track-rod end nut split pin should be used on refitting.*
1 Chock the rear wheels, apply the handbrake, then jack up the front of the vehicle and support securely on axle stands (see *"Jacking and Vehicle Support"*). Remove the roadwheels.
2 Move the steering wheel so that the front wheels are pointing in the straight-ahead position.
3 Working on one side of the vehicle, remove the split pin, then partially unscrew the castellated nut securing the track-rod end to the steering arm. Using a balljoint separator tool, separate the track-rod end from the steering arm **(see illustrations)**. Remove the nut. Discard the split pin - a new one must be used on refitting.
4 Repeat the procedure to disconnect the track-rod end on the other side of the vehicle.
5 Working in the engine bay at the bulkhead, remove the retaining nuts, lift off the retaining plates (where applicable) and peel back the gaiter from the steering shaft joint **(see illustration)**.
6 Mark the relationship between the steering shaft universal joint and the steering gear pinion **(see illustration)**, then slacken the clamp bolt and separate the joint from the steering gear pinion.

12.6 Slacken the clamp bolt (arrowed) and separate the universal joint from the steering gear pinion

7 Unscrew the bolts securing the steering gear mounting brackets to the bulkhead. Support the steering gear, then withdraw the brackets.

8 Rotate the steering gear, and manipulate it out through the right-hand wheel arch. Note that on left-hand-drive models, it will be necessary to lift the steering gear over the mounting brackets before it can be withdrawn.

Inspection

9 Examine the assembly for obvious signs of wear or damage.

10 Check the rack for smooth operation through its full stroke of movement, and check that there is no binding or free play.

11 Check the track-rods for deformation and cracks.

12 Check the condition of the steering gear rubber gaiters, and renew if necessary with reference to Section 13.

13 Examine the track-rod ends for wear or damage, and renew if necessary (Section 16).

Refitting

14 Ensure that the steering gear is centralised as follows:
  a) *Turn the pinion to rotate the steering from lock-to-lock, and count the number of turns of the pinion.*
  b) *With the steering on full lock, turn the pinion back through half the number of turns noted for lock-to-lock, to achieve the centralised position.*

15 Manoeuvre the steering gear into position through the right-hand wheel arch, then refit the mounting brackets (noting the orientation markings), and refit and tighten the securing bolts.

16 Engage the steering shaft universal joint with the steering gear pinion, then refit and tighten the clamp bolt. **Note:** *If the original steering gear is being refitted, the marks made during removal can be used to align the universal joint and pinion.*

17 Position the gaiter over the universal joint, fit the retaining plates (where applicable) then refit and tighten the securing nuts.

18 Working on one side of the vehicle, reconnect the track-rod end to the steering arm, then refit the castellated nut, and tighten to (at least) minimum specified torque.

19 If necessary, tighten the nut further (ensure that the maximum torque for the nut is not exceeded) until the nearest grooves in the nut are aligned with the split pin hole in the track-rod end, then fit a new split pin.

20 Repeat the procedure to reconnect the track-rod end on the other side of the vehicle.

21 Refit the roadwheels, and lower the vehicle to the ground.

Power steering gear

Removal

22 Chock the rear wheels, apply the handbrake, then jack up the front of the vehicle and support securely on axle stands (see *"Jacking and Vehicle Support"*). Remove the roadwheels.

23 Position a suitable container beneath the fluid feed pipe unions on the steering gear, then unscrew the union nut, and disconnect the pipe from the steering gear **(see illustration)**. Similarly, disconnect the fluid return hose from the steering gear. Drain the fluid into the container, then plug or cover the open ends of the pipe/hose and steering gear to reduce further fluid loss, and to prevent dirt ingress.

 HAYNES HiNT *Cut the fingertips from an old rubber glove and secure them with elastic bands over the open fluid pipes and steering gear ports - this will help to prevent the ingress of dirt and excessive fluid leakage.*

24 To improve access, remove the exhaust front section as described in the relevant Part of Chapter 4.

25 Working on one side of the vehicle, remove the split pin, then partially unscrew the castellated nut securing the track-rod end to the steering arm. Using a balljoint separator tool, separate the track-rod end from the steering arm (refer to illustrations 12.3a and 12.3b). Remove the nut. Discard the split pin - a new one must be used on refitting.

26 Repeat the procedure to disconnect the track-rod end on the other side of the vehicle.

27 Working in the engine bay at the bulkhead, remove the retaining nuts, lift off the retaining plates (where applicable) and peel back the gaiter from the steering shaft joint (refer to illustration 12.5)

12.29a Remove the bolts from the steering gear clamp brackets on the left . . .

12.23 Power steering gear fluid unions (arrowed)

28 Mark the relationship between the steering shaft universal joint and the steering gear pinion, then slacken the clamp bolt and separate the joint from the steering gear pinion (see illustration 12.6)

29 Unscrew the bolts securing the steering gear mounting brackets to the bulkhead **(see illustrations)**. Support the steering gear, then withdraw the brackets.

30 Manipulate the steering gear around the wiring harness (where applicable), then slide the assembly to the right-hand side of the vehicle, and withdraw the assembly from under the left-hand side of the vehicle.

Inspection

31 Clean the assembly thoroughly, then examine it for obvious signs of wear or damage.

32 Check the track-rods for deformation and cracks.

33 Check the condition of the steering gear rubber gaiters, and renew if necessary with reference to Section 13.

34 Examine the track-rod ends for wear or damage, and renew if necessary with reference to Section 16.

Refitting

35 Ensure that the steering gear is centralised as follows:
  a) *Turn the pinion to rotate the steering from lock-to-lock, and count the number of turns of the pinion.*
  b) *With the steering on full lock, turn the pinion back through half the number of turns noted for lock-to-lock, to achieve the centralised position.*

10

12.29b . . . and right hand sides

36 Manoeuvre the steering gear into position from under the left-hand side of the vehicle, then refit the mounting brackets (noting the orientation markings) and the securing bolts. **Note:** *Lightly tighten the lower clamp bolts (do not fully tighten the bolts at this stage), then fit and tighten all the clamp bolts to the specified torque in the sequence shown* **(see illustration)**

37 Where applicable, refit the exhaust front section with reference to the relevant Part of Chapter 4.

38 Engage the steering shaft universal joint with the steering gear pinion, then refit and tighten the clamp bolt. **Note:** *If the original steering gear is being refitted, the marks made during removal can be used to align the universal joint and pinion.*

39 Position the gaiter over the universal joint, fit the retaining plates (where applicable) then refit and tighten the securing nuts.

40 Working on one side of the vehicle, reconnect the track-rod end to the steering arm, then refit the castellated nut, and tighten to (at least) minimum specified torque.

41 If necessary, tighten the nut further (ensure that the maximum torque for the nut is not exceeded) until the nearest grooves in the nut are aligned with the split pin hole in the track-rod end, then fit a new split pin.

42 Repeat the procedure to reconnect the track-rod end on the other side of the vehicle.

43 Reconnect the fluid feed pipe and the return hose to the steering gear, observing the specified torque settings.

44 Refit the roadwheels, then bleed the power steering hydraulic system as described in Section 14.

45 On completion, lower the vehicle to the ground.

13 Steering gear rubber gaiters - renewal

Note: *New gaiter retaining clips should be used on refitting.*

1 Remove the relevant track-rod end as described in Section 16.

2 If not already done, unscrew the track-rod end locknut from the end of the track-rod.

3 Mark the correct fitted position of the gaiter on the track-rod, then release the gaiter securing clips. Slide the gaiter from the steering gear, and off the end of the track-rod.

4 Thoroughly clean the track-rod and the steering gear housing, using fine abrasive paper to polish off any corrosion, burrs or sharp edges, which might damage the new gaiter sealing lips on installation. Scrape off all the grease from the old gaiter, and apply it to the track rod inner balljoint. (This assumes that grease has not been lost or contaminated as a result of damage to the old gaiter. Use fresh grease if in doubt.)

5 Carefully slide the new gaiter onto the track-rod, and locate it on the steering gear

12.36 Power steering gear clamp bolts - tightening sequence
A Initial tightening   B Final tightening

H28758

housing. Align the outer edge of the gaiter with the mark made on the track-rod prior to removal, then secure it in position with new retaining clips.

6 Screw the track-rod end locknut onto the end of the track-rod.

7 Refit the track rod end as described in Section 17.

14 Power steering hydraulic system - bleeding

General

1 The following symptoms indicate that there is air present in the power steering hydraulic system:
a) *Generation of air bubbles in fluid reservoir.*
b) *"Clicking" noises from power steering pump.*
c) *Excessive "buzzing" from power steering pump.*

2 Note that when the vehicle is stationary, or while moving the steering wheel slowly, a "hissing" noise may be produced in the steering gear or the fluid pump. This noise is inherent in the system, and does not indicate any cause for concern.

Bleeding

3 Chock the rear wheels, apply the handbrake, then jack up the front of the vehicle and support securely on axle stands (see *"Jacking and Vehicle Support"*).

4 Check the fluid level in the power steering fluid reservoir (bear in mind that the vehicle will be tilted, so the level cannot be read accurately), and if necessary top-up to just above the relevant level mark.

5 Have an assistant turn the steering quickly from lock to lock, and observe the fluid level. If the fluid level drops, add more fluid, and repeat the operation until the fluid level no longer drops. Failure to achieve this within a reasonable period may indicate a leak in the system.

6 Start the engine and repeat the procedure described in the previous paragraph.

7 Once the fluid level has stabilised, and all air has been bled from the system, lower the vehicle to the ground.

15 Power steering pump - removal and refitting

Removal

Note: New sealing rings must be used when reconnecting the high-pressure fluid hose to the pump.

1 For improved access, apply the handbrake, then jack up the front of the vehicle, and support securely on axle stands (see *"Jacking and Vehicle Support"*).

2 Remove the pump drivebelt (Chapter 1).

3 Place a suitable container beneath the power steering pump, then unscrew the banjo bolt from the high-pressure fluid hose union, and disconnect the hose from the pump. Recover the sealing rings and discard them - new ones should be used on refitting. Drain the escaping fluid into the container. Plug or cover the open ends of the hose and pump, to reduce further fluid loss, and to prevent dirt ingress.

4 Similarly, disconnect the fluid return hose from the pump.

5 Unscrew the nut from the adjuster stud, then unscrew the two lower bolts securing the adjuster bracket to the engine, and withdraw the adjuster bracket assembly.

6 Turn the pump pulley until one of the holes in the pulley lines up with the through-bolt, then unscrew the nut from the end of the through-bolt, and recover any washers.

7 Support the pump, then withdraw the through-bolt, and manipulate the pump out from above the engine. Note that on certain models surrounding components may prevent the pump from being withdrawn from above - in this case, it will be necessary to unbolt the pump mounting bracket from the engine, and withdraw the pump from underneath the vehicle.

16.3 Counterhold the track-rod end using the flats provided, then loosen the track-rod end locknut

16.4 Alternatively, mark the relationship between the track-rod end and the track-rod using a dab of paint (arrowed)

Refitting

8 Refitting is a reversal of removal, but use new sealing rings when reconnecting the high-pressure fluid hose, and on completion, refit and tension the drivebelt as described in Chapter 1.

16 Track-rod end - removal and refitting

Removal

Note: *A balljoint separator tool will be required for this operation. A new track-rod end nut split pin should be used on refitting.*

1 Chock the rear wheels, apply the handbrake, then jack up the front of the vehicle and support on axle stands (see *"Jacking and Vehicle Support "*). Remove the relevant front roadwheel.

2 Remove the split pin, then partially unscrew the castellated nut securing the track-rod end to the steering arm. Using a balljoint separator tool, separate the track-rod end from the steering arm. Remove the nut. Discard the split pin - a new one must be used on refitting.

3 Counterhold the track-rod end using the flats provided, then loosen the track-rod end locknut **(see illustration)**.

4 Unscrew the track-rod end from the track-rod, counting the exact number of turns required to do so. Alternatively, mark the relationship between the track-rod end and the track-rod using a dab of paint **(see illustration)**.

Refitting

5 Carefully clean the track-rod end and the track-rod threads.

6 Renew the track-rod end if the rubber dust cover is cracked, split or perished, or if the movement of the balljoint is either sloppy or too stiff. Also check for other signs of damage

such as worn threads.

7 Screw the track-rod end onto the track-rod by the number of turns noted before removal.

8 Ensure that the balljoint taper is clean, then engage the taper with the steering arm on the hub carrier.

9 Refit the castellated nut, and tighten to the specified torque.

10 If necessary, tighten the nut further (ensure that the maximum torque for the nut is not exceeded) until the nearest grooves in the nut are aligned with the split pin hole in the track-rod end, then fit a new split pin.

11 Refit the roadwheel, and lower the vehicle to the ground.

12 Check the front wheel alignment as described in Chapter 1, and adjust if necessary, then tighten the track-rod end locknut. **Note:** *If the vehicle is to be driven to have the wheel alignment checked, the track-rod end locknut should be tightened before driving the vehicle.*

10

Chapter 11
Bodywork and fittings

Contents

Degrees of difficulty

Easy, suitable for novice with little experience	Fairly easy, suitable for beginner with some experience	Fairly difficult, suitable for competent DIY mechanic	Difficult, suitable for experienced DIY mechanic	Very difficult, suitable for expert DIY or professional

Specifications

Torque wrench settings	Nm	lbf ft
Front bumper bracket through-bolts	30	22
Rear bumper bracket through-bolts	30	22
Front seat securing bolts	50	37
Door hinge bolts:		
Coupe models	30	22
Hatchback and saloon models	40	30
Door lock striker bolts	15	11
Door latch screws	6	5
Tailgate strut upper mountings:		
3 dr hatchback	6	5
5 dr hatchback	15	11
Coupe	10	8
Tailgate strut lower mountings:		
3 dr hatchback	6	5
5 dr hatchback	15	11
Coupe	6	5

11

1 General information

The bodyshell is composed of pressed-steel sections which are welded together, although some use of structural adhesives is made. In addition, the front wings are bolted on.

The bonnet, door and some other panels vulnerable to corrosion are fabricated from zinc-coated metal. A coating of anti-chip primer, applied prior to paint spraying provides further protection.

Extensive use is made of plastic materials, mainly in the interior, but also in exterior components. The outer sections of the front and rear bumpers are injection-moulded from a synthetic material which is very strong, and yet light. Plastic components such as wheel arch liners are fitted to the underside of the vehicle, to improve the body's resistance to corrosion.

2 Maintenance - bodywork and underframe

The general condition of a vehicle's bodywork significantly affects its value. Maintenance is easy, but needs to be regular. Neglect, particularly after minor damage, can lead quickly to further deterioration and costly repair bills. It is important also to keep watch on those parts of the vehicle not immediately visible, for instance the underside, inside all the wheel arches, and the lower part of the engine compartment.

The basic maintenance routine for the bodywork is washing - preferably with a lot of water, from a hose. This will remove all the loose solids which may have stuck to the vehicle. It is important to flush these off in such a way as to prevent grit from scratching the finish. The wheel arches and underframe need washing in the same way, to remove any accumulated mud which will retain moisture and tend to encourage rust. Oddly enough, the best time to clean the underframe and wheel arches is in wet weather, when the mud is thoroughly wet and soft. In very wet weather, the underframe is usually cleaned of large accumulations automatically, and this is a good time for inspection.

Periodically, except on vehicles with a wax-based underbody protective coating, it is a good idea to have the whole of the underframe of the vehicle steam-cleaned, engine compartment included, so that a thorough inspection can be carried out to see what minor repairs and renovations are necessary. Steam-cleaning is available at many garages, and is necessary for the removal of the accumulation of oily grime, which sometimes is allowed to become thick in certain areas. If steam-cleaning facilities are not available, there are some excellent grease solvents available which can be brush-applied; the dirt can then be simply hosed off. Note that these methods should not be used on vehicles with wax-based underbody protective coating, or the coating will be removed. Such vehicles should be inspected annually, preferably just prior to Winter, when the underbody should be washed down, and any damage to the wax coating repaired using a proprietary brand of undershield. Ideally, a completely fresh coat should be applied. It would also be worth considering the use of such wax-based protection for injection into door panels, sills, box sections, etc, as an additional safeguard against rust damage, where such protection is not provided by the vehicle manufacturer.

After washing paintwork, wipe off with a chamois leather to give an unspotted clear finish. A coat of clear protective wax polish will give added protection against chemical pollutants in the air. If the paintwork sheen has dulled or oxidised, use a cleaner/polisher combination to restore the brilliance of the shine. This requires a little effort, but such dulling is usually caused because regular washing has been neglected. Care needs to be taken with metallic paintwork, as special non-abrasive cleaner/polisher is required to avoid damage to the finish. Always check that the door and ventilator opening drain holes and pipes are completely clear, so that water can be drained out. Brightwork should be treated in the same way as paintwork. Windscreens and windows can be kept clear of the smeary film which often appears, by the use of a proprietary glass cleaner. Never use any form of wax or other body or chromium polish on glass.

3 Maintenance - upholstery and carpets

Mats and carpets should be brushed or vacuum-cleaned regularly, to keep them free of grit. If they are badly stained, remove them from the vehicle for scrubbing or sponging, and make quite sure they are dry before refitting. Seats and interior trim panels can be kept clean by wiping with a damp cloth and a proprietary brand of cleaner. If they do become stained (which can be more apparent on light-coloured upholstery), use a little liquid detergent and a soft nail brush to scour the grime out of the grain of the material. Do not forget to keep the headlining clean in the same way as the upholstery. When using liquid cleaners inside the vehicle, do not over-wet the surfaces being cleaned. Excessive damp could get into the seams and padded interior, causing stains, offensive odours or even rot. If the inside of the vehicle gets wet accidentally, it is worthwhile taking some trouble to dry it out properly, particularly where carpets are involved. *Do not leave oil or electric heaters inside the vehicle for this purpose.*

4 Minor body damage - repair

Repairs of minor scratches in bodywork

If the scratch is very superficial, and does not penetrate to the metal of the bodywork, repair is very simple. Lightly rub the area of the scratch with a paintwork renovator, or a very fine cutting paste to remove loose paint from the scratch, and to clear the surrounding bodywork of wax polish. Rinse the area with clean water.

Apply touch-up paint to the scratch using a fine paint brush; continue to apply fine layers of paint until the surface of the paint in the scratch is level with the surrounding paintwork. Allow the new paint at least two weeks to harden, then blend it into the surrounding paintwork by rubbing the scratch area with a paintwork renovator or a very fine cutting paste. Finally, apply a good wax polish.

Where the scratch has penetrated right through to the metal of the bodywork, causing the metal to rust, a different repair technique is required. Remove any loose rust from the bottom of the scratch with a penknife, then apply rust-inhibiting paint to prevent the formation of rust in the future. Using a rubber or nylon applicator, fill the scratch with bodystopper paste. If required, this paste can be mixed with cellulose thinners to provide a very thin paste which is ideal for filling narrow scratches. Before the stopper-paste in the scratch hardens, wrap a piece of smooth cotton rag around the top of a finger. Dip the finger in cellulose thinners, and quickly sweep it across the surface of the stopper-paste in the scratch; this will ensure that the surface of the stopper-paste is slightly hollowed. The scratch can now be painted over as described earlier in this Section.

Repairs of dents in bodywork

When deep denting of the vehicle's bodywork has taken place, the first task is to pull the dent out until the affected bodywork almost attains its original shape. There is little point in trying to restore the original shape completely, as the metal in the damaged area will have stretched on impact, and cannot be reshaped fully to its original contour. It is better to bring the level of the dent up to a point which is about 3 mm below the level of the surrounding bodywork. In cases where the dent is very shallow anyway, it is not worth trying to pull it out at all. If the underside of the dent is accessible, it can be hammered out gently from behind, using a mallet with a wooden or plastic head. Whilst doing this, hold a suitable block of wood firmly against the outside of the panel, to absorb the impact from the hammer blows and thus prevent a large area of the bodywork from being "belled-out".

Should the dent be in a section of the bodywork which has a double skin, or some other factor making it inaccessible from behind, a different technique is called for. Drill several small holes through the metal inside the area - particularly in the deeper section. Then screw long self-tapping screws into the holes, just sufficiently for them to gain a good purchase in the metal. Now the dent can be pulled out by pulling on the protruding heads of the screws with a pair of pliers.

The next stage of the repair is the removal of the paint from the damaged area, and from an inch or so of the surrounding "sound" bodywork. This is accomplished most easily by using a wire brush or abrasive pad on a power drill, although it can be done just as effectively by hand, using sheets of abrasive paper. To complete the preparation for filling, score the surface of the bare metal with a screwdriver or the tang of a file, or alternatively, drill small holes in the affected area. This will provide a really good "key" for the filler paste.

To complete the repair, see the Section on filling and respraying.

Repairs of rust holes or gashes in bodywork

Remove all paint from the affected area, and from an inch or so of the surrounding "sound" bodywork, using an abrasive pad or a wire brush on a power drill. If these are not available, a few sheets of abrasive paper will do the job most effectively. With the paint removed, you will be able to judge the severity of the corrosion, and therefore decide whether to renew the whole panel (if this is possible) or to repair the affected area. New body panels are not as expensive as most people think, and it is often quicker and more satisfactory to fit a new panel than to attempt to repair large areas of corrosion.

Remove all fittings from the affected area, except those which will act as a guide to the original shape of the damaged bodywork (eg headlight shells, etc). Then, using tin snips or a hacksaw blade, remove all loose metal and any other metal badly affected by corrosion. Hammer the edges of the hole inwards, in order to create a slight depression for the filler paste.

Wire-brush the affected area to remove the powdery rust from the surface of the remaining metal. Paint the affected area with rust-inhibiting paint; if the back of the rusted area is accessible, treat this also.

Before filling can take place, it will be necessary to block the hole in some way. This can be achieved by the use of aluminium or plastic mesh, or aluminium tape.

Aluminium or plastic mesh, or glass-fibre matting, is probably the best material to use for a large hole. Cut a piece to the approximate size and shape of the hole to be filled, then position it in the hole so that its edges are below the level of the surrounding

bodywork. It can be retained in position by several blobs of filler paste around its periphery.

Aluminium tape should be used for small or very narrow holes. Pull a piece off the roll, trim it to the approximate size and shape required, then pull off the backing paper (if used) and stick the tape over the hole; it can be overlapped if the thickness of one piece is insufficient. Burnish down the edges of the tape with the handle of a screwdriver or similar, to ensure that the tape is securely attached to the metal underneath.

Bodywork repairs - filling and respraying

Before using this Section, see the Sections on dents, scratches, rust holes and gash repairs.

Many types of bodyfiller are available, but generally speaking, those proprietary brand kits which contain a tin of filler paste and a tube of resin hardener are best for this type of repair, or a proprietary brand of no-mix filler, which can be used directly from the tube. A wide, flexible plastic or nylon applicator will be found invaluable for imparting a smooth and well-contoured finish to the surface of the filler.

Mix up a little filler on a clean piece of card or board - measure the hardener carefully (follow the maker's instructions on the pack), otherwise the filler will set too rapidly or too slowly. Alternatively, a no-mix filler can be used straight from the tube without mixing, but daylight is required to cure it. Using the applicator, apply the filler paste to the prepared area; draw the applicator across the surface of the filler to achieve the correct contour and to level the surface. As soon as a contour that approximates to the correct one is achieved, stop working the paste - if you carry on too long, the paste will become sticky and begin to "pick-up" on the applicator. Continue to add thin layers of filler paste at 20-minute intervals, until the level of the filler is just proud of the surrounding bodywork.

Once the filler has hardened, the excess can be removed using a metal plane or file. From then on, progressively-finer grades of abrasive paper should be used, starting with a 40-grade production paper, and finishing with a 400-grade wet-and-dry paper. Always wrap the abrasive paper around a flat rubber, cork, or wooden block - otherwise the surface of the filler will not be completely flat. During the smoothing of the filler surface, the wet-and-dry paper should be periodically rinsed in water. This will ensure that a very smooth finish is imparted to the filler at the final stage.

At this stage, the "dent" should be surrounded by a ring of bare metal, which in turn should be encircled by the finely "feathered" edge of the good paintwork. Rinse the repair area with clean water, until all of the dust produced by the rubbing-down operation has gone.

Spray the whole area with a light coat of primer - this will show up any imperfections in the surface of the filler. Repair these imperfections with fresh filler paste or bodystopper, and once more smooth the surface with abrasive paper. If bodystopper is used, it can be mixed with cellulose thinners, to form a really thin paste which is ideal for filling small holes. Repeat this spray-and-repair procedure until you are satisfied that the surface of the filler, and the feathered edge of the paintwork, are perfect. Clean the repair area with clean water, and allow to dry fully.

The repair area is now ready for final spraying. Paint spraying must be carried out in a warm, dry, windless and dust-free atmosphere. This condition can be created artificially if you have access to a large indoor working area, but if you are forced to work in the open, you will have to pick your day very carefully. If you are working indoors, dousing the floor in the work area with water will help to settle the dust which would otherwise be in the atmosphere. If the repair area is confined to one body panel, mask off the surrounding panels; this will help to minimise the effects of a slight mis-match in paint colours. Bodywork fittings (eg chrome strips, door handles etc) will also need to be masked off. Use genuine masking tape, and several thicknesses of newspaper, for the masking operations.

Before commencing to spray, agitate the aerosol can thoroughly, then spray a test area (an old tin, or similar) until the technique is mastered. Cover the repair area with a thick coat of primer; the thickness should be built up using several thin layers of paint, rather than one thick one. Using 400-grade wet-and-dry paper, rub down the surface of the primer until it is really smooth. While doing this, the work area should be thoroughly doused with water, and the wet-and-dry paper periodically rinsed in water. Allow to dry before spraying on more paint.

Spray on the top coat again building up the thickness by using several thin layers of paint. Start spraying in the centre of the repair area, and then, using a circular motion, work outwards until the whole repair area and about 2 inches of the surrounding original paintwork is covered. Remove all masking material 10 to 15 minutes after spraying on the final coat of paint.

Allow the new paint at least two weeks to harden, then, using a paintwork renovator or a very fine cutting paste blend the edges of the paint into the existing paintwork. Finally, apply wax polish.

Plastic components

With the use of more and more plastic body components by the vehicle manufacturers (eg bumpers. spoilers, and in some cases major body panels), rectification of more serious damage to such items has become a matter of either entrusting repair work to a specialist in this field, or renewing complete

11

components. Repair of such damage by the DIY owner is not really feasible, owing to the cost of the equipment and materials required for effecting such repairs. The basic technique involves making a groove along the line of the crack in the plastic, using a rotary burr in a power drill. The damaged part is then welded back together, using a hot air gun to heat up and fuse a plastic filler rod into the groove. Any excess plastic is then removed, and the area rubbed down to a smooth finish. It is important that a filler rod of the correct plastic is used, as body components can be made of a variety of different types (eg polycarbonate, ABS, polypropylene).

Damage of a less serious nature (abrasions, minor cracks etc) can be repaired by the DIY owner using a two-part epoxy filler repair material, or a no-mix filler, which can be used directly from the tube. Once mixed in equal proportions (or applied directly from the tube in the case of the no-mix), this is used in similar fashion to the bodywork filler used on metal panels. The filler is usually cured in twenty to thirty minutes, ready for sanding and painting.

If the owner is renewing a complete component himself, or if he has repaired it with epoxy filler, he will be left with the problem of finding a suitable paint for finishing which is compatible with the type of plastic used. At one time, the use of a universal paint was not possible, owing to the complex range of plastics encountered in body component applications. Standard paints, generally speaking, will not bond to plastic or rubber satisfactorily, but paints to match any plastic or rubber finish, can be obtained from dealers. However, it is now possible to obtain a plastic body parts finishing kit which consists of a pre-primer treatment, a primer and coloured top coat. Full instructions are normally supplied with a kit, but basically, the method of use is to first apply the pre-primer to the component concerned, and allow it to dry for up to 30 minutes. Then the primer is applied, and left to dry for about an hour before finally applying the special-coloured top coat. The result is a correctly-coloured component, where the paint will flex with the plastic or rubber, a property that standard paint does not normally posses.

6.2a Remove the engine undertray fixings . . .

5 Major body damage - repair

Where serious damage has occurred, or large areas need renewal due to neglect, it means that complete new panels will need welding-in, and this is best left to professionals. If the damage is due to impact, it will also be necessary to check completely the alignment of the bodyshell, and this can only be carried out accurately by a Nissan dealer using special jigs. If the alignment of the bodyshell is not corrected, as the cars handling may be seriously affected. In addition, excessive stress may be imposed on the steering, suspension, tyres or transmission, causing abnormal wear or even complete failure.

6 Front bumper - removal and refitting

Removal

1 To improve access, chock the rear wheels, apply the handbrake, then jack up the front of the vehicle, and support on axle stands (see "Jacking and Vehicle Support").
2 Where applicable, remove the fixings and lower the engine bay undertrays from the vehicles underside (see illustrations).

6.2b . . . and lower the undertrays away from the vehicles underside

Saloon and Hatchback models

3 Working under one of the wheel arches, remove the securing screws and release the upper edge of the bumper from the body. Repeat the procedure on the remaining side of the vehicle (see illustration).
4 Remove the screws and detach the lower edge of the bumper from the bracing strut (see illustration).
5 Working under the front of the vehicle, unscrew the through-bolts that secure both bumper brackets to ends of the chassis rails (two on each side, either side of the transverse crossmember) (see illustration).
6 Where applicable, release the clips securing the plastic section of the bumper to the lower front body panel.
7 On models with front foglights, disconnect the battery negative lead, then disconnect the foglight wiring connectors.
8 Withdraw the bumper forwards from the vehicle and extract the bumper brackets from the bodywork. Hold the trailing edges of the bumper away from the bodywork as you do this to avoid scratching the paintwork (see illustrations).
9 If desired, release the securing clips to remove the plastic outer section of the bumper from the metal main section.

Coupe models

10 Remove the clips and screws and detach the wheel arch liners on both sides of the vehicle.

6.3 Remove the securing screws and release the upper edge of the bumper from the body

6.4 Remove the screws and detach the lower edge of the bumper from the bracing strut

6.5 Unscrew the bumper bracket through-bolts

6.8a Withdraw the bumper forwards from the vehicle . . .

11 Remove the clips that secure the lower edge of the front spoiler to the spoiler mounting bracket and vehicle body.
12 Slacken and withdraw the bolts that secure the upper edge of the front spoiler to the bumper.
13 Disconnect the battery negative lead, then disconnect the foglight wiring connectors.
14 Carefully separate the front spoiler moulding from the bumper.
15 Working inside the wheel arches, remove the nuts that secure both sides of the bumper moulding to the front edge of the wings (five nuts on each side).
16 Slacken and withdraw the bolts from the upper edge of the bumper moulding.
17 Withdraw the bumper moulding from the front of the vehicle.
18 If desired, the metal section of the bumper and the energy absorbing material can now be removed from the vehicle. The metal section of

6.8b . . . and extract the bumper brackets from the bodywork

the bumper is mounted on the bodywork by means of two brackets which are secured with through-bolts on each side, accessible from under the front edge of each wing.

Refitting
19 Refitting is a reversal of removal - ensure that the bumper bracket mounting bolts are tightened to the correct torque.

7 Rear bumper - removal and refitting

Removal
1 To improve access, chock the front wheels, apply the handbrake, then jack up the rear of the vehicle, and support on axle stands (see *"Jacking and Vehicle Support"*).

Saloon and Hatchback models
2 Working at the rear of the wheel arches, slacken and withdraw the screws that secure the leading edges of the bumper moulding to the wheel arch rim and the underside of the rear wing (two on each side) **(see illustrations)**.
3 Working in the luggage compartment, lift up the carpet panel, then prise out the rubber covers, and unscrew the bolts (two on each side) securing the bumper mounting brackets to the floor **(see illustrations)**.
4 Withdraw the bumper assembly and extract the mounting brackets from the bodywork **(see illustrations)**.
5 If desired, the bumper plastic moulding can be detached from the metal bumper section after releasing the plastic securing clips.

Coupe models
6 Remove the fixings and detach the number plate and its mounting bracket from the bumper moulding.
7 Working at the rear of the wheel arches, slacken and withdraw the screws that secure the leading edges of the bumper moulding to the wheel arch rims.
8 Extract the fixings and release the lower edge of the bumper moulding from the underside of the rear wing.
9 Working inside the load space, remove the bolts (one each side) that secure the flanks of the bumper to the side of the wing.
10 At the rear lower edge of the load space, remove the nuts that secure the upper edge of the bumper to the bodywork.

7.2a Remove the screws securing the leading edges of the bumper moulding to the rear wing . . .

7.2b . . . and the edge of the wheel arch rim

7.3a Working in the luggage compartment, prise out the rubber covers . . .

7.3b . . . and unscrew the bolts (arrowed) securing the bumper mounting brackets

7.4a Withdraw the bumper assembly . . .

7.4b . . . and extract the mounting brackets from the bodywork

11

11 Prise the bungs from the rear corners of the load space floor to expose the heads of the bumper mounting bracket through-bolts.
12 Slacken and with draw the through-bolts, then partially pull the bumper away from the rear of the vehicle. Disconnect the number plate wiring and remove the bumper assembly from the vehicle.

Refitting

13 Refitting is a reversal of removal. Ensure that the bumper mounting through-bolts are tightened to the specified torque.

8 Bonnet - removal, refitting and adjustment

Removal

1 Open the bonnet and have an assistant support it. Using a pencil or felt tip pen, mark the outline of each bonnet hinge relative to the bonnet, to use as a guide on refitting.
2 Disconnect the windscreen washer fluid supply hose from the connector under the bonnet, then release the hose from the clips under the bonnet.
3 Unscrew the bolts securing the bonnet to the hinges **(see illustration)** and, with the help of an assistant, carefully lift the bonnet clear. Store the bonnet out of the way in a safe place.
4 Inspect the bonnet hinges for signs of wear and free play at the pivots, and if necessary renew. Each hinge is secured to the body by two bolts.

Refitting

5 With the aid of an assistant, offer up the bonnet, and loosely fit the retaining bolts. Align the hinges with the marks made on removal, then tighten the retaining bolts to the specified torque.
6 Reconnect the windscreen washer fluid supply hose, and clip it into position under the bonnet.
7 Adjust the alignment of the bonnet as follows.

Adjustment

8 Close the bonnet, and check for alignment with the adjacent panels. If necessary, partially slacken the hinge bolts and re-align the bonnet to suit. Once the bonnet is correctly aligned, tighten the relevant hinge bolts to the specified torque.
9 Once the bonnet is correctly aligned, check that the bonnet lock meshes and releases in a satisfactory manner. Ideally, the lock should mesh when the leading edge of the bonnet is depressed 1.0-1.5 mm below the level of the wing panels. If adjustment is necessary, slacken the bonnet lock retaining bolts, and adjust the position of the lock to suit. Once the lock is operating correctly, securely tighten its retaining bolts.
10 If necessary, align the leading edge of the bonnet with the wing panels by turning the bump rubbers screwed into the body front panel, to raise or lower the front edge as required.

9 Bonnet release cable - removal and refitting

Removal

1 Open the bonnet.
2 If desired, to improve access, carefully pull the front grille panel from the front of the vehicle to release the securing clips.
3 Unscrew the three securing bolts, and remove the lock assembly from the body panel.
4 Pull the return spring to one side, then unhook the end of the bonnet release cable from the lock lever. Withdraw the lock assembly from the vehicle.
5 Where applicable, unscrew the cable securing clip from the front body panel.
6 Working in the driver's footwell, remove the securing screw from the footwell side trim panel. Release the plastic securing clip, then pull the weatherstrip from the edge of the panel. Pull the panel from the footwell to release the remaining securing clips.

7 Unscrew the two now-exposed securing bolt, and withdraw the bonnet release lever (the cable is integral with the lever moulding).
8 Note the routing of the cable, and release it from any clips in the engine compartment, then feed the cable through the bulkhead grommet into the engine compartment. On some models, it may be necessary to move certain components in the engine compartment to one side, to gain access to the cable clips. It is advisable to tie a length of string to the release lever end of the cable before removal, to aid refitting. Pull the cable through into the engine compartment, then untie the string and leave it place until the cable is to be refitted.

Refitting

9 Refitting is a reversal of removal, but use the string to pull the cable into position, and ensure that the bulkhead grommet is securely located. Make sure that the cable is routed as noted before removal, and reposition the cable in its securing clips in the engine compartment. Check the bonnet release mechanism for correct operation on completion.

10 Bonnet lock - removal and refitting

Removal

Hatchback and Saloon models

1 Open the bonnet.
2 Release the grille panel securing clips at either end by rotating them anticlockwise through quarter of a turn. Lift the grille panel from the bumper/bodywork
3 Unscrew the securing bolts, and remove the lock assembly from the body panel **(see illustration)**
4 Pull the return spring to one side, then unhook the end of the bonnet release cable from the lock lever, and withdraw the assembly from the vehicle.

8.3 Bonnet hinge securing bolts (arrowed)

10.3 Bonnet lock assembly securing bolts (arrowed)

Coupe models

5 Remove the front bumper moulding as described in Section 6.

6 Unscrew the securing bolts, and remove the lock assembly from the body panel.

7 Pull the return spring to one side, then unhook the end of the bonnet release cable from the lock lever, and withdraw the assembly from the vehicle.

Refitting

8 Refitting is a reversal of removal. Tighten the bonnet lock securing bolts to the specified torque.

---

11 Door - removal, refitting and adjustment

Note: *This procedure is applicable both to the front and rear doors.*

Removal

Note: *A new door check strap roll-pin will be required on refitting.*

1 Disconnect the battery negative lead.

2 Remove the inner trim panel (Section 12).

3 Disconnect all relevant wiring from the components inside the door, and unclip the wiring harnesses from inside the door. Take careful note of the way the wire is routed, to aid refitting.

4 Carefully feed the wiring through the aperture in the front edge of the door (pull out the grommet if necessary).

5 Using a suitable punch, drive out the roll-pin securing the door check strut to the body bracket **(see illustration)**.

6 Mark the positions of the hinges on the door, to aid alignment of the door on refitting.

7 Have an assistant support the door, then unscrew the bolts securing the door hinges to the door, and lift the door from the vehicle **(see illustration)**.

8 Examine the hinges for wear and damage. If necessary, the hinges can be unbolted from the body and renewed.

Refitting

9 Refitting is a reversal of removal, but align

11.5 Drive the roll-pin from the door check strut

the hinges with the marks made on the body before removal, and before finally tightening the hinge securing bolts, check the door adjustment as described in the following paragraphs. Use a new roll-pin to secure the door check strut to the body bracket.

Adjustment

10 Close the door **carefully**, in case the alignment is incorrect, which may cause scratching on the door or the body as the door is closed), and check the fit of the door with the surrounding panels.

11 If adjustment is required, loosen the hinge securing bolts (the hinge-to-door and the hinge-to-body bolt holes are elongated), and move the hinges as required to achieve satisfactory alignment. Tighten the securing bolts to the specified torque when the alignment is satisfactory.

12 Check the operation of the door lock. If necessary, slacken the securing bolts, and adjust the position of the lock striker on the body pillar to achieve satisfactory alignment. Tighten the bolts to the specified torque on completion.

---

12 Door inner trim panel - removal and refitting

Removal

1 Disconnect the battery negative lead.

11.7 Unscrew the door hinges bolts (arrowed)

2 On models with manual windows, use a length of bent wire to hook out the regulator handle wire clip (pass the wire down behind the handle, and press back the plastic trim plate) until the handle can be withdrawn **(see illustration)**. Recover the plastic trim plate.

3 Carefully prise the interior door handle surround from the door panel **(see illustration)**.

4 Lift off the caps and remove the screws, then prise out the door grab handle moulding **(see illustration)**.

5 Prise the electric window switch, or the blanking plate, as applicable from the armrest, to expose the door trim panel securing screw. Remove the securing screw.

6 Unscrew the remaining door panel securing screws, located around the outside edge of the door trim panel - note that some are concealed beneath plastic caps.

7 On coupe models, remove the panel securing screw located at the electric window switch module.

8 Using a suitable forked tool inserted between the door and the trim panel, release the press-stud clips located around the edge of the panel, then lift the trim panel upwards to release the central locating pawl.

9 Pull the panel from the door, and where applicable, separate the electric window and central locking wiring connectors. Note that the lower window aperture weatherstrip is integral with the trim panel, and must be released from the door as the panel is withdrawn.

12.2 Removing the regulator handle wire clip

12.3 Carefully prise the interior door handle surround from the door panel

12.4 Prise out the caps and remove the door grab handle screws

12.10 Removing the plastic sealing sheet from the inside of the door

10 If work is to be carried out on the door internal components, it will be necessary to remove the plastic sealing sheet from the inside of the door; start at one corner of the sheet and carefully peel it away **(see illustration)**. Try to keep the sealant intact as far as possible, to ease refitting.

Refitting

11 Refitting is a reversal of removal, bearing in mind the following points:
  a) Ensure that the sealing sheet is correctly refitted, and sealed around its edge. It should be possible to use the original mastic sealant, but if necessary, new sealant can be obtained from a Nissan dealer.
  c) Where applicable, before refitting the trim panel, feed the electric window switch wiring through the aperture in the front of the panel.

13.2 Detach the link rods (arrowed) from the latch mechanism

13.7 Door outside handle link rods and retaining nuts (arrowed)

  d) Make sure that the trim panel central securing pawl engages correctly with the bracket, and that the weatherstrip engages securely with the edge of the door and the trim panel as the panel is refitted.

13 Door latch, lock cylinder and handle components - removal and refitting

Door latch

Removal

1 Disconnect the battery negative cable and position it away from the terminal. Refer to Section 12 and remove the door inner trim panel.
2 Working inside the door aperture, detach the link rods from the latch mechanism **(see illustration)**.
3 Slacken and withdraw the latch mechanism retaining screws, at the rear outer edge of the door **(see illustration)**.
4 Remove the latch assembly, together with the central locking servo (where fitted).

Refitting

5 Refitting is a reversal of removal. Coat the threads of the latch retaining screws with locking fluid, then tighten the screws to the specified torque.

Lock cylinder and outside handle

Removal

6 Disconnect the battery negative cable and position it away from the terminal. Refer to Section 12 and remove the door inner trim panel.
7 Working inside the door aperture, detach the link rods from the handle actuating levers **(see illustration)**.
8 Slacken and remove the handle retaining nuts and lift the handle assembly from the door (refer to illustration 13.7).
9 Detach the link rod from the lock cylinder, then using a pair of pliers, prise the metal retaining clip from the rear of the cylinder **(see illustration)**. Extract the lock cylinder from the door.

13.9 Detach the link rod from the lock cylinder, then prise out the remaining clip

Refitting

10 Refitting is a reversal of removal.

Inside handle

Removal

11 Prise the outer trim from the door panel (refer to illustration 12.3)
12 Remove the retaining screw and pull the handle assembly out of the door panel **(see illustration)**.
13 Disconnect the link rod from the rear of the handle assembly.

Refitting

14 Refitting is a reversal of removal.

14 Door window glass and regulator - removal and refitting

Door window glass

Removal

1 Remove the door inner trim panel and the plastic sealing sheet, as described in Section 12.
2 Temporarily reconnect the electric window switch, and the battery negative lead, or refit the window regulator handle, as applicable.
3 Lower the window until the front bolt securing the lower edge of the window glass to the regulator mechanism is accessible through the hole in the inside of the door.

13.3 Latch mechanism retaining screws (arrowed)

13.12 Remove the retaining screw and pull the handle assembly out of the door panel

14.4 Remove the bolts (arrowed) securing the window glass to the regulator mechanism

14.10 Window winder mechanism bolts (arrowed) - models with manual windows

4 Support the glass, then remove the bolts securing the window glass to the regulator mechanism **(see illustration)**. Note that on coupe models, there is an additional bolt securing the window glass to the front guide rail runner.

5 Lift the glass out through the window aperture in the top of the door, manipulating the glass past the weatherstrips as it is withdrawn.

Refitting

6 Refitting is a reversal of removal, bearing in mind the following points:
a) *Take care not to dislodge the weatherstrips when fitting the glass.*
b) *Check the operation of the window mechanism before refitting the door inner trim panel.*
c) *Refit the door inner trim panel with reference to Section 12.*

Door window regulator - hatchback and saloon models

Removal

7 Separate the window glass from the regulator mechanism, as described earlier in this Section.

8 Fully raise the window glass, and secure the glass in position using suitable tape, or by wedging the glass in position using rags between the glass and the edge of the door - ensure that the glass cannot drop into the door. Alternatively, lift the glass panel out through the window aperture.

9 Where applicable, separate the two halves of the regulator motor wiring connector.

10 Unscrew the bolts securing the motor assembly/winder mechanism to the door **(see illustration)**.

11 Unscrew the two upper and the two lower regulator mechanism securing bolts, then manipulate the complete regulator assembly out through the aperture in the door **(see illustrations)**. The winder/motor assembly, together with its associated control cables remains connected to the regulator mechanism. **Note:** *Carefully mark the*

relationship between the guide rails and the door to ensure correct adjustment on refitting.

Refitting

12 Refitting is a reversal of removal, bearing in mind the following points:
a) *Take care not to dislodge the weatherstrips when fitting the glass.*
b) *Check the operation of the window mechanism before refitting the door inner trim panel.*
c) *Refit the door inner trim panel with reference to Section 12.*

Door window regulator - coupe models

Removal

13 Refer to Section 12 then remove the door window glass.

14 Separate the two halves of the regulator motor wiring connector.

15 Unscrew the bolts securing the window motor assembly to the door.

16 The regulator operates by scissor action and its movement is controlled by horizontal and vertical guide rails. Unscrew the securing bolts for both guide rails, then manipulate the complete regulator assembly out through the door aperture. **Note:** *Carefully mark the relationship between the guide rails and the door to ensure correct adjustment on refitting.*

Refitting

17 Refitting is a reversal of removal, bearing in mind the following points:
a) *Take care not to dislodge the weatherstrips when fitting the glass.*
b) *Check the operation of the window mechanism before refitting the door inner trim panel.*
c) *Refit the door inner trim panel with reference to Section 12.*

Rear door fixed window glass - 5 door hatchback models

Removal

18 Remove the sliding window glass, as described earlier in this Section.

19 Remove the three bolts and detach the rear guide rail from the door - support the fixed window glass as you do this.

20 Carefully pull the fixed window glass, complete with its surrounding weatherstrip, from the window aperture.

21 If desired, pull the weatherstrip from the edge of the window.

Refitting

22 Refitting is a reversal of removal, but ensure that the weatherstrip seals securely on both the window aperture and the window glass, and refit the sliding window glass as described previously in this Section.

14.11a Window regulator upper . . .

14.11b . . . and lower mounting bolts (arrowed)

15.5 Mark the outline of each boot hinge relative to the boot lid, before removal

15 Boot lid (Saloon models) - removal, refitting and adjustment

Boot lid

Removal

1 Disconnect the battery negative lead.
2 Open the boot lid, and have an assistant support it in the open position.
3 Release the securing clips, and remove the trim panel from the rear of the boot lid.
4 Working inside the boot lid, disconnect the wiring harness connector. Tie a length of string to the wiring connector, then prise the wiring harness grommet from the boot lid, and feed the wiring through the aperture. Untie the string from the wiring connector, and leave the string in place in the boot lid, to aid refitting.
5 Using a pencil or felt-tipped pen, mark the outline of each boot hinge relative to the boot lid, to use as a guide on refitting **(see illustration)**.
6 Unscrew the bolts securing the hinges to the boot lid, then lift the boot lid from the vehicle - take care not to scratch the bodywork as the boot lid is removed.

Refitting

7 With the aid of an assistant, offer up the boot lid, and loosely fit the retaining bolts. Align the hinges with the marks made on removal, then tighten the retaining bolts securely.

8 Tie the string to the wiring harness connector, and use the string to draw the wiring harness through the aperture, and into the boot lid.
9 Adjust the alignment of the boot lid as follows.

Adjustment

10 Close the boot lid **carefully**, in case the alignment is incorrect, which may cause scratching on the lid or the body as the boot lid is closed), and check for alignment with the adjacent panels. If necessary, slacken the hinge bolts and re-align the boot lid to suit. Once the boot lid is correctly aligned, tighten the hinge bolts to the specified torque.
11 Once the boot lid is correctly aligned, check that the boot lid fastens and releases in a satisfactory manner. If adjustment is necessary, slacken the boot lid lock retaining bolts, and adjust the position of the lock to suit. Once the lock is operating correctly, securely tighten its retaining bolts.

16 Tailgate and struts (Coupe and hatchback models) - removal, refitting and adjustment

Support struts

1 Open the tailgate and support it using a suitable prop.

Coupe and 5-door hatchback models

2 Slacken locknut, then unscrew the ball joint stud and withdraw it from the tailgate **(see illustration)**.

3-door hatchback models

3 At the upper end of the strut, slacken and remove the two mounting bracket bolts.

All models

4 Compress the strut slightly and detach it from the tailgate.

 Warning: The strut may still be under tension and could extend suddenly once detached from its mountings.

5 Unscrew the bracket mounting bolts and detach the lower end of the strut unit from the bodywork **(see illustration)**.

6 Refitting is a reversal of removal. Tighten all fixings to the specified torque settings.

Tailgate

Removal

7 Disconnect the battery negative lead.
8 Remove the tailgate interior trim panels as described in Section 25.
9 Working inside the tailgate, disconnect all wiring harness connectors and unbolt the earth lead(s). Check for any other wiring connectors which must be disconnected to facilitate tailgate removal. **Note:** *Carefully label each wiring harness connector to aid correct refitting.*
10 Tie a length of string to the wiring harness, then prise the wiring harness grommets from the edge of the tailgate, and feed the wiring through the aperture in the tailgate. Untie the string from the wiring connector, and leave the string in place in the tailgate, to aid refitting.
11 Where applicable, remove the fluid hose from the tailgate washer nozzle, then tie a length of string to the hose and draw it out of the tailgate using the procedure carried out on the wiring harness.
12 Have an assistant support the tailgate in the open position.
13 Using a pencil of felt tip pen, mark the outline of each hinge relative to the tailgate, to use as a guide on refitting.
14 Detach the upper ends of the support struts from the tailgate as described earlier in this Section.
15 Unscrew the bolts securing the hinges to the tailgate **(see illustration)**, then lift the tailgate from the vehicle.

Refitting

16 Refitting is a reversal of removal, bearing in mind the following points.
17 Tie the string to the wiring harness and use it to pull the harness through the aperture and into the tailgate. Where applicable, repeat the procedure on the washer fluid hose.
18 Do not fully tighten the hinge bolts until the tailgate adjustment has been checked, as described in the following paragraphs.

16.2 Unscrew the ball joint stud and withdraw it from the tailgate

16.5 Unscrew the mounting bolts and detach the lower end of the strut

16.15 Unscrew the bolts securing the hinges to the tailgate

Adjustment

19 Close the tailgate **carefully**, in case the alignment is incorrect, which may cause scratching on the tailgate or the body as the tailgate is closed), and check for alignment with the adjacent panels. If necessary, slacken the hinge bolts and re-align the tailgate to suit. Once the tailgate is correctly aligned, tighten the hinge bolts to the specified torque.
20 Once the tailgate is correctly aligned, check that the tailgate fastens and releases in a satisfactory manner. If adjustment is necessary, slacken the tailgate lock retaining bolts, and adjust the position of the lock to suit. Once the lock is operating correctly, securely tighten its retaining bolts.

17 Boot lid lock components (Saloon models) - removal and refitting

Boot lid lock

Removal

1 Using a suitable forked tool, prise out the plastic clips securing the trim panel, then unhook the panel from the rear of the boot lid.
2 Unclip the plastic cover from the lock.
3 Push out the plastic clip securing the luggage compartment light switch wiring connector to the inside of the boot lid.
4 Unscrew the two securing bolts, and withdraw the lock from the boot lid.
5 Using the key, operate the boot lid lock cylinder to allow the lock operating rod to be pushed back - this will provide clearance for the switch wiring connector to pass through.
6 Separate the two halves of the wiring connector, and withdraw the lock.

Refitting

7 Refitting is a reversal of removal.

Boot lid lock cylinder

Removal

8 Using a suitable forked tool, prise out the plastic clips securing the trim panel, then unhook the panel from the rear of the boot lid.
9 Release the securing clip, and disconnect the lock operating rod from the lock cylinder.
10 Using a suitable pair of pliers, pull out the metal lock cylinder securing clip, then withdraw the lock cylinder from outside the boot lid.

Refitting

11 Refitting is a reversal of removal, but ensure that the lock cylinder securing clip is securely refitted.

Boot lid lock striker

Removal

12 Pull the weatherstrip from the plastic trim panel at the rear of the boot, then pull the trim panel from the body.

13 Using a suitable forked tool, prise out the plastic clips securing the rear carpet trim panel to the body.
14 Mark the relationship between the lock striker and the bodywork by drawing around the outside of the striker with a marker pen. Unscrew the two securing bolts, then withdraw the lock striker assembly, and disconnect the boot lid release cable from the lever on the striker assembly.

Refitting

15 Refitting is a reversal of removal, but check the operation of the boot lid release mechanism before refitting the luggage compartment trim panels.

18 Tailgate lock and handle components - removal and refitting

Tailgate lock

Removal

1 Disconnect the battery negative lead.
2 Remove the tailgate inner trim panels as described in Section 25.
3 Disconnect the lock operating rods from the lock, noting their locations.
4 Separate the two halves of the door lock wiring connector.
5 Working at the lower edge of the tailgate, unscrew the two lock securing nuts, then manipulate the lock out through the aperture in the inside of the tailgate.

Refitting

6 Refitting is a reversal of removal, but ensure that the lock operating rods are correctly reconnected, and check the operation of the lock before refitting the trim panel.

Tailgate lock cylinder

Note: *A new gasket may be required when refitting the lock cylinder.*

Removal

7 Disconnect the battery negative lead, and remove the tailgate inner trim panel as described in Section 25.
8 Working inside the tailgate, unscrew the four nuts securing the tailgate outer trim/handle panel.
9 Release the outer trim/handle panel securing nuts and clips (accessible from the inside of the tailgate).
10 Disconnect the number plate wiring connectors.
11 Disconnect the operating rod from the exterior handle, then pull the panel from the outside of the tailgate, and pull the number plate light wiring grommets from their apertures in the tailgate.
12 Disconnect the operating rod from the lock cylinder.
13 Working inside the tailgate, remove the two securing nuts, then withdraw the lock cylinder from outside the tailgate, and recover the rubber gasket **(see illustration)**.

Refitting

14 Refitting is a reversal of removal, bearing in mind the following points:
a) *If necessary, use a new rubber gasket when refitting the lock cylinder.*
b) *Ensure that the lock operating rods are correctly reconnected.*
c) *Check the operation of the lock components before refitting the tailgate inner trim panel.*

Tailgate lock striker

Removal

15 Release the securing clips, and remove the luggage compartment rear trim panel.
16 Unscrew the two securing bolts, and remove the lock striker.

Refitting

17 Refitting is a reversal of removal.

Tailgate exterior handle

Removal

18 Proceed as described in paragraphs 7 to 11 inclusive.
19 Working at the rear of the tailgate outer trim/handle panel, remove the two securing screws, and withdraw the handle from the panel.

Refitting

20 Refitting is a reversal of removal, bearing in mind the following points:
a) *Ensure that the lock operating rods are correctly reconnected.*
b) *Check the operation of the lock components before refitting the tailgate inner trim panel.*

19 Central locking system components - removal and refitting

Driver's door lock switch

Removal

1 Remove the door lock as described in Section 13.
2 The switch is secured to the lock by two screws.

18.13 Remove the two securing nuts (arrowed), then withdraw the lock cylinder

Refitting

3 Refit the door lock as shown in Section 13.

Door lock motor

Removal

4 Remove the door lock as described in Section 13.

5 The motor is secured to the lock assembly by two screws.

Refitting

6 Refit the door lock as shown in Section 13.

Tailgate lock motor - Estate models

Removal

7 Disconnect the battery negative lead.

8 Remove the tailgate inner trim panel, as described in Section 25.

9 Working inside the tailgate, disconnect the wiring plug from the lock motor.

10 Disconnect the two lock operating rods from the motor, noting their locations.

11 Remove the two securing screws, and withdraw the motor from the tailgate.

Refitting

12 Refitting is a reversal of removal, but check the operation of the lock mechanism before refitting the tailgate trim panel.

20 Exterior mirror and associated components - removal and refitting

Mirror assembly

Removal

1 If working on an electric mirror, disconnect the battery negative lead. On models with manual mirror adjustment, remove the screw and detach the adjustment handle **(see illustration)**.

2 Remove the door inner trim panel, as described in Section 12.

3 Remove the two securing screws, and remove the mirror trim panel from the inside edge of the door.

4 Peel back the plastic sealing sheet from the front upper corner of the door.

20.1 On models with manual mirror adjustment, remove the screw and detach the adjustment handle

5 Reach through the aperture in the door, and disconnect the mirror wiring connector. Unclip the mirror wiring from the door, noting its routing.

6 Remove the securing screws **(see illustration)** and withdraw the mirror from the outside of the door.

Refitting

7 Refitting is a reversal of removal, ensuring that the mirror wiring is routed as noted before removal.

Mirror glass

Removal

8 On models with electrically-heated mirror glass, disconnect the battery negative lead.

9 Insert a suitable thin plastic or wooden tool between the mirror glass and the mirror body, and lever the glass forward to release the securing clips.

10 Where applicable, disconnect the wiring from the rear of the glass, and withdraw the glass from the mirror.

Refitting

 HAYNES HiNT *To aid refitting, lightly grease the securing clips on the rear of the mirror glass.*

11 Where applicable, reconnect the wires to the rear of the mirror glass, then push the glass into position to engage the securing clips.

21 Windscreen, tailgate and fixed windows - general information

These areas of glass are secured by the tight fit of the weatherstrip in the body aperture, and are bonded in position with a special adhesive. Renewal of such fixed glass is a difficult, messy and time-consuming task, which is beyond the scope of the home mechanic. It is difficult, unless one has plenty of practice, to obtain a secure, waterproof fit. Furthermore, the task carries a high risk of breakage; this applies especially to the laminated glass windscreen. In view of this,

20.6 Remove the mirror securing screws

owners are strongly advised to have this sort of work carried out by one of the many specialist windscreen fitters.

22 Sunroof - general information

Due to the complexity of the sunroof mechanism, considerable expertise is needed to repair, replace or adjust the sunroof components successfully. Removal of the roof first requires the headlining to be removed, which is a complex and tedious operation, and not a task to be undertaken lightly. Therefore, any problems with the sunroof should be referred to a Nissan dealer.

On models with an electric sunroof, if the sunroof motor fails to operate, first check the relevant fuse. If the fault cannot be traced and rectified, the sunroof can be opened and closed manually using a cranked Allen key (provided with the vehicles toolkit) to turn the motor spindle. To gain access to the motor spindle, ensure that the ignition key is in the "off" position, then remove the sunroof switch panel - refer to Chapter 12 for details. Engage the Allen key with the spindle, then push the centre of the spindle and turn clockwise to close the sunroof.

23 Body exterior fittings - removal and refitting

Front grille panel

1 Open the bonnet, and pull the grille panel forwards from the body release the securing clips by turning them through quarter of a turn with a flat bladed screwdriver **(see illustration)**.

2 Refitting is a reversal of removal. Note that the lower edge of the grille panel is located by pegs **(see illustration)**.

Wheel arch liners

3 The wheel arch liners are secured by a combination of self-tapping screws and plastic clips, and removal is self-evident.

23.1 Release the grille panel securing clips by turning them through quarter of a turn

23.2 The lower edge of the grille panel is located by pegs (arrowed)

Body trim strips and badges

4 The various body trim strips and badges are held in position with a special adhesive tape. Removal requires the trim/badge to be heated, to soften the adhesive, and then cut away from the surface. Due to the high risk of damage to the vehicle paintwork during this operation, it is recommended that this task should be entrusted to a Nissan dealer or a body repair specialist.

24 Seats - removal and refitting

Front seat

Removal

1 Disconnect the battery negative cable and position it away from the terminal.
2 Slide the seat fully forwards using the adjustment mechanism.
3 Unclip the trim cover from the rear corner of the seat outer rail.
4 Remove the securing screw, and remove the trim cover from the rear corner of the seat inner rail.
5 Unscrew the seat rail rear securing bolts.
6 Slide the seat fully rearwards, then unscrew the seat rail front securing bolts.
7 Tilt the seat backwards and unplug the wiring harness connectors from the underside.
8 Check that nothing remains connected to the seat, then lift it from the vehicle complete with the rails.

Refitting

9 Refitting is a reversal of removal, but tighten the securing bolts to the specified torque.

Rear seat back

Removal

10 Fold the relevant rear seat section forwards, then release the clips, and pull the trim panel from the rear edge of the seat back.
11 Remove the four nuts or bolts, as applicable (two on each side) securing the seat back to the hinges, or the hinges to the floor, as desired, then withdraw the seat back from the vehicle.

Refitting

12 Refitting is a reversal of removal.

Rear seat cushion

Removal

13 Fold the seat cushion forwards, then unscrew the four bolts securing the hinges to the floor, and withdraw the seat cushion, complete with the hinges.

Refitting

14 Refitting is a reversal of removal.

Rear seat back side bolster

Removal

15 Fold the relevant rear seat cushion forwards, and fold the seat back down.
16 Remove the securing screw from the bottom of the side bolster, then unhook the top of the side bolster and remove it from the vehicle.

Refitting

17 Refitting is a reversal of removal.

25 Interior trim panels - removal and refitting

General

1 The interior trim panels are secured by a combination of metal and plastic clips and screws. When releasing certain types of securing clips, a suitable forked tool will prove invaluable to avoid damage to the panel and clips. In some cases, it may be necessary to remove surrounding panels before a particular panel can be released.

Footwell trim panels

2 Using a screwdriver, carefully prise out the trim plate to reveal the trim panel securing screw. Remove the screw.
3 Twist the rear securing clip to release it, then withdraw the clip, and pull the trim panel from the footwell.
4 Refitting is a reversal of removal.

Sill trim panels

5 Where necessary, pull the weatherstrip from the edge of the panel, then pull the panel from the body to release the securing clips.
6 To refit the panel, simply push it back into position, ensuring that the retaining clips engage.

A-pillar trim panels

7 Carefully prise the weatherstrip from the edge of the panel, then pull the panel from the pillar.
8 Ensure that the weatherstrip is correctly seated on refitting.

Door inner trim panels

9 Refer to Section 12.

Rear parcel shelf - Saloon models

10 Remove the rear seat back side bolster, as described in Section 24.
11 Remove the two plastic clips securing the front of the parcel shelf.
12 Pull up the rear of the parcel shelf to release the rear securing clips, then withdraw the shelf.
13 If the shelf is to be removed completely, it will be necessary to unbolt the seat belt lower anchor, and pass the belt through the flap in the shelf belt surround plate.
14 Refitting is a reversal of removal, but where applicable, tighten the seat belt anchor bolt to the specified torque.

Luggage compartment trim panels - Saloon models

15 The rear luggage compartment trim panel can be removed by pulling the weatherstrip from the rear of the panel, then pulling the panel upwards to release the securing clips.
16 The luggage compartment carpet trim panels are secured by plastic clips, which are most easily released using a forked tool. Where applicable, remove the luggage strap brackets, and/or the luggage compartment light, to enable the panels to be removed.
17 Refitting is a reversal of removal.

Luggage compartment trim panels - hatchback and Coupe models

18 Prise out the plastic screw covers, and unscrew the four rear luggage compartment trim panel securing screws. Pull the panel from the body to release the securing clips.
19 If desired, the rear carpet trim panel can be removed as follows.
20 Lift up the rear of the luggage compartment carpet panel.
21 Using a suitable forked tool, prise out the plastic clips securing the rear carpet trim panel to the body (see illustration).
22 Refitting is a reversal of removal.

Boot lid inner trim panel - Saloon models

23 Using a forked tool, remove the plastic securing clips, then unhook the rear of the panel from the boot lid, and withdraw the panel.
24 Refitting is a reversal of removal.

25.21 Removing a trim panel press-stud plastic clip

25.25a Removing tailgate trim panel press-stud clip

25.25b Removing the tailgate trim panel

Tailgate inner trim panels - Hatchback models

Removal

25 Prise out the plastic covers, and remove the trim panel securing screws. Carefully pull the trim panel from the tailgate, using a forked tool to release the press stud clips concealed behind the trim panel (see illustrations).

Refitting

26 Refitting is a reversal of removal, but ensure that all clips are securely engaged and all screws are securely tightened.

26 Centre console - removal and refitting

Warning: *Later models are equipped with a Supplementary Restraint System (SRS) which incorporates a drivers air bag.* **One of the SRS collision sensors is mounted underneath the centre console. Make sure that the safety recommendations given below are followed, to prevent personal injury.**

26.4a Prise the cover plate from the top of the console . . .

a) *Do not attempt to check any of the air bag system components using meters or any other form of test equipment.*
b) *Before working near any of the SRS components, switch the ignition off, and disconnect the battery negative lead, then wait for at least 10 minutes before carrying out any further work.*
c) *Do not attempt to remove collision sensor, located under the centre console.*
d) *If the air bag warning light comes on, or any fault in the system is suspected, consult a Nissan dealer without delay.* **Do not** *attempt to carry out fault diagnosis, or any dismantling of the components.*

Removal

1 Disconnect the battery negative lead.
2 Prise out the plastic covers, then unscrew the console front securing screws.
3 Slide the front seats forward, then remove the console rear securing screws.
4 Prise the cover plate from the top of the console, and unscrew the console upper securing screws (see illustrations).
5 On models with manual transmission, unclip the gear lever gaiter surround from the top of the centre console.
6 On models with automatic transmission, unclip the selector lever cover from the centre console.

26.4b . . . and unscrew the console upper securing screws

7 Draw the console assembly away from the facia, towards the rear of the vehicle. Carefully lift the console up and manipulate it over the handbrake lever.

Refitting

8 Refitting is a reversal of removal, but ensure that the wiring plugs are correctly reconnected.

27 Facia panels - removal and refitting

Warning: *Later models are equipped with a Supplementary Restraint System (SRS) which incorporates a drivers air bag.* **One of the SRS collision sensors is mounted underneath the centre console. Make sure that the safety recommendations given below are followed, to prevent personal injury.**

a) *Do not attempt to check any of the air bag system components using meters or any other form of test equipment.*
b) *Before working near any of the SRS components, switch the ignition off, and disconnect the battery negative lead, then wait for at least 10 minutes before carrying out any further work.*
c) *Do not attempt to remove collision sensor, located under the centre console.*
d) *If the air bag warning light comes on, or any fault in the system is suspected, consult a Nissan dealer without delay.* **Do not** *attempt to carry out fault diagnosis, or any dismantling of the components.*

Glovebox

Removal

1 Working under the glovebox, remove the two securing screws (one each side of the glovebox), then lower the glovebox from the facia.

27.12a Unclip the trim plate from the ignition switch/steering column lock . . .

27.12b . . . and pull the lower shroud down to unclip it from the upper shroud

Refitting

2 Refitting is a reversal of removal.

Driver's side lower facia panel

Removal

3 Remove the securing screws from the upper and lower edges of the panel, then lower the panel from the facia.

Refitting

4 Refitting is a reversal of removal.

Facia centre switch housing

Removal

5 Disconnect the battery negative lead.
6 Unclip the gear/selector lever gaiter from the centre console assembly.
7 Remove the securing screws from both sides of the switch housing panel, then carefully pull switch the panel away from the facia.
8 Disconnect the switch wiring plugs, and withdraw the panel.
9 If further work is to be carried out, note the routing of the wiring harnesses, to ensure correct routing on refitting.

Refitting

10 Refitting is a reversal of removal, but ensure that the wiring is routed as noted before removal, and ensure that the air ducting engages correctly with the rear of the ventilation nozzles.

Steering column shrouds

Removal

11 Disconnect the battery negative lead.
12 Working under the steering column lower shroud, remove the six shroud securing screws, then unclip the trim plate from the ignition switch/steering column lock, and pull the lower shroud down to unclip it from the upper shroud (see illustrations).
13 Set both steering column switches to their lowest positions, then carefully manipulate the upper shroud from the column (on models with an adjustable steering column, this is aided by fully lowering the column).

Refitting

14 Refitting is a reversal of removal, but ensure that the shroud clips engage correctly.

Instrument panel surround/fresh air vent housing

Removal

15 Remove the steering column shrouds, as described previously in this Section.
16 To improve access, loosen the two steering column upper securing bolts, and lower the steering column slightly.
17 Unscrew the instrument panel shroud securing screws. Two screws are located at the top of the panel, two on the left, and one on the right (see illustrations).
18 Carefully unclip the housing from the facia (see illustration). If necessary, lower the steering column further to provide sufficient clearance.

Refitting

19 Refitting is a reversal of removal, but tighten the steering column upper securing bolts to the specified torque.

27.17a Unscrew the instrument panel shroud upper . . .

27.17b . . . and lower securing screws

27.18 Carefully unclip the housing from the facia (steering wheel removed for clarity)

11

Chapter 12
Body electrical systems

Contents

Degrees of difficulty

Easy, suitable for novice with little experience	Fairly easy, suitable for beginner with some experience	Fairly difficult, suitable for competent DIY mechanic	Difficult, suitable for experienced DIY mechanic	Very difficult, suitable for expert DIY or professional

Specifications

Bulb ratings	Watts
Headlights	60/55
Front driving light	55
Front foglight	55
Front direction indicator light	21
Front sidelight	5
Front direction indicator repeater light	5
Stop/tail light	21/5
Rear direction indicator light	21
Reversing light	21
Rear foglight	21
High-level stop-light:	
Saloon models	5
Hatchback models	2
Rear number plate light	5
Courtesy light	10
Map reading light	10
Luggage compartment light	5/3.4

1 General information and precautions

General information

The body electrical system consists of all lights, wash/wipe equipment, interior electrical equipment, and associated switches and wiring.

The electrical system is of the 12-volt negative earth type. Power to the system is provided by a 12-volt battery, which is charged by the alternator (see Chapter 5A).

The engine electrical system (battery, alternator, starter motor, ignition system, etc) is covered separately in Chapter 5.

Precautions

Caution: If the radio/cassette player fitted to the vehicle has an anti-theft security code, ensure that you have a copy of the code written down before disconnecting the battery.

Prior to wiring on any component in the electrical system, the battery negative lead should first be disconnected, to prevent the possibility of electrical short-circuits and/or fires.

 Warning: Before carrying out any work on the electrical system, read through the precautions given in "Safety first!" at the beginning of this manual, and in Chapter 5. Later models are equipped with an air bag system. When working on the electrical system, refer to the precautions given in Section 20, to avoid the possibility of personal injury.

12

2 Electrical fault-finding - general information

Note: *Refer to the precautions given in "Safety first!" and in Section 1 of this Chapter before starting work. The following tests relate to testing of the main electrical circuits, and should not be used to test delicate electronic circuits (such as anti-lock braking systems), particularly where an electronic control module is used.*

General

1 A typical electrical circuit consists of an electrical component, any switches, relays, motors, fuses, fusible links or circuit breakers related to that component, and the wiring and connectors which link the component to both the battery and the chassis. To help to pinpoint a problem in an electrical circuit, wiring diagrams are included at the end of this manual.

2 Before attempting to diagnose an electrical fault, first study the appropriate wiring diagram, to obtain a more complete understanding of the components included in the particular circuit concerned. The possible sources of a fault can be narrowed down by noting whether other components related to the circuit are operating properly. If several components or circuits fail at one time, the problem is likely to be related to a shared fuse or earth connection.

3 Electrical problems usually stem from simple causes, such as loose or corroded connections, a faulty earth connection, a blown fuse, a melted fusible link, or a faulty relay (refer to Section 3 for details of testing relays). Visually inspect the condition of all fuses, wires and connections in a problem circuit before testing the components. Use the wiring diagrams to determine which terminal connections will need to be checked, in order to pinpoint the trouble-spot.

4 The basic tools required for electrical fault-finding include a circuit tester or voltmeter (a 12-volt bulb with a set of test leads can also be used for certain tests); a self-powered test light (sometimes known as a continuity tester); an ohmmeter (to measure resistance); a battery and set of test leads; and a jumper wire, preferably with a circuit breaker or fuse incorporated, which can be used to bypass suspect wires or electrical components. Before attempting to locate a problem with test instruments, use the wiring diagram to determine where to make the connections.

5 To find the source of an intermittent wiring fault (usually due to a poor or dirty connection, or damaged wiring insulation), a "wiggle" test can be performed on the wiring. This involves wiggling the wiring by hand, to see if the fault occurs as the wiring is moved. It should be possible to narrow down the source of the fault to a particular section of wiring. This method of testing can be used in conjunction with any of the tests described in the following sub-Sections.

6 Apart from problems due to poor connections, two basic types of fault can occur in an electrical circuit - open-circuit, or short-circuit.

7 Open-circuit faults are caused by a break somewhere in the circuit, which prevents current from flowing. An open-circuit fault will prevent a component from working, but will not cause the relevant circuit fuse to blow.

8 Short-circuit faults are caused by a "short" somewhere in the circuit, which allows the current flowing in the circuit to "escape" along an alternative route, usually to earth. Short-circuit faults are normally caused by a breakdown in wiring insulation, which allows a feed wire to touch either another wire, or an earthed component such as the bodyshell. A short-circuit fault will normally cause the relevant circuit fuse to blow.

Finding an open-circuit

9 To check for an open-circuit, connect one lead of a circuit tester or voltmeter to either the negative battery terminal or a known good earth.

10 Connect the other lead to a connector in the circuit being tested, preferably nearest to the battery or fuse.

11 Switch on the circuit, bearing in mind that some circuits are live only when the ignition switch is moved to a particular position.

12 If voltage is present (indicated either by the tester bulb lighting or a voltmeter reading, as applicable), this means that the section of the circuit between the relevant connector and the battery is problem-free.

13 Continue to check the remainder of the circuit in the same fashion.

14 When a point is reached at which no voltage is present, the problem must lie between that point and the previous test point with voltage. Most problems can be traced to a broken, corroded or loose connection.

Finding a short-circuit

15 To check for a short-circuit, first disconnect the load(s) from the circuit (loads are the components which draw current from a circuit, such as bulbs, motors, heating elements, etc).

16 Remove the relevant fuse from the circuit, and connect a circuit tester or voltmeter to the fuse connections.

17 Switch on the circuit, bearing in mind that some circuits are live only when the ignition switch is moved to a particular position.

18 If voltage is present (indicated either by the tester bulb lighting or a voltmeter reading, as applicable), this means that there is a short-circuit.

19 If no voltage is present, but the fuse still blows with the load(s) connected, this indicates an internal fault in the load(s).

Finding an earth fault

20 The battery negative terminal is connected to "earth" - the metal of the engine/transmission and the car body - and most systems are wired so that they only receive a positive feed, the current returning via the metal of the car body. This means that the component mounting and the body form part of that circuit. Loose or corroded mountings can therefore cause a range of electrical faults, ranging from total failure of a circuit, to a puzzling partial fault. In particular, lights may shine dimly (especially when another circuit sharing the same earth point is in operation), motors (eg wiper motors or the radiator cooling fan motor) may run slowly, and the operation of one circuit may have an apparently-unrelated effect on another. Note that on many vehicles, earth straps are used between certain components, such as the engine/transmission and the body, usually where there is no metal-to-metal contact between components, due to flexible rubber mountings, etc.

21 To check whether a component is properly earthed, disconnect the battery, and connect one lead of an ohmmeter to a known good earth point. Connect the other lead to the wire or earth connection being tested. The resistance reading should be zero; if not, check the connection as follows:

22 If an earth connection is thought to be faulty, dismantle the connection, and clean back to bare metal both the bodyshell and the wire terminal or the component earth connection mating surface. Be careful to remove all traces of dirt and corrosion, then use a knife to trim away any paint, so that a clean metal-to-metal joint is made. On reassembly, tighten the joint fasteners securely; if a wire terminal is being refitted, use serrated washers between the terminal and the bodyshell, to ensure a clean and secure connection. When the connection is remade, prevent the onset of corrosion in the future by applying a coat of petroleum jelly or silicone-based grease, or by spraying on (at regular intervals) a proprietary brand of ignition sealer or a water-dispersant lubricant

3 Fuses and relays - general information

Fuses

1 Fuses are designed to break a circuit when a predetermined current is reached, in order to protect the components and wiring which could be damaged by excessive current flow. Any excessive current flow will be due to a fault in the circuit, usually a short-circuit (see Section 2).

2 The main fuses are located in the fusebox on the driver's side of the facia **(see illustration)**.

3.2 The main fuses are located in the fusebox on the driver's side of the facia

3.4 Additional fuses and circuit-breakers are located in an auxiliary fusebox(es) in the engine compartment

O.K   BLOWN

H27336

3.5 A blown fuse can be recognised from its melted or broken wire

3 For access to the fuses, pull open the cover flap.

4 Additional fuses and circuit-breakers are located in an auxiliary fusebox(es) in the engine compartment, attached to the inner wings **(see illustration)**.

5 A blown fuse can be recognised from its melted or broken wire **(see illustration)**.

6 To remove a fuse, first ensure that the relevant circuit is switched off.

7 Using the plastic tool clipped to the main fusebox lid, pull the fuse from its location.

8 Spare fuses are provided in the main fusebox.

9 Before renewing a blown fuse, trace and rectify the cause, and always use a fuse of the correct rating (fuse ratings are specified on the inside of the fusebox cover flap). Never substitute a fuse of a higher rating, or make temporary repairs using wire or metal foil; more serious damage, or even fire, could result.

10 Note that the fuses are colour-coded as follows. Refer to the wiring diagrams for details of the fuse ratings used and the circuits protected.

Colour	Rating
Orange	*5A*
Red	*10A*
Blue	*15A*
Yellow	*20A*
Clear or White	*25A*
Green	*30A*

11 The radio/cassette player fuse is located in the rear of the unit, and can be accessed after removing the radio/cassette player.

Relays

12 A relay is an electrically-operated switch, which is used for the following reasons:

a) *A relay can switch a heavy current remotely from the circuit in which the current is flowing, therefore allowing the use of lighter-gauge wiring and switch contacts.*

b) *A relay can receive more than one control input, unlike a mechanical switch.*

c) *A relay can have a timer function - for example, the intermittent wiper relay.*

13 Various relays are located behind the facia, next to the fusebox, and in various other locations, depending on model. Most of the engine-related relays are located in the relay box on the right-hand side of the engine compartment.

14 On most models, the direction indicator/hazard warning flasher unit is located on a bracket behind the facia and can be accessed once the driver's side lower facia panel has been removed (see Chapter 11).

15 The "headlights on" warning buzzer is screwed to a bracket behind the facia, above the direction indicator/hazard warning flasher unit (see paragraph 14).

16 Relays may be located in various other locations, depending on specification - for example, on models with ABS the ABS relays are mounted in a dedicated relay box in the engine bay.

17 If a circuit or system controlled by a relay develops a fault, and the relay is suspect, operate the system. If the relay is functioning, it should be possible to hear it "click" as it is energised, If this is the case, the fault lies with the components or wiring of the system. If the relay is not being energised, then either the relay is not receiving a main supply or a switching voltage, or the relay itself is faulty. Testing is by the substitution of a known good unit, but be careful - while some relays are identical in appearance and in operation, others look similar but perform different functions.

4.3a Slide the relevant switch from the bracket on the steering column . . .

18 To remove a relay, first ensure that the relevant circuit is switched off. The relay can then simply be pulled out from the socket, and pushed back into position.

---

4   Switches - removal and refitting

Note: *Disconnect the battery negative lead before removing any switch, and reconnect the lead after refitting the switch. Refer to the* **Caution** *in Section 1 if a security-coded radio/cassette player is fitted.*

Ignition switch/steering column lock

1 Refer to Chapter 10.

Steering column combination switches

Removal

2 Remove the steering column shrouds, as described in Chapter 10.

3 Remove the securing screws, then slide the relevant switch from the bracket on the steering column and disconnect the wiring plugs **(see illustrations)**.

Refitting

4 Refitting is a reversal of removal.

4.3b . . . and disconnect the wiring plugs

12

4.5 Remove the facia centre switch housing

4.7 Disconnect the switch wiring plug, then push the switch forwards from the panel to release it

5.3 Pull the wiring plug from the rear of the bulb

Centre facia-mounted pushbutton switches

Removal

5 Remove the facia centre switch housing as described in Chapter 11 (see illustration).
6 Working at the rear of the panel, disconnect the wiring plug from the relevant switch.
7 Push the switch forwards from the panel to release the securing clips (see illustration).

Refitting

8 Refitting is a reversal of removal.

Heater blower motor switch

Removal

9 Remove the heater/ventilation control unit as described in Chapter 3.
10 Carefully pull off the blower motor control knob. If using pliers, wrap a suitable piece of cloth or card around the knob to protect it.
11 Release the securing clips (two at the bottom and one at the top of the switch), using a screwdriver if necessary, then pull the blower motor switch from the rear of the control panel.

Refitting

12 Refit the switch using a reversal of the removal procedure, then refit the heater/ventilation control unit as described in Chapter 3.

Driver's side switch/ventilation panel-mounted switches

Removal

13 These switches include the electric door mirror switch, the instrument panel illumination switch, and the front foglight switch.
14 Remove the instrument panel surround, as described in Chapter 11.
15 Working at the rear of the panel, release the securing clips, then push the relevant switch out through the front of the panel. Disconnect the wiring harness at the connector.
16 Refit the switch by pushing it into position in the panel, then refit the panel with reference to Chapter 11.

Electric window switches

Removal

17 To remove a front door switch, simply prise the switch from the door trim panel, and disconnect the wiring connector. Note that the wiring connector is clipped to the inside of the door, and it may be necessary to remove the door inner trim panel (see Chapter 11) for access to the connector.

Refitting

18 Where applicable, refit the door inner trim panel as described in Chapter 11, and refit the switch by pushing it into position.

Electric sunroof switch

Removal

19 Carefully prise the switch housing from the headlining/sunroof mechanism casing using a small flat bladed screwdriver - pad the blade with PVC tape to avoid causing damage.
20 Disconnect the wiring plugs and remove the switch assembly.

Refitting

21 Refitting is a reversal of removal.

Courtesy light/door ajar warning switches

22 Open the door to expose the switch in the door B-pillar.
23 Remove the securing screw, then withdraw the switch from the door pillar. Disconnect the wiring connector as it becomes accessible.

 HAYNES HINT *Tape the wiring to the door pillar, or tie string to the wiring, to retrieve it if it falls back into the door pillar.*

24 Refitting is a reversal of removal, but ensure that the rubber gaiter is correctly seated on the switch.

5 Bulbs (exterior lights) - renewal

General

1 Whenever a bulb is renewed, note the following points:

a) Disconnect the battery negative lead before starting work.
b) Remember that, if the light has just been in use, the bulb may be extremely hot.
c) Always check the bulb contacts and holder, ensuring that there is clean metal-to-metal contact between the bulb and its live contact(s) and earth. Clean off any corrosion or dirt before fitting a new bulb.
d) Wherever bayonet-type bulbs are fitted, ensure that the live contact(s) bear firmly against the bulb contact.
e) Always ensure that the new bulb is of the correct rating (see Specifications), and that it is completely clean before fitting it; this applies particularly to headlight/foglight bulbs (see following paragraphs).

Headlight

2 Open the bonnet.
3 Squeeze the securing lugs, and disconnect the wiring plug from the rear of the bulb (see illustration).
4 Grasp the bulb housing cover and twist it anticlockwise to release it from the headlight unit.
5 Pull the rubber boot from the rear of the headlight unit.
6 Squeeze the retaining spring-clip lugs, and release the clip from the rear of the bulb.
7 Withdraw the bulb (see illustration).
8 When handling the new bulb, use a tissue or clean cloth, to avoid touching the glass with the fingers; moisture and grease from the skin can cause blackening and rapid failure of this type of bulb. If the glass is accidentally touched, wipe it clean using methylated spirit. Avoid knocking or shaking the bulb as this may weaken the filament.

5.7 Withdraw the headlight bulb

5.11 Squeeze the securing lugs and disconnect the sidelight wiring plug

5.15 Remove the upper securing screw from the direction indicator light unit

5.16 Using a screwdriver, release the lower balljoint (arrowed), carefully prise the light unit away from the wing

5.17 Twist the bulbholder anti-clockwise and withdraw it from the light unit

5.18 The bulb is a bayonet fit in the bulbholder

9 Install the new bulb, ensuring that its locating tabs are correctly located in the light unit cut-outs. Secure the bulb in position with the retaining clip, then refit the rubber boot and reconnect the wiring plug. Note the "TOP" mark on the rubber boot which should be uppermost.

Sidelight

10 Open the bonnet.
11 Squeeze the securing lugs, and disconnect the wiring plug from the rear of the headlight bulb (see illustration).
12 Twist the bulbholder to release it from the rear of the light unit.
13 The bulb is a push fit in the bulbholder.
14 Fit the new bulb using a reversal of the removal procedure.

Front direction indicator

15 Open the bonnet and remove the direction indicator light unit securing screw (located at the outer top corner of the light unit) (see illustration).
16 Using a suitable screwdriver to release the lower balljoint, carefully prise the light unit away from the front of the wing (see illustration).
17 Twist the bulbholder anti-clockwise and withdraw it from the light unit (see illustration).
18 The bulb is a bayonet fit in the bulbholder (see illustration).
19 Fit the new bulb, then refit the light assembly using a reversal of the removal

procedure. Ensure that the light unit lower balljoint is securely engaged and that the upper screw is securely tightened and that the upper locating peg engages with the lug on the bodywork (see illustration).

Front direction indicator side repeater

20 Slide the light unit towards the front of the vehicle and release it from the wing panel.
21 Withdraw the light unit, then twist the bulbholder anti-clockwise to release it from the light unit.
22 The bulb is a push fit in the bulbholder.
23 Fit the new bulb using a reversal of the removal procedure.

Front driving light

24 Remove the two driving light unit securing screws - do not turn either of the aim adjustment screws.
25 Withdraw the unit from the valance, then rotate the rear cover anticlockwise and remove it to expose the bulb.
26 Release the retaining clip from the rear of the bulb, then withdraw the bulb from the rear of the light unit, and unplug the wiring connector.
27 When handling the new bulb, use a tissue or clean cloth, to avoid touching the glass with the fingers; moisture and grease from the skin can cause blackening and rapid failure of this type of bulb. If the glass is accidentally touched, wipe it clean using methylated spirit.

5.19 Ensure that the light unit upper locating peg engages with the lug (arrowed) on the bodywork

Avoid knocking or shaking the bulb as this may weaken the filament.
28 Install the new bulb, ensuring that its locating tabs are correctly located in the light unit cut-outs.
29 Secure the bulb with the retaining clip and connect the wiring.
30 Refit the plastic cover, then fit the light unit to the valance and secure it position with the screws.

Front foglight

31 Remove the two foglight unit securing screws, then withdraw the unit - do not turn either of the aim adjustment screws.
32 Disconnect the wiring from the bulb, then release the spring clip, and withdraw the bulb from the rear of the light unit.
33 Fit the new bulb using a reversal of the removal procedure.

12

5.36 Withdraw the bulbholder from the rear of the light unit

5.37 The bulbs are a bayonet fit in the bulbholder

7.4 Unscrew the two headlight side securing bolts

Rear light cluster bulbs

34 Open the boot lid/tailgate.

35 Working at the side of the luggage compartment, release the securing clip, and open the flap in the load space trim panel.

36 Release the bulbholder securing clip, and withdraw the bulbholder from the rear of the light unit **(see illustration)**.

37 The bulbs are a bayonet fit in the bulbholder **(see Illustration)**.

38 Fit the new bulb using a reversal of the removal procedure. Note that the stop/tail light bulb has offset pins, to ensure correct orientation.

Rear number plate light

39 Remove the two securing screws, and withdraw the light unit lens from the boot lid/tailgate.

40 The bulb is a push fit in the light unit.

41 Fit the new bulb using a reversal of the removal procedure.

---

6 Bulbs (interior lights) - renewal

General

1 Whenever a bulb is renewed, note the following points:

a) *Disconnect the battery negative lead before starting work.*

b) *Remember that, if the light has just been in use, the bulb may be extremely hot.*

c) *Always check the bulb contacts and holder, ensuring that there is clean metal-to-metal contact between the bulb and its live contact(s) and earth. Clean off any corrosion or dirt before fitting a new bulb.*

d) *Wherever bayonet-type bulbs are fitted, ensure that the live contact(s) bear firmly against the bulb contact.*

e) *Always ensure that the new bulb is of the correct rating (see Specifications), and that it is completely clean before fitting it; this applies particularly to headlight/foglight bulbs (see following paragraphs).*

Courtesy light

2 Carefully prise the lens from the light unit (if necessary, carefully use a flat-bladed screwdriver).

3 The bulb is a push fit in the light unit.

4 Fit the new bulb using a reversal of the removal procedure.

Luggage compartment light

5 Open the tailgate/boot lid.

6 Unclip the lens from the light unit.

7 The bulb is a push fit in the light assembly.

8 Fit the new bulb using a reversal of the removal procedure.

---

7 Exterior light units - removal and refitting

Note: *Disconnect the battery negative lead before removing any light unit, and reconnect*

the lead after refitting the light. Refer to the caution in Section 1 if a security-coded radio/cassette player is fitted.

Headlight - Saloon and Hatchback models

Removal

1 Remove the adjacent direction indicator light as described in Section 5.

2 Release the securing clips and remove the front grille panel from the front of the vehicle.

3 Disconnect the headlight bulb wiring plug, then separate the two halves of the headlight unit wiring harness connector.

4 Unscrew the two headlight side securing bolts **(see illustration)**.

5 Similarly, unscrew the two headlight rear securing nuts **(see illustration)**.

6 Withdraw the headlight unit from the vehicle **(see illustrations)**.

Refitting

7 Refitting is a reversal of removal, but check that the direction indicator light unit lower balljoint is securely engaged. On completion, it is wise to have the headlight beam alignment checked with reference to Section 8.

Front direction indicator light

8 The procedure is described as part of the bulb renewal procedure in Section 5 **(see illustration)**.

Front direction indicator side repeater light

9 The procedure is described as part of the bulb renewal procedure in Section 5.

7.5 Similarly, unscrew the two headlight rear securing nuts

7.6 Withdraw the headlight unit from the vehicle

7.8 Front direction indicator wiring harness connection

7.12 Remove rear light cluster bulbholder assembly

7.13a Unscrew the light unit securing nuts . . .

7.13b . . . remove the trim mounting bracket . . .

Front foglight

10 The procedure is described as part of the bulb renewal procedure in Section 5.

Front driving lamp

11 The procedure is described as part of the bulb renewal procedure in Section 5.

Rear light cluster

Note: *A new light unit sealing strip will be required on refitting.*

Removal

12 Remove the bulbholder assembly, as described for the bulb renewal procedure in Section 5 **(see illustration)**.

13 Working inside the luggage compartment, unscrew the four securing nuts (one at each corner of the light unit), then pull the light unit from the rear of the vehicle **(see illustrations)**. Note that the light unit is held in place with a self-adhesive sealing compound.

Refitting

14 Before refitting the light unit, clean all traces of sealant from the light unit and the wing panel.

15 Apply the new sealing strip to the rear of the light unit (the sealing strip is supplied in rolls, and may have to be trimmed to the required length).

16 Refit the light unit using a reversal of the removal procedure. Tighten the securing screws securely.

8 Headlight beam alignment - general information

Accurate adjustment of the headlight beam is only possible using optical beam-setting equipment, and this work should therefore be carried out by a Nissan dealer or suitably-equipped workshop.

Certain models are equipped with a headlight beam adjustment switch, located on the facia, which allows the aim of the headlights to be adjusted to compensate for the varying loads carried in the vehicle. The switch should be positioned according to the load being carried in the vehicle - refer to the vehicles handbook for details.

9 Instrument panel - removal and refitting

Note: *This section is not applicable to models fitted with a Supplementary Restraint System (SRS).*

 Warning: For safety reasons, owners are strongly advised to entrust to an authorised Nissan dealer any work which involves disturbing the SRS components. Specialised test equipment is needed to check that the SRS is fully operational following reassembly.

Removal

1 Disconnect the battery negative cable and position it away from the terminal.

2 Remove the instrument panel surround as described in Chapter 11.

3 Remove the instrument panel securing screws **(see illustrations)**.

4 Working in the engine compartment, disconnect the speedometer cable from the gearbox (see Section 14), then push the cable through the engine compartment bulkhead sufficiently to enable the instrument panel to be pulled forwards.

5 Pull the instrument panel forwards, and disconnect the wiring plugs and the speedometer cable from the rear of the panel **(see illustration)**. Withdraw the instrument panel.

Refitting

6 Refitting is a reversal of removal, bearing in mind the following points:

a) *When reconnecting the speedometer cable, reconnect the cable to the speedometer, then pull the cable through the bulkhead, back into the engine compartment, until the instrument panel can be seated securely in the facia. Reconnect the speedometer to the gearbox with reference to Chapter 12.*

b) *After refitting the instrument panel surround, tighten the steering column upper securing bolts to the specified torque.*

7.13c . . . and withdraw the light unit

9.3 Remove the instrument panel securing screws (arrowed)

H 28760

9.5 To detach the speedometer cable, depress the lug and twist off the connector

10.4 Horn sounder mounting bolt

12.3a Lift up the wiper arm spindle nut cover (tailgate wiper shown)

12.3b On hatchback models, disconnect the washer hose union (tailgate wiper shown)

10 Horn - removal and refitting

Removal

1 Disconnect the battery negative lead.
2 Refer to Chapter 11 and remove the front grille panel.
3 Disconnect the wiring from the horn.
4 Unscrew the securing bolt(s), and withdraw the horn sounder(s), complete with the mounting bracket (see illustration).

Refitting

5 Refitting is a reversal of removal.

11 Speedometer drive cable - removal and refitting

Removal

1 Remove the instrument panel as described in Section 9.
2 Working in the engine compartment, unscrew the sleeve securing the cable end to gearbox, then pull the cable from gearbox.
3 Where applicable, release the cable from the brackets in the engine compartment bulkhead, then pull the cable through into the engine compartment. If necessary, pull the cable grommet from the bulkhead.

Refitting

4 Refitting is a reversal of removal, bearing in mind the following points:
a) Ensure that the bulkhead grommet is securely seated.
b) Refit the instrument panel with reference to Section 9.
c) Note that certain models have alignment marks on the cable outer for use when refitting. The marks should be aligned with the bulkhead bracket when the cable is correctly refitted and routed.

12 Wiper arm - removal and refitting

Removal

1 Operate the wiper motor, then switch it off so that the wiper arm returns to the at-rest/parked position.
2 If a windscreen or tailgate wiper is being removed, stick a piece of tape along the edge of the wiper blade, to use as an alignment aid on refitting.
3 Where applicable, lift up the wiper arm spindle nut cover, then slacken and remove the spindle nut (see illustrations). Lift the blade off the glass, and pull the wiper arm off its spindle. If necessary, the arm can be levered off the spindle using a suitable flat-bladed screwdriver. If both windscreen wiper arms are removed, note their locations, as different arms are fitted to the driver's and passenger's sides.

Refitting

4 Ensure that the wiper arm and spindle splines are clean and dry.
5 When refitting a windscreen or tailgate wiper arm, refit the arm to the spindle, aligning the wiper blade with the tape fitted before removal. If both windscreen wiper arms have been removed, ensure that the arms are refitted to their correct positions as noted before removal.
6 When refitting a headlight wiper arm, hold the arm below the stops at the bottom of the headlight unit, until the spindle nut has been refitted and tightened.
7 Refit the spindle nut, tighten it securely, and where applicable, clip the nut cover back into position. If refitting a headlight wiper arm, once the spindle nut has been tightened, position the wiper blade against the upper surfaces of the stops on the headlight.

13 Windscreen wiper motor and linkage - removal and refitting

Removal

1 Disconnect the battery negative lead.
2 Open the bonnet.
3 Pull the weatherstrip from the front edge of the bulkhead cowl panel.
4 Remove the securing screw(s) and plastic clip(s), and withdraw the cowl panel (see illustration).

12.3c Slacken and remove the spindle nut

13.4 Remove the plastic clips, and withdraw the cowl panel

13.5 Disconnect the wiring plug from the windscreen wiper motor

13.6a Unscrew the motor spindle nut, recover the washer . . .

5 Disconnect the motor wiring plug **(see illustration)**.
6 Unscrew the motor spindle nut and recover the washer **(see illustrations)**.
7 Slacken and withdraw the motor securing bolts and withdraw the motor.

Refitting

8 Refitting is a reversal of removal, but ensure that the motor drive is in the "parked" position before reconnecting the crank arm.

14 Tailgate wiper motor - removal and refitting

Removal

1 Disconnect the battery negative lead.
2 Remove the tailgate inner trim panel as described in Chapter 11.
3 Remove the wiper arm with reference to Section 15, disconnecting the integral washer hose where applicable.
4 Working inside the tailgate, disconnect the tailgate wiper motor wiring plug **(see illustration)**.
5 Unscrew the bolts securing the motor mounting bracket to the tailgate, noting that one of the bolts also secures an earth lead **(see illustration)**.
6 Withdraw the motor assembly through the aperture in the tailgate.
7 The motor is secured to the mounting bracket by three bolts, insulated with rubber grommets.

14.4 Disconnect the tailgate wiper motor wiring plug

13.6b . . . and detach the wiper linkage from the spindle

8 If desired, the motor spindle grommet can be pulled from the hole in the tailgate.

Refitting

9 Refitting is a reversal of removal, but where applicable, ensure that the grommet is correctly located in the tailgate, and refit the wiper arm with reference to Section 15.

15 Windscreen/tailgate washer system components - removal and refitting

Washer fluid reservoir

Removal

1 Working in the engine compartment, twist the reservoir filler neck clockwise, then pull it from the top of the reservoir.
2 Disconnect the battery negative lead.
3 Chock the rear wheels, apply the handbrake, then jack up the front of the vehicle and support securely on axle stands (see *"Jacking and Vehicle Support"*). Remove the front right-hand roadwheel.
4 Remove the wheel arch liner.
5 Disconnect the wiring plug(s) from the washer pump(s), and from the fluid level sensor, where applicable.
6 Disconnect the fluid hose(s) from the washer pump(s) - if the reservoir still contains fluid, be prepared for fluid spillage.
7 Where applicable, release the wiring harness from its clips, and move the harness

14.5 Unscrew the bolts securing the motor mounting bracket to the tailgate

to one side to allow sufficient clearance to remove the reservoir.
8 Working under the wheel arch, remove the reservoir securing screws, then lower the reservoir from under the wheel arch.

Refitting

9 Refitting is a reversal of removal.

Washer fluid reservoir and washer pump(s)

Removal

10 Proceed as described in the previous sub-Section, paragraphs 2 to 4.
11 Disconnect the wiring plug and the fluid hose from the relevant washer pump.
12 Pull the washer pump from the reservoir, and where applicable, recover the grommet. If the reservoir still contains fluid, be prepared for fluid spillage.

Refitting

13 Refitting is a reversal of removal.

Windscreen washer nozzle

Removal

14 Open the bonnet.
15 Working under the bonnet, release the securing tabs using a suitable screwdriver, then push the nozzle from the bonnet. Disconnect the fluid hose, and withdraw the nozzle.

Refitting

16 Refitting is a reversal of removal.

Tailgate washer nozzle - Hatchback models

Removal

17 The tailgate washer nozzle is screwed to the wiper arm. Remove the screw and separate the nozzle housing from the wiper arm. Disconnect the washer hose.

Refitting

18 Refitting is a reversal of removal, but ensure that the fluid hose is securely reconnected.

16 Radio/cassette player - removal and refitting

Caution: If the radio/cassette player fitted to the vehicle has an anti-theft security code (as does the unit fitted as standard), refer to the information given in the preliminary Sections of this manual before removing the unit.

Removal

1 Disconnect the battery negative lead.
2 Remove the facia centre switch housing as described in Chapter 11.
3 Remove the radio/cassette player securing screws.

16.4a Pull the unit forwards from the facia . . .

16.4b . . . then disconnect the wiring plugs and the aerial lead from the rear of the unit

17.2 Remove the loudspeaker housing securing screws (arrowed)

4 Pull the unit forwards from the facia, then disconnect the wiring plugs and the aerial lead from the rear of the unit **(see illustrations)**.

5 Note the bayonet fuse, which is a push fit in the rear of the unit.

Refitting

6 Refitting is a reversal of removal, ensuring that the wiring is freely routed behind the unit.

17 Loudspeakers - removal and refitting

Front door-mounted loudspeakers

Removal

1 Remove the door inner trim panel as described in Chapter 11.

2 Remove the four securing screws, and withdraw the loudspeaker housing from the door, then disconnect the wiring plug **(see illustration)**.

3 If desired, the loudspeaker can be withdrawn from the housing after removing the four securing screws.

Refitting

4 Refitting is a reversal of removal, refit the inner door trim panel with reference to Chapter 11.

Front footwell-mounted loudspeakers

Removal

5 Disconnect the battery negative lead.

6 Open the relevant front door, and pull the weatherstrip from the edge of the body pillar trim panel.

7 Carefully pull the trim panel from the pillar to release the securing clips.

8 Remove the two screws securing the loudspeaker to the pillar, then lift out the loudspeaker, and separate the two halves of the wiring connector (where necessary, pull the insulating foam from the connector).

Refitting

9 Refitting is a reversal of removal.

Rear loudspeakers

Saloon models

10 Disconnect the battery negative lead.

11 Remove the parcel shelf, as described in Chapter 11.

12 Remove the four securing screws, then withdraw the loudspeaker from the body panel, and disconnect the wiring plug (where necessary, release the wiring harness from the securing clips).

13 Refitting is a reversal of removal.

Hatchback models

14 Disconnect the battery negative lead.

15 At the relevant luggage compartment side/parcel shelf support panel, unscrew the four loudspeaker securing screws, then withdraw the loudspeaker from the mounting bracket, and disconnect the wiring plug.

16 Refitting is a reversal of removal.

18 Radio aerial - removal and refitting

Rear window aerial

1 Certain models may have a radio aerial incorporated in the rear window glass, with the heating element. In the event of a suspected fault, consult a Nissan dealer for advice.

Rear wing-mounted aerial

Removal

2 Disconnect the battery negative lead.

3 Remove the carpet panel from the floor of the luggage compartment.

4 Release the securing clips, and pull the carpet trim panel from the side of the luggage compartment.

5 Working through the aperture in the body panel, disconnect the aerial motor wiring connector.

6 Remove the screw securing the aerial earth lead to the body.

7 Unclip the aerial lead from the body, and disconnect the lead from the aerial.

8 Working outside the vehicle, unscrew the securing nut from the top of the aerial **(see illustration)**.

9 Working in the luggage compartment, remove the two screws securing the aerial assembly to the body.

10 Manipulate the assembly out through the aperture in the body, and disconnect the water drain tube from the bottom of the assembly.

Refitting

11 Refitting is a reversal of removal, bearing in mind the following points:

a) Ensure that the drain hose is reconnected to the aerial before manipulating the assembly into position.

b) Refit the screws securing the assembly to the body, but do not fully tighten them until the top securing nut has been refitted and tightened.

Roof-mounted aerial

Removal

12 Working on the roof of the vehicle, remove the two securing screws, then carefully pull the aerial from the roof, and disconnect the aerial lead.

Refitting

13 Refitting is a reversal of removal, but ensure that the aerial housing is securely engaged with the roof panel.

18.8 Unscrew the aerial mast

Front windscreen pillar-mounted aerial

Removal

14 Working on the roof of the vehicle, remove the securing screws, then carefully pull the aerial shaft from the roof, and disconnect the aerial lead.

Refitting

15 Refitting is a reversal of removal, but ensure that the aerial housing is securely engaged with the roof panel. Tighten the retaining screw securely.

19 Heated front seat components - general information

Certain models may be with heated front seats. The seats are heated by electrical elements built into the seat cushions.

For access to the heating elements, the seats must be dismantled, and this work should be entrusted to a Nissan dealer.

20 Air bag system - general information and precautions

General information

Certain later models are fitted with a Supplementary Restraint System (SRS), incorporating driver and front seat passenger air bags to help prevent chest and head injuries in the event of an accident.

The system is armed when the ignition key is in the "ON" or "START" positions (note that the system remains armed for at least ten minutes after the ignition is switched off), and is activated by one of a number of "g" sensor (deceleration sensor) mounted inside the vehicle. The system is controlled by an electronic control unit mounted under the steering column.

For safety reasons, owners are strongly advised to entrust to an authorised Nissan dealer any work which involves disturbing the SRS components.

Specialised test equipment is needed to check that the SRS is fully operational following reassembly.

Precautions

 Warning: The following precautions must be observed when working on vehicles with an air bag system, to prevent the possibility of personal injury.

a) *Do not attempt to check any of the air bag system components using meters or any other form of test equipment.*

b) *Before working on any vehicle components located near air bag system components (steering wheel, steering column, facia and centre console), switch the ignition off, and disconnect the battery negative lead, then wait for at least 10 minutes before carrying out any further work.*

c) *Do not attempt to remove the system electronic control unit (located under the steering column), or the sensor (located under the centre console).*

d) *Do not attempt to turn the steering wheel or column with the steering gear removed.*

e) *If the air bag warning light comes on, or any fault in the system is suspected, consult a Nissan dealer without delay.* **Do not** *attempt to carry out fault diagnosis, or any dismantling of the components.*

Wiring diagrams commence on page 12•12

Key to symbols

Connecting wires	
Connection to other circuits (e.g. diagram 3/grid location B2).	**3/B2** **3/B2**
Direction of arrow denotes current flow.	
Solenoid actuator	
Wire-battery positive potential (double line)	
Wire-battery negative potential (thick line)	
Wire-interconnecting (thin line)	

Bulb
Switch
Fuse F13
Item no. 7
Pump/motor M
Earth
Resistor
Variable resistor
Diode

Wire colours

B	Black	BR	Brown
w	White	OR	Orange
R	Red	P	Pink
G	Green	PU	Purple
L	Blue	GY	Grey
Y	Yellow	SB	Sky blue
LG	Light green		

Key to items

1 Battery
2 Starter motor
3 Ignition switch
4 Ignition relay
5 Inhibitor relay (auto. trans.)
6 Inhibitor switch (auto. trans.)
7 Alternator
8 Accessory relay
9 Heater blower relay
10 Fusible links

FUSIBLE LINK AND FUSEBOX

F28 20A	FL (H) 30A	FL (F) 30A	FL (E) 30A	FL (D) 30A	FL (C) 30A	FL (B) 25A
F27 10A						
F26 15A						
F25 15A	F24 10A	F23 15A	FL (G) 75A			

PASSENGER FUSEBOX

F1 10A	F2 15A	F3 10A	F4 10A	F5 10A	F6 10A	F7 15A	F8 10A	F9 15A	F10 10A	F11 10A
F12 10A	F13 10A	F14 10A	F15 20A	F16 15A	F17 10A	F18 20A	F19 10A	F20 10A	F21 15A	F22 15A

FUSES IN RELAY BOX

F31 15A
F29 10A

Notes

1. Wires may interconnect between diagrams and are located by using a grid reference e.g. 2/A1 denotes a position on diagram 2 grid location A1.
2. Brackets show how circuits may be wired in more than one way.
3. Not all items are fitted to all models.

Diagram 1 : Notes, fuses, key to symbols, typical starting, charging and power supply

Diagram 2 : Typical engine management - DE models

Key to items	
11	Fuel pump relay
12	Air regulator
13	Fuel pump
14	Spark plugs
15	Distributor
16	Power transistor
17	Condenser/resistor
18	Ignition coil
19	E.C.C.S. relay
20	Crank angle sensor
21	Air flow meter
22	Exhaust gas sensor
23	Fuel injectors
24	A.A.C. valve
25	Diagnostic connector
26	Power steering oil pressure switch
27	Neutral switch (manual trans.)
28	Throttle sensor
29	Engine temperature sensor
30	E.C.C.S. control unit

Wire colours			
B	Black	BR	Brown
W	White	OR	Orange
R	Red	P	Pink
G	Green	PU	Purple
L	Blue	GY	Grey
Y	Yellow	SB	Sky blue
LG	Light green		

Ignition on/start 1/J5

H29221
T.M.MAPKE

Cooling fan signal 7/F4

Tacho signal 6/J7

Warning light 6/F7

Automatic transmission 1/F8

Ignition start 1/J6

Battery +ve 1/B7

Ignition on/start 1/J5

12

Key to items

14	Spark plugs	32	Air fuel ratio control valve
15	Distributor	33	Fuel cut valve
16	Power transistor	34	Accelerator pump control valve
17	Condenser/resistor	35	Idle-up control valve
18	Ignition coil	36	F.I.C.D. solenoid valve
19	E.C.C.S. relay	37	A.I.V. control solenoid valve
20	Crank angle sensor	38	E.G.R. and canister control valve
22	Exhaust gas sensor	39	Mixture heater relay
25	Diagnostic connector	40	Mixture heater
26	Power steering oil pressure switch	41	Throttle valve switch
27	Neutral switch (manual trans.)	42	Clutch switch
29	Engine temperature sensor	43	Boost pressure sensor
30	E.C.C.S. control unit		
31	Diode		

Wire colours

B	Black	BR	Brown
W	White	OR	Orange
R	Red	P	Pink
G	Green	PU	Purple
L	Blue	GY	Grey
Y	Yellow	SB	Sky blue
LG	Light green		

Diagram 3 : Typical engine management - DS models

Diagram 4 : Typical anti-lock brakes, overdrive cancel, heated rear window and dim/dip lighting

Key to items

44 ABS control unit
45 LH front wheel sensor
46 RH front wheel sensor
47 LH rear wheel sensor
48 RH rear wheel sensor
49 Actuator relay
50 Motor relay
51 Actuator
52 Overdrive cancel switch
53 Overdrive cancel solenoid
54 Heated rear window switch
55 Heated rear window
56 Condenser
57 Lighting switch
58 Dim-dip unit
59 RH headlight
60 LH headlight

Wire colours

B Black
W White
R Red
G Green
L Blue
Y Yellow
LG Light green
BR Brown
OR Orange
P Pink
PU Purple
GY Grey
SB Sky blue

12

Diagram 5 : Typical side, stop, reversing, fog and direction indicator lights

Key to items

57 Lighting switch
61 LH front sidelight
62 RH front sidelight
63 Number plate light
64 LH tail light
65 RH tail light
66 LH stop-light
67 RH stop-light
68 High level stop-light
69 LH reversing light
70 RH reversing light
71 Reversing light switch (manual trans.)
72 Rear foglight relay
73 LH rear foglight
74 RH rear foglight
75 Rear foglight switch
76 Hazard switch
77 Flasher unit
78 Turn signal switch
79 LH front indicator
80 LH indicator repeater
81 LH rear indicator
82 RH front indicator
83 RH indicator repeater
84 RH rear indicator
85 Stop light switch

Wire colours

B   Black   BR Brown
W   White   OR Orange
R   Red   P   Pink
G   Green   PU Purple
L   Blue   GY Grey
Y   Yellow   SB Sky blue
LG Light green

Diagram 6 : Typical interior lighting, warning lights, gauges horn and cigar lighter

Key to items

86 Diode (models with electric windows only)
87 Interior light
88 Driver's door switch
89 Passenger's door switch
90 LH rear door switch
91 RH rear door switch
92 Luggage comp. light
93 Luggage comp. light switch
94 Cigar lighter illumination
95 Ashtray illumination
96 Auto. trans.switch stage illumination
97 Illumination control
98 Instrument illumination
99 Clock illumination
100 Instrument cluster
  a = charge warning light
  b = washer level warning light
  c = oil pressure warning light
  d = brake warning light
  e = engine warning light
  f = door warning light
  g = ABS warning light
  h = overdrive warning light
  i = headlight warning light
  j = LH dir. ind. warning light
  k = RH dir. ind. warning light
  l = low fuel warning light
  m = fuel gauge
  n = temperature gauge
  o = tachometer
  p = digital clock
101 Washer level sensor
102 Oil pressure switch
103 Handbrake warning switch
104 Brake fluid level switch
105 Fuel gauge sender
106 Temperature gauge sender
107 Lights on buzzer
108 Cigar lighter
109 Horn
110 Horn switch
111 Horn relay

12

Diagram 7 : Typical heater blower, radiator cooling fan, and wash/wipe

Key to items

112 Heater blower switch
113 Heater blower motor
114 Heater blower resistors
115 Radiator cooling fan relay
116 Radiator cooling fan switch
117 Radiator cooling fans
118 Front wiper switch
119 Front wiper motor
120 Front washer pump
121 Wiper delay amplifier
122 Wiper delay rheostat
123 Rear wash/wipe switch
124 Rear washer pump
125 Rear wiper motor
126 Rear wiper relay
127 Rear wiper amplifier

Wire colours

B Black   BR Brown
w White   OR Orange
R Red   P Pink
G Green   PU Purple
L Blue   GY Grey
Y Yellow   SB Sky blue
LG Light green

Key to items

128 Door mirror switch
129 LH mirror assembly
130 RH mirror assembly
131 Heated mirror relay
132 Circuit breaker
133 Driver's door switch
134 Main switch
135 Driver's window motor
136 LH rear window motor
137 RH rear window motor
138 Passenger's window motor
139 LH rear window switch
140 RH rear window switch
141 Passenger's window switch
142 Passenger's door lock
143 RH rear door lock
144 LH rear door lock
145 Radio/cassette
146 RH door speaker
147 LH door speaker
148 RH rear speaker
149 LH rear speaker

Wire colours

B	Black	BR	Brown
w	White	OR	Orange
R	Red	P	Pink
G	Green	PU	Purple
L	Blue	GY	Grey
Y	Yellow	SB	Sky blue
LG	Light green		

Radio/cassette

Window aerial

Rod aerial

Ignition acc/on

Battery +ve

Heated/electric door mirrors

MIRROR SWITCH

CHANGE-OVER SWITCH

Ignition on/start

Heated rear window

Door switch

Ignition on/start

Battery +ve

Central locking and electric windows

Lighting

ILLUM.

Diagram 8 : Typical electric door mirrors, central locking and electric windows

H29227
T.M.MARKE

12

Dimensions and Weights

Note: *All figures are approximate, and may vary according to model. Refer to manufacturer's data for exact figures.*

Dimensions

Overall length:
  Saloon models . . . . 4230 mm
  3-door Hatchback . . . . 4975 mm
  5-door Hatchback . . . . 4145 mm
Overall width . . . . 1670 mm
Overall height (unladen) . . . . 1395 mm

Weights

Kerb weight . . . . 960 to 1030 kg*
Towing weight:
  Saloon/Hatchback 1.4 litre . . . . 840 to 900 kg
  Saloon/Hatchback 1.6 litre . . . . 1160 to 1250 kg
  Coupe . . . . 1000 to 1200 kg
Maximum trailer nose weight . . . . 75 kg

Depending on model and specification.

Conversion Factors

Length (distance)

Inches (in)	25.4	= Millimetres (mm)	x 0.0394	= Inches (in)
Feet (ft)	0.305	= Metres (m)	x 3.281	= Feet (ft)
Miles	1.609	= Kilometres (km)	x 0.621	= Miles

Volume (capacity)

Cubic inches (cu in; in³)	x 16.387	= Cubic centimetres (cc; cm³)	x 0.061	= Cubic inches (cu in; in³)
Imperial pints (Imp pt)	x 0.568	= Litres (l)	x 1.76	= Imperial pints (Imp pt)
Imperial quarts (Imp qt)	x 1.137	= Litres (l)	x 0.88	= Imperial quarts (Imp qt)
Imperial quarts (Imp qt)	x 1.201	= US quarts (US qt)	x 0.833	= Imperial quarts (Imp qt)
US quarts (US qt)	x 0.946	= Litres (l)	x 1.057	= US quarts (US qt)
Imperial gallons (Imp gal)	x 4.546	= Litres (l)	x 0.22	= Imperial gallons (Imp gal)
Imperial gallons (Imp gal)	x 1.201	= US gallons (US gal)	x 0.833	= Imperial gallons (Imp gal)
US gallons (US gal)	x 3.785	= Litres (l)	x 0.264	= US gallons (US gal)

Mass (weight)

Ounces (oz)	x 28.35	= Grams (g)	x 0.035	= Ounces (oz)
Pounds (lb)	x 0.454	= Kilograms (kg)	x 2.205	= Pounds (lb)

Force

Ounces-force (ozf; oz)	x 0.278	= Newtons (N)	x 3.6	= Ounces-force (ozf; oz)
Pounds-force (lbf; lb)	x 4.448	= Newtons (N)	x 0.225	= Pounds-force (lbf; lb)
Newtons (N)	x 0.1	= Kilograms-force (kgf; kg)	x 9.81	= Newtons (N)

Pressure

Pounds-force per square inch (psi; lbf/in²; lb/in²)	x 0.070	= Kilograms-force per square centimetre (kgf/cm²; kg/cm²)	x 14.223	= Pounds-force per square inch (psi; lbf/in²; lb/in²)
Pounds-force per square inch (psi; lbf/in²; lb/in²)	x 0.068	= Atmospheres (atm)	x 14.696	= Pounds-force per square inch (psi; lbf/in²; lb/in²)
Pounds-force per square inch (psi; lbf/in²; lb/in²)	x 0.069	= Bars	x 14.5	= Pounds-force per square inch (psi; lbf/in²; lb/in²)
Pounds-force per square inch (psi; lbf/in²; lb/in²)	x 6.895	= Kilopascals (kPa)	x 0.145	= Pounds-force per square inch (psi; lbf/in²; lb/in²)
Kilopascals (kPa)	x 0.01	= Kilograms-force per square centimetre (kgf/cm²; kg/cm²)	x 98.1	= Kilopascals (kPa)
Millibar (mbar)	x 100	= Pascals (Pa)	x 0.01	= Millibar (mbar)
Millibar (mbar)	x 0.0145	= Pounds-force per square inch (psi; lbf/in²; lb/in²)	x 68.947	= Millibar (mbar)
Millibar (mbar)	x 0.75	= Millimetres of mercury (mmHg)	x 1.333	= Millibar (mbar)
Millibar (mbar)	x 0.401	= Inches of water (inH₂O)	x 2.491	= Millibar (mbar)
Millimetres of mercury (mmHg)	x 0.535	= Inches of water (inH₂O)	x 1.868	= Millimetres of mercury (mmHg)
Inches of water (inH₂O)	x 0.036	= Pounds-force per square inch (psi; lbf/in²; lb/in²)	x 27.68	= Inches of water (inH₂O)

Torque (moment of force)

Pounds-force inches (lbf in; lb in)	x 1.152	= Kilograms-force centimetre (kgf cm; kg cm)	x 0.868	= Pounds-force inches (lbf in; lb in)
Pounds-force inches (lbf in; lb in)	x 0.113	= Newton metres (Nm)	x 8.85	= Pounds-force inches (lbf in; lb in)
Pounds-force inches (lbf in; lb in)	x 0.083	= Pounds-force feet (lbf ft; lb ft)	x 12	= Pounds-force inches (lbf in; lb in)
Pounds-force feet (lbf ft; lb ft)	x 0.138	= Kilograms-force metres (kgf m; kg m)	x 7.233	= Pounds-force feet (lbf ft; lb ft)
Pounds-force feet (lbf ft; lb ft)	x 1.356	= Newton metres (Nm)	x 0.738	= Pounds-force feet (lbf ft; lb ft)
Newton metres (Nm)	x 0.102	= Kilograms-force metres (kgf m; kg m)	x 9.804	= Newton metres (Nm)

Power

Horsepower (hp)	x 745.7	= Watts (W)	x 0.0013	= Horsepower (hp)

Velocity (speed)

Miles per hour (miles/hr; mph)	x 1.609	= Kilometres per hour (km/hr; kph)	x 0.621	= Miles per hour (miles/hr; mph)

Fuel consumption*

Miles per gallon (mpg)	x 0.354	= Kilometres per litre (km/l)	x 2.825	= Miles per gallon (mpg)

It is common practice to convert from miles per gallon (mpg) to litres/100 kilometres (l/100km), where mpg x l/100 km = 282

Temperature

Degrees Fahrenheit = (°C x 1.8) + 32

Degrees Celsius (Degrees Centigrade; °C) = (°F - 32) x 0.56

Spare parts are available from many sources, including maker's appointed garages, accessory shops, and motor factors. To be sure of obtaining the correct parts, it may sometimes be necessary to quote the vehicle identification number. If possible, it can also be useful to take the old parts along for positive identification. Items such as starter motors and alternators may be available under a service exchange scheme - any parts returned should always be clean.

Our advice regarding spare part sources is as follows.

Officially-appointed garages

This is the best source of parts which are peculiar to your car, and are not otherwise generally available (eg badges, interior trim, certain body panels, etc). It is also the only place at which you should buy parts if the vehicle is still under warranty.

Accessory shops

These are very good places to buy materials and components needed for the maintenance of your car (oil, air and fuel filters, spark plugs, light bulbs, drivebelts, oils and greases, brake pads, touch-up paint, etc). Parts like this sold by a reputable shop are of the same standard as those used by the car manufacturer.

Motor factors

Good factors will stock all the more important components which wear out comparatively quickly and can sometimes supply individual components needed for the overhaul of a larger assembly. They may also handle work such as cylinder block reboring, crankshaft regrinding and balancing, etc.

Tyre and exhaust specialists

These outlets may be independent or part of a local or national chain. They frequently offer competitive prices compared with a main dealer or local garage, but it pays to get several quotes before making a decision. Also ask what 'extras' may be added to the quote - for instance, fitting a new valve and balancing the wheel are both often charged on top of the price of a new tyre.

Other sources

Beware of parts or materials obtained from market stalls, car boot sales or similar outlets. Such items are not invariably sub-standard, but there is little chance of compensation if they do prove unsatisfactory. In the case of safety-critical components such as brake pads there is the risk not only of financial loss but also of an accident causing injury or death.

Vehicle Identification

Modifications are a continuing and unpublicised process in vehicle manufacture, quite apart from major model changes. Spare parts lists are compiled upon a numerical basis, the individual vehicle identification numbers being essential to correct identification of the component concerned.

When ordering spare parts, always give as much information as possible. Quote the car model, year of manufacture, body and engine numbers, as appropriate.

The Vehicle Identification Number (VIN) plate is riveted to the engine compartment bulkhead, and can be seen with the bonnet open. The plate carries the VIN, vehicle weight information, and paint and trim colour codes. The vehicle identification number is also stamped into the bulkhead next to the plate.

The *Engine number* is stamped on a machined surface on the front side of the cylinder block, at the flywheel end. The first part of the engine number gives the engine code - eg "GA16DE".

The *Transmission number* is on top of the bellhousing on manual transmission models, and on the governor cap on top of the bellhousing on automatic transmission models.

Vehicle Identification Number stamped into bulkhead (1) and VIN plate (2)

Whenever servicing, repair or overhaul work is carried out on the car or its components, it is necessary to observe the following procedures and instructions. This will assist in carrying out the operation efficiently and to a professional standard of workmanship.

Joint mating faces and gaskets

When separating components at their mating faces, never insert screwdrivers or similar implements into the joint between the faces in order to prise them apart. This can cause severe damage which results in oil leaks, coolant leaks, etc upon reassembly. Separation is usually achieved by tapping along the joint with a soft-faced hammer in order to break the seal. However, note that this method may not be suitable where dowels are used for component location.

Where a gasket is used between the mating faces of two components, ensure that it is renewed on reassembly, and fit it dry unless otherwise stated in the repair procedure. Make sure that the mating faces are clean and dry, with all traces of old gasket removed. When cleaning a joint face, use a tool which is not likely to score or damage the face, and remove any burrs or nicks with an oilstone or fine file.

Make sure that tapped holes are cleaned with a pipe cleaner, and keep them free of jointing compound, if this is being used, unless specifically instructed otherwise.

Ensure that all orifices, channels or pipes are clear, and blow through them, preferably using compressed air.

Oil seals

Oil seals can be removed by levering them out with a wide flat-bladed screwdriver or similar tool. Alternatively, a number of self-tapping screws may be screwed into the seal, and these used as a purchase for pliers or similar in order to pull the seal free.

Whenever an oil seal is removed from its working location, either individually or as part of an assembly, it should be renewed.

The very fine sealing lip of the seal is easily damaged, and will not seal if the surface it contacts is not completely clean and free from scratches, nicks or grooves. If the original sealing surface of the component cannot be restored, and the manufacturer has not made provision for slight relocation of the seal relative to the sealing surface, the component should be renewed.

Protect the lips of the seal from any surface which may damage them in the course of fitting. Use tape or a conical sleeve where possible. Lubricate the seal lips with oil before fitting and, on dual-lipped seals, fill the space between the lips with grease.

Unless otherwise stated, oil seals must be fitted with their sealing lips toward the lubricant to be sealed.

Use a tubular drift or block of wood of the appropriate size to install the seal and, if the seal housing is shouldered, drive the seal down to the shoulder. If the seal housing is unshouldered, the seal should be fitted with its face flush with the housing top face (unless otherwise instructed).

Screw threads and fastenings

Seized nuts, bolts and screws are quite a common occurrence where corrosion has set in, and the use of penetrating oil or releasing fluid will often overcome this problem if the offending item is soaked for a while before attempting to release it. The use of an impact driver may also provide a means of releasing such stubborn fastening devices, when used in conjunction with the appropriate screwdriver bit or socket. If none of these methods works, it may be necessary to resort to the careful application of heat, or the use of a hacksaw or nut splitter device.

Studs are usually removed by locking two nuts together on the threaded part, and then using a spanner on the lower nut to unscrew the stud. Studs or bolts which have broken off below the surface of the component in which they are mounted can sometimes be removed using a stud extractor. Always ensure that a blind tapped hole is completely free from oil, grease, water or other fluid before installing the bolt or stud. Failure to do this could cause the housing to crack due to the hydraulic action of the bolt or stud as it is screwed in.

When tightening a castellated nut to accept a split pin, tighten the nut to the specified torque, where applicable, and then tighten further to the next split pin hole. Never slacken the nut to align the split pin hole, unless stated in the repair procedure.

When checking or retightening a nut or bolt to a specified torque setting, slacken the nut or bolt by a quarter of a turn, and then retighten to the specified setting. However, this should not be attempted where angular tightening has been used.

For some screw fastenings, notably cylinder head bolts or nuts, torque wrench settings are no longer specified for the latter stages of tightening, "angle-tightening" being called up instead. Typically, a fairly low torque wrench setting will be applied to the bolts/nuts in the correct sequence, followed by one or more stages of tightening through specified angles.

Locknuts, locktabs and washers

Any fastening which will rotate against a component or housing during tightening should always have a washer between it and the relevant component or housing.

Spring or split washers should always be renewed when they are used to lock a critical component such as a big-end bearing retaining bolt or nut. Locktabs which are folded over to retain a nut or bolt should always be renewed.

Self-locking nuts can be re-used in non-critical areas, providing resistance can be felt when the locking portion passes over the bolt or stud thread. However, it should be noted that self-locking stiffnuts tend to lose their effectiveness after long periods of use, and should be renewed as a matter of course.

Split pins must always be replaced with new ones of the correct size for the hole.

When thread-locking compound is found on the threads of a fastener which is to be re-used, it should be cleaned off with a wire brush and solvent, and fresh compound applied on reassembly.

Special tools

Some repair procedures in this manual entail the use of special tools such as a press, two or three-legged pullers, spring compressors, etc. Wherever possible, suitable readily-available alternatives to the manufacturer's special tools are described, and are shown in use. In some instances, where no alternative is possible, it has been necessary to resort to the use of a manufacturer's tool, and this has been done for reasons of safety as well as the efficient completion of the repair operation. Unless you are highly-skilled and have a thorough understanding of the procedures described, never attempt to bypass the use of any special tool when the procedure described specifies its use. Not only is there a very great risk of personal injury, but expensive damage could be caused to the components involved.

Environmental considerations

When disposing of used engine oil, brake fluid, antifreeze, etc, give due consideration to any detrimental environmental effects. Do not, for instance, pour any of the above liquids down drains into the general sewage system, or onto the ground to soak away. Many local council refuse tips provide a facility for waste oil disposal, as do some garages. If none of these facilities are available, consult your local Environmental Health Department, or the National Rivers Authority, for further advice.

With the universal tightening-up of legislation regarding the emission of environmentally-harmful substances from motor vehicles, most current vehicles have tamperproof devices fitted to the main adjustment points of the fuel system. These devices are primarily designed to prevent unqualified persons from adjusting the fuel/air mixture, with the chance of a consequent increase in toxic emissions. If such devices are encountered during servicing or overhaul, they should, wherever possible, be renewed or refitted in accordance with the vehicle manufacturer's requirements or current legislation.

OIL CARE
FOLLOW THE CODE

OIL BANK LINE
0800 66 33 66

Note: It is antisocial and illegal to dump oil down the drain. To find the location of your local oil recycling bank, call this number free.

The jack supplied with the vehicle tool kit should only be used for changing the roadwheels - see *"Wheel changing"* at the front of this manual. When carrying out any other kind of work, raise the vehicle using a hydraulic (or "trolley") jack, and always supplement the jack with axle stands positioned under the vehicle jacking points **(see illustrations)**.

When using a hydraulic jack or axle stands, always position the jack head or axle stand head under one of the relevant jacking points (note that the jacking points for use with the vehicle jack are different from those for a hydraulic trolley jack). Nissan recommend the use of adapters when supporting the vehicle with axle stands - the adapters are grooved, and fit over the sill edge to prevent the vehicle weight damaging the sill **(see illustration)**. **Do not** jack the vehicle under the sump or any of the steering or suspension components other than those indicated.

Never work under, around, or near a raised vehicle, unless it is adequately supported on stands.

Jacking and supporting points
1 *Vehicle jack and axle stand location points*
2 *Hydraulic jack locating points*

H29447

H29448

Nissan special adapters for use when supporting vehicle on axle stands. Fit the adapter to the stand, and position it underneath the vehicle so the sill edge is located in the adapter groove (arrowed)
1 *Adapter*   2 *Axle stand*

H.2876!

The vehicle jack fits over the sill edge (there are two jacking points on each side of the vehicle, indicated by a notch on the sill)

Tools and Working Facilities

Introduction

A selection of good tools is a fundamental requirement for anyone contemplating the maintenance and repair of a motor vehicle. For the owner who does not possess any, their purchase will prove a considerable expense, offsetting some of the savings made by doing-it-yourself. However, provided that the tools purchased meet the relevant national safety standards and are of good quality, they will last for many years and prove an extremely worthwhile investment.

To help the average owner to decide which tools are needed to carry out the various tasks detailed in this manual, we have compiled three lists of tools under the following headings: *Maintenance and minor repair*, *Repair and overhaul*, and *Special*. Newcomers to practical mechanics should start off with the *Maintenance and minor repair* tool kit, and confine themselves to the simpler jobs around the vehicle. Then, as confidence and experience grow, more difficult tasks can be undertaken, with extra tools being purchased as, and when, they are needed. In this way, a *Maintenance and minor repair* tool kit can be built up into a *Repair and overhaul* tool kit over a considerable period of time, without any major cash outlays. The experienced do-it-yourselfer will have a tool kit good enough for most repair and overhaul procedures, and will add tools from the *Special* category when it is felt that the expense is justified by the amount of use to which these tools will be put.

Maintenance and minor repair tool kit

The tools given in this list should be considered as a minimum requirement if routine maintenance, servicing and minor repair operations are to be undertaken. We recommend the purchase of combination spanners (ring one end, open-ended the other); although more expensive than open-ended ones, they do give the advantages of both types of spanner.

- ☐ *Combination spanners:*
  Metric - 8 to 19 mm inclusive
- ☐ *Adjustable spanner - 35 mm jaw (approx.)*
- ☐ *Spark plug spanner (with rubber insert) - petrol models*
- ☐ *Spark plug gap adjustment tool - petrol models*
- ☐ *Set of feeler gauges*
- ☐ *Brake bleed nipple spanner*
- ☐ *Screwdrivers:*
  Flat blade - 100 mm long x 6 mm dia
  Cross blade - 100 mm long x 6 mm dia
- ☐ *Combination pliers*
- ☐ *Hacksaw (junior)*
- ☐ *Tyre pump*
- ☐ *Tyre pressure gauge*
- ☐ *Oil can*
- ☐ *Oil filter removal tool*
- ☐ *Fine emery cloth*
- ☐ *Wire brush (small)*
- ☐ *Funnel (medium size)*

Repair and overhaul tool kit

These tools are virtually essential for anyone undertaking any major repairs to a motor vehicle, and are additional to those given in the *Maintenance and minor repair* list. Included in this list is a comprehensive set of sockets. Although these are expensive, they will be found invaluable as they are so versatile - particularly if various drives are included in the set. We recommend the half-inch square-drive type, as this can be used with most proprietary torque wrenches.

The tools in this list will sometimes need to be supplemented by tools from the *Special* list:

- ☐ *Sockets (or box spanners) to cover range in previous list (including Torx sockets)*
- ☐ *Reversible ratchet drive (for use with sockets)*
- ☐ *Extension piece, 250 mm (for use with sockets)*
- ☐ *Universal joint (for use with sockets)*
- ☐ *Torque wrench (for use with sockets)*
- ☐ *Self-locking grips*
- ☐ *Ball pein hammer*
- ☐ *Soft-faced mallet (plastic/aluminium or rubber)*
- ☐ *Screwdrivers:*
  Flat blade - long & sturdy, short (chubby), and narrow (electrician's) types
  Cross blade – Long & sturdy, and short (chubby) types
- ☐ *Pliers:*
  Long-nosed
  Side cutters (electrician's)
  Circlip (internal and external)
- ☐ *Cold chisel - 25 mm*
- ☐ *Scriber*
- ☐ *Scraper*
- ☐ *Centre-punch*
- ☐ *Pin punch*
- ☐ *Hacksaw*
- ☐ *Brake hose clamp*
- ☐ *Brake/clutch bleeding kit*
- ☐ *Selection of twist drills*
- ☐ *Steel rule/straight-edge*
- ☐ *Allen keys (inc. splined/Torx type)*
- ☐ *Selection of files*
- ☐ *Wire brush*
- ☐ *Axle stands*
- ☐ *Jack (strong trolley or hydraulic type)*
- ☐ *Light with extension lead*

Sockets and reversible ratchet drive

Valve spring compressor

Spline bit set

Piston ring compressor

Clutch plate alignment set

Special tools

The tools in this list are those which are not used regularly, are expensive to buy, or which need to be used in accordance with their manufacturers' instructions. Unless relatively difficult mechanical jobs are undertaken frequently, it will not be economic to buy many of these tools. Where this is the case, you could consider clubbing together with friends (or joining a motorists' club) to make a joint purchase, or borrowing the tools against a deposit from a local garage or tool hire specialist. It is worth noting that many of the larger DIY superstores now carry a large range of special tools for hire at modest rates.

The following list contains only those tools and instruments freely available to the public, and not those special tools produced by the vehicle manufacturer specifically for its dealer network. You will find occasional references to these manufacturers' special tools in the text of this manual. Generally, an alternative method of doing the job without the vehicle manufacturers' special tool is given. However, sometimes there is no alternative to using them. Where this is the case and the relevant tool cannot be bought or borrowed, you will have to entrust the work to a dealer.

☐ Valve spring compressor
☐ Valve grinding tool
☐ Piston ring compressor
☐ Piston ring removal/installation tool
☐ Cylinder bore hone
☐ Balljoint separator
☐ Coil spring compressors (where applicable)
☐ Two/three-legged hub and bearing puller
☐ Impact screwdriver
☐ Micrometer and/or vernier calipers
☐ Dial gauge
☐ Stroboscopic timing light
☐ Dwell angle meter/tachometer
☐ Universal electrical multi-meter
☐ Cylinder compression gauge
☐ Hand-operated vacuum pump and gauge
☐ Clutch plate alignment set
☐ Brake shoe steady spring cup removal tool
☐ Bush and bearing removal/installation set
☐ Stud extractors
☐ Tap and die set
☐ Lifting tackle
☐ Trolley jack

Buying tools

Reputable motor accessory shops and superstores often offer excellent quality tools at discount prices, so it pays to shop around.

Remember, you don't have to buy the most expensive items on the shelf, but it is always advisable to steer clear of the very cheap tools. Beware of 'bargains' offered on market stalls or at car boot sales. There are plenty of good tools around at reasonable prices, but always aim to purchase items which meet the relevant national safety standards. If in doubt, ask the proprietor or manager of the shop for advice before making a purchase.

Care and maintenance of tools

Having purchased a reasonable tool kit, it is necessary to keep the tools in a clean and serviceable condition. After use, always wipe off any dirt, grease and metal particles using a clean, dry cloth, before putting the tools away. Never leave them lying around after they have been used. A simple tool rack on the garage or workshop wall for items such as screwdrivers and pliers is a good idea. Store all normal spanners and sockets in a metal box. Any measuring instruments, gauges, meters, etc, must be carefully stored where they cannot be damaged or become rusty.

Take a little care when tools are used. Hammer heads inevitably become marked, and screwdrivers lose the keen edge on their blades from time to time. A little timely attention with emery cloth or a file will soon restore items like this to a good finish.

Working facilities

Not to be forgotten when discussing tools is the workshop itself. If anything more than routine maintenance is to be carried out, a suitable working area becomes essential.

It is appreciated that many an owner-mechanic is forced by circumstances to remove an engine or similar item without the benefit of a garage or workshop. Having done this, any repairs should always be done under the cover of a roof.

Wherever possible, any dismantling should be done on a clean, flat workbench or table at a suitable working height.

Any workbench needs a vice; one with a jaw opening of 100 mm is suitable for most jobs. As mentioned previously, some clean dry storage space is also required for tools, as well as for any lubricants, cleaning fluids, touch-up paints etc, which become necessary.

Another item which may be required, and which has a much more general usage, is an electric drill with a chuck capacity of at least 8 mm. This, together with a good range of twist drills, is virtually essential for fitting accessories.

Last, but not least, always keep a supply of old newspapers and clean, lint-free rags available, and try to keep any working area as clean as possible.

Micrometer set

Dial test indicator ("dial gauge")

Stroboscopic timing light

Compression tester

Stud extractor set

This is a guide to getting your vehicle through the MOT test. Obviously it will not be possible to examine the vehicle to the same standard as the professional MOT tester. However, working through the following checks will enable you to identify any problem areas before submitting the vehicle for the test.

Where a testable component is in borderline condition, the tester has discretion in deciding whether to pass or fail it. The basis of such discretion is whether the tester would be happy for a close relative or friend to use the vehicle with the component in that condition. If the vehicle presented is clean and evidently well cared for, the tester may be more inclined to pass a borderline component than if the vehicle is scruffy and apparently neglected.

It has only been possible to summarise the test requirements here, based on the regulations in force at the time of printing. Test standards are becoming increasingly stringent, although there are some exemptions for older vehicles. For full details obtain a copy of the Haynes publication Pass the MOT! (available from stockists of Haynes manuals).

An assistant will be needed to help carry out some of these checks.

The checks have been sub-divided into four categories, as follows:

1 Checks carried out **FROM THE DRIVER'S SEAT**

2 Checks carried out **WITH THE VEHICLE ON THE GROUND**

3 Checks carried out **WITH THE VEHICLE RAISED AND THE WHEELS FREE TO TURN**

4 Checks carried out on **YOUR VEHICLE'S EXHAUST EMISSION SYSTEM**

1 Checks carried out **FROM THE DRIVER'S SEAT**

Handbrake

☐ Test the operation of the handbrake. Excessive travel (too many clicks) indicates incorrect brake or cable adjustment.
☐ Check that the handbrake cannot be released by tapping the lever sideways. Check the security of the lever mountings.

☐ Check that the brake pedal is secure and in good condition. Check also for signs of fluid leaks on the pedal, floor or carpets, which would indicate failed seals in the brake master cylinder.
☐ Check the servo unit (when applicable) by operating the brake pedal several times, then keeping the pedal depressed and starting the engine. As the engine starts, the pedal will move down slightly. If not, the vacuum hose or the servo itself may be faulty.

Footbrake

☐ Depress the brake pedal and check that it does not creep down to the floor, indicating a master cylinder fault. Release the pedal, wait a few seconds, then depress it again. If the pedal travels nearly to the floor before firm resistance is felt, brake adjustment or repair is necessary. If the pedal feels spongy, there is air in the hydraulic system which must be removed by bleeding.

Steering wheel and column

☐ Examine the steering wheel for fractures or looseness of the hub, spokes or rim.
☐ Move the steering wheel from side to side and then up and down. Check that the steering wheel is not loose on the column, indicating wear or a loose retaining nut. Continue moving the steering wheel as before, but also turn it slightly from left to right.
☐ Check that the steering wheel is not loose on the column, and that there is no abnormal

movement of the steering wheel, indicating wear in the column support bearings or couplings.

Windscreen and mirrors

☐ The windscreen must be free of cracks or other significant damage within the driver's field of view. (Small stone chips are acceptable.) Rear view mirrors must be secure, intact, and capable of being adjusted.

Seat belts and seats

Note: *The following checks are applicable to all seat belts, front and rear.*

☐ Examine the webbing of all the belts (including rear belts if fitted) for cuts, serious fraying or deterioration. Fasten and unfasten each belt to check the buckles. If applicable, check the retracting mechanism. Check the security of all seat belt mountings accessible from inside the vehicle.

☐ The front seats themselves must be securely attached and the backrests must lock in the upright position.

Doors

☐ Both front doors must be able to be opened and closed from outside and inside, and must latch securely when closed.

2 Checks carried out WITH THE VEHICLE ON THE GROUND

Vehicle identification

☐ Number plates must be in good condition, secure and legible, with letters and numbers correctly spaced – spacing at (A) should be twice that at (B).

☐ The VIN plate and/or homologation plate must be legible.

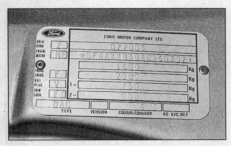

Electrical equipment

☐ Switch on the ignition and check the operation of the horn.

☐ Check the windscreen washers and wipers, examining the wiper blades; renew damaged or perished blades. Also check the operation of the stop-lights.

☐ Check the operation of the sidelights and number plate lights. The lenses and reflectors must be secure, clean and undamaged.

☐ Check the operation and alignment of the headlights. The headlight reflectors must not be tarnished and the lenses must be undamaged.

☐ Switch on the ignition and check the operation of the direction indicators (including the instrument panel tell-tale) and the hazard warning lights. Operation of the sidelights and stop-lights must not affect the indicators - if it does, the cause is usually a bad earth at the rear light cluster.

☐ Check the operation of the rear foglight(s), including the warning light on the instrument panel or in the switch.

Footbrake

☐ Examine the master cylinder, brake pipes and servo unit for leaks, loose mountings, corrosion or other damage.

☐ The fluid reservoir must be secure and the fluid level must be between the upper (**A**) and lower (**B**) markings.

☐ Inspect both front brake flexible hoses for cracks or deterioration of the rubber. Turn the steering from lock to lock, and ensure that the hoses do not contact the wheel, tyre, or any part of the steering or suspension mechanism. With the brake pedal firmly depressed, check the hoses for bulges or leaks under pressure.

Steering and suspension

☐ Have your assistant turn the steering wheel from side to side slightly, up to the point where the steering gear just begins to transmit this movement to the roadwheels. Check for excessive free play between the steering wheel and the steering gear, indicating wear or insecurity of the steering column joints, the column-to-steering gear coupling, or the steering gear itself.

☐ Have your assistant turn the steering wheel more vigorously in each direction, so that the roadwheels just begin to turn. As this is done, examine all the steering joints, linkages, fittings and attachments. Renew any component that shows signs of wear or damage. On vehicles with power steering, check the security and condition of the steering pump, drivebelt and hoses.

☐ Check that the vehicle is standing level, and at approximately the correct ride height.

Shock absorbers

☐ Depress each corner of the vehicle in turn, then release it. The vehicle should rise and then settle in its normal position. If the vehicle continues to rise and fall, the shock absorber is defective. A shock absorber which has seized will also cause the vehicle to fail.

Exhaust system

☐ Start the engine. With your assistant holding a rag over the tailpipe, check the entire system for leaks. Repair or renew leaking sections.

3 Checks carried out **WITH THE VEHICLE RAISED AND THE WHEELS FREE TO TURN**

Jack up the front and rear of the vehicle, and securely support it on axle stands. Position the stands clear of the suspension assemblies. Ensure that the wheels are clear of the ground and that the steering can be turned from lock to lock.

Steering mechanism

☐ Have your assistant turn the steering from lock to lock. Check that the steering turns smoothly, and that no part of the steering mechanism, including a wheel or tyre, fouls any brake hose or pipe or any part of the body structure.
☐ Examine the steering rack rubber gaiters for damage or insecurity of the retaining clips. If power steering is fitted, check for signs of damage or leakage of the fluid hoses, pipes or connections. Also check for excessive stiffness or binding of the steering, a missing split pin or locking device, or severe corrosion of the body structure within 30 cm of any steering component attachment point.

Front and rear suspension and wheel bearings

☐ Starting at the front right-hand side, grasp the roadwheel at the 3 o'clock and 9 o'clock positions and shake it vigorously. Check for free play or insecurity at the wheel bearings, suspension balljoints, or suspension mountings, pivots and attachments.
☐ Now grasp the wheel at the 12 o'clock and 6 o'clock positions and repeat the previous inspection. Spin the wheel, and check for roughness or tightness of the front wheel bearing.

☐ If excess free play is suspected at a component pivot point, this can be confirmed by using a large screwdriver or similar tool and levering between the mounting and the component attachment. This will confirm whether the wear is in the pivot bush, its retaining bolt, or in the mounting itself (the bolt holes can often become elongated).

☐ Carry out all the above checks at the other front wheel, and then at both rear wheels.

Springs and shock absorbers

☐ Examine the suspension struts (when applicable) for serious fluid leakage, corrosion, or damage to the casing. Also check the security of the mounting points.
☐ If coil springs are fitted, check that the spring ends locate in their seats, and that the spring is not corroded, cracked or broken.
☐ If leaf springs are fitted, check that all leaves are intact, that the axle is securely attached to each spring, and that there is no deterioration of the spring eye mountings, bushes, and shackles.

☐ The same general checks apply to vehicles fitted with other suspension types, such as torsion bars, hydraulic displacer units, etc. Ensure that all mountings and attachments are secure, that there are no signs of excessive wear, corrosion or damage, and (on hydraulic types) that there are no fluid leaks or damaged pipes.
☐ Inspect the shock absorbers for signs of serious fluid leakage. Check for wear of the mounting bushes or attachments, or damage to the body of the unit.

Driveshafts (fwd vehicles only)

☐ Rotate each front wheel in turn and inspect the constant velocity joint gaiters for splits or damage. Also check that each driveshaft is straight and undamaged.

Braking system

☐ If possible without dismantling, check brake pad wear and disc condition. Ensure that the friction lining material has not worn excessively, (A) and that the discs are not fractured, pitted, scored or badly worn (B).

☐ Examine all the rigid brake pipes underneath the vehicle, and the flexible hose(s) at the rear. Look for corrosion, chafing or insecurity of the pipes, and for signs of bulging under pressure, chafing, splits or deterioration of the flexible hoses.
☐ Look for signs of fluid leaks at the brake calipers or on the brake backplates. Repair or renew leaking components.
☐ Slowly spin each wheel, while your assistant depresses and releases the footbrake. Ensure that each brake is operating and does not bind when the pedal is released.

☐ Examine the handbrake mechanism, checking for frayed or broken cables, excessive corrosion, or wear or insecurity of the linkage. Check that the mechanism works on each relevant wheel, and releases fully, without binding.

☐ It is not possible to test brake efficiency without special equipment, but a road test can be carried out later to check that the vehicle pulls up in a straight line.

Fuel and exhaust systems

☐ Inspect the fuel tank (including the filler cap), fuel pipes, hoses and unions. All components must be secure and free from leaks.

☐ Examine the exhaust system over its entire length, checking for any damaged, broken or missing mountings, security of the retaining clamps and rust or corrosion.

Wheels and tyres

☐ Examine the sidewalls and tread area of each tyre in turn. Check for cuts, tears, lumps, bulges, separation of the tread, and exposure of the ply or cord due to wear or damage. Check that the tyre bead is correctly seated on the wheel rim, that the valve is sound and

properly seated, and that the wheel is not distorted or damaged.

☐ Check that the tyres are of the correct size for the vehicle, that they are of the same size and type on each axle, and that the pressures are correct.

☐ Check the tyre tread depth. The legal minimum at the time of writing is 1.6 mm over at least three-quarters of the tread width. Abnormal tread wear may indicate incorrect front wheel alignment.

Body corrosion

☐ Check the condition of the entire vehicle structure for signs of corrosion in load-bearing areas. (These include chassis box sections, side sills, cross-members, pillars, and all suspension, steering, braking system and seat belt mountings and anchorages.) Any corrosion which has seriously reduced the thickness of a load-bearing area is likely to cause the vehicle to fail. In this case professional repairs are likely to be needed.

☐ Damage or corrosion which causes sharp or otherwise dangerous edges to be exposed will also cause the vehicle to fail.

4 Checks carried out on YOUR VEHICLE'S EXHAUST EMISSION SYSTEM

Petrol models

☐ Have the engine at normal operating temperature, and make sure that it is in good tune (ignition system in good order, air filter element clean, etc).

☐ Before any measurements are carried out, raise the engine speed to around 2500 rpm, and hold it at this speed for 20 seconds. Allow

the engine speed to return to idle, and watch for smoke emissions from the exhaust tailpipe. If the idle speed is obviously much too high, or if dense blue or clearly-visible black smoke comes from the tailpipe for more than 5 seconds, the vehicle will fail. As a rule of thumb, blue smoke signifies oil being burnt (engine wear) while black smoke signifies unburnt fuel (dirty air cleaner element, or other carburettor or fuel system fault).

☐ An exhaust gas analyser capable of measuring carbon monoxide (CO) and hydrocarbons (HC) is now needed. If such an instrument cannot be hired or borrowed, a local garage may agree to perform the check for a small fee.

CO emissions (mixture)

☐ At the time of writing, the maximum CO level at idle is 3.5% for vehicles first used after August 1986 and 4.5% for older vehicles. From January 1996 a much tighter limit (around 0.5%) applies to catalyst-equipped vehicles first used from August 1992. If the CO level cannot be reduced far enough to pass the test (and the fuel and ignition systems are otherwise in good condition) then the carburettor is badly worn, or there is some problem in the fuel injection system or catalytic converter (as applicable).

HC emissions

☐ With the CO emissions within limits, HC emissions must be no more than 1200 ppm (parts per million). If the vehicle fails this test at idle, it can be re-tested at around 2000 rpm; if the HC level is then 1200 ppm or less, this counts as a pass.

☐ Excessive HC emissions can be caused by oil being burnt, but they are more likely to be due to unburnt fuel.

Diesel models

☐ The only emission test applicable to Diesel engines is the measuring of exhaust smoke density. The test involves accelerating the engine several times to its maximum unloaded speed.

Note: *It is of the utmost importance that the engine timing belt is in good condition before the test is carried out.*

☐ Excessive smoke can be caused by a dirty air cleaner element. Otherwise, professional advice may be needed to find the cause.

Fault Finding

Engine 1

- ☐ Engine fails to rotate when attempting to start
- ☐ Engine rotates, but will not start
- ☐ Engine difficult to start when cold
- ☐ Engine difficult to start when hot
- ☐ Starter motor noisy or rough in engagement
- ☐ Engine starts, but stops immediately
- ☐ Engine idles erratically
- ☐ Engine misfires at idle speed
- ☐ Engine misfires throughout the driving speed range
- ☐ Engine hesitates on acceleration
- ☐ Engine stalls
- ☐ Engine lacks power
- ☐ Engine backfires
- ☐ Oil pressure warning light illuminated with engine running
- ☐ Engine runs-on after switching off
- ☐ Engine noises

Cooling system 2

- ☐ Overheating
- ☐ Overcooling
- ☐ External coolant leakage
- ☐ Internal coolant leakage
- ☐ Corrosion

Fuel and exhaust systems 3

- ☐ Excessive fuel consumption
- ☐ Fuel leakage and/or fuel odour
- ☐ Excessive noise or fumes from exhaust system

Clutch 4

- ☐ Pedal travels to floor - no pressure or very little resistance
- ☐ Clutch fails to disengage (unable to select gears)
- ☐ Clutch slips (engine speed increases, with no increase in vehicle speed)
- ☐ Judder as clutch is engaged
- ☐ Noise when depressing or releasing clutch pedal

Manual transmission 5

- ☐ Noisy in neutral with engine running
- ☐ Noisy in one particular gear
- ☐ Difficulty engaging gears
- ☐ Jumps out of gear
- ☐ Vibration
- ☐ Lubricant leaks

Automatic transmission 6

- ☐ Fluid leakage
- ☐ Transmission fluid brown, or has burned smell
- ☐ General gear selection problems
- ☐ Transmission will not downshift (kickdown) with accelerator fully depressed
- ☐ Engine will not start in any gear, or starts in gears other than Park or Neutral
- ☐ Transmission slips, shifts roughly, is noisy, or has no drive in forward or reverse gears

Driveshafts 7

- ☐ Clicking or knocking noise on turns (at slow speed on full-lock)
- ☐ Vibration when accelerating or decelerating

Braking system 8

- ☐ Vehicle pulls to one side under braking
- ☐ Noise (grinding or high-pitched squeal) when brakes applied
- ☐ Excessive brake pedal travel
- ☐ Brake pedal feels spongy when depressed
- ☐ Excessive brake pedal effort required to stop vehicle
- ☐ Judder felt through brake pedal or steering wheel when braking
- ☐ Brakes binding
- ☐ Rear wheels locking under normal braking

Suspension and steering systems 9

- ☐ Vehicle pulls to one side
- ☐ Wheel wobble and vibration
- ☐ Pitching and/or rolling around corners, or when braking
- ☐ Wandering or general instability
- ☐ Excessively-stiff steering
- ☐ Excessive play in steering
- ☐ Lack of power assistance
- ☐ Tyre wear excessive

Electrical system 10

- ☐ Battery will only hold a charge for a few days
- ☐ Ignition/no-charge warning light remains illuminated with engine running
- ☐ Ignition/no-charge warning light fails to come on
- ☐ Lights inoperative
- ☐ Instrument readings inaccurate or erratic
- ☐ Horn inoperative, or unsatisfactory in operation
- ☐ Windscreen/tailgate wipers inoperative, or unsatisfactory in operation
- ☐ Windscreen/tailgate washers inoperative, or unsatisfactory in operation
- ☐ Electric windows inoperative, or unsatisfactory in operation
- ☐ Central locking system inoperative, or unsatisfactory in operation

Introduction

The vehicle owner who does his or her own maintenance according to the recommended service schedules should not have to use this section of the manual very often. Modern component reliability is such that, provided those items subject to wear or deterioration are inspected or renewed at the specified intervals, sudden failure is comparatively rare. Faults do not usually just happen as a result of sudden failure, but develop over a period of time. Major mechanical failures in particular are usually preceded by characteristic symptoms over hundreds or even thousands of miles. Those components which do occasionally fail without warning are often small and easily carried in the vehicle.

With any fault-finding, the first step is to decide where to begin investigations. Sometimes this is obvious, but on other occasions, a little detective work will be necessary. The owner who makes half a dozen haphazard adjustments or replacements may be successful in curing a fault (or its symptoms), but will be none the wiser if the fault recurs, and ultimately may have spent more time and money than was necessary. A calm and logical approach will be found to be more satisfactory in the long run. Always take into account any warning signs or abnormalities that may have been noticed in the period preceding the fault - power loss, high or low gauge readings, unusual smells, etc - and remember that failure of components such as fuses or spark plugs may only be pointers to some underlying fault.

The pages which follow provide an easy-reference guide to the more common problems which may occur during the operation of the vehicle. These problems and their possible causes are grouped under headings denoting various components or systems, such as Engine, Cooling system, etc. The Chapter and/or Section which deals with the problem is also shown in brackets. Whatever the fault, certain basic principles apply. These are as follows:

Verify the fault. This is simply a matter of being sure that you know what the symptoms are before starting work. This is particularly important if you are investigating a fault for someone else, who may not have described it very accurately.

Don't overlook the obvious. For example, if the vehicle won't start, is there fuel in the tank? (Don't take anyone else's word on this particular point, and don't trust the fuel gauge either!) If an electrical fault is indicated, look for loose or broken wires before using the test gear.

Cure the disease, not the symptom. Substituting a flat battery with a fully-charged one will get you off the hard shoulder, but if the underlying cause is not attended to, the new battery will go the same way. Similarly, changing oil-fouled spark plugs for a new set will get you moving again, but remember that the reason for the fouling (if it wasn't simply an incorrect grade of plug) will have to be established and corrected.

Don't take anything for granted. Particularly, don't forget that a "new" component may itself be defective (especially if it's been rattling around in the boot for months), and don't leave components out of a fault diagnosis sequence just because they are new or recently-fitted. When you do finally diagnose a difficult fault, you'll probably realise that all the evidence was there from the start.

1 Engine

Engine fails to rotate when attempting to start

- ☐ Battery terminal connections loose or corroded (Chapter 1).
- ☐ Battery discharged or faulty (Chapter 5).
- ☐ Broken, loose or disconnected wiring in the starting circuit (Chapter 5).
- ☐ Defective starter solenoid or switch (Chapter 5).
- ☐ Defective starter motor (Chapter 5).
- ☐ Starter pinion or flywheel/driveplate ring gear teeth loose or broken (Chapter 2A or 5).
- ☐ Engine earth strap broken or disconnected (Chapter 2A).
- ☐ Automatic transmission not in Park/Neutral position or starter inhibitor switch faulty (Chapter 7B).

Engine rotates, but will not start

- ☐ Fuel tank empty.
- ☐ Battery discharged (engine rotates slowly) (Chapter 5).
- ☐ Battery terminal connections loose or corroded (Chapter 1).
- ☐ Ignition components damp or damaged (Chapter 1 and 5).
- ☐ Broken, loose or disconnected wiring in the ignition circuit (Chapters 1 and 5).
- ☐ Worn, faulty or incorrectly-gapped spark plugs (Chapter 1).
- ☐ Carburettor/fuel injection system fault (Chapter 4A or 4B).
- ☐ Major mechanical failure (eg camshaft drive) (Chapter 2B).

Engine difficult to start when cold

- ☐ Battery discharged (Chapter 5).
- ☐ Battery terminal connections loose or corroded (Chapter 1).
- ☐ Worn, faulty or incorrectly-gapped spark plugs (Chapter 1).
- ☐ Choke mechanism faulty - carburettor models (Chapter 4A).
- ☐ Faulty fuel cut-off solenoid - carburettor models (Chapter 4A).
- ☐ Fuel injection system fault - fuel-injected models (Chapter 4B).
- ☐ Other ignition system fault (Chapters 1 and 5).
- ☐ Low cylinder compressions (Chapter 2A).

Engine difficult to start when hot

- ☐ Air filter element dirty or clogged (Chapter 1).
- ☐ Choke mechanism faulty - carburettor models (Chapter 4A).
- ☐ Faulty fuel cut-off solenoid - carburettor models (Chapter 4A).
- ☐ Fuel injection system fault - fuel-injection models (Chapter 4B).
- ☐ Ignition system fault (Chapters 1 and 5).
- ☐ Low cylinder compressions (Chapter 2A).

Starter motor noisy or rough in engagement

- ☐ Starter pinion or flywheel/driveplate ring gear teeth loose or broken (Chapter 2A or 5).
- ☐ Starter motor mounting bolts loose or missing (Chapter 5).
- ☐ Starter motor internal components worn or damaged (Chapter 5).

Engine starts, but stops immediately

- ☐ Loose or faulty connections in the ignition circuit (Chapters 1 and 5).
- ☐ Vacuum leak at the carburettor/throttle body or inlet manifold (Chapter 4A or 4B).
- ☐ Faulty carburettor (Chapter 4A).
- ☐ Fuel injection system fault (Chapter 4B).

Engine idles erratically

- ☐ Air filter element clogged (Chapter 1).
- ☐ Vacuum leak at the carburettor/throttle body, inlet manifold or associated hoses (Chapter 4A or 4B).
- ☐ Worn, faulty or incorrectly-gapped spark plugs (Chapter 1).
- ☐ Uneven or low cylinder compressions (Chapter 2A).
- ☐ Camshaft lobes worn (Chapter 2A).
- ☐ Timing chain(s) incorrectly fitted (Chapter 2A).
- ☐ Faulty carburettor (Chapter 4A).
- ☐ Fuel injection system fault (Chapter 4B).

Engine misfires at idle speed

- ☐ Worn, faulty or incorrectly-gapped spark plugs (Chapter 1).
- ☐ Faulty spark plug HT leads (Chapter 1).
- ☐ Vacuum leak at the carburettor/throttle body, inlet manifold or associated hoses (Chapter 4A or 4B).
- ☐ Faulty carburettor (Chapter 4A).
- ☐ Fuel injection system fault (Chapter 4B).
- ☐ Distributor cap cracked or tracking internally (Chapter 1).
- ☐ Uneven or low cylinder compressions (Chapter 2A).
- ☐ Disconnected or leaking crankcase ventilation hoses (Chapter 4).

Engine misfires throughout the speed range

- ☐ Fuel filter choked (Chapter 1).
- ☐ Fuel pump faulty, or delivery pressure low (Chapter 4A or 4B).
- ☐ Fuel tank vent blocked, or fuel pipes restricted (Chapter 4A or 4B).
- ☐ Vacuum leak at the carburettor/throttle body, inlet manifold or associated hoses (Chapter 4A or 4B).
- ☐ Worn, faulty or incorrectly-gapped spark plugs (Chapter 1).
- ☐ Faulty spark plug HT leads (Chapter 1).
- ☐ Distributor cap cracked or tracking internally (Chapter 1).
- ☐ Faulty ignition coil (Chapter 5B).
- ☐ Uneven or low cylinder compressions (Chapter 2A).
- ☐ Faulty carburettor (Chapter 4A).
- ☐ Fuel injection system fault (Chapter 4B).

Engine hesitates on acceleration

- ☐ Worn, faulty or incorrectly-gapped spark plugs (Chapter 1).
- ☐ Vacuum leak at the carburettor/throttle body, inlet manifold or associated hoses (Chapter 4A or 4B).
- ☐ Faulty carburettor (Chapter 4A).
- ☐ Fuel injection system fault (Chapter 4B).

1 Engine (continued)

Engine stalls

☐ Vacuum leak at the carburettor/throttle body, inlet manifold or associated hoses (Chapter 4A or 4B).
☐ Fuel filter choked (Chapter 1).
☐ Fuel pump faulty, or delivery pressure low (Chapter 4A or 4B).
☐ Fuel tank vent blocked, or fuel pipes restricted (Chapter 4A or 4B).
☐ Faulty carburettor (Chapter 4A).
☐ Fuel injection system fault (Chapter 4B).

Engine lacks power

☐ Fuel filter choked (Chapter 1).
☐ Fuel pump faulty, or delivery pressure low (Chapter 4A or 4B).
☐ Uneven or low cylinder compressions (Chapter 2A).
☐ Worn, faulty or incorrectly-gapped spark plugs (Chapter 1).
☐ Vacuum leak at the carburettor/throttle body, inlet manifold or associated hoses (Chapter 4A or 4B).
☐ Faulty carburettor (Chapter 4A).
☐ Fuel injection system fault (Chapter 4B).
☐ Brakes binding (Chapters 1 and 9).
☐ Clutch slipping - manual transmission models (Chapter 6).

Engine backfires

☐ Vacuum leak at the carburettor/throttle body, inlet manifold or associated hoses (Chapter 4A or 4B).
☐ Faulty carburettor (Chapter 4A).
☐ Fuel injection system fault (Chapter 4B).

Oil pressure warning light illuminated with engine running

☐ Low oil level, or incorrect oil grade (Chapter 1).
☐ Faulty oil pressure sensor (Chapter 5).
☐ Worn engine bearings and/or oil pump (Chapter 2A or 2B).
☐ Excessively high engine operating temperature (Chapter 3).
☐ Oil pressure relief valve defective (Chapter 2A).
☐ Oil pick-up strainer clogged (Chapter 2A).

Engine runs-on after switching off

☐ Excessive carbon build-up in engine (Chapter 2A or 2B).
☐ High engine operating temperature (Chapter 3).
☐ Faulty carburettor (Chapter 4A).
☐ Faulty fuel injection system fault (Chapter 4B).

Engine noises

Pre-ignition (pinking) or knocking during acceleration or under load

☐ Ignition timing incorrect/ignition system fault (Chapters 1 and 5).
☐ Incorrect grade of spark plug (Chapter 1).
☐ Incorrect grade of fuel (Chapter 1).
☐ Vacuum leak at carburettor/throttle body, inlet manifold or associated hoses (Chapter 4A or 4B).
☐ Excessive carbon build-up in engine (Chapter 2A or 2B).
☐ Faulty carburettor (Chapter 4A).
☐ Fuel injection system fault (Chapter 4B).

Whistling or wheezing noises

☐ Leaking inlet manifold or carburettor/throttle body gasket (Chapter 4A or 4B).
☐ Leaking exhaust manifold gasket or pipe-to-manifold joint (Chapter 4A or 4B).
☐ Leaking vacuum hose (Chapters 4A, 4B, 5B and 9).
☐ Blowing cylinder head gasket (Chapter 2A).

Tapping or rattling noises

☐ Worn valve gear or camshaft (Chapter 2A).
☐ Incorrect valve clearances (Chapter 1)
☐ Ancillary component fault (water pump, alternator, etc) (Chapters 3, 5A, etc).

Knocking or thumping noises

☐ Worn big-end bearings (regular heavy knocking, perhaps less under load) (Chapter 2B).
☐ Worn main bearings (rumbling and knocking, perhaps worsening under load) (Chapter 2B).
☐ Piston slap (most noticeable when cold) (Chapter 2B).
☐ Ancillary component fault (water pump, alternator, etc) (Chapters 3, 5A, etc).

2 Cooling system

Overheating

☐ Auxiliary drivebelt broken - or incorrectly adjusted (Chapter 1).
☐ Insufficient coolant in system (Chapter 1).
☐ Thermostat faulty (Chapter 3).
☐ Radiator core blocked, or grille restricted (Chapter 3).
☐ Electric cooling fan or thermostatic switch faulty (Chapter 3).
☐ Pressure cap faulty (Chapter 3).
☐ Ignition timing incorrect, or ignition system fault (Chapters 1 and 5).
☐ Inaccurate temperature gauge sender unit (Chapter 3).
☐ Airlock in cooling system (Chapter 1).

Overcooling

☐ Thermostat faulty (Chapter 3).
☐ Inaccurate temperature gauge sender unit (Chapter 3).

External coolant leakage

☐ Deteriorated or damaged hoses or hose clips (Chapter 1).
☐ Radiator core or heater matrix leaking (Chapter 3).
☐ Pressure cap faulty (Chapter 3).
☐ Water pump internal seal leaking (Chapter 3).
☐ Water pump seal leaking (Chapter 3).
☐ Boiling due to overheating (Chapter 3).
☐ Core plug leaking (Chapter 2B).

Internal coolant leakage

☐ Leaking cylinder head gasket (Chapter 2A).
☐ Cracked cylinder head or cylinder block (Chapter 2A or 2B).

Corrosion

☐ Infrequent draining and flushing (Chapter 1).
☐ Incorrect coolant mixture or inappropriate coolant type (Chapter 1).

3 Fuel and exhaust systems

Excessive fuel consumption

- ☐ Air filter element dirty or clogged (Chapter 1).
- ☐ Faulty carburettor (Chapter 4A).
- ☐ Fuel injection system fault (Chapter 4B).
- ☐ Ignition timing incorrect or ignition system fault (Chapters 1 and 5).
- ☐ Tyres under-inflated (Chapter 1).

Fuel leakage and/or fuel odour

- ☐ Damaged fuel tank, pipes or connections (Chapters 1 and 4).
- ☐ Faulty carburettor (Chapter 4A).

Excessive noise or fumes from exhaust system

- ☐ Leaking exhaust system or manifold joints (Chapters 1, 4A or 4B).
- ☐ Leaking, corroded or damaged silencers or pipe (Chapters 1, 4A or 4B).
- ☐ Broken mountings causing body or suspension contact (Chapter 4A or 4B).

4 Clutch

Pedal travels to floor - no pressure or very little resistance

- ☐ Broken clutch cable (Chapter 6).
- ☐ Incorrect clutch cable adjustment (Chapter 6).
- ☐ Broken clutch release bearing or fork (Chapter 6).
- ☐ Broken diaphragm spring in clutch pressure plate (Chapter 6).

Clutch fails to disengage (unable to select gears)

- ☐ Incorrect clutch cable adjustment (Chapter 6).
- ☐ Clutch disc sticking on splines (Chapter 8).
- ☐ Clutch disc sticking to flywheel or pressure plate (Chapter 8).
- ☐ Faulty pressure plate assembly (Chapter 8).
- ☐ Clutch release mechanism worn or poorly assembled (Chapter 8).

Clutch slips (engine speed increases, with no increase in vehicle speed)

- ☐ Incorrect clutch cable adjustment (Chapter 6).
- ☐ Clutch disc linings excessively worn (Chapter 6).
- ☐ Clutch disc linings contaminated with oil or grease (Chapter 6).
- ☐ Faulty pressure plate or weak diaphragm spring (Chapter 6).

Judder as clutch is engaged

- ☐ Clutch disc linings contaminated with oil or grease (Chapter 6).
- ☐ Clutch disc linings excessively worn (Chapter 6).
- ☐ Clutch cable sticking or frayed (Chapter 6).
- ☐ Faulty or distorted pressure plate or diaphragm spring (Chapter 6).
- ☐ Worn or loose engine or transmission mountings (Chapter 2A).
- ☐ Clutch disc hub or shaft splines worn (Chapter 6).

Noise when depressing or releasing clutch pedal

- ☐ Worn clutch release bearing (Chapter 6).
- ☐ Worn or dry clutch pedal bushes (Chapter 6).
- ☐ Faulty pressure plate assembly (Chapter 6).
- ☐ Pressure plate diaphragm spring broken (Chapter 6).
- ☐ Broken clutch disc cushioning springs (Chapter 6).

5 Manual transmission

Noisy in neutral with engine running

- ☐ Input shaft bearings worn (noise apparent with clutch pedal released, but not when depressed) (Chapter 7A).*
- ☐ Clutch release bearing worn (noise apparent with clutch pedal depressed, possibly less when released) (Chapter 6).

Noisy in one particular gear

- ☐ Worn, damaged or chipped gear teeth (Chapter 7A).*

Difficulty engaging gears

- ☐ Clutch fault (Chapter 6).
- ☐ Oil level low (Chapter 1).
- ☐ Worn or damaged gear linkage (Chapter 7A).
- ☐ Incorrectly-adjusted gear linkage (Chapter 7A).
- ☐ Worn synchroniser units (Chapter 7A).*

Jumps out of gear

- ☐ Worn or damaged gear linkage (Chapter 7A).
- ☐ Incorrectly-adjusted gear linkage (Chapter 7A).
- ☐ Worn synchroniser units (Chapter 7A).*
- ☐ Worn selector forks (Chapter 7A).*

Vibration

- ☐ Lack of oil (Chapter 1).
- ☐ Worn bearings (Chapter 7A).*

Lubricant leaks

- ☐ Leaking oil seal (Chapter 7A).
- ☐ Leaking housing joint (Chapter 7A).*
- ☐ Leaking input shaft oil seal (Chapter 7A).*

*Although the corrective action necessary to remedy the symptoms described is beyond the scope of the home mechanic, the above information should be helpful in isolating the cause of the condition, so that the owner can communicate clearly with a professional mechanic.

6 Automatic transmission

Note: *Due to the complexity of the automatic transmission, it is difficult for the home mechanic to properly diagnose and service this unit. For problems other than the following, the vehicle should be taken to a dealer service department or automatic transmission specialist.*

Fluid leakage

☐ Automatic transmission fluid is usually deep red in colour. Fluid leaks should not be confused with engine oil, which can easily be blown onto the transmission by air flow.
☐ To determine the source of a leak, first remove all built-up dirt and grime from the transmission housing and surrounding areas, using a degreasing agent or by steam-cleaning. Drive the vehicle at low speed, so that air flow will not blow the leak far from its source. Raise and support the vehicle, and determine where the leak is coming from. The following are common areas of leakage.

a) Oil pan (Chapter 7B).
b) Dipstick tube (Chapter 7B).
c) Transmission-to-fluid cooler fluid pipes/unions (Chapter 7B).

Transmission fluid brown, or has burned smell

☐ Transmission fluid level low, or fluid in need of renewal (Chapter 1).

General gear selection problems

☐ The most likely cause of gear selection problems is a faulty or poorly-adjusted gear selector mechanism. The following are common problems associated with a faulty selector mechanism.

a) Engine starting in gears other than Park or Neutral.
b) Indicator on gear selector lever pointing to a gear other than the one actually being used.
c) Vehicle moves when in Park or Neutral.
d) Poor gear shift quality, or erratic gear changes.

☐ Refer any problems to a Nissan dealer, or an automatic transmission specialist.

Transmission will not downshift (kickdown) with accelerator pedal fully depressed

☐ Low transmission fluid level (Chapter 1).
☐ Incorrect selector cable adjustment (Chapter 7B).
☐ Incorrect kickdown cable adjustment (Chapter 7B).

Engine will not start in any gear, or starts in gears other than Park or Neutral

☐ Incorrect starter inhibitor switch adjustment (Chapter 7B).
☐ Incorrect selector cable adjustment (Chapter 7B).

Transmission slips, shifts roughly, is noisy, or has no drive in forward or reverse gears

☐ There are many probable causes for the above problems, but the home mechanic should be concerned with only one possibility - fluid level. Before taking the vehicle to a dealer or transmission specialist, check the fluid level and condition of the fluid as described in Chapter 1. Correct the fluid level as necessary, or change the fluid and filter if needed. If the problem persists, professional help will be necessary.

7 Driveshafts

Clicking or knocking noise on turns (at slow speed on full-lock)

☐ Lack of constant velocity joint lubricant, possibly due to damaged gaiter (Chapter 8).
☐ Worn outer constant velocity joint (Chapter 8).

Vibration when accelerating or decelerating

☐ Worn inner constant velocity joint (Chapter 8).
☐ Bent or distorted driveshaft (Chapter 8).

8 Braking system

Note: *Before assuming that a brake problem exists, make sure that the tyres are in good condition and correctly inflated, that the front wheel alignment is correct, and that the vehicle is not loaded with weight in an unequal manner.*

Vehicle pulls to one side under braking

☐ Worn, defective, damaged or contaminated front or rear brake pads/shoes on one side (Chapters 1 and 9).
☐ Seized or partially-seized front or rear brake caliper/wheel cylinder piston (Chapter 9).
☐ A mixture of brake pad/shoe lining materials fitted between sides (Chapter 9).
☐ Brake caliper mounting bolts loose (Chapter 9).
☐ Worn or damaged steering or suspension components (Chapters 1 and 10).

Noise (grinding or high-pitched squeal) when brakes applied

☐ Brake pad or shoe friction lining material worn down to metal backing (Chapters 1 and 9).
☐ Excessive corrosion of brake disc/drum - may be apparent after the vehicle has been standing for some time (Chapters 1 and 9).

Excessive brake pedal travel

☐ Inoperative rear brake self-adjust mechanism - rear drum brake models (Chapters 1 and 9).
☐ Faulty master cylinder (Chapter 9).
☐ Air in hydraulic system (Chapter 9).
☐ Faulty vacuum servo unit (Chapter 9).

Brake pedal feels spongy when depressed

☐ Air in hydraulic system (Chapter 9).
☐ Deteriorated flexible rubber brake hoses (Chapters 1 and 9).
☐ Master cylinder mountings loose (Chapter 9).
☐ Faulty master cylinder (Chapter 9).

Excessive brake pedal effort required to stop car

☐ Faulty vacuum servo unit (Chapter 9).
☐ Disconnected, damaged or insecure brake servo vacuum hose (Chapters 1 and 9).
☐ Primary or secondary hydraulic circuit failure (Chapter 9).
☐ Seized brake caliper/wheel cylinder piston(s) (Chapter 9).
☐ Brake pads/shoes incorrectly fitted (Chapter 9).
☐ Incorrect grade of brake pads/shoes fitted (Chapter 9).
☐ Brake pads/shoes contaminated (Chapter 9).

8 Braking system (continued)

Judder felt through brake pedal or steering wheel when braking
- [ ] Excessive run-out or distortion of brake disc/drum (Chapter 9).
- [ ] Brake pad/shoe linings worn (Chapters 1 and 9).
- [ ] Brake caliper/rear brake backplate mounting bolts loose (Chapter 9).
- [ ] Wear in suspension or steering components or mountings (Chapters 1 and 10).

Brakes binding
- [ ] Seized brake caliper/wheel cylinder piston(s) (Chapter 9).
- [ ] Incorrectly-adjusted handbrake mechanism (Chapter 9).
- [ ] Faulty master cylinder (Chapter 9).

Rear wheels locking under normal braking
- [ ] Rear brake shoe linings contaminated (Chapters 1 and 9).
- [ ] Faulty brake pressure regulator (Chapter 9).

9 Suspension and steering

Note: *Before diagnosing suspension or steering faults, be sure that the trouble is not due to incorrect tyre pressures, mixtures of tyre types, or binding brakes.*

Vehicle pulls to one side
- [ ] Defective tyre (Chapter 1).
- [ ] Excessive wear in suspension or steering components (Chapters 1 and 10).
- [ ] Incorrect front wheel alignment (Chapter 10).
- [ ] Accident damage to steering or suspension components (Chapters 1 and 10).

Wheel wobble and vibration
- [ ] Front roadwheels out of balance (vibration felt mainly through the steering wheel) (Chapter 10).
- [ ] Rear roadwheels out of balance (vibration felt throughout the vehicle) (Chapter 10).
- [ ] Roadwheels damaged or distorted (Chapter 10).
- [ ] Faulty or damaged tyre (Chapter 1).
- [ ] Worn steering or suspension joints, bushes or components (Chapters 1 and 10).
- [ ] Wheel bolts loose (Chapter 10).

Pitching and/or rolling on corners, or when braking
- [ ] Defective shock absorbers (Chapters 1 and 10).
- [ ] Broken or weak coil spring and/or suspension component (Chapters 1 and 10).
- [ ] Worn or damaged anti-roll bar or mountings (Chapter 10).

Wandering or general instability
- [ ] Incorrect front wheel alignment (Chapter 10).
- [ ] Worn steering or suspension joints, bushes or components (Chapters 1 and 10).
- [ ] Roadwheels out of balance (Chapter 10).
- [ ] Faulty or damaged tyre (Chapter 1).
- [ ] Wheel bolts loose (Chapter 10).
- [ ] Defective shock absorbers (Chapters 1 and 10).

Excessively-stiff steering
- [ ] Lack of steering gear lubricant (Chapter 10).
- [ ] Seized track rod end balljoint or suspension balljoint (Chapters 1 and 10).

- [ ] Broken or incorrectly adjusted auxiliary drivebelt (Chapter 1).
- [ ] Incorrect front wheel alignment (Chapter 10).
- [ ] Steering rack or column bent or damaged (Chapter 10).

Excessive play in steering
- [ ] Worn steering column universal joint(s) (Chapter 10).
- [ ] Worn steering track rod end balljoints (Chapters 1 and 10).
- [ ] Worn rack-and-pinion steering gear (Chapter 10).
- [ ] Worn steering or suspension joints, bushes or components (Chapters 1 and 10).

Lack of power assistance
- [ ] Broken or incorrectly-adjusted auxiliary drivebelt (Chapter 1).
- [ ] Incorrect power steering fluid level (Chapter 1).
- [ ] Restriction in power steering fluid hoses (Chapter 1).
- [ ] Faulty power steering pump (Chapter 10).
- [ ] Faulty rack-and-pinion steering gear (Chapter 10).

Tyre wear excessive

Tyres worn on inside or outside edges
- [ ] Tyres under-inflated (wear on both edges) (Chapter 1).
- [ ] Incorrect camber or castor angles (wear on one edge only) (Chapter 10).
- [ ] Worn steering or suspension joints, bushes or components (Chapters 1 and 10).
- [ ] Excessively-hard cornering.
- [ ] Accident damage.

Tyre treads exhibit feathered edges
- [ ] Incorrect toe setting (Chapter 10).

Tyres worn in centre of tread
- [ ] Tyres over-inflated (Chapter 1).

Tyres worn on inside and outside edges
- [ ] Tyres under-inflated (Chapter 1).
- [ ] Worn shock absorbers (Chapters 1 and 10).

Tyres worn unevenly
- [ ] Tyres out of balance (Chapter 1).
- [ ] Excessive wheel or tyre run-out (Chapter 1).
- [ ] Worn shock absorbers (Chapters 1 and 10).
- [ ] Faulty tyre (Chapter 1).

10 Electrical system

Note: *For problems associated with the starting system, refer to the faults listed under "Engine" earlier.*

Battery will only hold a charge for a few days
- [ ] Battery defective internally (Chapter 5).
- [ ] Battery electrolyte level low - where applicable (Chapter 1).

- [ ] Battery terminal connections loose or corroded (Chapter 1).
- [ ] Auxiliary drivebelt worn - or incorrectly adjusted (Chapter 1).
- [ ] Alternator not charging at correct output (Chapter 5).
- [ ] Alternator or voltage regulator faulty (Chapter 5).
- [ ] Short-circuit causing continual battery drain (Chapters 5 and 12).

10 Electrical system (continued)

Ignition/no-charge warning light remains illuminated with engine running

- ☐ Auxiliary drivebelt broken, worn, or incorrectly adjusted (Chapter 1).
- ☐ Alternator brushes worn, sticking, or dirty (Chapter 5).
- ☐ Alternator brush springs weak or broken (Chapter 5).
- ☐ Internal fault in alternator or voltage regulator (Chapter 5).
- ☐ Broken, disconnected, or loose wiring in charging circuit (Chapter 5).

Ignition/no-charge warning light fails to come on

- ☐ Warning light bulb blown (Chapter 12).
- ☐ Broken, disconnected, or loose wiring in warning light circuit (Chapter 12).
- ☐ Alternator faulty (Chapter 5).

Lights inoperative

- ☐ Bulb blown (Chapter 12).
- ☐ Corrosion of bulb or bulbholder contacts (Chapter 12).
- ☐ Blown fuse (Chapter 12).
- ☐ Faulty relay (Chapter 12).
- ☐ Broken, loose, or disconnected wiring (Chapter 12).
- ☐ Faulty switch (Chapter 12).

Instrument readings inaccurate or erratic

Instrument readings increase with engine speed

- ☐ Faulty voltage regulator (Chapter 12).

Fuel or temperature gauges give no reading

- ☐ Faulty gauge sender unit (Chapters 3 and 4).
- ☐ Wiring open-circuit (Chapter 12).
- ☐ Faulty gauge (Chapter 12).

Fuel or temperature gauges only give maximum reading

- ☐ Faulty gauge sender unit (Chapters 3 and 4).
- ☐ Wiring short-circuit (Chapter 12).
- ☐ Faulty gauge (Chapter 12).

Horn inoperative, or unsatisfactory in operation

Horn operates all the time

- ☐ Horn contacts permanently bridged or horn push stuck down (Chapter 12).

Horn fails to operate

- ☐ Blown fuse (Chapter 12).
- ☐ Cable or cable connections loose, broken or disconnected (Chapter 12).
- ☐ Faulty horn (Chapter 12).

Horn emits intermittent or unsatisfactory sound

- ☐ Cable connections loose (Chapter 12).
- ☐ Horn mountings loose (Chapter 12).
- ☐ Faulty horn (Chapter 12).

Windscreen/tailgate wipers inoperative, or unsatisfactory in operation

Wipers fail to operate, or operate very slowly

- ☐ Wiper blades stuck to screen, or linkage seized or binding (Chapters 1 and 12).
- ☐ Blown fuse (Chapter 12).
- ☐ Cable or cable connections loose, broken or disconnected (Chapter 12).
- ☐ Faulty relay (Chapter 12).
- ☐ Faulty wiper motor (Chapter 12).

Wiper blades sweep over too large or too small an area of the glass

- ☐ Wiper arms incorrectly positioned on spindles (Chapter 1).
- ☐ Excessive wear of wiper linkage (Chapter 12).
- ☐ Wiper motor or linkage mountings loose or insecure (Chapter 12).

Wiper blades fail to clean the glass effectively

- ☐ Wiper blade rubbers worn or perished (Chapter 1).
- ☐ Wiper arm springs broken, or arm pivots seized (Chapter 12).
- ☐ Insufficient windscreen washer additive to adequately remove road film (Chapter 1).

Windscreen/tailgate washers inoperative, or unsatisfactory in operation

One or more washer jets inoperative

- ☐ Blocked washer jet (Chapter 1).
- ☐ Disconnected, kinked or restricted fluid hose (Chapter 12).
- ☐ Insufficient fluid in washer reservoir (Chapter 1).

Washer pump fails to operate

- ☐ Broken or disconnected wiring or connections (Chapter 12).
- ☐ Blown fuse (Chapter 12).
- ☐ Faulty washer switch (Chapter 12).
- ☐ Faulty washer pump (Chapter 12).

Washer pump runs for some time before fluid is emitted from jets

- ☐ Faulty one-way valve in fluid supply hose (Chapter 12).

Electric windows inoperative, or unsatisfactory in operation

Window glass will only move in one direction

- ☐ Faulty switch (Chapter 12).

Window glass slow to move

- ☐ Regulator seized or damaged, or in need of lubrication (Chapter 11).
- ☐ Door internal components or trim fouling regulator (Chapter 11).
- ☐ Faulty motor (Chapter 11).

Window glass fails to move

- ☐ Blown fuse (Chapter 12).
- ☐ Faulty relay (Chapter 12).
- ☐ Broken or disconnected wiring or connections (Chapter 12).
- ☐ Faulty motor (Chapter 11).

Central locking system inoperative, or unsatisfactory in operation

Complete system failure

- ☐ Blown fuse (Chapter 12).
- ☐ Faulty relay (Chapter 12).
- ☐ Broken or disconnected wiring or connections (Chapter 12).
- ☐ Faulty control unit (Chapter 11).

Latch locks but will not unlock, or unlocks but will not lock

- ☐ Faulty switch (Chapter 12).
- ☐ Broken or disconnected latch operating rods or levers (Chapter 11).
- ☐ Faulty relay (Chapter 12).
- ☐ Faulty control unit (Chapter 11).

One solenoid/motor fails to operate

- ☐ Broken or disconnected wiring or connections (Chapter 12).
- ☐ Faulty solenoid/motor (Chapter 11).
- ☐ Broken, binding or disconnected latch operating rods or levers (Chapter 11).
- ☐ Fault in door latch (Chapter 11).

A

ABS (Anti-lock brake system) A system, usually electronically controlled, that senses incipient wheel lockup during braking and relieves hydraulic pressure at wheels that are about to skid.

Air bag An inflatable bag hidden in the steering wheel (driver's side) or the dash or glovebox (passenger side). In a head-on collision, the bags inflate, preventing the driver and front passenger from being thrown forward into the steering wheel or windscreen.

Air cleaner A metal or plastic housing, containing a filter element, which removes dust and dirt from the air being drawn into the engine.

Air filter element The actual filter in an air cleaner system, usually manufactured from pleated paper and requiring renewal at regular intervals.

Air filter

Allen key A hexagonal wrench which fits into a recessed hexagonal hole.

Alligator clip A long-nosed spring-loaded metal clip with meshing teeth. Used to make temporary electrical connections.

Alternator A component in the electrical system which converts mechanical energy from a drivebelt into electrical energy to charge the battery and to operate the starting system, ignition system and electrical accessories.

Ampere (amp) A unit of measurement for the flow of electric current. One amp is the amount of current produced by one volt acting through a resistance of one ohm.

Anaerobic sealer A substance used to prevent bolts and screws from loosening. Anaerobic means that it does not require oxygen for activation. The Loctite brand is widely used.

Antifreeze A substance (usually ethylene glycol) mixed with water, and added to a vehicle's cooling system, to prevent freezing of the coolant in winter. Antifreeze also contains chemicals to inhibit corrosion and the formation of rust and other deposits that would tend to clog the radiator and coolant passages and reduce cooling efficiency.

Anti-seize compound A coating that reduces the risk of seizing on fasteners that are subjected to high temperatures, such as exhaust manifold bolts and nuts.

Asbestos A natural fibrous mineral with great heat resistance, commonly used in the composition of brake friction materials. Asbestos is a health hazard and the dust created by brake systems should never be inhaled or ingested.

Axle A shaft on which a wheel revolves, or which revolves with a wheel. Also, a solid beam that connects the two wheels at one end of the vehicle. An axle which also transmits power to the wheels is known as a live axle.

Axleshaft A single rotating shaft, on either side of the differential, which delivers power from the final drive assembly to the drive wheels. Also called a driveshaft or a halfshaft.

B

Ball bearing An anti-friction bearing consisting of a hardened inner and outer race with hardened steel balls between two races.

Bearing The curved surface on a shaft or in a bore, or the part assembled into either, that permits relative motion between them with minimum wear and friction.

Bearing

Big-end bearing The bearing in the end of the connecting rod that's attached to the crankshaft.

Bleed nipple A valve on a brake wheel cylinder, caliper or other hydraulic component that is opened to purge the hydraulic system of air. Also called a bleed screw.

Brake bleeding Procedure for removing air from lines of a hydraulic brake system.

Brake bleeding

Brake disc The component of a disc brake that rotates with the wheels.

Brake drum The component of a drum brake that rotates with the wheels.

Brake linings The friction material which contacts the brake disc or drum to retard the vehicle's speed. The linings are bonded or riveted to the brake pads or shoes.

Brake pads The replaceable friction pads that pinch the brake disc when the brakes are applied. Brake pads consist of a friction material bonded or riveted to a rigid backing plate.

Brake shoe The crescent-shaped carrier to which the brake linings are mounted and which forces the lining against the rotating drum during braking.

Braking systems For more information on braking systems, consult the *Haynes Automotive Brake Manual*.

Breaker bar A long socket wrench handle providing greater leverage.

Bulkhead The insulated partition between the engine and the passenger compartment.

C

Caliper The non-rotating part of a disc-brake assembly that straddles the disc and carries the brake pads. The caliper also contains the hydraulic components that cause the pads to pinch the disc when the brakes are applied. A caliper is also a measuring tool that can be set to measure inside or outside dimensions of an object.

Camshaft A rotating shaft on which a series of cam lobes operate the valve mechanisms. The camshaft may be driven by gears, by sprockets and chain or by sprockets and a belt.

Canister A container in an evaporative emission control system; contains activated charcoal granules to trap vapours from the fuel system.

Canister

Carburettor A device which mixes fuel with air in the proper proportions to provide a desired power output from a spark ignition internal combustion engine.

Castellated Resembling the parapets along the top of a castle wall. For example, a castellated balljoint stud nut.

Castor In wheel alignment, the backward or forward tilt of the steering axis. Castor is positive when the steering axis is inclined rearward at the top.

Catalytic converter A silencer-like device in the exhaust system which converts certain pollutants in the exhaust gases into less harmful substances.

Catalytic converter

Circlip A ring-shaped clip used to prevent endwise movement of cylindrical parts and shafts. An internal circlip is installed in a groove in a housing; an external circlip fits into a groove on the outside of a cylindrical piece such as a shaft.

Clearance The amount of space between two parts. For example, between a piston and a cylinder, between a bearing and a journal, etc.

Coil spring A spiral of elastic steel found in various sizes throughout a vehicle, for example as a springing medium in the suspension and in the valve train.

Compression Reduction in volume, and increase in pressure and temperature, of a gas, caused by squeezing it into a smaller space.

Compression ratio The relationship between cylinder volume when the piston is at top dead centre and cylinder volume when the piston is at bottom dead centre.

Constant velocity (CV) joint A type of universal joint that cancels out vibrations caused by driving power being transmitted through an angle.

Core plug A disc or cup-shaped metal device inserted in a hole in a casting through which core was removed when the casting was formed. Also known as a freeze plug or expansion plug.

Crankcase The lower part of the engine block in which the crankshaft rotates.

Crankshaft The main rotating member, or shaft, running the length of the crankcase, with offset "throws" to which the connecting rods are attached.

Crankshaft assembly

Crocodile clip See Alligator clip

D

Diagnostic code Code numbers obtained by accessing the diagnostic mode of an engine management computer. This code can be used to determine the area in the system where a malfunction may be located.

Disc brake A brake design incorporating a rotating disc onto which brake pads are squeezed. The resulting friction converts the energy of a moving vehicle into heat.

Double-overhead cam (DOHC) An engine that uses two overhead camshafts, usually one for the intake valves and one for the exhaust valves.

Drivebelt(s) The belt(s) used to drive accessories such as the alternator, water pump, power steering pump, air conditioning compressor, etc. off the crankshaft pulley.

Accessory drivebelts

Driveshaft Any shaft used to transmit motion. Commonly used when referring to the axleshafts on a front wheel drive vehicle.

Drum brake A type of brake using a drum-shaped metal cylinder attached to the inner surface of the wheel. When the brake pedal is pressed, curved brake shoes with friction linings press against the inside of the drum to slow or stop the vehicle.

E

EGR valve A valve used to introduce exhaust gases into the intake air stream.

Electronic control unit (ECU) A computer which controls (for instance) ignition and fuel injection systems, or an anti-lock braking system. For more information refer to the *Haynes Automotive Electrical and Electronic Systems Manual*.

Electronic Fuel Injection (EFI) A computer controlled fuel system that distributes fuel through an injector located in each intake port of the engine.

Emergency brake A braking system, independent of the main hydraulic system, that can be used to slow or stop the vehicle if the primary brakes fail, or to hold the vehicle stationary even though the brake pedal isn't depressed. It usually consists of a hand lever that actuates either front or rear brakes mechanically through a series of cables and linkages. Also known as a handbrake or parking brake.

Endfloat The amount of lengthwise movement between two parts. As applied to a crankshaft, the distance that the crankshaft can move forward and back in the cylinder block.

Engine management system (EMS) A computer controlled system which manages the fuel injection and the ignition systems in an integrated fashion.

Exhaust manifold A part with several passages through which exhaust gases leave the engine combustion chambers and enter the exhaust pipe.

F

Fan clutch A viscous (fluid) drive coupling device which permits variable engine fan speeds in relation to engine speeds.

Feeler blade A thin strip or blade of hardened steel, ground to an exact thickness, used to check or measure clearances between parts.

Feeler blade

Firing order The order in which the engine cylinders fire, or deliver their power strokes, beginning with the number one cylinder.

Flywheel A heavy spinning wheel in which energy is absorbed and stored by means of momentum. On cars, the flywheel is attached to the crankshaft to smooth out firing impulses.

Free play The amount of travel before any action takes place. The "looseness" in a linkage, or an assembly of parts, between the initial application of force and actual movement. For example, the distance the brake pedal moves before the pistons in the master cylinder are actuated.

Fuse An electrical device which protects a circuit against accidental overload. The typical fuse contains a soft piece of metal which is calibrated to melt at a predetermined current flow (expressed as amps) and break the circuit.

Fusible link A circuit protection device consisting of a conductor surrounded by heat-resistant insulation. The conductor is smaller than the wire it protects, so it acts as the weakest link in the circuit. Unlike a blown fuse, a failed fusible link must frequently be cut from the wire for replacement.

G

Gap The distance the spark must travel in jumping from the centre electrode to the side electrode in a spark plug. Also refers to the spacing between the points in a contact breaker assembly in a conventional points-type ignition, or to the distance between the reluctor or rotor and the pickup coil in an electronic ignition.

Adjusting spark plug gap

Gasket Any thin, soft material - usually cork, cardboard, asbestos or soft metal - installed between two metal surfaces to ensure a good seal. For instance, the cylinder head gasket seals the joint between the block and the cylinder head.

Gasket

Gauge An instrument panel display used to monitor engine conditions. A gauge with a movable pointer on a dial or a fixed scale is an analogue gauge. A gauge with a numerical readout is called a digital gauge.

H

Halfshaft A rotating shaft that transmits power from the final drive unit to a drive wheel, usually when referring to a live rear axle.

Harmonic balancer A device designed to reduce torsion or twisting vibration in the crankshaft. May be incorporated in the crankshaft pulley. Also known as a vibration damper.

Hone An abrasive tool for correcting small irregularities or differences in diameter in an engine cylinder, brake cylinder, etc.

Hydraulic tappet A tappet that utilises hydraulic pressure from the engine's lubrication system to maintain zero clearance (constant contact with both camshaft and valve stem). Automatically adjusts to variation in valve stem length. Hydraulic tappets also reduce valve noise.

I

Ignition timing The moment at which the spark plug fires, usually expressed in the number of crankshaft degrees before the piston reaches the top of its stroke.

Inlet manifold A tube or housing with passages through which flows the air-fuel mixture (carburettor vehicles and vehicles with throttle body injection) or air only (port fuel-injected vehicles) to the port openings in the cylinder head.

J

Jump start Starting the engine of a vehicle with a discharged or weak battery by attaching jump leads from the weak battery to a charged or helper battery.

L

Load Sensing Proportioning Valve (LSPV) A brake hydraulic system control valve that works like a proportioning valve, but also takes into consideration the amount of weight carried by the rear axle.

Locknut A nut used to lock an adjustment nut, or other threaded component, in place. For example, a locknut is employed to keep the adjusting nut on the rocker arm in position.

Lockwasher A form of washer designed to prevent an attaching nut from working loose.

M

MacPherson strut A type of front suspension system devised by Earle MacPherson at Ford of England. In its original form, a simple lateral link with the anti-roll bar creates the lower control arm. A long strut - an integral coil spring and shock absorber - is mounted between the body and the steering knuckle. Many modern so-called MacPherson strut systems use a conventional lower A-arm and don't rely on the anti-roll bar for location.

Multimeter An electrical test instrument with the capability to measure voltage, current and resistance.

N

NOx Oxides of Nitrogen. A common toxic pollutant emitted by petrol and diesel engines at higher temperatures.

O

Ohm The unit of electrical resistance. One volt applied to a resistance of one ohm will produce a current of one amp.

Ohmmeter An instrument for measuring electrical resistance.

O-ring A type of sealing ring made of a special rubber-like material; in use, the O-ring is compressed into a groove to provide the sealing action.

Overhead cam (ohc) engine An engine with the camshaft(s) located on top of the cylinder head(s).

Overhead valve

Overhead valve (ohv) engine An engine with the valves located in the cylinder head, but with the camshaft located in the engine block.

Oxygen sensor A device installed in the engine exhaust manifold, which senses the oxygen content in the exhaust and converts this information into an electric current. Also called a Lambda sensor.

P

Phillips screw A type of screw head having a cross instead of a slot for a corresponding type of screwdriver.

Plastigage A thin strip of plastic thread, available in different sizes, used for measuring clearances. For example, a strip of Plastigage is laid across a bearing journal. The parts are assembled and dismantled; the width of the crushed strip indicates the clearance between journal and bearing.

Plastigage

Propeller shaft The long hollow tube with universal joints at both ends that carries power from the transmission to the differential on front-engined rear wheel drive vehicles.

Proportioning valve A hydraulic control valve which limits the amount of pressure to the rear brakes during panic stops to prevent wheel lock-up.

R

Rack-and-pinion steering A steering system with a pinion gear on the end of the steering shaft that mates with a rack (think of a geared wheel opened up and laid flat). When the steering wheel is turned, the pinion turns, moving the rack to the left or right. This movement is transmitted through the track rods to the steering arms at the wheels.

Radiator A liquid-to-air heat transfer device designed to reduce the temperature of the coolant in an internal combustion engine cooling system.

Refrigerant Any substance used as a heat transfer agent in an air-conditioning system. R-12 has been the principle refrigerant for many years; recently, however, manufacturers have begun using R-134a, a non-CFC substance that is considered less harmful to the ozone in the upper atmosphere.

Rocker arm A lever arm that rocks on a shaft or pivots on a stud. In an overhead valve engine, the rocker arm converts the upward movement of the pushrod into a downward movement to open a valve.

Rotor In a distributor, the rotating device inside the cap that connects the centre electrode and the outer terminals as it turns, distributing the high voltage from the coil secondary winding to the proper spark plug. Also, that part of an alternator which rotates inside the stator. Also, the rotating assembly of a turbocharger, including the compressor wheel, shaft and turbine wheel.

Runout The amount of wobble (in-and-out movement) of a gear or wheel as it's rotated. The amount a shaft rotates "out-of-true." The out-of-round condition of a rotating part.

S

Sealant A liquid or paste used to prevent leakage at a joint. Sometimes used in conjunction with a gasket.

Sealed beam lamp An older headlight design which integrates the reflector, lens and filaments into a hermetically-sealed one-piece unit. When a filament burns out or the lens cracks, the entire unit is simply replaced.

Serpentine drivebelt A single, long, wide accessory drivebelt that's used on some newer vehicles to drive all the accessories, instead of a series of smaller, shorter belts. Serpentine drivebelts are usually tensioned by an automatic tensioner.

Serpentine drivebelt

Shim Thin spacer, commonly used to adjust the clearance or relative positions between two parts. For example, shims inserted into or under bucket tappets control valve clearances. Clearance is adjusted by changing the thickness of the shim.

Slide hammer A special puller that screws into or hooks onto a component such as a shaft or bearing; a heavy sliding handle on the shaft bottoms against the end of the shaft to knock the component free.

Sprocket A tooth or projection on the periphery of a wheel, shaped to engage with a chain or drivebelt. Commonly used to refer to the sprocket wheel itself.

Starter inhibitor switch On vehicles with an automatic transmission, a switch that prevents starting if the vehicle is not in Neutral or Park.

Strut See MacPherson strut.

T

Tappet A cylindrical component which transmits motion from the cam to the valve stem, either directly or via a pushrod and rocker arm. Also called a cam follower.

Thermostat A heat-controlled valve that regulates the flow of coolant between the cylinder block and the radiator, so maintaining optimum engine operating temperature. A thermostat is also used in some air cleaners in which the temperature is regulated.

Thrust bearing The bearing in the clutch assembly that is moved in to the release levers by clutch pedal action to disengage the clutch. Also referred to as a release bearing.

Timing belt A toothed belt which drives the camshaft. Serious engine damage may result if it breaks in service.

Timing chain A chain which drives the camshaft.

Toe-in The amount the front wheels are closer together at the front than at the rear. On rear wheel drive vehicles, a slight amount of toe-in is usually specified to keep the front wheels running parallel on the road by offsetting other forces that tend to spread the wheels apart.

Toe-out The amount the front wheels are closer together at the rear than at the front. On front wheel drive vehicles, a slight amount of toe-out is usually specified.

Tools For full information on choosing and using tools, refer to the *Haynes Automotive Tools Manual.*

Tracer A stripe of a second colour applied to a wire insulator to distinguish that wire from another one with the same colour insulator.

Tune-up A process of accurate and careful adjustments and parts replacement to obtain the best possible engine performance.

Turbocharger A centrifugal device, driven by exhaust gases, that pressurises the intake air. Normally used to increase the power output from a given engine displacement, but can also be used primarily to reduce exhaust emissions (as on VW's "Umwelt" Diesel engine).

U

Universal joint or U-joint A double-pivoted connection for transmitting power from a driving to a driven shaft through an angle. A U-joint consists of two Y-shaped yokes and a cross-shaped member called the spider.

V

Valve A device through which the flow of liquid, gas, vacuum, or loose material in bulk may be started, stopped, or regulated by a movable part that opens, shuts, or partially obstructs one or more ports or passageways. A valve is also the movable part of such a device.

Valve clearance The clearance between the valve tip (the end of the valve stem) and the rocker arm or tappet. The valve clearance is measured when the valve is closed.

Vernier caliper A precision measuring instrument that measures inside and outside dimensions. Not quite as accurate as a micrometer, but more convenient.

Viscosity The thickness of a liquid or its resistance to flow.

Volt A unit for expressing electrical "pressure" in a circuit. One volt that will produce a current of one ampere through a resistance of one ohm.

W

Welding Various processes used to join metal items by heating the areas to be joined to a molten state and fusing them together. For more information refer to the *Haynes Automotive Welding Manual.*

Wiring diagram A drawing portraying the components and wires in a vehicle's electrical system, using standardised symbols. For more information refer to the *Haynes Automotive Electrical and Electronic Systems Manual.*

Note: *References throughout this index are in the form - "Chapter number" • "page number"*

N

Number plate light - 12•6

O

Oil
engine - 0•11, 0•16, 1•6
filter - 1•2, 1•6
transmission - 0•16, 1•9, 1•10, 1•18
pressure warning light switch - 5A•4
pump - 2A•17
Oil seals
automatic transmission - 7B•4
crankshaft - 2A•19
general - REF•4
manual transmission - 7A•2

P

Parts - REF•3
PCV filter - 1•17
Pedals
accelerator - 4A•5, 4B•3
brake - 9•14
clutch - 6•2
Piston rings - 2B•12, 2B•15
Piston/connecting rod - 2B•10, 2B•12, 2B•18
Power steering
bleeding - 10•14
fluid - 0•16, 1•9
pump drivebelt - 1•11
pump - 10•14
Punctures - 0•8

R

Radiator - 3•2
Radio/cassette player - 12•9
Rear light bulb - 12•6
Rear light unit - 12•7
Relays - 12•2
Respraying - 11•3
Reversing light switch - 7A•3, 7B•4
Routine maintenance and servicing - 1•1 et seq
Rust - 11•3

S

Safety first - 0•5
Screenwasher fluid - 0•12
Seat belt check - 1•15
Seats - 11•13
Seats heated - 12•11
Servo unit - 9•15
Short circuit - 12•2

Spare parts - REF•3
Spark plugs - 1•2, 1•8
Speakers - 12•10
Specifications - see Chapter headings
Speedometer cable - 12•8
Speedometer drive - 7A•4
Starter motor - 5A•4
Starting and charging systems - 5A•1 et seq
Starting problems - 0•6, 5B•2
Starting system testing - 5A•3
Steering - 10•1 et seq
check - 1•13, 1•15
column - 10•12
column lock - 10•11
fault finding - REF•12, REF•17
front hub bearings - 10•2
gear - 10•12
gear rubber gaiters - 10•14
power steering bleeding - 10•14
power steering fluid - 0•16, 1•9
power steering pump - 10•14
power steering pump drivebelt - 1•11
rear hub bearings - 10•6
track-rod end - 10•15
wheel - 10•11
Stop-light switch - 9•17
Sump - 2A•16
Sunroof - 11•12
Suspension - 10•1 et seq
anti-roll bar - 10•6
check - 1•13, 1•15
fault finding - REF•12, REF•17
lower arm - 10•5
components - 10•7
strut front - 10•3
Switches
cooling system - 3•4
handbrake 'on' warning light - 9•17
ignition - 10•11
oil pressure warning light - 5A•4
removal and refitting - 12•3
reversing light - 7A•3, 7B•4
starter inhibitor switch - 7B•4
stop-light - 9•17

T

Tailgate - 11•10
Tailgate lock - 11•11
TDC - 2A•4
Temperature gauge sender - 3•4
Temperature sensor - 3•4
Thermostat - 3•3
Throttle cable - 4A•5, 4B•3
Throttle pedal - 4A•5, 4B•3
Timing, ignition - 5B•5

Timing chain - 2A•6, 2A•9
Tools - REF•4, REF•6
Top dead centre (TDC) - 2A•4
Towing - 0•9
Trim panels - 11•13
Tyre pressures - 0•16
Tyres - 0•13

U

Underbody views - 1•4, 1•5
Underbonnet views - 0•10, 1•4
Unleaded petrol - 4A•5, 4B•3
Upholstery - 11•2

V

Valves - 2A•2, 2A•13, 2B•1, 2B•9
Vehicle identification - REF•3
Ventilation components - 3•5

W

Washer fluid - 0•12
Washer system components - 12•9
Weekly checks - 0•10
Wheel alignment - 1•14
Wheel arch liners - 11•12
Wheel changing - 0•8
Wheel cylinder - 9•13
Window regulator - 11•8
Windscreen - 11•12
Wiper arm - 12•8
Wiper blades - 0•14
Wiper motors - 12•8, 12•9
Wiring diagrams - 12•12 et seq

Preserving Our Motoring Heritage

< The Model J Duesenberg Derham Tourster. Only eight of these magnificent cars were ever built – this is the only example to be found outside the United States of America

Almost every car you've ever loved, loathed or desired is gathered under one roof at the Haynes Motor Museum. Over 300 immaculately presented cars and motorbikes represent every aspect of our motoring heritage, from elegant reminders of bygone days, such as the superb Model J Duesenberg to curiosities like the bug-eyed BMW Isetta. There are also many old friends and flames. Perhaps you remember the 1959 Ford Popular that you did your courting in? The magnificent 'Red Collection' is a spectacle of classic sports cars including AC, Alfa Romeo, Austin Healey, Ferrari, Lamborghini, Maserati, MG, Riley, Porsche and Triumph.

A Perfect Day Out

Each and every vehicle at the Haynes Motor Museum has played its part in the history and culture of Motoring. Today, they make a wonderful spectacle and a great day out for all the family. Bring the kids, bring Mum and Dad, but above all bring your camera to capture those golden memories for ever. You will also find an impressive array of motoring memorabilia, a comfortable 70 seat video cinema and one of the most extensive transport book shops in Britain. The Pit Stop Cafe serves everything from a cup of tea to wholesome, home-made meals or, if you prefer, you can enjoy the large picnic area nestled in the beautiful rural surroundings of Somerset.

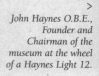

> John Haynes O.B.E., Founder and Chairman of the museum at the wheel of a Haynes Light 12.

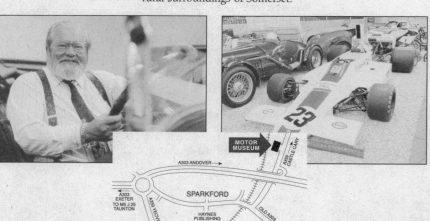

< Graham Hill's Lola Cosworth Formula 1 car next to a 1934 Riley Sports.

The Museum is situated on the A359 Yeovil to Frome road at Sparkford, just off the A303 in Somerset. It is about 40 miles south of Bristol, and 25 minutes drive from the M5 intersection at Taunton.
Open 9.30am - 5.30pm (10.00am - 4.00pm Winter) 7 days a week, *except Christmas Day, Boxing Day and New Years Day*
Special rates available for schools, coach parties and outings Charitable Trust No. 292048